Desh Pardesh

The South Asian Presence in Britain

ROGER BALLARD (*editor*)
MARCUS BANKS
RACHEL DWYER
KATY GARDNER / ABDUS SHUKUR
JOHN R. HINNELLS
KIM KNOTT
PHILIP LEWIS
ELEANOR NESBITT
ALISON SHAW
STEVEN VERTOVEC
SHRIKALA WARRIER

HURST & COMPANY, LONDON

First published in the United Kingdom by
C. Hurst & Co. (Publishers) Ltd.,
38 King Street, Covent Garden, London WC2E 8JT
© 1994 by C. Hurst & Co. (Publishers) Ltd.

Printed in India

ISBNs
1–85065–091–8 (cased)
1–85065–092–6 (paper)

Distributed in North America by the
University of British Columbia Press,
6344 Memorial Road,
Vancouver, British Columbia V6T 1Z2

CONTENTS

Preface and Acknowledgements   *page* vii

Notes on Contributors   xii

Introduction: The Emergence of Desh Pardesh
                                        Roger Ballard   1

The Pakistani Community in Oxford   *Alison Shaw*   35

Being Muslim and Being British: The Dynamics of
   Islamic Reconstruction in Bradford   *Philip Lewis*   58

Differentiation and Disjunction among the Sikhs
                                        Roger Ballard   88

Valmikis in Coventry: The Revival and Reconstruction
   of a Community   *Eleanor Nesbitt*   117

"I'm Bengali, I'm Asian, and I'm Living Here": The
   Changing Identity of British Bengalis
                             Katy Gardner and Abdus Shukur   142

Caste, Religion and Sect in Gujarat: Followers of
   Vallabhacharya and Swaminarayan   *Rachel Dwyer*   165

Gujarati Prajapatis in London: Family Roles and
   Sociability Networks   *Shrikala Warrier*   191

The Gujarati Mochis in Leeds: From Leather Stockings
   to Surgical Boots and Beyond   *Kim Knott*   213

Jain Ways of Being   *Marcus Banks*   231

Parsi Zoroastrians in London   *John R. Hinnells*   251

Caught in an Ethnic Quandary: Indo-Carribean Hindus
   in London   *Steven Vertovec*   272

Bibliographical Key   291

Index   293

v

MAPS

1. The Indian Subcontinent   xvi
2. The Punjab Region   xvi
3. The Gujarat Region   xvii
4. Northeast Bangladesh   xvii
5. Distribution of Britain's Asian Population   xviii

PREFACE

This book has been a long while in the making. It had its origins in a small gathering held at Manchester University's Hollyroyd Conference Centre in March 1989; most of the papers presented there have found their way into the book, although they have been supplemented by additional contributions which were later sought to fill the principal gaps in our coverage.

A volume such as this is necessarily constructed around a number of compromises, for which I as editor take full responsibility. But while choices have to be made, coming to a decision is by no means easy, not least because anyone who writes about the South Asian presence in Britain necessarily finds the experience like mounting a tightrope. Given the yawning knowledge deficit among the remainder of the population, there can be no dispute about the urgent need for the production of descriptively accurate and analytically sophisticated accounts of the minority presence. Even so, it does not follow that the production of such accounts will in itself provide any kind of solution to Britain's increasing problems of racial and ethnic polarisation. The reason is obvious. Although valuable in its own right, knowledge changes nothing. Real solutions — when and if they occur — will of necessity be the outcome of political process, in which the minorities themselves will be the principal actors; and as these processes unfold, the new minorities will represent their own interests in their own ways.

Yet although we are under no illusion that writers and academic analysts such as ourselves can or should expect to have anything more than a marginal role in any deals which are ultimately struck, we are very conscious that a book such as this can potentially play a role in establishing the parameters of the conceptual space within which such deals might be struck; and by the same token it might equally well have the opposite effect. It is our awareness of these responsibilities which has, among other things, slowed the publication of this book.

Within that context we certainly hope that this volume will become a major source to which students from a wide range of disciplines will turn to inform themselves about the South Asian presence in Britain, but even so we are well aware of the dilemmas which accompany that goal. Whatever that audience might expect, we have not attempted to present everything that non-Asian Britons might want to know about their new neighbours' religions, cultures and lifestyles, not least because that would take an encyclopedia. Our objectives here are much more limited. What we have sought to present is a reasonably comprehensive picture of the quality and character of the self-created worlds of South Asian settlers and their British-born offspring, and of the changes and developments which are taking place within them. In doing so we have of course been selective, not just in terms of the groups and communities which we have chosen to highlight, but also in terms of the phenomena we have addressed. Most contributors to this book are anthropologists by training, and hence our accounts tend to highlight those aspects of behaviour and experience with which anthropologists have always been primarily concerned: family and kinship, religion and morality, and the networks of obligation and reciprocity which lie at the heart of any sense of community. By the same token, most contributors place rather less emphasis on the kinds of issues on which sociologists habitually focus, such as exploitation and social inequality.

Critics of the anthropological approach — of whom there are many — will no doubt seek to suggest that a book entitled *Desh Pardesh* will by definition amount to little more than a systematic peddling of arcane exotica, and will therefore provide an escape route to those who wish to dodge the real issue: the pervasive tendency to racism which is so deeply institutionalised in British society. Hence our critics may well argue that racism, not cultural exoticism, is the issue which matters.

We would beg to differ — although not over the issue of whether or not racism is a deeply entrenched feature of the British social order. As readers will soon discover, every single contributor to this volume makes it clear that this is indeed so; thus the constraints which people of colour constantly encounter form a backdrop to all our analyses. What we would dispute, however, is whether an approach which focuses *solely* on processes of ethnic and racial exclusion can ever do justice to the experience of its victims — no matter how vicious those processes of exclusion may become. If public discussion is allowed to focus on victimhood alone, as is the case in reams of sociological literature, its impact can be both dangerous and patronising, above all because it leads to the representation of the objects of exclusionism as helpless pawns, whose fate, experience, perceptions and circumstances are entirely determined by the injustices which are heaped upon them.

Of course the existence of such injustices must be kept constantly in focus, both because they are a constant constraint, and because members of Britain's white majority have every interest in ignoring this dimension of their behaviour. But as every chapter in this volume serves to show, Britain's South Asian settlers have been neither cowed nor overwhelmed by these experiences. Rather they have risen to the challenge and pressed forward *despite* the exclusionism they have encountered, and in doing so have relied extensively on the strengths and resiliences generated within their own self-created worlds. Given the importance of these processes, and given the reluctance of socio-logical commentators even to acknowledge their existence, we make no apologies for adopting a broadly anthropological agenda. It is precisely by means of those processes which an anthropological perspective serves to highlight — such as the maintenance of family and kinship ties, and the generation of a sense of communal solidarity on the basis of common religious inspiration and kin-specific moral loyalties — that South Asian settlers have constructed such a strong sense of personal and social confidence that they have been able not just to survive but actively to prosper in an adverse and often hostile British environment. Hence far from being mere deprived pawns, the new minorities have begun actively to *resist* the racial and ethnic exclusionism they still routinely encounter.[1]

Our concern here is not, however, to give a comprehensive account of the contemporary dialectics of racial and ethnic polarisation, or to describe every single aspect of the South Asian experience in Britain. Given our interest in the settlers' own self-created worlds, our em-phasis here is on both detail and distinctiveness: each contributor has therefore written about the specific community and the specific local context with which he or she is most familiar. A great deal has therefore been left out. Given the exceedingly diverse character of the South Asian presence in Britain, this book would have had to run to several hundred chapters if all its components had been explored to a similar depth — always given that several hundred anthro-pologists had actually carried out the necessary studies! Thus while every effort has been made to include a representative selection of the total range of South Asian communities in this volume, we have been restricted by space, by a paucity of ethnographic studies, and by the ability and willingness of those who had been invited to make a contribution being able to respond — especially in the light of the much shorter deadline initially envisaged. The end-product is there-fore as much a reflection of the availability of good-quality ethno-graphic material as of a conscious decision to include specific groups and communities.

Last but not least there is also the question of the personal and social identity of ourselves as contributors. On that score we vary: by gender, by social class, by ancestry and nationality — and of

[1] These arguments, together with a critique of current sociological orthodoxy, are more fully worked out in Roger Ballard, "New Clothes for the Emperor? The con-ceptual nakedness of Britain's Race Relations Industry", *New Community*, vol. 18 (1992), pp. 481–2.

course by whether or not we are ourselves members of any of the communities highlighted here. What difference does this make? There is, of course, a widespread view that insiders' accounts are somehow more "authentic" than those constructed by external analysts. Although there is undoubtedly some force in such arguments — not least because excluded minorities rightly resent the prospect of others speaking on their behalf — there is also something to be said for the currently less fashionable view: that reflective objectivity is best achieved by an observer who can achieve distance from that which is observed. But it is not a matter of either/or, for there are no right answers.

Hence although our objective has been to make the accounts we present as authentic and as objective as possible, we would reject the proposition that comprehensive authenticity or total objectivity can ever be attained. Regardless of whether the author is an insider or an outsider, these will always be targets worth striving for; those who convince themselves that they have reached that goal will, we think, always be deluding themselves. As for ourselves, it is up to our readers to make their own judgements about the quality of our offerings, and the extent to which particular contributors' personal groundings have coloured their analysis and presentation. All that I myself would seek to emphasise is that we are a mixed bunch. And while I would have been very pleased had I been able to draw in a greater number of minority contributors — not least because minority voices are still so rarely heard in Britain — I make no apologies at all for offering a mixture.

But the bottom line is clear. While we can only hope that those whose lifestyles are described here will at least recognise themselves in our depictions, we do not speak — and certainly do not seek to speak — on their behalf. Ours may be a literary representation of values, styles and strategies of South Asian Britain, but it is not a representation of what their political interests and concerns might be, and should never be so regarded. In political terms the new minorities are capable of speaking for themselves. It is their voices, not ours, which demand an audience.

Nevertheless the prospect of such a dialogue being opened is likely to be greatly facilitated when those who stand outside have at least some inkling of what may be happening on the other side of ethnic boundaries, and it is above all to the opening of such dialogues that we hope this volume will contribute. However unfamiliar, *Desh Pardesh* is close at hand: its inhabitants are your neighbours. Bridges can be built across the divide, provided that each side treats the other with respect. The more this volume helps to unblock communications and to facilitate such discourse, the better pleased we will be. That is what we would regard as an authentic and positive response to our efforts in constructing this volume.

Finally I would like to thank my fellow contributors for their immense patience in what turned out to be a lengthy editorial process; the publisher Christopher Hurst for his work on the manuscript; Sebastian Ballard and Virinder Kalra, who drew the maps; and finally my wife Tahirah, who knows better than anyone what was involved in putting together this volume.

University of Manchester ROGER BALLARD
September 1994

NOTES ON CONTRIBUTORS

Roger Ballard is a Lecturer in Comparative Religion at the University of Manchester. Since he gained a doctorate in Sociology at the University of Delhi in 1970, his primary research interest has been in the changing character of the Punjabi presence in Britain, and in the increasingly plural character of the British social order. He has supplemented his long-standing acquaintance with the South Asian communities in Leeds and Bradford with substantial periods of fieldwork in Jullundur District in India, and in Mirpur District across the border in Pakistan.

Marcus Banks received his doctorate in Social Anthropology from the University of Cambridge in 1985 and went on to train as a documentary filmmaker at the National Film and Television School, Beaconsfield. His doctoral thesis examined the social and religious organization of Jains in India and England, and he has published a monograph and numerous articles on the subject. More recently he has been researching and publishing in the field of visual representation, and is currently co-editing a volume of essays on aspects of visual anthropology. Until recently he taught social anthropology at the University of Oxford.

Rachel Dwyer is Lecturer in Gujarati at the School of Oriental and African Studies, University of London. She took her B.A. in Sanskrit at S.O.A.S., followed by a M.Phil in General Linguistics and Comparative Philology at Oxford. Her current doctoral research is focused on the lyrics of Dayaram (1777–1853), a follower of Vallabhacharya. Author of a new *Teach Yourself Gujarati* course, she also convenes courses on the Literatures of South Asia, and on Indian Cinema and Society.

Katy Gardner is Lecturer in Social Anthropology at the University of Sussex. She took her doctorate, which was based on fieldwork in Bangladesh, at the London School of Economics, after which she worked as an assistant social adviser for the British Overseas Development Association, and taught at the University of Kent. She is the author of *Songs at the River's Edge: Stories from a Bangladesh Village*, and *Londoni-gram: Migration and Transformation in Rural Bangladesh*. She is currently co-authoring a book about Development and Anthropology.

John R. Hinnells is Professor of Comparative Religion in the University of London and head of the Department for the Study of Religions at the School of Oriental and African Studies. His original research was on ancient Zoroastrian teaching and its impact on Judaism and Christianity, but since 1973 he has specialised on the Parsis of British India, and from 1985 on the contemporary global Parsi diaspora. He is editor of *The Handbook of Living Religions* and *The Penguin Dictionary of Religions*, as well as *Who's Who of World Religions*.

Kim Knott is Senior Lecturer in the Department of Theology and Religious Studies at the University of Leeds, and Director of the Community Religions project. Her teaching and research interests lie in modern Hinduism, religion and gender, and the religions of South Asians in Britain. Her publications include *Hinduism in Leeds*, and *My Sweet Lord*, a book on the Hare Krishna Movement. She is currently writing a book on women and destiny.

Philip Lewis is currently Adviser on Inter-Faith Issues to the Bishop of Bradford. Having spent six years in Pakistan studying Sufism and the specific profile of South Asian Islam, his special area of interest is in Muslim-Christian relations. His recently completed doctoral thesis on Muslims in Bradford is soon to be published as *Islamic Britain: Religion, Politics and Identity amongst British Muslims*. His central interest is in the capacity of religious traditions to cope creatively and constructively with religious and ideological diversity.

Eleanor Nesbitt is currently senior Research Fellow on the Religious Education and Community Project in the Faculty of Social Studies at the University of Warwick. She studied at the Universities of Cambridge and Oxford, and has also been a teacher in Nainital (North India) and Coventry. Her interests include the ethnographic study of religious nurture and the religious traditions of Britain's Punjabi and Gujarati communities. Co-author with Robert Jackson of *Hindu Children in Britain*, she is also reviews editor of the *International Journal of Punjab Studies*.

Abdus Shukur is Head of Equality Services at the Royal Hospitals Trust, and was elected to Tower Hamlets Council from Shadwell Ward in May 1994. Having arrived in Britain from Bangladesh in 1966, he went on to take his B.Ed. at Avery Hill College. Before taking up his present appointment he was heavily involved in Community Development work with young Bengalis, as well as working as a Law Centre adviser on Immigration and Nationality.

Alison Shaw is currently teaching social anthropology at the University of Oxford. Her doctoral research was conducted among the local Pakistani community, and led to the publication of *A Pakistani Com-*

munity in Britain. Between finishing her research and returning once again to Oxford, she directed a community relations project teaching Urdu to non-Pakistani adults in South London.

Steve Vertovec is Principal Research Fellow at the Centre for Research on Ethnic Relations at the University of Warwick. Having gained his M.A. in Religious Studies from the University of California, he went on to take a doctorate in Social Anthropology at Oxford, for which he conducted a study of religion and ethnicity among the Indians in Trinidad. He has since conducted research with Hindu and Muslim groups in Britain, with particular emphasis on their organisation and relationships with local authorities. Author and editor of a number of books on Trinidad, the South Asian Diaspora and Muslim minorities in Europe, he was Humboldt Fellow in the Free University of Berlin during 1983–4.

Srikala Warrier is a sociologist with a doctorate from the University of London. After a career in teaching at universities in India, she joined the National Health Service, becoming a Senior Manager with the South East Thames Regional Health Authority in London, responsible for research on policy issues emerging from the recent reforms. She now works as an independent consultant on health issues, and has a particular interest in mental health, learning disabilities and user empowerment.

MAPS

1. The Indian Subcontinent

2. The Punjab Region

xvi

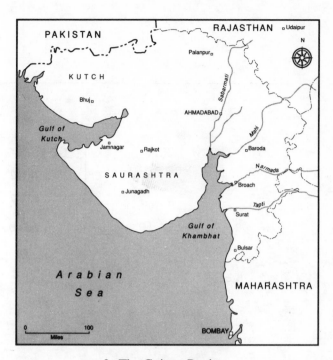

3. The Gujarat Region

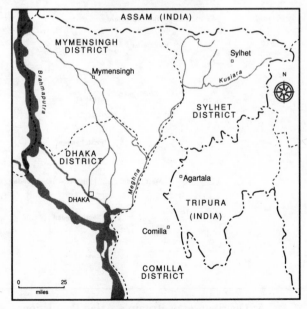

4. Northeast Bangladesh

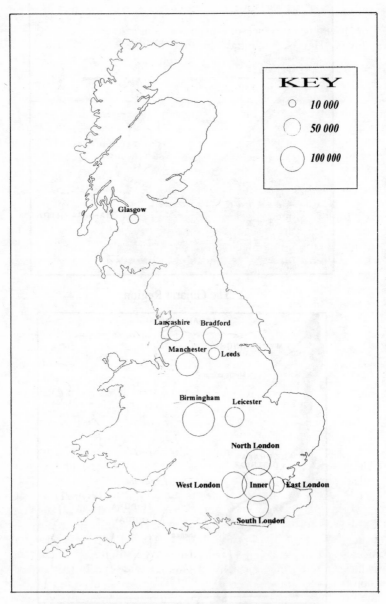

5. Distribution of Britain's Asian Population

INTRODUCTION

THE EMERGENCE OF *DESH PARDESH*

Roger Ballard

Although our central concern in this book is to explore the way in which migrants from India, Pakistan and Bangladesh have set about making themselves at home in Britain, it is well worth remembering that immigration itself is anything but an unprecedented phenomenon. Throughout its history Britain has been a recipient of immigrant inflows, as with the Celts, Anglo-Saxons and Normans in the relatively distant past, supplemented by the more recent arrival of substantial numbers of Irish, Jewish and Eastern European settlers. Thus while the most recent wave of arrivals — in which migrant workers were drawn in from the Indian subcontinent and the islands of the Caribbean to fill the yawning gaps that emerged in the British labour market during the years of the post-war boom — is in some senses nothing but the latest episode in a long chain of developments, it has nevertheless brought about a profound and indeed irreversible change in the whole character of the British social order. First, Britain is now a visibly *multi-racial* society, in the sense that its citizens now include 2.7 million people who are either wholly or partly of non-European ancestry. Secondly, and just as important, it has become a much more overtly *poly-ethnic* society. Inspired as they are by cultural, religious and linguistic traditions whose roots lie far beyond the boundaries of Europe, the new minorities have significantly expanded the range of diversities covered by local British lifestyles.

Nevertheless it seems doubtful that any of us — whether we belong to the white majority or the new visible minorities — have yet come fully to grips with the momentous implications of these developments. Although a careful reading of Britain's past history could have provided plenty of evidence that immigration tends to have a long-term impact on the local social and cultural order, and although it is now nearly half a century since the inflow from South Asia and the Caribbean began, and more than twenty years since it reached its peak, remarkably little serious thought has yet been given to considering either the extent, or indeed the irreversibility, of the changes it has wrought. Paradoxically, it was for many years regarded as thoroughly alarmist — at least in liberal circles — even to consider the possibility that any such changes might occur at all. My own view, by contrast, is that future historians may well conclude that the

1

impact of the arrival of South Asian and Afro-Caribbean settlers on the British social and cultural order will eventually prove almost as great as that precipitated by the arrival of William of Normandy in 1066.

Of course there are also many differences. South Asian and Afro-Caribbean migrants arrived as workers, not as rulers; hence although they also hoped to make their fortunes, their starting point was quite different. Most found they had little alternative but to accept manual employment in an industrial economy which subsequently went into rapid decline, clearly a far cry from their Norman predecessors' privileged position as victorious conquerors. And while the Normans may have taken pride in their ancestry, neither they nor any of many other European migrant groups who arrived in Britain before or since were a *visible* minority, quite unlike their South Asian and Afro-Caribbean successors.

Nevertheless there are also some striking parallels between the adaptive strategies devised by these otherwise disparate groups. Just as the newly established Norman-French élite continued to draw inspiration from their own distinctive linguistic, religious, and cultural traditions for several generations after their arrival in England, so too does the current group of South Asian and Afro-Caribbean settlers — as indeed did the Irish and Jewish migrants who arrived in even larger numbers in the late nineteenth century. And just as the religious, linguistic and cultural impact of the Norman irruption eventually had a profoundly creative impact on the local social order, so there is every reason to expect that the consequences of the arrival of the latest group of migrants will be just as far-reaching.

Even so, that process is still only at its earliest stage. As the growth of ever more dynamic ethnic colonies in most of Britain's industrial towns and cities clearly demonstrates, all the new minorities are strongly committed to cultural and religious reconstruction. Nevertheless the minority impact on mainline social and cultural institutions has so far remained largely peripheral, and confined to a few specific areas, such as popular music, professional football, small retail outlets and the fast-food trade. What their presence *has* precipitated, however, is some intense hostility among Britain's white natives.[1]

Right from the outset, non-European settlers found themselves subjected to racial exclusionism, and to this day skin-colour remains an inescapable social marker. Yet despite its widespread use as a trigger for exclusionary behaviour, physical appearance is of much less significance than it once was as a target of white hostility. Instead

[1] Ernest Cashmore, *The Logic of Racism* (London: Allen & Unwin, 1987), provides a vigorous and richly descriptive account of a range of white reactions to the growth of the minority presence.

the focus has shifted to the minorities' religious and ethnic distinctiveness. Besides being regarded as wholly unreasonable, their very ethnicity is widely perceived as presenting a dangerous and indeed unacceptable challenge to the established social and cultural order.

Desh Pardesh: The South Asian Dimension

There is of course much more that could be said about the logic and dynamics of racial and ethnic polarisation, and the way in which such tensions might be resolved, let alone about parallel developments elsewhere, both today and in the past. What is clear, however, is that the United Kingdom is by definition a multi-national society, even if it is one within which the English have long enjoyed a position of almost unquestioned hegemony. Likewise the charge that a minority ethnic presence constitutes an unacceptable threat to the religious and cultural integrity of the nation is in no way novel, since the growth of Irish Catholic and Jewish ethnic colonies precipitated equally great popular hostility.[2]

Yet although we must always keep these wider issues in view — for they provide a constant backdrop to our discussion — the focus of this book is much narrower: it is restricted to those people, or rather those *communities*, who trace their ancestral roots to one part or another of the Indian subcontinent. To that end it draws together eleven specially written ethnographic accounts exploring current processes of social, religious and cultural adaptation within a specific, and usually highly localised, British South Asian community.

As befits an ethnographic account, we pay relatively little attention to the quantitative aspects of the South Asian presence, about which a growing body of statistical data can be found elsewhere. Our aim, instead, is to highlight the *qualitative* characteristics of the new South Asian settlements, and to emphasise that however similar all "Asians" may seem to outsiders, they actually constitute a far more diverse population category than is commonly realised. Even so, the accounts presented here are far from comprehensive: as readers will soon realise, that diversity is so great that we could not hope to encompass all its dimensions within a single volume.

Nevertheless the accounts presented here are wide in range. They include an exploration of the experiences of Pakistani Muslims in both Oxford and Bradford; high-caste Punjabi Sikhs in Leeds; low-caste Valmikis in Coventry; Sylhetis in London's East End; the growing popularity of Hindu devotional movements among emigrants

---

[2] See Colin Holmes, *A Tolerant Country?: immigrants, refugees and minorities in Britain* (London: Faber, 1991).

from Gujarat; two caste-based Gujarati communities, Prajapatis in London and Mochis in Leeds; two more religiously-based communities Jains in Leicester and Parsis in London; and last but not least the experiences of Indo-Caribbean Hindu migrants from Trinidad and Guyana who have settled in London. Though by definition far from exhaustive, these accounts nevertheless highlight the most important dimensions of the South Asian presence in Britain, while also demonstrating how vigorous — and how varied — the processes of cultural reconstruction which they have set in train.

A further consequence of our approach is that it serves to demonstrate the difficulty of making generalisations which apply with equal force to every section of Britain's "Asian" population. Nor does moving down to the next level of differentiation — such as national origins — in search of a "community" about which to generalise necessarily constitute much of an advance. Thus while most people will fairly willingly identify themselves either as "Indians", "Pakistanis" or "Bangladeshis" when asked to do so, it would be a great mistake to assume that those so identified will show any great degree of commonality among themselves, or that they will ever interact in a sufficiently coherent way to merit being described as a community.

Far from it. If one regards a community as a body of people whose feelings of mutual identification are strong enough to precipitate an active and ongoing sense of solidarity, the great majority of Britain's ethnic colonies rest on much more parochial foundations than is commonly supposed. Thus while common religious affiliation — whether to Hinduism, Sikhism or Islam — has undoubtedly proved a far more effective vehicle for large-scale mobilisation than mere nationality, such solidarities have still tended to be relatively short-lived, and linked to specific issues, such as the *Satanic Verses* affair. In contrast the networks of reciprocity which provide the framework for most settlers' everyday lives are largely grounded in much narrower loyalties of caste, sect and descent-group. Hence if we are to make sense of their preferred strategies we need to take careful note of what *jati* and *biraderi* membership entails. It is only then that one can begin to understand why these loyalties have been such an effective foundation for the networks of reciprocity which lie at the heart of any sense of community.

Yet although we have therefore sought to highlight both the detail and the increasingly varied character of British South Asian lifestyles, we are also committed to teasing out the common elements which underlie this variety. Our aim is therefore to identify the adaptive strategies which *all* South Asian settlers, regardless of their precise affiliation, have devised as a means of coping with their new environment, for despite the dangers of reckless generalisation, it is possible to identify a number of common elements behind what might appear at first sight to be ever-burgeoning diversity. Thus even though we do indeed focus on specific communities, our aim is not just to pile up ever more detailed descriptions of one little group after another, but rather to develop an analytical perspective on the ways in which those involved have settled down and made themselves at home in Britain.

This takes us straight back into the choppy waters of the issues raised right at the outset. Contrary to the expectations of most of Britain's white natives, settling down has not taken the form of a comprehensive process of assimilation, or even an approximation to it. Thus, as every subsequent chapter shows, both the older generation of settlers and their British-born offspring are continuing to find substantial inspiration in the resources of their own particular cultural, religious and linguistic inheritance, which they are actively and creatively reinterpreting in order to rebuild their lives *on their own terms*. Hence, among other things, the title we have chosen.

Why *Desh Pardesh*? At first the phrase is unlikely to make much impact. Few readers, except those of South Asian origin themselves, will be familiar with either Hindi, Urdu, Punjabi, Gujarati or Bangla, even though these are now widely-spoken British languages. However as speakers of any of these tongues will already appreciate, the phrase *Desh Pardesh* has a double meaning, for it can equally well be translated both as "home from home" and as "at home abroad". As such it sums up the central theme of this book: despite the many obstacles they have encountered, Britain's *Desh Pardeshis* still remain strongly committed to the pursuit of their own self-determined goals.

The Growth of the South Asian Presence in Britain

Although our principal concern in this book is to explore the qualitative character of Britain's South Asian ethnic colonies, at least some mention of their quantitative dimensions is clearly also required, if only because public debate on this subject is often as ill-informed as it is heated. Although a large-scale South Asian presence is very much a post-war phenomenon, its history is very much longer, for a small number of adventurers had begun to find their way to Britain in the seventeenth century.[3] Occasional visitors continued to arrive thereafter, but once seamen began to be hired in Bombay and Calcutta to serve on British steamships, numbers increased. By the end of the nineteenth century small settlements of Indian seamen awaiting re-

---

[3] Rosina Visram, *Ayahs, Lascars and Princes* (London: Pluto, 1986).

employment could be found in most of Britain's major ports,[4] and these in turn served as bridgeheads through which the subsequent large-scale inflow was organised.

Mass migration was dependent on plentiful employment opportunities, which only became available after the end of the Second World War. Thereafter the inflow from the subcontinent began to escalate rapidly. From the early 1950s until the end of the 1970s, the British economy was acutely short of labour. The post-war boom was proceeding apace, but reservoirs from which additional workers had been recruited during previous periods of expansion — Ireland and Eastern Europe — could no longer satisfy its demands. Hence migrant workers began to be drawn in from much further afield, especially from the islands of the Caribbean and from the Indian subcontinent.

The subsequent growth of Britain's South Asian population has been affected by many factors, including the boom, and then in the 1980s the equally rapid decline in the demand for unskilled industrial labour; the imposition of ever more draconian immigration rules, which primarily targeted people of non-European descent; the arrival of British passport-holders of South Asian origin from Britain's newly-independent colonies in East Africa; the reunion of families, as wives came with their children to join their husbands; and, most recently of all, the emergence of a burgeoning British-born second generation.

Tracing the precise growth pattern of Britain's South Asian population poses a number of problems, for it was not until 1991 that a properly posed ethnic question was included in the Census. Hence the figures in the final column of Table 1.1 can be regarded as broadly reliable, while those to the left of them are the best available estimates for the three previous decades.

Although South Asians still only make up a small proportion of the population as a whole, their total numbers have grown rapidly since the early 1950s. At the outset growth was largely a consequence of further immigration, but since the imposition of ever-tighter controls on settlement from the mid-1960s onwards, the South Asian inflow has steadily declined, and has now been reduced to little more than a trickle. This has not halted population growth, however, mainly because of the demographic characteristics of this section of the population. Most South Asian migrants arrived in Britain as young adults, and their inflow reached its peak in the late 1960s, with the result that it is still only the early pioneers who have reached retire-

---

[4] Joseph Salter, *The Asiatic in London* (London: Seely, 1873) provides many illuminating details of seamen in the late nineteenth century. Paul Fryer, *Staying Power: the history of black people in Britain* (London: Pluto, 1984) offers a masterly overview.

ment age. But if South Asian pensioners are still few, the pattern is reversed at the other end of the age spectrum. Not only did most settlers first arrive as young adults, but their families tended to be relatively large, with their wives sustaining this higher rate of fertility following their arrival in Britain. All the indications are that fertility rates are now declining sharply, especially among the rising British-born generation. Even so, Britain's South Asian population is now so heavily skewed towards youth that substantial growth is inevitable, if only because births will substantially outnumber deaths for many years to come. It can therefore be predicted that Britain's South Asian population will eventually stabilise at roughly twice its present size.[5]

Table 1.1. GROWTH OF BRITAIN'S SOUTH ASIAN POPULATION

Country of birth/ethnicity[6]	1961	1971	1981	1991
India	81,400	240,730	673,704	823,821
Pakistan	24,900	127,565	295,461	449,646
Bangladesh[7]	–	–	64,562	157,881
East Africa[8]	–	44,860	181,321	–
Total S. Asian population	106,300	413,155	1,215,048	1,431,348
% S. Asians in U.K. population	0.23%	0.85%	2.52%	3.04%

Sources: 1961: E.J.B. Rose (ed.), *Colour and Citizenship* (Oxford University Press, 1969), p. 97. 1971, 1981 and 1991: O.P.C.S. Census Reports, London H.M.S.O.

Yet even if that prediction proves correct, South Asians would still only make up some 6% of the total population, far short of the "swamping" level which some alarmists have predicted. Even so, the national average obscures much local variation, for the South Asian

[5] Roger Ballard and Virinder Singh Kalra, *The Ethnic Dimensions of the 1991 Census* (Manchester University: Manchester Census Group, 1994).
[6] The figures in the final column are the most reliable, since they are based on responses to a genuine ethnic question. The figures in the preceding columns are "best estimates", based either on country of birth data (1961 and 1971), or data on residents in households headed by persons born in the countries specified (1981).
[7] Bangladesh only broke away from Pakistan after the 1971 civil war, so separate figures for Bangladeshis are only available from 1981 onwards.
[8] No reliable figures for East African Asians are available for 1961. By 1991, when an ethnic question was posed, the majority of East African Asians appear to have identified themselves as Indian.

population is by no means evenly distributed. Rather its members are still heavily concentrated in those towns and cities which experienced acute labour shortages during the 1960s and 1970s — i.e. London, the industrial Midlands, and the textile towns on either side of the Pennines; and within each of those areas, South Asian settlers are further concentrated in particular residential localities, usually — although not always — in inner-city areas. In these contexts their presence is much more prominent. In both Birmingham and Bradford, for example, nearly a quarter of all school entrants are now of South Asian descent, and in certain neighbourhoods they form the over-whelming majority. Hence in the areas which the settlers have made their own, *Desh Pardesh* is much more than a social and cultural expression: it has also become a spatial reality.

Many of Britain's white natives undoubtedly view the rapid growth of such ethnic colonies with alarm, particularly when they emerge in or close to the neighbourhoods in which they themselves once lived. Nor are their fears assuaged by well-meaning but increasingly thread-bare arguments that such developments are nothing but a temporary way-station in a more long-term process of assimilation. That thesis is no longer valid. Like it or not, Britain has been changed, and decisively so, as a consequence of post-war immigration.

Yet just what has changed? There is of course a visible difference: several million of Britain's inhabitants have the kind of skin colour which its white natives would like to acquire on expensive tropical holidays, but would be horrified to inherit. But while that difference is literally only skin-deep, the changes precipitated by the new min-orities' *ethnicity* — that is their commitment to their own religious, linguistic, and cultural traditions — have been far more fundamental. Since their ethnicity is intrinsic to their very being, the resultant loyalties are a major resource in the construction of survival strategies: hence they are unlikely to be abandoned. If this is so, it follows that short of comprehensive ethnic cleansing — which one hopes is not an option — nothing can alter the fact that the new minorities have become an integral part of the British social order, and they have done so *on their own terms*. Hence the underlying challenge is simple: how — and how soon — can Britain's white natives learn to live with difference, and to respect the right of their fellow-citizens to organise their lives on their own preferred terms, whatever their historical and geographical origins?

We do not suggest that responding to this challenge will be easy: indeed, given the cultural impact of Britain's imperial past, it is likely to be exceedingly difficult. It is the aim of this book to help readers confront these issues and find some answers to them.

The Dilemmas of Migration

Nevertheless our central concern here is not with white sensitivities, but rather with the settlers' experiences, and in this context it is worth emphasising that however much alarm their arrival may have caused among Britain's white majority, they themselves found the experience yet more perplexing, confronted as they were by what seemed to be a never-ending series of puzzles, contradictions and dilemmas. These often started from the moment migrants planned their departure, sharpened with their arrival overseas, and grew more complex the longer they stayed away. Thus even the most well-settled may suddenly find themselves faced with irresolvably contradictory pressures, as when they have to balance their obligations to care for ageing parents in the subcontinent against an equally strong commitment to support their British-based offspring. Likewise their children may face equally intractable dilemmas as they seek to balance their obligation to fulfil their parents' expectations of respect and support against the contrary imperatives arising from their involvement in a much wider British world.

Such dilemmas become more poignant when migrants find that despite all their new opportunities, they still remain aliens at their destination. No matter how bad the social and material conditions they may have left behind, and no matter how great their achievements abroad, migrants invariably feel a grievous sense of loss. They miss — and therefore long once again to experience — the familiar sights, sounds and smells of their birthplace, and the warmth and conviviality of everyday domestic life. All of them yearn for closer contact with their now-distant kin, and for closer involvement with the linguistic, cultural and religious world which once gave comprehensive meaning and purpose to their everyday lives; no wonder, therefore, that most make every effort to construct a more meaningful world in their otherwise alien destination.

A Flight from Poverty?

Yet if the social and emotional costs of migration were so great, why did so many settlers come to Britain in the first place? Material inequality was undoubtedly a spur; unless the financial rewards to which they might gain access are very tempting, the counter-attraction of the known and familiar will never be overcome. Even so, long-distance migrants are rarely drawn from the poorest families, and for good reason. Migration is above all an *entrepreneurial* activity, in which success usually depends on making substantial initial investment, so that those with minimal social and financial assets cannot hope to get very far. Overseas travel strains the resources of even the most prosperous of Indian villagers, so overseas migration is normally way beyond the means of the landless poor: for them buying a railway ticket to Dhaka, Bombay or Karachi is the only realistic way of finding employment elsewhere. Overseas migrants are therefore usually drawn from families of middling status, whose members are neither sufficiently prosperous to be wholly content with their lot, nor so poor as to be unable to afford the migrant's ticket, passport and visa.

Much the same is true of the particular areas in India, Pakistan and Bangladesh from which most migrants have come. While some parts of the subcontinent do indeed suffer from the grinding poverty of popular stereotypes, this is far from true in the three regions from which the vast majority of Britain's South Asian settlers have been drawn — Punjab, straddling the border between India and Pakistan in the north-west; Gujarat, on the western seacoast north of Bombay; and Sylhet District in north-eastern Bangladesh. Punjab and Gujarat are both noted for their agricultural prosperity; Sylhet might seem at first sight to conform more closely to the stereotype, given its location in poverty-stricken Bangladesh, but this does not stand up to closer examination.

First, Bengal has not always been in its present parlous economic condition. Its fabled wealth made it an early target of the East India Company, and its current penury must therefore be seen in the context of a long history of British colonial exploitation, more recently compounded by rapid population growth. Secondly, as Gardner and Shukkur show in their chapter, the marked concentration of emigration in Sylhet District was not a consequence of the Sylhetis' greater poverty, but rather of a historical anomaly which made cultivators in the District the *owners* rather than mere tenants of their land. This highlights a further major characteristic of South Asian migration to Britain: whether Punjabi, Gujarati or Sylheti, the majority of settlers are from *peasant farming* families. Not only did this mean that they were people who had proudly and autonomously owned and cultivated the land from which they made their living, but the sense of psychological and financial independence which this status gave them has proved crucial to their success both as migrants and settlers.

Not all migrants were peasant farmers, however. Some were craftsmen, and the inflow also included a small but significant leaven of urbanites who were much more likely to have commercial skills and/or professional qualifications. Migration to Britain has therefore in no way been a means of escaping destitution. Most of the urbanites saw the move as a step towards career advancement, and although the peasants were undoubtedly attracted by the money they could earn in Britain, they did not seek access to this new source of wealth to meet their families' everyday expenses; that came from the land. Employment overseas was more usually the means of supplementing the family's *capital* resources: the migrant's savings would be invested in building a new house, buying more land or a tractor, installing a tube-well, or providing a daughter or a sister with a larger and more attractive dowry. Hence the initial objective of most migrants, especially the peasant-farmers, was to raise their family's standing in the local social hierarchy.

Migration and Kinship

In such a context migration is a far less individualistic activity than is often supposed. First, few left without the active support of their extended families, who often provided the migrant with his ticket, passport and visa. Secondly, most migrants regarded their continued membership of their extended families as axiomatic. Not only did they expect to share the fruits of their labour with the group as a whole, but their physical absence had little impact on their position in their extended family. Even if they returned penniless (which heaven forbid), it was taken for granted that they would and should immediately resume all the social roles and rights which they had enjoyed before they left.

Nor was this the only way in which kinship reciprocities had a major impact on the migratory process. As Shaw's account of the Pakistani settlement in Oxford shows, only a tiny minority of newcomers arrived in Britain as lone adventurers with no prior contacts whatsoever. Of course the very earliest pioneers must indeed have done so long ago. But this phase did not last long. Having established themselves, each of these early pioneers soon became a bridgehead through which the entry of a whole stream of kinsmen and fellow-villagers was facilitated. Hence the vast majority of migrants arrived not as unconnected individuals, but in cascading chains along increasingly well-worn paths of kinship and friendship. These processes have had a comprehensive impact on patterns of settlement. As the following chapters show in abundance, chain migration has given Britain's South Asian settlements a far more parochial character than most outsiders are aware, for specific and highly localised castes, sects and kinship groups in the subcontinent have given rise to — and are now umbilically linked with — equally tightly structured British-based ethnic colonies.

From Sojourners to Settlers

Despite the material advantages to which they gained access as a result of going to Britain, few rural migrants at first envisaged that they might become permanent settlers. Indeed since their aim was above all to earn and save as much as possible as quickly as possible before returning home, they could at that stage best be described as *sojourners* rather than settlers. Had that initial objective remained unchanged, the South Asian presence in Britain would have developed very differently. But that was not to be. While a few sojourners did return once they had met their initial financial targets, the vast majority stayed on much longer. At first this delay could be interpreted as only a temporary deferral of their original goal, to save just a little bit more. But just as many other migrant groups in a similar position the world over have discovered — not least the native English as they built up their own vast overseas diaspora — such a habit can turn addictive. So too the South Asian sojourners: the longer they stayed, the more rooted and at ease they felt in their new British environment.

Although few ceased to dream about returning home permanently, many began to enjoy the greater personal autonomy they enjoyed in Britain, as well as the steadily increasing influence their new-found role as wealth-producers gave them within their extended families. From the 1960s onwards the cost of air travel fell sharply, so regular visits back home became much easier. This was a major boon. It allowed migrants to re-establish face-to-face contact with their families, to oversee the investment of their savings, and above all to savour some of the fruits of their labours as unskilled manual workers in a wet, dirty, and far-away world. But if cheap tickets allowed them to make much more frequent visits to the world they valued most, they also made it far easier to return for another spell on the treadmill. Little by little and almost unaware of it themselves, transient sojourners were undergoing a metamorphosis: they were gradually being transformed into more or less permanent settlers.

Yet the further along the route they went, the more their dilemmas were compounded. Years of residence abroad made them ever more aware of their alienation from the warmth and conviviality of family life, for even though visits back home were now much easier to make — and often became extended holidays of a year or more — each round-trip made them more poignantly conscious of the extent of their sacrifice, most heart-rendingly so when dearly loved and much remembered children failed even to recognise their long-absent fathers.

Meanwhile migrants' experience of Britain was also changing fast. As numbers grew rapidly during the 1950s and '60s, chain migration led to the reconstitution of large parts of many sojourners' kinship networks, so that many of those who lived nearby, and alongside whom they worked in the mill or foundry, were either kinsmen or fellow villagers. Hence rather than being a social and cultural no-man's-land, as it had been at first, Britain — or rather those parts of each industrial city into which they had been drawn by the demands of the labour market — was gradually becoming an arena for ethnic colonisation, as all the human material needed to support such an enterprise was converging within it.[9] This was welcome, for it made Britain a less alien place in which to live. But it also opened up a new dilemma: had Britain become an arena suitable for the resumption of family life? Attractive as that prospect might be, many sojourners were still sceptical.

Settlers' Perceptions of the Lifestyles of the Native English

From their perspective, Britain was a country riddled with contradictions. Materially, there was much to recommend it: living standards were substantially higher than in the subcontinent, and despite the ever-present blight of racial exclusionism, free access to health care and education was much appreciated. Even so, these obvious benefits had to be set against the sojourners' unanimous view that local *moral* values had little to recommend them. The English might be well-off materially, but the more migrants saw of their white neighbours' lifestyles, their standards (or lack of them) of personal hygiene, the apparent absence of any sense of personal dignity, and the individualism and hedonism of their everyday lives, the more scandalised they became.

In their own scheme of things, such values were absolutely crucial. Not to maintain a sense of *izzat* (personal honour) was to ignore an essential aspect of human dignity, while to ignore the emotional and material reciprocities due within the extended family was to pass up one's most fundamental obligations. Yet the native English appeared to have no such concerns. As the sojourners saw it — and most of those who have since settled down permanently see little need to change their opinions — people who expected that their sons and daughters should become financially self-supporting (and therefore socially autonomous) the moment they left school lacked any serious sense of family life. It also appeared that their children were never taught to behave with any sense of honour or respect — hence their tendency to behave like farmyard animals flaunting their bodies, and kissing and cuddling on the street. Nor was their treatment of elderly

---

[9] Excellent accounts of this early period can be found in Gurdip Aurora, *The New Frontiersmen* (Bombay: Popular Prakashan, 1967), and in Reshmi Desai, *Indian Immigrants in Britain* (Oxford University Press, 1963).

people any better: far from treating their elders with respect, they appeared to be figures of fun, and were bundled off into oblivion in old people's homes when they ceased to be able to look after themselves. As for *izzat*, the English seemed to lack all comprehension of what it meant. From all of this the sojourners drew the obvious inference. This was *not* a culture worthy of emulation, nor one to whose corrupting influence their nearest and dearest should be exposed.

If this was not enough, they reached similar conclusions over matters of personal hygiene. Thus while the white majority were (and are) all too ready to perceive migrants as "dirty" because of unfamiliar cooking smells and their preference for eating with their fingers instead of knives and forks, migrants' judgements of native English practices were far more scathing. For them, people who used toilet paper and not water to clean themselves, who rejected showers in favour of infrequent baths, and who even failed to wash after sexual activity were manifestly uncivilised and quite beyond the pale.

Survival in an Alien World

While such perceptions enabled the settlers to draw a clear boundary between themselves and their white neighbours, and thus reinforced their sense of ethnic solidarity, they nevertheless generated further dilemmas. If the surrounding social order was based on values so antithetical to their own, how could they hope to survive within it — especially in the longer term?

The reactions of the early pioneers are easy to describe. Because their families were not with them, their own exposure to local values was not regarded as particularly dangerous, since they saw themselves as having fallen only temporarily among barbarians. Indeed like many other expatriates — such as Europeans working on contract in Saudi Arabia and the Gulf — they took great pride in their capacity to survive despite having to let everything they really valued fall temporarily into abeyance. Saving was their only goal, since the more swiftly their bank balances grew, the sooner they could return to a world where the fruits of their labour could be sensibly enjoyed. Given this frame of mind, it is easy to see why sojourners were prepared to work long hours: twelve-hour shifts six or even seven days a week were quite normal, especially in the early days. And if shift work on this scale maximised earnings, crowding together into all-male households where a day and a night shift worker might even share the same bed made equal sense: expenditure was minimised. While no-one regarded this as a "proper" way to live and work, it nevertheless provided the quickest way of getting back to a land where civilised behaviour could be resumed.[10]

Yet contrary developments were taking place at the same time. As the inflow continued, chain migration brought kinsmen and fellow villagers together in ever larger residential and occupational clusters. And just as their own networks of reciprocity had facilitated the initial process of migration, so they also offered sojourners an equally positive means of surviving adversity, all the more so since the outside English world was so hostile and alien. Thus even though it had been no part of their initial plan, they gradually began to reconstruct a familiar social order around themselves, complete with all its associated cultural norms. All of a sudden conformity mattered. Behaviour which had previously passed without comment — as when lonely men sought comfort and relief with local prostitutes — ceased to be regarded as reasonable. Instead a very different tendency emerged. As conventional norms were re-established, deviance invited criticism and ridicule. Those who mimicked English ways too closely began to be accused of being *be-izzat* — without honour. *Desh Pardesh* was beginning to emerge.

Family Reunion

Since each settlement had become an arena within which honour could be sustained, life within it was transformed. The maintenance of personal and familial honour was of great concern to every migrant, especially since the need to restore their family's good standing in the local social hierarchy by increasing its material resources had often been the original spur to migration itself.

From this perspective *izzat* emerges not as something fixed and permanent, but as a matter of relative standing which generates constant competition, both between individuals and even more between closely related families. It follows that as soon as competition for *izzat* takes off, there can be no escape: anyone who fails to play the game will by definition lose face. Hence the emergence of Britain as an arena for status competition soon brought about a radical transformation of sojourners' lifestyles, because an ever higher premium gradually began to be placed on moral conformity.

This changed everything, for now at long last migrants began to regard the resumption of family life in Britain as a realistic possibility.

[10] Badr Dahya's account of "The nature of Pakistani ethnicity in Industrial cities in Britain", in Abner Cohen (ed.), *Urban Ethnicity* (London: Tavistock, 1974)) gives an excellent portrait of lifestyles during this period.

But they did so not because they had begun to take a more positive view of local cultural conventions, but rather because of a growing confidence that it was possible to recreate a fully moral social universe in Britain. Today such a conclusion might seem unexceptional, given the scale and success of Britain's many South Asian ethnic colonies; but for the early pioneers it was a major leap of faith. Moreover, given the far-reaching implications of the decision, it was not a step which every group took at the same speed. English lifestyles and moral conventions were still viewed as negatively as always, and it was precisely because of the threat which these were held to pose to their own most deeply-held values that the more cautious groups concluded that family reunion could *not* be justified; and had they been right, family reunion would indeed have been a disaster. Hence the more pessimistic groups — most of them Muslim — remained very doubtful about the wisdom of the whole enterprise long after the more easygoing communities had taken the decisive step.[11]

Changing Patterns of Investment and Expenditure

Whether the move towards family reunion took place quickly or slowly, the arrival of wives and children rapidly transformed the character of each community. Almost immediately, the all-male households which had been so prominent in the earlier period broke up, as settlers bought separate houses to accommodate their families. But although real kinship replaced quasi-kinship as the basis of domestic life, intense frugality remained the cornerstone of most families' financial strategies. Hence they preferred to buy cheap terraced houses in run-down areas, and to equip with a minimum amount of furniture, itself often secondhand. While to outside observers it often seemed that the settlers were too deprived and poverty-stricken to do any better, they themselves often saw things differently: their preferred lifestyles reflected their determination to save, despite the much greater cost of maintaining a family in Britain.

Even so, buying and furnishing a house, even on this basis, was a radical change in financial strategy, since the proportion of their income they could save dropped sharply. Moreover, as time passed, they gradually began to spend more on enhancing their local standard of living. The first step was usually to turn the front room into a comfortably and relatively expensively furnished *baithak* where

---

[11] A more detailed exploration of the factors underlying differential rates of family reunion can be found in Roger Ballard, "Emigration in a wider context", *New Community*, 1983, and in Roger Ballard "Migration and Kinship" in Colin Clarke (ed.), *South Asians Overseas* (Cambridge University Press, 1990).

guests could be entertained in style: as always, enhancing the family's *izzat* was a central priority. Thereafter change became ever more pervasive. Most families installed a telephone to keep in touch with kin, and a VCR to watch Hindi movies. Many then refurbished and redecorated their properties (often with the help of Local Authority improvement grants, of which they took more advantage than most), before finally buying new furniture, laying down fitted carpets, and installing central heating. Last but not least, the more affluent families began to abandon the inner-city areas, where initial settlement had invariably occurred, in favour of more expensive suburban properties.

As this went on, the rate at which they were able to put money aside dropped sharply, as did their propensity to remit — much to the alarm of kin back home. Yet although sojourners-turned-settlers were now by their own standards behaving in an increasingly pro-fligate way, their overall financial strategies were still broadly in keeping with their original objectives, but were certainly much more frugal than those of their white neighbours. Thanks to their peasant origins, they remained strongly committed to social and financial autonomy, and refused to be seduced by the credit-driven expectations of consumer capitalism. Hence they placed a high premium on proper-ty ownership, and regarded all forms of tenancy — even if the landlord was a Local Authority — as humiliating. They took an equally negative view of indebtedness, so when terraced houses in so-called "slums" could be bought for no more than a few hundred pounds — as was possible in many industrial cities right up to the late 1960s — many seized the opportunity to do so, often cash down. Since then property prices have spiralled upwards, leaving little alternative to taking out a mortgage, but even so their commitment to capital accumulation remained intense. Anyone who paid off a loan before its due date was much admired. Everyday household finances were also just as frugally organised: not only was hire-purchase avoided like the plague, but extended families took every possible advantage of economies of scale: all but the most perishable of food was — and still is — bought by the gross, sack or box.[12]

The Reconstruction of Social and Religious Institutions

As sojourners became settlers, so their lifestyles changed — although this was largely a matter of their revising, rather than abandoning,

---

[12] This has confused many sociological commentators, for in "objective" terms the new minorities have given and often still give every appearance of suffering from severe deprivation. But appearances can be deceptive. Because most South Asian settlers have studiously avoided the values of consumer capitalism, they have survived adversity far more successfully than their white working-class peers.

their initial aims and objectives. They remained almost as frugal as ever, even if Britain, rather than their home village, became the principal arena of saving and capital investment. And as settlers began to put down local roots, they made vigorous efforts to rebuild almost every aspect of their social and cultural traditions. Thus while religious observance had previously slid into abeyance, family reunion soon precipitated a resurgence in this area. Indeed, as every subsequent chapter shows, shared religious and sectarian commitments have for the most part proved to be the catalyst around which most South Asian communities have coalesced. Hence as numbers grew, a network of mosques, gurdwaras and mandirs began to spread across the country, each attracting an ever larger and more committed congregation.

The rapid re-establishment of religious institutions, and the growing vigour of *izzat*-competition, had a major impact on the behaviour of settlers, who found themselves under growing pressure to conform (or at least give the appearance of conforming) to the ideal norms of their own particular group. Former pleasures — such as smoking, drinking, and occasional adventures with white women — were now perceived as shameful and dishonourable. Sikhs began to regrow their hair and readopt the turban, Muslims to forswear alcohol, and many Hindus to become more strictly vegetarian.

Another major consequence of family reunion was that life-cycle rituals, especially those associated with marriage and birth, could now be celebrated in Britain. The implications of this development were far-reaching. Large numbers of guests are invited to such celebrations, which therefore become important arenas for social interaction. And besides the fact that they are joyful events, the elaborateness with which they were celebrated had always been the central means whereby families competed to secure and advance their relative *izzat*. Thus from simple beginnings, marriage and births came to be celebrated in an ever more elaborate way: in every community rituals have grown longer and more complex, and the scale of gift-giving larger. Hence the cost of participation has steadily escalated, leading to what can only be described as conspicuous consumption among the most affluent and firmly rooted communities.[13] Nothing more clearly confirms the settlers' commitment to ethnic colonisation than these developments.

[13] Both Parminder Bhachu, *The Twice Migrants* (London: Tavistock, 1986), and Pnina Werbner, *The Migration Process* (London: Berg, 1989) provide detailed accounts of well-established South Asian communities, with a particular emphasis on the elaborate processes of gift exchange which now accompany marriage among East African Ramgarhia Sikhs on the one hand, and affluent Pakistani businessmen on the other.

Difference and Diversity

Yet although all the various components of Britain's South Asian population have been involved in these processes of ethnic colonisation, and thus in the construction of their own *Desh Pardesh*, their trajectories of adaptation have varied greatly. Hence while the accounts presented in this volume reveal many common features, they also highlight how much South Asian communities differ from each other, and that many of those differences were established during the process of migration itself. Thus while chain migration facilitated ethnic colonisation by bringing kinsmen together in specific neighbourhoods, it also generated differentiation, since each cascading stream brought migrants from a specific region, caste and community to an equally specific location in Britain. While all the new arrivals had to cope with similar forms of racial and ethnic exclusionism, it was above all to the specific resources of their own group that they looked for inspiration as they set about devising strategies for survival. The results of all this are now becoming obvious. Since each little group of settlers rebuilt its life around their own religious, cultural and linguistic resources, and since the precise character of these resources varied enormously from group to group, so too have the ways — and the speed — with which they have adapted to their new environment.

First and foremost, the migrants were very varied in their *geographical origins*. Leaving those who arrived as "twice-migrants" from elsewhere in the diaspora to one side for a moment, the vast majority of direct migrants came from just three relatively compact geographical regions in Punjab, Gujarat, and finally from Sylhet District in Bangladesh (see maps, pp. xvi and xvii). Of the three, Punjab has provided by far the largest inflow, for around two-thirds of Britain's South Asians are of Punjabi ancestry.[14] Even so Punjabis are not a homogeneous group. Although as regards language, behaviour and culture they have much in common, religious and caste differentiation has increased sharply during the past century. Hence Independence in 1947 was accompanied by a vicious process of religious and ethnic polarisation. Several hundred thousand people died, and the killing only stopped after several million Hindus and Sikhs living in areas allocated to Pakistan took refuge in India, while a similar number of Muslims in east Punjab fled west to Pakistan.[15]

[14] While the 1991 Census figures quoted earlier give a much more accurate estimate than ever before of the total size of Britain's South Asian population, the numbers are of little help when it comes to making a more precise regional and religious breakdown.
[15] A useful introduction to the events of this period can be found in Khushwant Singh, *A History of the Sikhs* (Oxford University Press, 1991).

Of the Punjabis in Britain, rather less than half are from the Indian side of the border, and of these the great majority are from the central and eastern parts of the Jullundur Doab. Most Indian Punjabis are Sikhs, although perhaps a quarter are Hindus; and while the great majority of the Pakistani Punjabis are Muslims, they also include a small Christian minority, most of whom are of Untouchable descent.[16] No less than their Indian counterparts, Britain's Punjabi Muslim settlers are also predominantly of rural origin, and once again with specific regional concentrations. As many as two-thirds originate from the Potohar region south-west of Rawalpindi, especially from Mirpur District in Azad Kashmir. The remainder trace their roots either to the Chhach District (formerly known as Campbellpur), the city of Lahore, or the canal colonies of northern and central Punjab.

Gujarat has been the next most important source of immigrants, and roughly a quarter of British Asians have Gujarati connections of some kind. As in Punjab, the social order in Gujarat is deeply divided by religion, so although Hindus form the majority of Gujarati settlers in Britain, they also include a significant Muslim minority. Moreover, as Dwyer shows, Gujaratis have a long history of emigration to both Africa and the Middle East, so as many as half of Britain's Gujaratis have East African connections of some sort. Over and above all this the Gujarati social order is further fragmented by a large number of religious, sectarian and caste disjunctions, and while a comprehensive account of these is beyond our scope, the descriptions of specific Gujarati communities in Dwyer's, Warrier's and Knott's chapters show how great that variation may be.

Sylhet District in north-east Bangladesh is the third-largest source of immigration from South Asia, and here Gardner and Shukur's account breaks much new ground, since few other researchers have yet paid much attention to the Sylhetis. As already noted, Sylhet may be slightly more prosperous than other parts of Bangladesh, but it is still a great deal less so than Punjab or Gujarat. Partly because of this, the Sylhetis have moved more slowly from the sojourner to the settler phase than any other group; indeed, in their case family reunion is still taking place. Hence they are currently by far the poorest component of the South Asian presence in Britain, and also have the highest rate of population growth.

Religion is also a major source of differentiation, and all of South Asia's faiths are now represented in Britain. Of these the Muslims are by far the most numerous, since all the Sylhetis, over half the Punjabis, and perhaps a fifth of the Gujaratis are followers of Islam.

---

[16] Patricia Jeffery, *Migrants and Refugees* (Cambridge University Press, 1976) provides an excellent account of Pakistani Christians and some of their dilemmas.

Yet although Islam has now become a significant vehicle for collective mobilisation, as Shaw's account of Pakistanis in Oxford, as well as Gardner and Shukur's discussion of East London Sylhetis shows, Islam in Britain is in fact far less homogeneous than outsiders commonly suppose, a point well underlined by Lewis's analysis of sectarian developments in Bradford. Nor are these contradictions unique to the Muslims. Thus while Dwyer indicates that a parallel form of neo-Hindu revivalism is attracting widespread interest in Britain, as it currently does in India itself, her focus on Hindu sectarianism also shows that Hindus are no more religiously united in Britain than they are in India itself. Caste and sectarian differentiation remains deeply entrenched, as — even more so — does the disjunction between the Gujarati majority and Punjabi minority. Ballard's analysis of Sikh disunity takes up the same theme, while Nesbitt's account of Valmiki revivalism shows how organised resistance to upper-caste hegemony leads to what can best be regarded as the creation of a whole new religion.

Over and above the sectarian fragments of which the Sikh, Hindu and Muslim presence is constituted, South Asian migrants have also brought a number a smaller and less well-known religious traditions to Britain. Of these the Jains and the Zoroastrian Parsis are discussed in latter chapters; lack of space has forced us arbitrarily to exclude the Buddhists and the Indian Christians, who themselves embrace a wide range of diversities. Punjabi Protestants, Catholics from Goa, and Syrian Christians from South India have all formed small but very active ethnic colonies of their own.

As for social class, it has already been indicated that the vast majority of migrants were of rural rather than urban origin, and that most belonged to peasant farming families, though with a significant leaven of skilled craftsmen. On arrival in Britain the industrial jobs which migrants took led some analysts to identify them uncritically as "working-class", but that term should be applied with caution. Structurally, settlers did indeed stand at the bottom of the ladder; but on the other hand their aspirations, strategies and expectations differed sharply from those of their white working-class neighbours. The social hierarchy of an Indian village cannot be mapped over that of urban industrial Britain.

Even so, it is clear that although everyone started out at the bottom of the social order, some groups have achieved much more upward mobility than others. How is this to be accounted for? In crude statistical terms there is now evidence that British Muslims have attained a much lower average level of achievement than the Hindus and Sikhs, let alone the Jains and the Parsis. Given that Islam is popularly regarded as inculcating narrow-mindedness, inflexibility and authoritarianism among its followers, the obvious conclusion is often drawn: that the correlation must be causal. However this conclusion cannot be sustained, above all because it fails to take any account of levels of economic development in the areas from which migrants have been drawn. Mirpur and Sylhet districts — from which the majority of Muslim migrants have been drawn — are relatively poverty-stricken, certainly as compared with West Punjab and Gujarat. It is this, rather than commitment to Islam *per se*, which accounts for most of those differentials.

If differential levels of rural economic development have affected patterns of upward mobility, being of urban origin has had still greater impact. As we have seen, only a small proportion of the total inflow was made up of urbanites, but since most came with educational or professional qualifications of some sort, their expectations and aspirations were much higher. Most were therefore distressed to find that despite their hopes of a professional career, they were no better placed on the labour market than the villagers, and that there was little alternative to taking unskilled manual jobs. Despite the bitter humiliation which this entailed, few allowed their hopes to be entirely dashed. Some have since established themselves in professional careers, but many more have sidestepped exclusionism in the labour market by starting their own businesses — and have thus achieved upward social mobility. In the early days some of those successes were spectacular. As Hinnells recounts, the tiny Parsi community saw no less than three Members of Parliament elected from among its ranks in the early twentieth century.

Later the situation became much tougher, and the experiences of the few people with professional qualifications who arrived in the midst of the much larger inflow of labour migrants were chequered.[17] Some, like the doctors, made progress towards the middle ranks of their professional hierarchies. Promotion to more senior positions largely eluded them, however, and the experience of racial exclusionism has gradually led to a change in their adaptive strategies. In the early years of settlement most professionals made great efforts to distance themselves from the mass of their fellow-countrymen and their ethnic colonies, hoping that their greater commitment to assimilation would serve to ward off exclusionism. However years of bitter experience has persuaded most of them to change their minds, so that in addition to the close ties they have long maintained among

---

[17] So much research has been devoted to charting the experiences of the labour-migrant majority that those of the professional minority have been largely overlooked. In the United States this pattern is reversed, and the experiences of its mostly professional settlers is ably charted in Arthur and Usha Helweg, *An Immigrant Success Story* (London: Hurst, 1991).

themselves, many South Asian professionals have established closer relationships with upwardly mobile labour-migrant families, especially if they are of similar regional, religious and caste origins.

Migrants and Twice Migrants

The final source of differentiation, which cuts across all the others discussed so far, is that between those who came directly to Britain from the subcontinent, and those who had previously lived elsewhere in the South Asian diaspora — a group which has been graphically dubbed by Parminder Bhachu as *"Twice Migrants"*.[18]

Bhachu herself is concerned solely with those twice-migrants who arrived by way of East Africa. Besides forming by far the largest such group in Britain, they do appear to differ strikingly from their once-migrant peers. Besides being heavily involved in ethnic reconstruction long before their involuntary departure from East Africa, the circumstances of their arrival in Britain were quite different. Most entered as more or less complete family units, and they had by definition rejected the option of an immediate return to India. Hence they were settlers rather than sojourners right from the outset. In addition they were also better equipped for economic survival: most had educational qualifications of some sort, many spoke English fluently, and most men (and some women) either had experience of professional, technical or commercial employment, or had run their own businesses before leaving Africa.

Despite these advantages, East African Asians soon met the same problems of racial exclusionism as their once-migrant peers. Few were dispirited, however, and by dint of hard work, reinforced by skill, determination and mutual co-operation, they have made rapid progress, both in paid (and often professional) employment, and by starting their own businesses. Even though many families lost most of their savings during their involuntary departure from Africa, by common consent the East Africans now form the most prosperous segment of the South Asian presence in Britain. Yet although they tend to feel themselves to be a cut above the rest, it is uncertain how long this sense of East African and twice-migrant distinctiveness will be sustained. Despite their greater affluence and more "westernised" material lifestyles, they also have a strong commitment to religious and ethnic reconstruction, and are thus much less different from the other settlers than is commonly supposed, since they belong to the very same communities and castes as do the once-migrants. Thus while the African connection remains a source of pride and not a little

[18] Parminder Bhachu, *ibid.*

prestige, its distinctiveness is inevitably fading. Kinship, caste and sect are proving far more effective as unifying agents than the experience of being a twice-migrant.

This is not true of all twice-migrants, however, as Vertovec's chapter demonstrates. In sharp contrast to every other group discussed, the Indo-Caribbean population of Guyana and Trinidad did not move overseas as voluntary migrants, but were transported there as indentured labourers in conditions of near-slavery. They were part of a replacement labour force recruited after the formal abolition of slavery; many thousands of Indian "coolies" thus found themselves working for a pittance in a whole string of tropical colonies.[19] Given the harshness of their conditions of employment, the indentured labourers found it much more difficult to sustain a coherent sense of cultural continuity than did their free migrant counterparts, and Indo-Caribbeans therefore differ strikingly in their lifestyles from all other British South Asians. Their links with the subcontinent have become so attenuated that few retain fluency in their ancestral language, and many aspects of their speech and lifestyle have been heavily influenced by contact with their Afro-Caribbean neighbours. However in religious terms they still identify themselves as Hindus, even if their practices have been influenced by Protestant Christianity, while the significance of caste divisions — which are still salient within all other South Asian groups — is also much diminished.

On the face of it, the Indo-Caribbeans differ sharply from everyone else, not least because for them those characteristics which the others regard as the very heart of their "Asianness" are severely atrophied. Yet it would be unwise to dismiss the Indo-Caribbean experience as wholly exceptional, for their adaptive strategies may well foreshadow the shape of things to come. Certainly, material conditions in contemporary Britain are much less adverse than those experienced by Caribbean cane-cutters, and cheap travel makes it easier for settlers to keep in touch with kin in the subcontinent; but the pressures to which the second and third generation in Britain are subjected, and their sense of distance from the subcontinent, echo the Indo-Caribbean experience. Before long their response to exile may seem much less aberrant than it does at present.

Caste

There is, however, one sphere in which no other groups have yet followed Indo-Caribbean practice: that of caste. As every subsequent

---

[19] A detailed account of the indenture system can be found in Hugh Tinker, *A New System of Slavery* (Oxford University Press, 1974).

chapter shows, caste remains a crucial feature of social organisation in almost every settlement. Yet despite its centrality, nothing provokes more bafflement and indignation among outsiders. It is therefore vital to look briefly at both the ideological foundations and the practical consequences of this most Indian of institutions.

In ideological terms, both differentiation and the functional inter-dependence of the component parts so differentiated is basic to the Hindu vision of the logic of the cosmic order. Hence the social order (which is itself viewed as a microcosm of the wider universe) is conceived of not as a collection of autonomous individuals all pur-suing their own independent goals, but rather as a complex system of interdependence where every component makes its own unique but necessary contribution to the operation of the whole. What this means in practice is that Hindu society is seen as arising from the interactions between a multiplicity of occupational specialists, where Brahmins perform rituals to please the gods, kings rule, merchants trade, farmers cultivate their land, and craftsmen of many kinds exercise their skills, while polluted menials serve all their superiors by removing the impurities which the latter continuously accumulate as a result of cosmic, local and personal entropy.[20]

Although this system emphasises cooperation and reciprocity, it is also explicitly hierarchical. Brahmins, as the epitome of ritual purity, stand at the top; rulers, traders, farmers and craftsmen are spread out along a steadily descending scale, down to groups right at the bottom which are often described as "Untouchable" — although "irretrievably impure" is a more exact term. Hence throughout the subcontinent the population of every village is divided between a number of hereditary, endogamous and occupationally linked groups known as *zat* or *jati*, or in English as castes. At least in principle, every such caste has a fixed and unchangeable rank, while its boun-daries are maintained both by the hereditary ascription of occupational specialism and by a rule of endogamy which requires that all mar-riages must take place within the *jati*. Yet although the tight closure and lack of flexibility which all this implies often leads Western observers to conclude that the whole system is morally objectionable, a closer examination of how it actually operates shows that it is actually much more fluid than first impressions might suggest.

First, each caste is a fully-fledged community of kin, whose mem-bers sustain horizontal links with like groups in neighbouring villages; and while individual mobility from one caste to another is unthink-able, *collective* mobility, where an entire locally-based *jati* moves

[20] Excellent accounts of the formal logic of the caste system can be found in Louis Dumont, *Homo Hierarchicus* (London: Allen and Unwin, 1970), and in Declan Quigley, *The Interpretation of Caste* (Oxford University Press, 1991).

upwards (or downwards) through the social scale, is indeed possible
Nor is this new; there is widespread agreement that such collective
mobility has always been a feature of the caste system.

Seen in this perspective, caste solidarity is much less puzzling: its
core feature is no more than a closing of ranks among those with
common interests. Stripped of exoticism, caste reveals itself as a
highly effective form of collective bargaining, and thus akin to a
system of guilds. However it gains a strongly Indian character because
in this case occupational specialists use rules of endogamy and commensality to reinforce further the effectiveness of their closed shops.
The nominal fixity of caste rank is therefore rather misleading. While
change is rarely speedy, the rank ascribed to any caste ultimately
depends on the effectiveness of its bargaining power within the
immediate local context. Thus, as Dwyer shows for pre-British
Gujarat, merchant castes took advantage of a political vacuum to
engineer an improved rank for themselves; meanwhile Nesbitt provides equally clear evidence that those whose bargaining power declines can suffer exactly the opposite fate.

The Dynamics of Caste in the Diaspora

Although caste systems have always been more flexible in practice
than the formal ideology suggests, it is still widely assumed that com-
mercialisation, urbanisation and migration would inevitably undermine the whole system. Much has indeed changed. In urban India the
formal division of labour and the resulting structures of interdependence have largely collapsed, and such patterns are even more alien
to life in the diaspora. Yet in Britain as in urban India, caste disjunctions and caste loyalties are still almost as active as they ever were.

Why should this be so? While the hereditary allocation of occupational specialisation may have been swept away, the rules of endogamy are still just as strictly followed in the diaspora as in the
subcontinent. As a result, all kinship networks remain firmly caste-
specific. By itself this would be of little significance, were it not that
kinship reciprocities still offer the most effective means of organising
mutual support, especially in fiercely competitive urban environments. Thus whenever migrants have helped each other gain access
to jobs, housing and other scarce resources, and whenever they have
sought to protect their gains (however limited) from encroachment,
they have invariably found that kinship ties provided the most effective base for collective mobilisation. So although rapid economic
change may indeed have eroded the caste system's traditional foundations, it has been re-invigorated by its role as a channel for kinship
reciprocities, no less in Birmingham than in Bombay.

The collapse of the traditional rank order has had a further paradoxical consequence: the intensification of inter-caste competition for status. As almost every subsequent chapter shows, many settlers are still almost obsessively concerned with issues of rank; members of "higher" castes still go to considerable lengths to preserve and maintain their status, while those further down the scale are if anything even more concerned to catch up.

Caste, Religion and Sect

Since caste is above all a Hindu ideological construct, and since the very idea is nominally repugnant to the Muslim, Sikh, Jain, Parsi and Indian Christian traditions, it might be thought that such a generalisation would not be widely applicable amongst non-Hindu settlers. In practice, however, few if any of the subcontinent's non-Hindu communities have remained immune from its influence.

The Sikhs provide a good illustration. On a strictly theological level, the Sikhs can and do argue that their Gurus flatly rejected the ideology of caste. But despite this, neither the Gurus nor their followers seriously challenged either the hereditary ascription of occupational specialism, or the principle of *zat* endogamy. And while those who followed the Gurus' teaching may thereby have been able to discount the Brahmins' claims to ritual superiority, their ideas about ritual impurity remained largely unchanged. From the viewpoint of those at the bottom of the pile, the conversion of their patrons to Sikhism made little difference; in the face of continued upper-caste chauvinism, many felt they had no alternative but to strike out separately on their own account, as Nesbitt shows for the Valmikis.

Similar tendencies can also be observed among the Muslims, most of whom are also converts from Hinduism. In most rural communities occupational roles are still hereditarily ascribed, and give rise to *zat* divisions of a manifestly caste-like character, while the tendency towards closure is further reinforced by a widespread preference for cousin-marriage. Thus even though Muslims are much less bothered about rules of endogamy, their *biraderis* tend to be even more tightly introverted than most *jatis* — and, as Shaw demonstrates, they are just as effective as vehicles for mutual support.

Finally, if the Sikhs and Muslims are internally divided by caste, the Jains and the Parsis discussed by Banks and Hinnells offer a neat contrast. In this context both can be seen as acting as castes in their own right, for although they can and do argue that they are not concerned with issues of caste, each group has a long history of occupational specialisation, as well as a strong commitment to (religious) endogamy. Hence wherever one stands in the debate about whether it is legitimate to regard them as "castes", there can be no dispute that Jain and Parsi strategies of closure have a strongly caste-like character.

The Construction of South Asian Communities in Britain

What consequences, then, has all this diversity had for the construction of *Desh Pardesh*? Although there can be little doubt that settlers' lifestyles have changed a great deal since their arrival in Britain, in understanding this adjustment two very different sets of factors must be borne in mind. On the one hand they have all followed a broadly similar strategy of rejecting assimilation, and have instead relied to a large extent on their own resources as a means of building themselves a home from home. But even though they have all therefore been following broadly parallel trajectories, each group has drawn on its own specific set of human and cultural resources while doing so.

Given that those resources were themselves diverse, this has given rise to a wide range of outcomes. Close examination soon reveals much variation in the speed with which the switch from the sojourner to the settler mode has taken place, the kinds of housing they chose to live in and the jobs they were able and prepared to accept, and the vigour and success with which they sought to press their way upwards through the employment and housing markets and the educational system. As a result wide differences in achievement can often be observed between groups whose regional and occupational background might seem at first sight very similar. So, for example, the dual impact of differing levels of economic development back in the subcontinent, together with some arcane differences in marriage rules which might otherwise seem wholly insignificant, can help to explain the striking differences now observable between Jullunduri and Mirpuri settlers, even though their homes lie little more than 100 miles apart in Punjab; if two relatively similar groups differ so much, it follows that we must expect a yet wider variation still amongst the South Asian population as a whole.

This volume yet further underlines these diversities. As subsequent chapters show, "Asian" experience now ranges all the way from Sylheti families in Spitalfields, East London, crowded together in decaying council tenements and faced by high levels of unemployment and racial harassment, to wealthy East African Gujarati Hindus who have moved into comfortable suburban neighbourhoods where they are courted by senior members of the Conservative Party, and some of whom were even invited to a special celebration dinner at 10 Downing Street by Mrs Thatcher herself. Yet while any generalisation about "Asians" must take these variations into account, we still have far to go in understanding how they have arisen, let alone how permanent they will prove to be. Since all settlers have met similar patterns of structural constraint, such differences are manifestly the outcome of cultural factors. However, it would be a mistake to regard the less successful groups as suffering from a cultural handicap of any sort, or to see their present position as fixed and immutable. What every subsequent chapter serves to emphasise is not only how much every little community *differs* from the next, but also that each is following its own distinctive dynamic. From this perspective the members of each colony are best understood as being in the midst of a vigorous process of adaptation, and thus busily engaged in deploying their own particular set of cultural, linguistic, religious and kinship resources to plot a better future for themselves. The result is both steady progress and ever-growing diversity.

Those in search of simple generalisations will undoubtedly be disappointed by our approach, for we offer no instant nostrums and no simple and easily measurable variables. What we ourselves would argue is that if one adopts this kind of perspective, there is no simple way of understanding either the quality of South Asian lifestyles in Britain or the scale and character of the active solidarities which form the basis of any sense of community. Indeed once it is accepted that meaningful solidarities must be grounded in active networks, it follows that to talk of an "Asian" community — or even of "Indian", "Pakistani" or "Bangladeshi" ones — is often to reinforce a fiction. Real communities are much more parochially organised, and have been generated from the specific skills, understandings and loyalties which each little network makes available to its members. *Desh Pardesh* — the embodiment of the self-created worlds of Britain's South Asian settlers — is therefore anything but homogeneous; it is precisely the rich and diverse nature of its many faces which we seek to highlight here.

Between Two Cultures?

Before closing, this Introduction must also review the developments associated with the emergence of a British-born generation. While its members are certainly major contributors to the process of ethnic colonisation, they are also much more deeply involved in transactions across the ethnic boundary than their parents ever were. Almost all the significant social interactions of older settlers take place within the local ethnic colony; to be sure, it is hard to avoid any relationships at all with members of the indigenous majority, but when such transactions do occur they are usually strongly instrumental in character, and are invested with little moral or emotional force.

Their offspring, and more specifically those who have spent the greater part of their childhood in Britain, usually participate much more actively in the wider social order — at school and college, at work, and in a wide range of leisure activities. Hence in contrast to their parents they are constantly on the move between a wide variety of social arenas, which are often organised around differing, and sometimes radically contradictory, moral and cultural conventions.

How do they cope with this? To many outside observers, the answer seems obvious enough. Given that majority and minority value-systems differ so sharply, those young people who are expected to conform to both must constantly be struggling with the resulting contradictions, or so it is believed. Thus, for example, teachers, social workers and youth workers who regularly encounter South Asians among their clientele can often be heard discussing the insufferable contradictions which these young people are thought to face through being trapped "between two cultures".[21] Indeed this vocabulary has become so widespread that young Asians have themselves adopted it; instant sympathy can certainly be expected if they ascribe all their personal difficulties to their condition of "culture conflict".

Real though the dilemmas of the rising British-born generation may be, does this terminology enable their experiences to be adequately grasped? Does active participation in two or more social and cultural arenas necessarily cause psychological confusion? If not, what kind of analytical perspective should we use instead?

Code Switching and Cultural Navigation

Perhaps the best way in which we can make some progress here is by drawing an analogy between bilingualism and bi- and multi-culturalism, not just as attributes of the wider social order, but also in terms of the degree of linguistic and cultural competence which individuals may or may not possess. For most members of Britain's monolingual majority, bilingualism remains an unusual and mysterious skill, of which they have little or no first-hand experience. Had their experience been more cosmopolitan, they might have been more aware that in global terms bilingualism is a far less unusual phenomenon than they suppose. More important still, the capacity to

---

[21] It is also most unfortunate that an earlier and extremely influential compendium on the minority presence in Britain, James Watson's *Between Two Cultures* (Oxford: Blackwell, 1977), used this phrase in its title. The term therefore appeared to have been given academic and analytical credence, even though none of the contributors to that volume made any further use of it.

switch from one linguistic and conceptual code to another is not a recipe for psychological confusion. Quite the contrary: the ability to express oneself with equal fluency in two or more languages is a wholly normal human capacity, with which our brains can cope with ease.

As with language, so with culture. Just as individuals can be bilingual, so they can also be multicultural, with the competence to behave appropriately in a number of different arenas, and to switch codes as appropriate. If this is so, the popular view that young people of South Asian parentage will inevitably suffer from "culture conflict" as a result of their participation in a number of differently structured worlds can be dismissed. Rather they are much better perceived as skilled cultural navigators, with a sophisticated capacity to manoeuvre their way to their own advantage both inside and outside the ethnic colony. While such a perspective radically transforms the conventional understanding of the experience of young British Asians, it would nevertheless be idle to suggest that code-switching is a means by which they can short-circuit all their problems and dilemmas. Far from it. Just because they do not follow a single given set of conventions, all cultural navigators must constantly decide how best to behave in any given context, while also finding some means of switching smoothly from one to the next.

While such strategic decisions can indeed be difficult, to call them *"culture* conflict" is surely mistaken. If that culture were in some way a comprehensive determinant of behaviour, an individual's participation in two different arenas might indeed give rise to irresolvable contradictions. But multiculturalism freezes behaviour no more than bilingualism inhibits speech. Cultures, like languages, are *codes*, which actors use to express themselves in a given context; and as the context changes, so those with the requisite competence simply switch code.

In this perspective a switch of arena, along with an associated switch of linguistic and cultural codes, can be quite straightforward. But problems may arise when one is *known* to have switched codes, and where behaviour in the second arena takes a form which is regarded as unacceptable from the perspective of the first. For example, if many Asian parents knew exactly how their daughters behaved once safely out of sight at school or college, they would be horrified — just as those same young women would be equally embarrassed if their English school-friends were more aware of how they behaved once they re-entered the ethnic colony. Thus, code-switching is much more a problem for the beholders than for the actors themselves. Hence if one can keep all the arenas in which one is an actor apart, so that information does not flow inappropriately and unexpectedly from one to the next, no problems will arise. When difficulties do occur, they are more likely to be a result of unexpected information leakage than of code-switching in itself.

Such code-switching is of course not unique to South Asians, or even to immigrants, for one can expect to encounter such activities in all contexts of cultural plurality, no matter how lightly marked. But although code switch is best regarded as a universal phenomenon — for few people live in such a homogeneous world that they have no experience whatsoever of stepping back and forth across such boundaries — such navigational skills are far from uniformly distributed. Because a central privilege of dominance is the power to insist that all one's interactions should be ordered on one's own terms, it is members of excluded and devalued groups who have a far greater need to develop and use such skills.

Yet although most young Britons of South Asian descent have therefore become very skilled in moving back and forth between all manner of "English" and "Asian" arenas, they still face all sorts of dilemmas. These arise not so much because the underlying value-premises of the arenas in which they participate are different, but rather because each side has such a markedly negative perception of the other — as we saw at the outset.

This contradiction has far-reaching consequences. Because most aspects of their domestic lifestyles are viewed so negatively by the native English, most young Asians find themselves under constant pressure to distance themselves from their parents' and their communities' linguistic, religious and cultural conventions. It is therefore hardly surprising that many go out of their way to present themselves as if majority lifestyles were also their own preferred option whenever they feel themselves to be in sight of a white audience. Yet few feel wholly relaxed in such a role. First, presenting oneself in this way is always in a sense a living lie, since it entails a constant denial of the legitimacy and validity of one's heritage, and of the warm emotional support offered by one's family and kin. Secondly skin colour remains an inescapable barrier. No matter how well-practised one's navigational skills, the prospect of being written off as a "Paki" can never be eliminated. Total acceptance is therefore out of the question.

Yet if participation in majority arenas is beset by contradictions, most young people are involved in battles of the very opposite kind on their own home territory. These are much more complex than most outsiders imagine. Contrary to pessimistic external assumptions, few young people experience any difficulty in conforming to their parents' styles and expectations within the four walls of their home: besides the large debt of gratitude they feel they owe to their elders, the values with which they are expected to conform are those into which they have been socialised since childhood. By contrast, difficulties are far more likely to arise over young people's extra-domestic activities, as when worried and over-authoritarian parents take the view that even the smallest infiltration of English norms will result in a swift and comprehensive slide into anglicisation, especially where daughters are concerned. The resulting conflicts are played out in a wide variety of ways, but the results are rarely as disastrous as external observers predict; if parents are prepared not to ask too searching questions, and their offspring are prepared to do their code-switching well out of sight of their elders, some wide contradictions can be bridged with surprising ease.

Yet although similar "blind-eye" strategies can also be observed on the other side of the ethnic boundary, it would be wrong to conclude that cultural navigators will always conform to the norms expected in their immediate environment, or even that they are faced with a straight choice between majority and minority codes. On the contrary, strategic advantages can often be gained by those who deliberately code their behaviour inappropriately. For example, young men or women who begin to act in an over-anglicised way at home may well simply be seeking to assert themselves: efforts to resist parental hegemony should not be misread as "culture conflict". Exactly the reverse of this process occurs when young people set out to make space for themselves in majority contexts. Hence to switch "inappropriately" into Urdu or Punjabi speech, to wear a turban or *shalwar kamiz*, to condemn the publication of *The Satanic Verses*, to praise arranged marriages — or indeed to reject any other aspect of Western orthodoxy — is a particularly effective way of re-establishing personal dignity in the face of racial and ethnic denigration. To interpret such behaviour as psycho-pathological, as a vocabulary of "culture conflict" and "identity crisis" inevitably suggests, is seriously misleading, for the essentially political dimension of these interactions is thereby obscured.

Desh Pardesh Renews Itself: The Younger Generation

Exploring the behavioural strategies of the rising British-born generation takes us into a world of considerably greater complexity than that inhabited by its parents. As we have seen — and as every subsequent chapter further emphasises — the older generation of migrants' commitment to ethnic colonisation largely reflected an intense concern to insulate domestic and personal life from the perceived corrosive impact of the social and cultural mores of the host society. Yet even though the surrounding environment may have had far more influence on settlers' lifestyles than they themselves are aware of, the boundaries around their own domestic worlds are still sharply drawn. In these circumstances a descriptive account which regards life within such internal "Asian" arenas as being grounded in cultural premises which are entirely separate from those of the surrounding white majority may cut some analytical corners, but it does so without too much injustice to empirical reality.

Once we turn to the rising generation of young adults, however, such an approach ceases to be sustainable. First, the internal/external distinction almost disappears: those who have grown up in Britain are as much at ease in many majority environments as they are within the ethnic colony, and their everyday lives involve constant movement between a wide variety of differently structured arenas. But such manoeuvres give rise to much more than a simple either/or choice. Young British Asians may indeed be just as much at home in their parents' world as they are among their white peers, but at the same time they are actively and creatively engaged in carving out *new* styles of interaction among themselves. Thus it is also apparent that members of the rising generation are best understood as extremely mobile in linguistic, religious and cultural terms, and often taking delight in drawing eclectically on every tradition available to them. In this respect the musical inventiveness of Apache Indian, the Birmingham-born pop star whose ironic lyrics seamlessly mixing English with Punjabi are declaimed rap-style against a beat which itself weaves *bhangra* with reggae, may well be a pointer to the future.

With the younger generation bringing further layers of differentiation over and above those introduced by the first generation of migrants, any attempt to present a general overview of current developments is hazardous. Yet there is one point on which we can be clear. Most of the rising generation are acutely aware of how much they differ from both their parents *and* from the surrounding white majority, and as a result they are strongly committed to ordering their own lives on their own terms. Just what those terms will be, and how they will rejig and reinterpret and reinvent the premises on which they choose to organise their lives, is yet to be seen. But the vigour with which young people insist that "We're British and we're here to stay" makes it clear that the commitment to building *Desh Pardesh* is in no way limited to the first generation.

THE PAKISTANI COMMUNITY
IN OXFORD

Alison Shaw

Given their marked reluctance to adopt Western attitudes and their tenacious retention of traditional beliefs and lifestyles, Pakistanis in Britain are often seen as deeply resistant to assimilation. Apart from theories about the alleged impact of "Islamic fundamentalism", the most usual way of explaining these tendencies is to point to what Anwar has graphically identified as a *myth of return*[1] — the expectation that the central purpose of migration was not to achieve permanent settlement in Britain, but to accumulate sufficient wealth to make possible an eventual return to Pakistan. In that context, retention of social and economic links with their home villages, as well as repeated return visits, could all be seen as part of a longer-term strategy to resist all changes which might impede their eventual return.[2] It follows that if Pakistani settlers' commitment to the myth were ever to weaken, then the religious and cultural values whereby they organised their lives would — so the theory implies — become much more much open to Western influence.

In the 1990s, more than forty years after settlement began, it is increasingly clear that the myth of return has almost ceased to be a central feature of British Pakistanis' perceptions and ideologies. Most men have long since been joined by their wives and children, and because of the scale of their local financial commitments, few if any are now in a position to invest large sums of money in Pakistan, support relatives there, or finance return visits. Even so, traditional beliefs and styles of life are still very much alive in every Pakistani community in Britain. Also most young people, while giving the appearance of being thoroughly "westernised" in the sense of being fluent English-speakers and holders of educational and professional qualifications, are often still committed to cultural distinctiveness and upholding their community's moral and religious identity. So in spite

---

[1] Mohammed Anwar, *The Myth of Return: Pakistanis in Britain* (London: Heinemann Educational Books, 1979).
[2] Badr Dahya, "Pakistanis in England", *New Community*, vol. 2, no. 1 (1972–3); Patricia Jeffery, *Migrants and Refugees: Muslim and Christian Pakistani Families in Bristol* (Cambridge University Press, 1976).

of cultural persistence, the myth of return has ceased to be a credible explanation of how and why that should be so.

The persistence of Pakistani culture in Britain is indeed rooted in the social structure of migrants' families, as well as in the long-established tradition of overseas emigration from rural Pakistan. However, the myth of return highlights only one dimension of this tradition, namely that whereby the movement of individuals and groups has been powerfully shaped by kinship loyalties. Hence far from being an undifferentiated aggregate of exploited and excluded migrant workers — as most sociological accounts of their arrival suggest — the pioneer settlers who arrived in Britain during the 1950s and '60s must also be seen as representatives and upholders of specific moral and social traditions, which in turn had a substantial impact on subsequent processes of settlement and adaptation. And while the myth of return was indeed a key factor in the maintenance and justification of Pakistani cultural traditions in the early phase of settlement, some very different arguments have been deployed for the same broad ends since the early 1980s.

As the force of the myth of return has declined, there has been a corresponding increase in settlers' perceptions of themselves as a *religious* minority, and thus a growing concern with the issue of Muslim identity. Yet despite the different emphasis, the current concern with religious identity can be seen as serving a very similar purpose to that which the myth of return once did. It, too, represents an effective way for migrants to maintain and control their distinctive culture and social structure.

The concern of this chapter is not, however, with the entire Pakistani presence in Britain, but rather with a specific local community — that in East Oxford.[3] In exploring what has gone on within this limited and therefore more manageable local arena, our discussion falls into three main parts. The first traces the history of emigration from Pakistan to Britain, emphasising that this has never involved individuals leaving their families to seek fame and fortune for themselves alone, but has rather been perceived as a means whereby the kinship group as a whole could improve its collective lot. Thus although the initial migratory movement might only involve a single individual, the impetus for departure was invariably provided by the entire extended family. Nor did the migrant feel that he had stepped outside the family. Their loyalties and expectations were those which ruled within the wider kinship group or *biradari* as well as in the family. Such loyalties also had a powerful impact on all aspects of the subsequent processes of migration and settlement.

[3] Alison Shaw, *A Pakistani Community in Britain* (Oxford: Basil Blackwell, 1988).

The second part of the chapter looks at the implications of this tradition now that both families and *biradaris* are firmly re-established in Britain. Links between kin had a major impact on patterns of migration, since kinsmen invariably assisted each other to find work and accommodation. Not only is the organisation of each settlement therefore *biradari*-specific, but these same ties have had a strongly conservative influence over settlers' lifestyles, a tendency yet further reinforced when women and children began to arrive in Britain in the late 1960s and early '70s. The resultant transformation of an all-male settlement into a family-based community also led to many other changes, including more home-ownership, a shift from waged work to self-employment (often in small businesses), and substantial local modifications to traditional caste rankings. Women also began to play an increasing social role, particularly in the organisation and development of *biradari* membership.

The third and last part of our discussion explores the way in which the community, and especially its British-born second generation, increasingly stresses its Muslim identity, and how religiously-based symbols and ideologies have usurped the myth of return as a means of articulating the British Pakistani community's sense of social and moral distinctiveness.

Traditions of Migration

Compared to industrial towns in the Midlands and North of England, Oxford's 2,000 strong Pakistani community[4] is small. But like all other such communities in Britain, its members are drawn from just a few areas in Pakistan: mainly from Faisalabad and Jhelum Districts in Punjab, Mirpur District in Azad (Free) Kashmir, and Attock District in the North West Frontier Province. The majority of the settlers in Oxford are from Jhelum District, with the remainder drawn in roughly equal numbers from Faisalabad, Mirpur and the North West Frontier. The majority are of rural rather than urban origins.

Why have they come only from these areas? Closer examination reveals that they fall into two differing geographical regions, each with a long and distinctive tradition of migration. The first is made up of long-settled rainfall-dependent districts, such as Mirpur, Jhelum, Attock, Rawalpindi and most of the North West Frontier. In this area peasant-farming families have only been able to gain a meagre livelihood from their small and unirrigated landholdings; for generations men from this region have sought employment elsewhere

---

[4] For further details about Pakistanis in Oxford, and a review of the number, distribution and regions of origin of Pakistanis in Britain as a whole, see Shaw, *ibid.*

in order to supplement family incomes. Indeed the whole area became a favoured recruiting ground for the (British) Indian Army, which considered certain Punjabi castes, such as the Mughals, Jats and Rajputs to have special military capacities. The Royal Indian Navy recruited heavily in Attock (then Campbellpur) District, leaving Mirpur to the merchant navy. Men from this area were also recruited as construction labourers when Punjab's railways were being built, and later took similar jobs on the Kenya-Uganda railway during the last quarter of the nineteenth century.

By contrast with the relative poverty of these districts, Faisalabad is often described as the "Manchester of Pakistan" as well as its "bread-basket". A busy textile-manufacturing centre, it lies at the heart of the irrigated, agriculturally prosperous plains of central Punjab. Before the establishment of British rule it was largely barren, but during the latter part of the nineteenth century Punjab's ancient irrigation systems were massively extended in a huge canal-building program. Land in the new "canal colonies" was then distributed to peasant-farmers, most of whom were recruited from densely settled parts of north and east Punjab such as the Jullundur Doab. Just as the Army sought recruits from particular castes, so the canal colonists were "drawn only from the best agricultural tribes"[5] — notably the Jat Sikhs and the Muslim Arains. Every recruit was subjected to a physical inspection, and careful steps were taken to prevent families gaining more than one 25-acre plot by putting forward several representatives.

Most migrants to the canal colonies saw the move as an investment, for a plot bought for a nominal sum held the promise of radically improving the living standard of the entire family. As among migrants to Britain, pioneer colonists often left their wives and children behind in their villages of origin, at least for the first few years, while they brought the virgin land into production. Every so often they returned home with their savings, and the money they brought back had a significant impact on the local economy. Families built new houses of kiln-baked bricks rather than mud, bought better cattle and seed, and deposited any excess in the local village bank.[6]

The restlessness and the desire for social advancement generated by all this was later to influence migration to Britain. For instance, Saleem, an Arain from Faisalabad, regarded his coming to Britain in 1958 as a continuation of a family tradition of migration dating back to his grandfather's move from Gurdaspur to Faisalabad (then known as Lyallpur) in the 1890s. Two men from his family moved down to

[5] Malcolm Lyall Darling, *The Punjab Peasant in Prosperity and Debt* (Oxford University Press, 1928), p. 133.
[6] *Ibid.*, pp. 160–1.

the new colony at first, though they maintained close links with the rest of the family who stayed in Gurdaspur. With the Partition of Punjab in 1947, however, Gurdaspur was allocated to India, and inter-religious hostility became so severe that all Punjabi Muslims who found themselves on the wrong side of the border soon found there was no alternative to fleeing to Pakistan, just as all the many Sikh and Hindu settlers in Lyallpur fled to India.

By the time Saleem himself was born, his grandfather's original plot in Faisalabad had been divided between his many sons and grandsons. As Saleem explained, "That's why my father encouraged and paid for me to go to England — he wanted our family to buy more land again, just as we had done when my grandfather moved from Gurdaspur." Migration had become an integral part of his family tradition.

The Process of Chain Migration

There can be little doubt that service in the Army and Navy, together with their experience of work abroad and of the opportunities of colonisation, gave Punjabis the confidence to become long-distance migrants. However, these factors alone cannot provide a *sufficient* explanation for their departure, since the pattern of emigration was far from random even within these two main regions of out-migration. In some villages almost every family has sent someone abroad, while in an adjacent village it may be that hardly anyone has emigrated. Such patterns are the result of a marked tendency for migration to be organised in "chains". The chain would begin when a group of close kin pooled their savings in order to send just one man abroad; having found work, this man would then use his savings to sponsor another relative, and the two of them could then pool their resources to bring over yet more of their kin. Earlier migrants would help later ones to find accommodation and work, with the effect that relatives from the same village in Pakistan tended to live close together in Britain.

In Oxford, almost all the Faisalabadi migrants can be accounted for in terms of two chains. Twelve men, later joined by their wives, moved to Oxford from two adjacent villages south of Faisalabad city. The first link in this chain was Shakeel, who had gone to Glasgow during the Second World War, and helped three of his kinsmen to migrate during the early 1950s. They in turn sponsored a number of their relatives from their own and adjacent villages; one of these was Saleem, whose family's involvement in the canal colonies has already been described. He visited Oxford in 1959, and since employment prospects appeared better there than in Glasgow, he decided to stay; on hearing of his success, several friends and more distant relatives soon joined him from Scotland. Saleem also sponsored his cousin Iqbal's migration from Pakistan in 1962; on arrival Iqbal sponsored his brother Zahoor, while one of Saleem's friends sponsored two brothers and a brother-in-law.[7]

While Saleem's chain accounts for twelve of Oxford's Faisalabadi families, almost all the rest can be accounted for in terms of another chain, once again rooted in a single village. Here the chain's founder was an ex-soldier who stayed briefly in Newcastle after his arrival in Britain in 1957, and reached Oxford in 1958. He was then in a position to sponsor his sister's husband in 1959, and two of his brothers in 1962. These two then sponsored a third brother in 1964 and a fourth in 1965.

As migrants entered Britain in steadily increasing numbers, so other factors, not least the impact of government decisions, began to have an effect — often of a paradoxical kind. For example, when tighter controls on entry imposed by the first Commonwealth Immigrants Act came into force in 1962, a rush of new migrants entered Britain in an effort to "beat the ban". The very threat of controls — which was widely publicised by travel agents in Pakistan — meant that some men who might otherwise not have migrated took up what seemed like a "last-chance" opportunity; likewise the voucher system briefly introduced under the 1962 Act also positively encouraged chain migration, since men with kinsmen who already had jobs in Britain had much the best chance of obtaining a voucher. The voucher system also reinforced the existing pattern of emigration from districts with traditions of service in the Army and Navy, since men who had served in the armed forces during the war were also offered preferential treatment. Thus while changes in immigration law helped to shape the timing and extent of the migration, they did not alter the basic strategies which prompted Pakistanis to act on their long-standing traditions. Faced with the choice of moving immediately or not at all, many chose to move, regardless of the possible difficulties and dangers.

Kinship and Biradari: Welfare and Social Control

The reciprocities of kinship which underlay the dynamics of chain migration have also had a major effect on the subsequent development of Pakistani communities overseas. Since newcomers always made their way to towns where friends and relatives had already settled, and since jobs were often secured through a kinsman putting in a word of recommendation to his foreman, Pakistani settlements in

[7] For details of this chain, see Shaw, *op. cit.*, pp. 22–4.

Britain have tended to develop along lines of kinship and common villages of origin. This is why migrants' villages and areas of origin are not randomly represented in different British towns: each Pakistani settlement has its own specific characteristics.

Once again Saleem's experience provides a convenient example. He first found work in Oxford in 1958, and during a brief holiday in Glasgow the following year met five fellow-villagers who were temporarily unemployed. Four of them went back with him to Oxford, where he helped them to find work. But finding work was only a small part of the deal, since migrants helped each other with form-filling, general welfare and finding accommodation, and often shared their lodgings with relatives and friends. Thus Amjad came to Oxford because a cousin had arranged his accommodation, though in conditions which would have been regarded as excessively overcrowded to most English observers, for as Amjad recalls, "We lived in a two-bedroomed house. There were seventeen of us, including myself, my cousin from our village, and Anwar from a village near us." His experience was far from unique, for the typical form of residence during this period was a multi-occupied lodging house. Male shift-workers sometimes shared beds as well as rooms, but living frugally in exceedingly cramped conditions enabled them to maximise their savings and thus the volume of remittances back to Pakistan.

The presence of relatives and fellow-villagers also exerted a strongly conservative influence over the men's lifestyles, ensuring that however much they might be tempted to enjoy themselves, most continued to conform to the expectations held of them by their families back in Pakistan. This was sustained even when settlers grew more familiar with local procedures for obtaining mortgages, employment and welfare, so that they were less directly dependent on one another, and despite the fact that some men took to drinking alcohol and visiting prostitutes. In sharp contrast to later developments, these last two activities were little criticised, always provided that what was seen as a consequence of "bachelor lifestyle" did not threaten the interests of the *biradari*. However, a much dimmer view was taken of men who established long-term relationships with European women, since the more permanent financial obligations in which they then became entangled were seen as a major threat to the most crucial activity of all: saving money.

The Arrival of Women and Children

A major turning point in the character of the settlement came about in the late 1960s onwards, when wives and children finally began to join men already settled in Britain. For many observers this development seems to have been something of a puzzle. If migrants regarded living and working in Britain as a means of improving their living standards in Pakistan, why did they bring non-working wives and daughters to a country where the cost of living was much higher, and where they would also be exposed to the potentially corrupting influence of Western culture?

One factor was undoubtedly the increasing pressure of immigration control, so that "bringing the whole family to Britain enables the man to ensure that he can be replaced by his son when he wants to return to Pakistan".[8] Even so, this does not explain why the majority of women stayed on in Britain, for they could have chosen to return to Pakistan after a brief interval. Could a further consequence of the introduction of controls have been to shift migrants' intentions away from the myth of return, and towards a greater commitment to permanent residence in Britain? By the late 1960s the question of whether or not to reunite one's family in Britain was becoming increasingly complex. Some male informants did indeed mention the wish to continue the chain of male wage-earners in Britain as a factor in family reunion, though many also cited the superior educational and health facilities in Britain.

However, women often advanced a very different set of explanations. For example, Amina heard through her husband's brother that her husband Amjad had married an English girl — and she immediately resolved to go to England herself. Likewise, when Zahida's husband Zafar's remittances became increasingly irregular, she became worried that he might have married again, having heard of other migrant men doing just that. Rumours of this kind, which all too often reflected real developments in Britain, spread like wildfire in Pakistan, and many families began to resolve that it was now time for lone male migrants to be joined by their wives. Amina's relatives helped to raise the money to enable her and her children to go to Britain, and they all lived together for a while with Amjad and his (common law) English wife — who eventually left. Zahida was more fortunate: she too moved to Britain as soon as possible, and although her husband had been squandering his money, she was relieved to find he had not established a relationship with another woman. But these stories and many others like them were soon being regarded as cautionary tales, with the result that more and more families began to arrange marriages for their unmarried migrant sons, and for them to be joined by their new brides as soon as possible. Several years later, some of these brides were quite explicit that one of the motives behind the arrangement of their marriages had been the family's wish to place a check on their husbands' activities.

[8] Jeffery, *op. cit.*, pp. 49 and 67.

Hence it becomes clear that the key to the arrival of women and children lay in the expectations of the *biradari* back in Pakistan. It was not simply a question of men bringing wives over, or of male migrants changing their strategies in response to new legislation. Since they assume migrants to be autonomous individuals, such explanations ignore the crucial influence of the *biradari* and its values, and above all the interests of women and the vigour with which they can be expected to protect these interests when they appear to be seriously threatened. Viewed thus, the explanations for the arrival of women and children routinely advanced by men are best seen as *post hoc* rationalisations, while changes in the immigration laws are reduced in this context to something of a red herring. Moreover the gender-specific character of the two main waves of immigration, with "bachelor status" men being joined later by their wives and children, is exactly what their tradition of migration would lead us to expect. In the Punjab, male migrants have always been recruited as a result of a combination of external demand and selection within the *biradari*; and their subsequent marriages and family histories have similarly been ordered both external by changing patterns of opportunity and by the ongoing internal dynamics of *biradari*.

Nevertheless the myth of return did have an important function. It provided a means of ensuring that male migrants would continue to fulfill the objective their families held for them — to earn and save for the *biradari*'s benefit; and it served to preserve the *biradari* from the corrosive effects of Western influence. The arrival of women and children is best seen not so much as a departure from these objectives, but as a further means of preserving and protecting them in response to changing circumstances; the most immediate effect of women's arrival was the re-imposition of *biradari* control over male sexuality. Thereafter most relationships with English women soon ceased, and those few men who kept up such relationships came to be regarded as morally peripheral. The reunion of families was thus in no way indicative of a change in migrants' fundamental intentions; rather, it was a positive means of ensuring that *biradari* obligations would continue to be fulfilled. To understand these continuities, we must next explore in greater detail the three main features of the resulting social structure: caste, *biradari* and the practice of reciprocal gift-giving known as *lena-dena*.

Caste and Caste Status

Given Islam's strong ideological commitment to social egalitarianism, most Pakistanis vehemently reject the idea that their society is divided by a caste hierarchy in anything like the manner so charac-

teristic of their Hindu neighbours. Nevertheless the social structure
of the villages from which most migrants are drawn closely parallels
that of a Hindu caste system, for the local population is invariably
made up of a number of largely endogamous and nominally occupa-
tionally-linked descent groups, usually described either as *zat* (the
Punjabi pronunciation of *jati*) or *biradari*. The name by which each
biradari is known is identical to that of Hindu and Sikh Punjabi *jati*
with a similar occupational specialism; and they can also be ranked
in three broad categories: *ashraf* (nobles), *zamindar* (landowners) and
kammi (craftsmen and artisans).

To this day a person's traditional caste status remains a subject of
great interest and curiosity to most Oxford Pakistanis, but this ascribed status is now overlaid by new criteria, such as property ownership, professional success, and the amount of wealth acquired since
settlement in Britain; those who have become prosperous in Oxford
are by no means always from high-caste families, or from those which
had a dominant position in the village hierarchy.

Let us take Mohammed Yacoub as an example. Yacoub was one
of the first Pakistanis to settle in Oxford (he arrived in 1957), and he
was later joined by his five brothers. They are Gujjars, a group
traditionally associated with cattle-herding, and although generally
regarded as low-ranking *zamindar* (landowning) *zat*, some of their
rivals assert that they are merely *kammi*. Soon after arriving in Britain,
Yacoub pooled his resources with one of his brothers and bought a
house; later he became sole landlord of one of Oxford's more notorious all-male lodging houses. In this position he gained status in
relation to his fellow-countrymen, particularly new arrivals to whom
he acted as patron. By the mid-1970s, Yacoub and his brother owned
ten properties and two thriving businesses, and although they were
known to be Gujjars, their early entry into property ownership had
allowed them to enhance their status considerably.

By contrast, Rashid Shah, who arrived in Oxford from the same
village as Yacoub during the early 1960s, belonged to an *ashraf*
family of higher rank than the *zamindars*, but has failed to secure a
dominant position in the local socio-economic hierarchy. Rashid
came to Oxford because fellow-villagers were already settled there,
but his closest kin in Britain established themselves in London. So
when his wife and children joined him in the mid-1970s, they were
put in the humiliating position — in terms of the traditional hierarchy
— of becoming Mohammed Yacoub's tenants until Rashid had saved
enough to buy a house of his own. By the mid-1980s Rashid and his
sons owned three houses. Although respected as being of a good
family and caste, this was not sufficient in itself to give them a
particularly high rank in the local status hierarchy.

The Structure and Functions of the Biradari

While social status depends partly on the family's background in Pakistan, further tempered by the extent of its local economic success and property ownership in Oxford, it is social exchanges organised by and through female members of the family which are particularly crucial in maintaining and developing *biradari* membership, in the inclusion (or exclusion) of more distant kin, or even non-kin, into the *biradari*, as well as in structuring movements within and between different Pakistani communities in Britain.

Although the great majority of Pakistani households in Oxford are physically nuclear and are thus composed of a man, his wife and their children, most such households have other close relatives living near-by: this may include as many as ten further households. Extended kinship networks of this kind are normally identified as a *biradari*, but the term is so widely used in Pakistani Muslim contexts that it calls for further elaboration.

As Alavi[9] has stressed, the *biradari* is best understood as a con-text-dependent idea, rather than a rigid and concrete entity. Thus besides its local manifestation as a network of co-resident kin, it may also include relatives elsewhere in Britain, and at its widest extent may span different countries, and so include members resident in Britain, Pakistan and the Middle East; indeed when only few members live locally, a family may well consider this trans-national network of relatives as constituting its *biradari*. But when this is so, women may also build closer ties with fellow-villagers, or with neighbours to whom they had no prior ties, and these often blossom so intensely that they begin to treat each other as if they were true hereditary *biradari* members. At the very least they will begin to address each other with the appropriate kinship terms, and when their socio-economic interests and status are sufficiently close, the association may be further stabilised by marriage, even though the two sides did not previously belong to the same *biradari*.

One such marriage between a previously unrelated couple was regarded as thoroughly acceptable since both were of similar social and economic standing, and both belonged to the same Arain caste. Indeed precisely because mutually advantageous local reciprocities would be strengthened by the match, the bride's father preferred to accept his new neighbours' proposal for his daughter's hand rather than the many parallel offers he received from closer but much poorer kin in Pakistan. In another case a marriage across caste boundaries

[9] Hamza Alavi, "Kinship in West Punjabi Villages", *Contributions to Indian Sociology*, (N.S.) 6, pp. 1–27.

was justified on the grounds that both families were of *ashraf* status. It also confirmed the view held by the heads of the two families that because they had shared lodgings in the early days, and subsequently set up business together, they now belonged to the same *biradari*. Thus while *biradari* ties are nominally hereditary, in practice boundaries are defined with sufficient flexibility to allow the incorporation of new members. This may even involve the construction of whole new *biradaris*.

Lena-dena and the Role of Women

Networks of formal and informal social activity and mutual support organised and run by women play just as a critical role in shaping and maintaining the *biradari* as does the more public activity of men. These woman-centred networks embrace all potential *biradari* members both locally and further afield, and draw non-relatives into ties of quasi-kinship. Informal socialising of this kind typically occurs in the back room of the house, where women casually entertain their female visitors; the front room is normally reserved for male visitors, so allowing the ideals of *purdah* to be maintained in the new setting. However, it would be wrong to assume that women are therefore relegated like helpless pawns, to the back room. On the contrary it is in this informal arena that all activities in the formal sector are minutely discussed, and all the most telling judgments are made about the social worth of the participants. So although decisions are nominally taken in the front room, every important element will usually have been thrashed out already in the back room.

One of the most important aspects of formal social activity is the organisation of family rituals — including the celebration of birth, circumcision, a child's first completed Qur'an reading, marriage and arrivals from or departures for abroad. These events are normally celebrated either in the evening or at the weekend, and although they involve all family members they are primarily organised by women. Since men are generally the wage-earners — in Oxford few Pakistani women have taken paid employment outside the home — it is they who normally provide the funds for food, gifts and new clothes, and if large numbers of guests have been invited, as for a wedding reception or in celebration of a child's first completed Qur'an reading, it is again the men who arrange the hire of a suitable hall and send out invitations, collect relatives and drive their families to events at which they themselves are guests. But it is the women who organise the food, have new clothes made, decide who should be invited to the events they convene and to whom gifts of food should be distributed, and, most crucially of all, manage and record the gift-giving which is such a striking feature of these events.

The gifts routinely offered include sums of money ranging from £1 to £30, articles of clothing such as women's *shalwar-kameez* (baggy trousers and long blouse) and *dupatta* (headscarf), handbags, men's shirts and socks and children's clothes. Such gifts are given to celebrate family rituals of all kinds, including birth, circumcision, children's birthdays, a child's first completed reading of the Qur'an, and of course marriage. At birth, the baby's parents receive gifts for themselves and for the baby, and distribute sweets to their friends and relatives; at a circumcision and at a wedding the hosts receive cash and goods from all the guests — not infrequently numbered in hundreds — for whom they provide a meal. Likewise all arrivals and departures, whether to Pakistan or for *hajj* (the pilgrimage to Mecca), are similarly marked by hosting dinners and giving gifts to the travellers.

These transactions, collectively known as *lena-dena* (literally "taking-giving"), put the recipient family under an obligation to return a similar gift to the donor on the next appropriate occasion. The expectation of return is explicit, for gifts are viewed as goods or sums of money owing. Hence the return gift should be similar in kind to the one received, but with a slight increase in value: thus instead of wiping out the debt, it creates a new one. Maintaining such exchanges articulates the vitality of the underlying relationship, so a failure to reciprocate implies both social withdrawal and a loss of status, since the maintenance of a large number of relationships is a mark of high status. A family's success in handling *lena-dena* is at its most obvious when daughters are married, when the gifts received from friends and relatives by the bride's parents — often worth several hundred pounds — are not only an important part of the bride's dowry, but are also a very public measure of the family's standing in the community at large.

Although traditionally grounded in *biradari* membership, *lena-dena* exchanges in Britain also draw in non-relatives, as well as families belonging to other castes.[10] Nor are *lena-dena* transactions necessarily spatially restricted, so those involved will normally include guests drawn in from a number of far-away British towns, either because they are real *biradari* members from Pakistan, or because they are servicing new, British-based relationships. Like the *biradari* itself, *lena-dena* is a flexible vehicle. It can be initiated with strangers, provided they know the rules, and the relationship continues as long as an appropriate return is made; and because it is based on trust and

[10] See Shaw, *ibid.*, chapter 6, especially pp. 113–14.

the expectation of return, *lena-dena* is also a means by which families can judge one another's wealth, generosity and status. Since this enables previously unrelated families to develop links with each other, it can also have important implications for stabilising joint business ventures and cementing new marriage prospects.

Among Pakistanis in Oxford — as indeed among many Muslim groups in the Middle East — the preferred form of marriage is with a first cousin or, failing that, with a rather more distantly related member of one's *biradari*. The routine exercise of such a choice powerfully reinforces both the solidarity and the exclusivity of each *biradari*, and beyond that the *zat*. However, matches do occasionally cross these boundaries, their acceptability depending partly on the rank of the two castes and partly on the relative socio-economic status of the two immediate families and *biradaris*. Occasional marriages with non-kin bring certain advantages, for they widen the family's social network and, given careful strategic planning, can also enhance its status. Widening networks in this way is a tricky business. Most families play safe most of the time, and the majority of marriages are therefore still arranged within the caste and *biradari*. However, links with non-kin, when carefully reinforced by *lena-dena* exchanges, can gradually become sufficiently strong to risk a radical extension of kinship. Without *lena-dena* to pave the way, however, few families would dare take such a risk.

The Rise of Islam and the Eclipse of the Myth of Return

On the face of it, the arrival of women and children had a strongly conservative impact on lifestyles within the community. Family, *biradari* and caste structures as well as the *lena-dena* exchanges through which they are articulated, were all strongly reinforced through family reunion, and this served both to sustain community distinctiveness and to shelter its members from Western influence. Yet although the underlying reasons for family reunion were thoroughly in keeping with migrants' initial goals, its achievement rapidly undermined the myth of return; when reunited families began to acknowledge that their future necessarily lay in Britain, its appeal simply evaporated. Nevertheless the functions which the myth had served still needed to be fulfilled, and settlers became even more concerned to find an effective means of protecting and articulating their collective interests. Thus at the same time as the myth of return has faded, its role has been replaced by concerns about the issue of Muslim identity, with the result that the mosque has gradually become an increasingly important focus for religious, social and political activity.

Oxford's first mosque, opened in 1965 in a converted warehouse, was established as a result of the fund-raising efforts of a Pakistani and a Bangladeshi who had together founded an Oxford branch of the Pakistan Welfare Association in 1961. Although not everyone attended, especially in the early days, the mosque provided a focus for regular worship, and was also a symbol of settlers' unity and common purpose. Sectarian differences were therefore played down as much as possible.

Religious practice slowly began to change, however, since the arrival of women and children was accompanied by a gradually increasing awareness of the need to preserve the community's Islamic identity. Male attendance at the mosque increased sharply: while some men now attend daily — if not for all five times, then at least for evening prayers — many more come to Friday congregational prayers, while virtually everyone attends the annual celebration of *Id u'l Fitr* and *Id u'l Zoha*. Providing religious instruction for children is also important: each mosque employs an *imam*, whose duties include holding Qur'an classes for children and leading congregational prayers. There is a large attendance at these classes. In any one week about 400 children — mainly boys but also some girls below the age of twelve — attend one of Oxford's two main Sunni mosques, where they are taught to read and recite the Qur'an, the basic principles of Islam, and how to pray.

Women do not attend the mosque but pray at home. Even so, they play an important educational role, for they often supplement the *imam*'s teaching by supervising their children's reading from the Qur'an and correcting their Arabic pronunciation, and by giving instruction to girls over the age of twelve who are deemed too old to be allowed to attend classes at the mosque. Some women teach Urdu (the national language of Pakistan) to their own and their neighbours' children, supplementing the Saturday morning community classes — which offer both religious instruction and "mother-tongue" teaching for Pakistani children. Women also regularly engage in collective religious activities on their own account. One popular ritual is the *Khatm-i-Qur'an*, where a number of women gather in the sponsor's home to read the entire Qur'an in one sitting; the task is divided between the participants, each of whom takes one or more of the Qur'an's thirty sections, which are then recited simultaneously. Such a reading is convened for religious merit, especially in times of illness or danger, and when it is completed the convener provides a meal for the participants.

With the growing intensity of religious practice among both women and men, there has also been a marked increase in their concern with Muslim issues in broader political contexts. So, for example, the threatened closure of Oxford's only single-sex girls' secondary school precipitated vigorous opposition right across the Muslim community, and the political pressure generated was so strong that the plan was abandoned. Nor was it just a concern for educational issues which brought them together. Organisationally, their perception of the school's closure as a threat to Islamic values was the key to their success, so much so that even those parents who sent their daughters to mixed schools gave enthusiastic support to the campaign. And while outrage at the publication of Salman Rushdie's *The Satanic Verses* did not give rise to organised protests in Oxford, the vast majority of local Muslims were nonetheless united in regarding the book as an insult to Islam.

Sectarian Conflicts

Yet although Oxford's Pakistani Muslims regularly present themselves as wholly united on these and many other issues, they are in no sense a monolithic community, even in religious terms. We have already noted the principal internal diversities of regional, caste and *biradari* affiliation, and emphasised that while these diversities were largely overlooked in the early phase of all-male settlement, they grew steadily with the later consolidation of village and kinship networks. In much the same way, differences in sectarian affiliation overlooked in the early days have since become more pronounced. In Oxford as in every Pakistani settlement in Britain, fierce theological disputes over the proper forms of religious practice have erupted, thus underlining and deepening long-standing sectarian divisions.

Until 1984 there was only a single mosque in Oxford, but between 1982 and that year a violent dispute tore the city's Muslims into two factions, and this was only resolved with the founding of a second mosque. The dispute revolved around the activities of a new *imam*, whose opponents were accused of trying to engineer a "Wahhabi" takeover of the mosque. Behind the dispute was the long-standing ideological rivalry between the so-called "Wahhabis" (followers of the Deobandi tradition), on the one hand, and followers of the Barelvi tradition on the other.

The majority of Oxford's Pakistani Muslims are Sunnis, and if pressed would broadly associate themselves with the Barelvi tradition, which takes its name from the religious school founded by Ahmad Raza Khan at Bareilly in the late nineteenth century. One of this tradition's distinctive features is a belief in the miraculous powers of the Prophet Mohammed, as well as in the capacity of *pirs* to act as spiritual intermediaries between men and Allah. *Pirs* are ascribed super human qualities, e.g. that they have the capacity to influence almost any part of the lives of their *murids* or followers, and in the

Barelvi tradition the tombs of *pirs* are regarded as important and legitimate places of worship. By contrast the Deobandi school, founded in 1867 following the decline of Muslim fortunes brought about by the imposition of British rule in India, is strongly opposed to these beliefs and practices. It is highly critical of local customs, rejecting as un-Islamic belief in the occult powers of *pirs*, worship at their tombs, and the ascription of superhuman qualities to the Prophet.

Despite the richness and vitality of their devotional commitment to the *pirs* and the Prophet, Barelvis in Oxford have been driven on to the defensive by Deobandi criticism, which they often feel is so comprehensive as to cast doubt on their being Muslims at all. Hence they seek to give as good as they get by dubbing their opponents "Wahhabi", after the eighteenth-century reformist sect which currently occupies a dominant position in Saudi Arabia, and whose theological stance is close to that of the Deobandis. The Barelvis deliberately employ the term "Wahhabi" as an insult — with the result that this usage is both rejected and resented by most Deobandis.

The differences go so deep that co-operation on religious issues is almost impossible. Thus the dispute in 1982–4 was only resolved when the smaller Deobandi group moved off to establish a separate mosque of its own. The division has been sustained to this day, for although the two mosques do not represent an utterly rigid ideological division — thus believers in the powers of *pirs* can and do offer prayers in the "Deobandi" mosque — the problem is never far beneath the surface. When those committed to two rival positions feel their interests are threatened, the resulting disputes can be vigorous and emotional.

A third mosque has been set up by the Ahmadiyya community, to which some twenty local households belong. Ahmadiyyas regard their founder Mirza Ghulam Ahmad, born in India in 1835, as the promised messiah — a belief most other Muslims regard as a serious heresy on the grounds that Mohammed is by definition the last of the Prophets. In Pakistan opposition to the Ahmadiyyas has been strong; in Oxford they have been subject to criticism and attack in the Urdu press, and most local Barelvis and Deobandis reject outright their claim to be considered Muslims at all.

Issues of Common Concern

Given the depth of these divisions, what is it that unites the Pakistani Muslims in Oxford? Issues of shared concern can be identified, and they fall into two broad categories. First there are family issues, especially the control of girls' behaviour; and secondly there are more general concerns arising from the community's Muslim identity. Issues which have been taken up at one time or another by community "leaders"[11] have included opposition to the closure of the local all-girls secondary school and to the provision of sex education, and demands that Muslim girls should be exempted from physical education, that they be allowed to wear *shalwar-kameez* as school uniform, and for Urdu language teaching to be introduced in Local Authority schools. Although primarily focused on educational issues — especially where girls are concerned — all these demands relate to a more general concern for the maintenance of Muslim identity, and the perceived threat to it posed by Western influence. Such concerns were certainly brought into particularly sharp focus in the furore over *The Satanic Verses*, but the underlying issue was far from new. The controversy simply provided an opportunity for the articulation of pre-existing worries.

Such perception of external danger is not, of course, the only issue around which members of rival sects can unite in common concern. The Barelvis and Deobandis are at one in their hatred of the Ahmadiyyas, for instance, but members of all three groups share concerns about the issues cited above, in which fear of Western influence seems to stir particularly strong emotional fervour. Indeed "fear of the West" appears to have taken over from the "myth of return" as the major force through which the community organises itself and consolidates its boundaries. Hence the concern to maintain a Muslim identity is at heart a defensive strategy.

Fear of Western Influences

Yet just why has Muslim identity become so important, and how does it relate to the tradition of migration? For Pakistanis the passage to Britain has always been associated with danger, particularly with decadence and moral corruption. In Pakistan, Britain is much admired for its wealth, education and health service. Fairness of skin is also much admired for its association with high-caste status. But Pakistanis in Britain now regard English people with growing ambivalence. Britain's administrative and political system has steadily betrayed immigrants' citizenship rights through successive changes in immigration law. Many of the younger generation now speak more openly — and more bitterly — of racial discrimination than do their parents. But the most deep-rooted source of these ambivalent feelings about English people and their ways is the sharp perceived contradiction

---

[11] A fuller discussion of the nature of community leadership can be found in Shaw, *ibid.*, chapter 7.

between Western social and sexual mores on the one hand, and Islamic values of *purdah* and sexual segregation on the other. From a Pakistani Muslim angle, Western society is one where pork is eaten and alcohol is drunk, where women shamelessly fail to observe the niceties of *purdah* and where sexual activity is wholly uncontrolled. Most Pakistanis therefore find little to admire in British social and sexual mores. As one man put it, "English women are like toys for men to play with. They are outside, out on the streets, in shops, or on the television. They are cheap, and there for anyone to take." His wife showed me what she thought of English women by pulling her *shalwar* tight across her buttocks, loosening her hair and swaying her hips.

Yet there are many paradoxes here. As we saw earlier, the arrival of wives and children can be seen as means by which families and *biradaris* protected themselves from corrupting English influences, and most especially from the threat of Pakistani men establishing liaisons with English women. Yet family reunion brought the dangers of living in England into even sharper focus, for both wives and daughters — and indeed the whole of the next generation — now face the "corrupting influences" to which only the men were previously exposed. In these circumstances it is hardly surprising that public concern about the community's Muslim identity has grown steadily more explicit, and that the protection of the community from Western influence, and the preservation and assertion of its distinctive identity has now become the dominant concern of many Pakistani Muslims. Both the strength and the character of these fears were particularly clearly articulated in a letter of appeal which the local Pakistan Welfare Association sent to the heads of state of a number of Islamic countries, appealing for money to build an Islamic Cultural Centre in Oxford:

You are well aware that the Muslim minority in Britain is in the grip of a materialistic culture, cut adrift from its moral moorings. The entire media of instruction champions the cause of a bestially nude society which considers all ethnical [*sic*] values outdated . . . The ideas of virtue and sin in this country have merged into one dark spot, too hazy to recognize. We consider it our duty to realise and express our fears that if the present Muslim generation remain blind to its duty and responsibility, and fail to keep abreast of the time, there won't be a single Muslim in Britain beyond the next two generations.

As this extract shows, controlling the activities of young men and women — the next generation of Muslim adults — is now widely perceived as the essence of the community's problem in protecting itself from corrosive Western influences. Ironically, most first-generation migrants seem to share the commonplace belief among the white majority that the British-born and British-educated second generation will find it impossible to resist the temptation to assimilate. But if most members of the white majority look forward to such a prospect, it offers nothing but a nightmare of foreboding and fear to the older generation of Pakistanis.

The Second Generation

Yet how realistic are these fears and expectations? While the concern to maintain a sense of Muslim identity undoubtedly offers ideological validation for the *biradari*'s efforts to control the activities of its younger members, both male and female, how effectively is that objective being achieved? The local newspaper has documented attempts by several Pakistani girls to escape arranged marriages. For example Nafisa, who had eloped with her boyfriend, was eventually found by her parents, who promptly took her back to Pakistan to arrange her marriage. Jamila not only eloped with but married her Pakistani boyfriend, although she returned to her parents' house a few days later; they too took her to Pakistan where she married a cousin. But although such incidents are still rare, how much of a challenge do they represent to the authority of the *biradari* and the ideologies which sustain it?

Because they undermine the arranged marriage system, elopements are certainly major challenges to the institution of the *biradaris*. Indeed, without arranged marriages, embedded as they are in *lena-dena* exchanges, *biradaris* would soon cease to exist, at least in their present form. Yet despite the challenge it offers to the *biradari* and all it stands for, elopement is not solely a response to Western influence: similar illicit romances also occur in Pakistan. Moreover the more closely one explores the details of such escapades, the more obvious it becomes that they are more likely to be ordered in terms of South Asian than Western romantic idioms, and to involve a Pakistani (or other South Asian) partner rather than anyone else. Such affairs are better understood as passionate engagements in traditional idioms than as a product of Western liberal attitudes.[12]

Moreover, no elopement which I have actually encountered led to a final break with the *biradari*. Nafisa, whose family took her to Pakistan after her elopement, is now contentedly awaiting an arranged marriage. Her elopement proved far less romantic than she expected, and she soon felt so miserable that she telephoned her family, asking them to fetch her. Jamila is now married to her cousin, who has joined

---

[12] See also Shaw, *A Pakistani Community in Britain*, pp. 167–76.

her in Britain, and they have two children. She speaks of her love affair as an unreal episode, which she regards as having come about because she had been "brainwashed" by watching too many romantic Urdu and Hindi films. In sharp contrast to outsiders' widely-held assumptions, elopements are not only infrequent but when they do occur they rarely pose a fundamental threat to the system of arranged marriages or to the *biradari*. On the contrary, it is striking that on a whole range of issues — ranging from attitudes to work through to expectations about family and marriage and to the maintenance of a Muslim identity — most members of the second generation adopt positions still broadly in line with those of their parents.

Young women's attitudes towards their future careers and the prospects of having arranged marriages provide a good example of these continuities, for I found that the great majority of schoolgirls accepted the roles which their families and *biradaris* expected them to fulfil with few, if any, questions. As they moved through their teens, their interest in schoolwork declined as they gradually began to take on more responsible roles both at home and in the community at large. Although it was routinely expected that once they had left school they would help to look after younger children, and possibly also work in the family business while awaiting their marriages, most still felt that this provided them with a strong sense of their own identity. A few girls took up paid work outside the home until their marriages, and indeed some continued to do so thereafter — and although this was initially considered somewhat scandalous, it is rapidly becoming unexceptional. Hitherto only a small minority of girls have gained higher educational qualifications, but they too have largely stayed within the orbit of the family and *biradari*, thus far finding few problems in combining the pursuit of a career with an arranged marriage and participation in family and community events.

Attitudes towards the prospect of women working and pursuing a career vary considerably, and are the subject of intense debate. While some argue that a Muslim woman's domestic responsibilities are incompatible with a career, others argue just as passionately that it is possible for a woman to combine a career with marrying and raising a family without in any way compromising Islamic values. It was also striking that there was no straightforward correlation between these viewpoints and a difference of generation. A number of younger women were happy to conform to traditional expectations, while attitudes among the parental generation were by no means unanimous. Although such variations were broadly associated with differences in class and caste status, at least some older people held strikingly "modern" views.

Since different families in the same *biradari* often take up different positions, it is virtually impossible to classify particular *biradaris*, or even particular families, as more or less "traditional" than any other, and as Yasmin's case shows, what happens to any particular individual is usually the outcome of practical considerations rather than the prior ideological stance of his or her family. Having persuaded her parents to delay her marriage so that she could finish her "A" levels and secure a university place, Yasmin gradually manoeuvred them, by means of many hints and suggestions, into accepting that she might also study away from home. In doing so she used her own and her parents' ambitions as a bargaining point, for she well knew that medicine was a high prestige career. She also tried to ensure that her parents would be persuaded by relatives and friends not only that it was acceptable within Islam for her to go to university, but also that there was little alternative to studying in a distant city if she was to achieve her objectives. Thus despite their initial reservations, Yasmin's family were persuaded to allow her to continue, not least because this could be expected radically to improve the prospects of her making a strategically advantageous marriage.

While young men have followed an even wider variety of educational and career paths, few have deviated far from parental values and expectations. Even among the British-born, most young men have adopted essentially similar lifestyles to those of their fathers. Of those who left school at sixteen, most work in factories and family shops, their leisure time is largely spent in the company of their Pakistani peers, and they remain heavily involved in the social and religious activities of the community. A few have embarked on business or professional careers, but it is striking that they too have usually remained strongly committed to the extended family, sometimes pooling wages with manual-worker brothers and fathers to advance collectively-based projects.

Yet there are also clear differences underlying these continuities. Thus while young people may justify their career choice — be it in law, engineering, or medicine — by suggesting that these qualifications would still be useful if ever the family returned to Pakistan, they themselves have little or no independent commitment to returning. For them the myth of return is essentially a fiction, which they maintain largely for their parents' benefit. At the same time, although they now perceive themselves as British-based, such young people are far from being comprehensively anglicised. Most maintain close links with relatives, friends and peers, and still routinely participate in family and community events. They also take for granted the obligation to support and take care of their parents. However, they rarely if ever use the myth of return to justify their respect for their parents and their commitment to jointness and co-operation within the family, preferring instead to appeal to the religious values of Islam.

Thus even those younger people whose educational success and upward occupational mobility might have been expected to set them apart from their parents still prove, on closer inspection, to share most of their elders' values rather than to have rebelled against them. Moreover where there are differences between the generations — for they do occur — it is striking that young people usually justify their views with reference to Islamic rather than to Western values. Thus the commonplace assumption that second-generation Pakistanis must by definition be "torn between two cultures" is both inappropriate and misleading, and the implied dichotomy between "modern" and "traditional" is in fact quite unsustainable.

Given the strength of these religious and cultural continuities, it follows that commitment to a Muslim identity now provides young Pakistanis with a powerful and ideologically effective justification for the maintenance of family and *biradari* solidarity. In this perspective the growth of a commitment to Islam among the younger generation is best understood as a recent variant of a much more long-standing process, in which the social function of this commitment — the maintenance and control of the community's social structure — remains the same as ever. Hence it is not surprising that the eclipse of the myth of return has not proved to be an advance signal for rapid cultural assimilation. Pakistani settlers' own traditions, and particularly the *biradari*'s capacity to control its members' activities despite rapid and radical changes of circumstance, are far too strong, dynamic and resilient for that to be a realistic prospect.

BEING MUSLIM AND BEING BRITISH

THE DYNAMICS OF ISLAMIC RECONSTRUCTION
IN BRADFORD

Philip Lewis

Before the controversy surrounding the publication of Salman Rushdie's novel *The Satanic Verses*, most discussions of the South Asian presence in Britain paid only the most perfunctory attention to the religious dimension of the settlers' personal lives, and still less to the extent to which Islam might provide them with a vehicle for the expression and mobilisation of their collective interests.[1] But the public and passionate campaign British Muslims launched and sustained against the book has changed all that. The media have become fascinated by something called "fundamentalist Islam", so much so that this phenomenon — whose nature and meaning are assumed to be as self-evident as its implications are sinister — has become a routine component of the journalistic lexicon. Witness, for example, the political editor of the *Sunday Times* reassuring his readers that "so far as Bradford is concerned the line has been held against Muslim fundamentalists who want to . . . bolster ethnic separatism."[2] Islam, according to this increasingly popular view, is an uncompromising monolith, with Muslims considered a homogeneous community intent on establishing a theocracy.

These easy and self-serving generalisations tell us more about the values and anxieties of the observers than about the beliefs and motivations of the observed, and while it would be illuminating to explore why they should so rapidly have established themselves as received opinion even in the most liberal quarters of white society,[3]

---

[1] In *Race and Ethnicity* (Milton Keynes: Open University Press 1986), John Rex includes the generic term "religion" in his index; three references are given, but none to specific religious traditions. Meanwhile, Vaughan Robinson in *Transients, Settlers and Refugees* (Oxford University Press, 1986), the most ambitious attempt so far to inject some methodological rigour into the subject, omits any reference to religion in his subject index.

[2] Michael Jones, "Time for Britain to show its true colours", *Sunday Times*, 3 September 1989.

[3] See Fay Weldon, *Sacred Cows: A portrait of Britain, post-Rushdie, pre-Utopia* (London: Chatto and Windus, 1989), a liberal response, and the eloquent rejoinder to such works by Rana Kabbani, *Letter to Christendom* (London: Virago Press, 1989).

that is not the focus of this chapter. Nor is it intended to rehearse the historical pattern of Muslim migration to and settlement in Bradford, since that has been discussed in detail elsewhere.[4] The aim, instead, is to focus specifically on the religious dimensions of that presence by exploring the role Islam has played and is playing in the formation of the local community and its institutions.

Islam is less homogeneous and less static than outsiders commonly suppose: Bradford's Islamic institutions have changed as settlers have set about using and developing their religious resources, the better to establish themselves in their new environment. Although these processes are still in full swing, some clear patterns of change can already be identified. Badr Dahya, in an early and seminal article on Bradford's Pakistani communities,[5] outlined a two-stage process of community formation where the initial tendency towards fusion — with pioneer settlers associating together regardless of their regional, caste or sectarian origins — gradually gave way, as numbers grew, to fission and segmentation. Within this second stage of fragmentation, ties of village-kinship and sectarian affiliation grew steadily more significant as a basis of communal aggregation. More recent events suggest, however, that a third stage of co-operation has now begun to manifest itself. Having found its initial institutional expression in the creation of the Bradford Council for Mosques in 1981, this impulse, which grew steadily in strength in the years that followed, has been quickened by the *Satanic Verses* affair. Now more than ever, Bradford Muslims feel that they have a common cause, and that without co-operation and unity they will never be successful in the pursuit of their collective interests.

Yet, however desirable that goal may be, Islamic unity is proving hard to achieve. Many factors militate against it. First Islam itself is not a monolith: Bradford's Muslims may be no more divided over issues of belief and practice than are Muslims in any other part of the world, but in the absence of an understanding of the sources of these differences little sense can be made of current developments. Secondly, these religious divisions are complicated by a variety of regional, caste and *biradari* affiliations. Thirdly, these developments have been accompanied by an even more radical set of changes: as members of a "semi-industrialised, newly urbanised working class

---

[4] For the Pakistanis see Verity Saifullah-Khan, "The Pakistanis: Mirpuri Villagers at Home and in Bradford", in James L. Watson (ed.), *Between Two Cultures* (Oxford, 1977), and for Bangladeshis, Stephen William Barton, *The Bengali Muslims of Bradford* (Community Religions Project, Dept of Theology and Religious Studies, University of Leeds, 1986).

[5] "The Nature of Pakistani Ethnicity in Industrial Cities in Britain", in Abner Cohen (ed.), *Urban Ethnicity* (London: Tavistock, 1974).

community that is only one generation away from rural peasantry",[6] settlers are still struggling to come to terms with the radical changes in their own lives. Meanwhile they are also having to cope with the "strategies for survival"[7] being developed by a second and third generation, whose life experiences — urban, secular-educated and English-speaking — differ radically from those of their parents.

Sufism and South Asian Islam

To understand the building bricks of Islamic reconstruction in Bradford we must briefly explore a characteristic institution of normative[8] Islam in South Asia and consider how it fared with the collapse of Mughal power and the imposition of the British Raj. This latter is the context which saw the creation of that repertoire of sectarian options which the South Asian settlers carried with them to Britain. If we follow a distinguished historian of Islam and describe normative Islam as a pluriform *Sunni-Shari'a-Sufi* [9] tradition, in South Asian Islam the critical institution is the Sufi order, the *silsila*.[10] The consolidation and spread of Islam in South Asia turned on the activities of the Sufis, who followed in the wake of the Turkish and Afghan armies from central Asia which swept into India through the northern and western passes and established the Delhi Sultanate (1206–1555). While elsewhere in the Muslim world Sufism, differentiated into a

---

[6] Tariq Modood, "British Asian Muslims and the Rushdie Affair", *Political Quarterly*, vol. 61 (1990), p. 145.

[7] Kim Knott, "Strategies for Survival among Asian Religions in Britain: Parallel Developments, Conflicts and Cooperation", in *Conflict and Cooperation Between Contemporary Religious Groups* (Tokyo: Chuo Academic Research Institute, Editor and Publisher, 1988).

[8] "Normative" seems a better description for Islam than "orthodox", since the latter term belongs to the Christian tradition with its councils and synods, vested with authority to distinguish between true and false doctrine. Islam knows no such authority, and law and right practice are central preoccupations rather than doctrine. See part 4, "Muslim Orthodoxy", of the illuminating essay by George Makdisi, "Hanbalite Islam", in Merlin L. Swartz (ed.), *Studies on Islam* (Oxford University Press, 1981).

[9] "The complex of views contained in *Sunni-Shar'ia-Sufi* Islam never became a formal system. Islam has no master science as Christianity has in theology, and no unified definition of itself. Within the Sunni complex there are numerous collections of hadith, several equally valid versions of the law, several acceptable theological positions, and different schools of mysticism." Ira M. Lapidus, *A History of Islamic Societies* (Cambridge University Press, 1988), pp. 221–2. The term Sunni is a shorthand for *ahl us sunna wa'l jama'a*, the people of the (prophetic) custom and the community, the majority of Muslims, who accept the authority of the first four Caliphs and the companions of the Prophet, in contrast to the Shi'a, who regard the fourth Caliph, Ali (d. 661 AD), and his heirs, as the only legitimate successors of the Prophet's authority.

[10] "Chain" (of descendants) through whom a Sufi traces his spiritual and/or physical ancestry back to the founder of his order, via Abu Bakr or Ali, to the Prophet himself.

number of orders, was the late flower of Islamic culture, it is almost co-terminous with the consolidation of Islam in South Asia, which thus bears its distinctive impress.[11]

At the heart of Sufism is the relationship between the saint, often referred to as *shaikh* or *pir*,[12] and the devotee, the *murid*. Since the saint is considered to be close to God, the devotee is expected to approach him with respect and unquestioning obedience. In the words of the eleventh century saint Hujwiri, "the sufi *shaikhs* are physicians of men's souls . . . the Apostle [Muhammad] said: The *shaikh* in his tribe is like the prophet in his nation."[13] The saints of Islam were God's elect, able to perform miracles to validate the truth of Muhammad's ministry, and organised into an invisible hierarchy who maintained the process of nature and guaranteed Muslim victories.[14] They were revered by their devotees as mediators between man and God and bearers of God's healing. Their tombs became an accessible and alternative focus for pilgrimage. They and their devotees generated a rich vernacular tradition of devotional hymns and thus rooted Islam in the hearts and minds of the majority, who were either unlettered or not acquainted with the languages of high Islamic culture. They were the creators and custodians of regional languages and culture. The activities of saintly dynasties, centred on their shrines, were the key element in a process of the gradual Islamisation of Hindu tribes.[15]

The devotion they could command from their followers soon translated into landed wealth and power. Warrior saints could be found in frontier zones. With the eclipse of Muslim political power, the saints could function as a nucleus of regional opposition to non-Muslim power, and whoever has captured power has sought to enlist their support. In the creation of Pakistan the Muslim League had to wean many of the *pirs* of the Punjab away from their traditional support for the Unionist party, an inter-communal party of landlords,[16] and in 1980 General Zia convened a one-day conference of the country's leading *pirs* to seek their endorsement of his policy of Islamisation, since the "majority of the population is not only under your influence but in a way under your command".[17]

[11] See Bruce B. Lawrence, *Notes form a Distant Flute: The Extant Literature of pre-Mughal Indian Sufism* (Tehran: Imperial Iranian Academy of Philosophy, 1978).
[12] The Arabic and Persian terms, respectively, for elder, used for a Sufi teacher. The Arabic *murshid*, guide, is also widely used.
[13] *The Kashf al-Mahjub, the Oldest Persian Treatise on Sufism*, by al-Hujwiri, translated by Reynold A. Nicholson, 1911 (reprint, Lahore: Al-Maarif, 1976), p. 55.
[14] *Ibid.*, pp. 213–14.
[15] See the seminal study by Richard M. Eaton, *The Sufis of Bijapur, 1300–1700: Social roles of Sufis in medieval India* (Princeton University Press, 1978).
[16] See Ian Talbot, "The growth of the Muslim League in the Punjab, 1937–46", *Journal of Commonwealth and Comparative Politics*, vol. 20, 1982.
[17] *Pakistan Times*, 23 September 1980.

Sufism has always had its critics, not least from within the movement itself. Thus Hujwiri's celebrated handbook on Sufism, *Kashf al Mahjub* (Unveiling the Veiled), contains explicit warnings against antinomianism and charlatans:

The outward and the inward aspects [of faith] cannot be divorced. The exoteric aspect of Truth without the esoteric is hypocrisy, and the esoteric without the exoteric is heresy. So, with regard to the Law, mere formality is defective, while mere spirituality is vain . . . ignorant pretenders to sufism . . . who have never associated with a spiritual director (*pir*), nor learned discipline from a *sheikh*, [and] without any experience have thrown themselves among the people . . . and trodden the path of unrestraint.[18]

These criticisms have been rehearsed down the centuries, and reform movements within Sufism periodically emerged to insist on the centrality of Islamic law and the need to remove customs which smack of *bid'a*, reprehensible novelty. It is not without irony that Hujwiri's shrine in Lahore has itself become the centre of a thriving cult. Popularly known as Data Ganj Bakhsh (the Master who gives treasure), he is regarded as the patron saint of Lahore, who enjoyed "supreme authority over the saints of India, and . . . no new saint entered the country without first obtaining permission from his spirit".[19]

Reformers of Sufism emerged from within the movement itself — too often a false dichotomy has been drawn between saint and scholar, overlooking the fact that many an *'alim*[20] is, and was, also a Sufi, or the devotee of one.[21]

Muslim Responses to Colonialism

The collapse of Mughal power in India and the gradual imposition of British control was deeply unsettling for Muslims. All religions began a process of re-evaluation of their ideals, organisation, priorities and practice. The colonial encounter precipitated the formation of a wide range of new sectarian developments.[22] Muslims were no exception.

If contemporary expressions of Islam in South Asia are largely the

---

[18] Nicholson, *op. cit.*, pp. 14 and 17.

[19] Annemarie Schimmel, *Islam in the Indian Subcontinent* (Leiden: E.J. Brill, 1980), p. 8.

[20] An *'alim* (plural *'ulema*) is a scholar specialising in one or all of the three traditional Islamic disciplines: *qur'an*, the traditions (*hadith*) and jurisprudence (*fiqh*).

[21] See Makdisi, *op. cit.*, and Barbara D. Metcalf, *Islamic Revival in British India: Deoband, 1860–1900* (Princeton University Press, 1982).

[22] For an excellent overview of these developments, see Kenneth Jones, *Socio-Religious Movements in British India* (Cambridge University Press, 1989).

product of this encounter, Muslims in Bradford have sought to plant them in a very different environment. Here four movements are of particular significance: the reformist Deobandis, the quietist and revivalist Tablighi Jamaat, the conservative and populist Barelvis and the neo-Islamic Jamaat-i-Islami.

The Deobandis. The Islamic seminary from which this group takes its name was founded in 1867 in Deoband, a small town 100 miles north of Delhi. Its founders, Muhammad Qasim Nanautawi (d. 1877) and Rashid Ahmad Gangohi (d. 1905), were acutely conscious of the extent to which power had shifted away from the Muslims to a new British and Christian élite, and their aim was above all to preserve and promote an Islamic identity in a changing world. Although both were classically trained *'ulema*, they were dissatisfied with the quality of the Islamic education then available. Their seminary not only re-emphasised traditional standards through the study of Hanafi law, but sought to use this as a bulwark against the inroads of non-Islamic influences. Their movement also promoted a distinctive ethos, which

. . . de-emphasised purely local ties in favour of the separate unity and identity of the whole group of Deobandis, whatever their geographic origin . . . fostering a style of Islam that preferred universal practices and beliefs to local cults and customs . . . and emphasising the diffusion of scripturalist practices and the cultivation of an inner spiritual life.[23]

They were no mere traditionalists, however. Besides drawing upon British educational institutions and missionary societies as a source of organisational inspiration for their seminary, the Deobandis also made extensive use of the press, the postal service and the rapidly expanding railway network to spread their message, and elicit subscriptions from far and wide. Thus freed from the obligation to respond to the whims of a few local benefactors — and hence from the vagaries of family control which had reduced so many of its rivals to crippling dependence — the seminary in Deoband was soon setting new standards of scholarly excellence and institutional continuity for North Indian Islam. This position was further reinforced by the movement's consistent use of Urdu rather than Persian as a *lingua franca*.

The founders of Deoband were reformist Sufis, as well as *'ulema*. As spiritual guides to many of their students they saw themselves as exemplars rather than as intercessors. They took their responsibilities as Sufi directors seriously:

The granting of initiation took place only after a period of contact in which the good intentions of the disciple, the spiritual perfections of the *shaikh*,

[23] Barbara Metcalf, "The Madrasa at Deoband: A Model for Religious Education in Modern India", *Modern Asian Studies*, vol. 12 (1978), pp. 132–4.

and the personal compatibility of both were shown. Often there would be a prolonged stay with the *shaikh* and substantial instruction in the disciplines and traditions of the order.[24]

As reformist Sufis, Deobandi scholars opposed much of the shrine cult as an unacceptable accommodation to a non-Muslim environment. Maulana Ashraf Ali Thanawi (d. 1943), a rector of Deoband and considered one of the leading Sufis of his generation, in his encyclopaedic Urdu work *Bihishti Zewar* (Heavenly Ornaments), reminds his readers that to sacrifice an animal, fast or take a vow in the name of a saint, amounts to *kufr* (disbelief) and *shirk* (associating another with God). It is similarly *shirk*, he contends, to believe that saints can relieve all ills. Finally, Thanawi seeks to undercut the function of saints as intercessors by insisting that only those who have received a promise from God and Muhammad will unequivocally enter heaven.[25]

While the Deobandis consequently set out to be reformists, the all-embracing Islamic unity they hoped to generate proved elusive. It is not difficult to see why. Most of their initial support came from the *ashraf*, the well-born Muslim élites, who claimed descent from outside India[26] and drew their income from land, trade or government service. Yet a principal target of their reformist activities consisted of the beliefs and practices of the rural peasantry. Here the efforts of the twentieth-century revivalist movement, Tablighi Jamaat, were to complement their work.

Tablighi Jamaat.   The founder of the faith movement, popularly referred to as Tablighi Jamaat, the preaching party, was Maulana Ilyas (1885–1944). He himself was a Sufi and *'alim* who had trained at Deoband and taught at the Deobandi seminary in Saharanpur.[27] Ilyas was concerned to develop the work of his father in Delhi, who had sought to preach the basics of Islam to the Meos, Muslims from Mewat, south of Delhi, who had come into the city in search of work. The Meos were Muslim in little more than name, largely ignorant of Islam and sharing many Hindu names and customs. Such groups were potentially vulnerable to the efforts of the Hindu Arya Samaj movement to reconvert Hindus who had become Muslim or Christian.[28]

[24] Metcalf, *Islamic Revival*, pp. 162–3.
[25] See the abridged translation by M.M. Khan, *Heavenly Ornaments* (Lahore: Al-Kitab, 1979), pp. 16–23 and 393.
[26] The *sayyids*, the descendants of the Prophet; the *shaikhs*, the descendants of his companions; and the Mughals and Pathans, descendants of Turk and Afghan rulers of India.
[27] See M. Amwarul Haq, *The Faith Movement of Mawlana Muhammad Ilyas* (London: George Allen & Unwin, 1972).
[28] See Z.H. Faruqi, "The Tablighi Jama'at" in S.T. Lokhandwalla (ed.), *India and*

Ilyas was aware that neither the traditional Sufi hospice nor the Islamic seminary was organised to touch the lives of such people. Most Meos could not be expected to spend eight years or more in a seminary, and Sufis were not in the habit of going out of their hospices on preaching and teaching tours. Thus in the 1920s and 1930s he developed his innovative movement, which sought inspiration from the methods used by the Prophet at the beginning of Islam, when neither seminary nor Sufi hospice existed.

The aim of his movement was to embody and commend the Qur'anic injunction of *sura* 3:104: 'that there might grow out of you a community [of people] who invite unto all that is good, and enjoin the doing of what is right and forbid the doing of what is wrong'. In pursuit of this aim Ilyas eschewed all controversial issues and avoided political involvement. His emphasis was on individual moral and spiritual renewal — the precondition, he contended, for any authentically Islamic endeavour in the public domain.

What was striking about Tablighi Jamaat was its expectation that all Muslims should devote time to door-to-door revivalist activities and thereby contribute to creating an Islamic environment. The discipline, mutual service, congregational worship, prescribed study and shared activity created the movement's distinctive style of self-reformation, within a supportive and egalitarian context. Its minimalist six-point programme reflects its Sufi ethos.[29] 'Its mobility has provided a medium of religious education on a mass scale. It may be termed as a unique experiment in adult education.'[30] Many Muslim scholars have recognised its value and involved themselves and their students with the movement. Sayyid Abul Hasan Ali Nadwi, the rector of India's prestigious Muslim academy Nadwatu'l Ulama, gave an address in 1944 warning *'ulema* that if they did not participate in Ilyas' venture they would become 'an untouchable minority to whose culture and way of life the common people would become total strangers; even their language and ideas would be unfamiliar to the general public necessitating a translator between the two.'[31] It is

---

Contemporary Islam (Simla: Indian Institute of Advanced Study, 1971), p. 68.

[29] 1. the profession of faith — a reminder of God's oneness and His Lordship; 2. the five daily prayers; 3. knowledge and remembrance — knowledge of God's commands and remembrance, *zikr*, a technical term for Sufi devotional practices; 4. respect for every Muslim — an attempt to transcend the virulent sectarianism of South Asian Islam; 5. sincerity of intention — to prefer the Hereafter and divine approval to the luxuries of the present, transitory world; 6. to spare time — for training and revivalist activities. The six points and the interpretation are taken from Sadruddin Amir Ansari, *Six Points of Tabligh* (New Delhi: Saleem Book Depot, 1978).

[30] Faruqi, *op. cit.*, p. 68.

[31] Anwarul Haq, *op. cit.*, p. 133.

evident that many have listened, for one recent scholar regards it as being 'the most influential movement, in terms of numbers, among Muslims in the subcontinent and perhaps the world'.[32]

The Barelvis. The Barelvi tradition is the most local and contextual of the various expressions of Islam in South Asia. It takes its name from the home town of its founder, Ahmad Raza Khan (1856–1921) of Bareilly, a member of the Qadiri Sufi order, who used his considerable scholarship to defend the legitimacy of the popular world of saints and shrines, where devotees come to seek the help of saints (living and dead), as intercessors between themselves and God. The central importance of having a *pir*, spiritual guide, is reflected in the Urdu language, where to be *be-pir*, without a *pir*, has the connotation of being vicious, cruel and pitiless.

Deobandi criticisms notwithstanding, it was the *pirs* and their devotees who constituted the very core of popular Islam. It was they who generated and propagated devotional songs in vernacular languages, and who thus rooted Islamic teachings in the minds of the rural majority, most of whom had no access to the languages of high Islamic culture — Arabic and Persian. The shrines became the centre of a rich annual cycle of religious festivals — celebrating the Prophet's birthday, his ascension, *mi'raj*, and the death anniversaries of the founder of the order and of many other saints.

All these practices were much more defensible in Qur'anic terms than Deobandi textualism might seem to suggest, for the disagreements between the two groups ultimately turned on distinct exegetical traditions, which supported their very different interpretations of the nature of God, the status of the Prophet and the saints. Ahmad Raza, using well-established Sufi arguments, insisted that the Prophet had "knowledge of the unseen" and was the bearer of God's light, which the saints also reflected. For the Deobandis, however, such claims were deemed excessive and encroached on prerogatives belonging to God alone. Such theological differences, passionately held, continue to generate a luxuriant sectarian literature, and mutual recrimination can flare up into open conflict.[33]

---

[32] Barbara D. Metcalf, *Perfecting Women: Maulana Ashraf Ali Thanawi's Bihishti Zewar*, a partial translation and commentary (Berkeley: University of California Press, 1990), p. 5.

[33] See Metcalf, *Islamic Revival*; Muhammad Munir, *From Jinnah to Zia* (Lahore: Vanguard Books, 1980); Alison Shaw, *A Pakistani Community in Britain* (Oxford: Basil Blackwell, 1988), pp. 149–53. Mohammad S. Raza, *Islam in Britain: Past, Present and The Future* (Leicester: Volcano Press, 1991) insists that "the mosques have been turned into medieval sectarian fortresses" (p. 35).

The Jamaat-i-Islami. The Jamaat-i-Islami, the Islamic Organisation, is of rather more recent origin than the other movements. It was founded in 1941 by Maulana Maududi (1903–79), a journalist rather than the product of an Islamic seminary. For Maududi Islam was an ideology, an activist creed and legal system, which aspired to regulate all aspects of life. He criticised the *'ulema* for obscuring Islam's dynamism with medieval commentary, fossilised law and devotion to holy men. He was no less scathing in his attacks on those who sought to introduce alien, especially Western, ideologies such as communism, socialism, capitalism and nationalism into the Muslim world. All these, he argued, threatened to fragment and destroy the transnational Muslim community, the *ummah*; for him westernisation was the new barbarism, threatening to return Muslims to the very *jahiliyya*[34] — the emotive term for pre-Islamic paganism — from which the Prophet's message had rescued them.

But Maududi was no mere ideologue; the Jamaat-i-Islami was a politico-religious party whose aim was to place trained cells of the righteous in positions of social and political leadership, with the object of transforming Muslim countries into Islamic states. Maududi's prolific writings have been translated into many languages, including English and Arabic. He had a considerable following in the Muslim Brotherhood and was courted by the Saudi Arabian government.[35]

Back home in Pakistan, however, the party's fortunes have been more mixed. It appeals to the products of expanded tertiary education in the cities,

. . . successful but unsatisfied people. Separated by their education from traditional communities, they are not part of the political elite. Like the uprooted peasants and bazaaris, these strata turn to Islam to symbolize their anxieties, their hostilities to the powers, domestic and foreign, that thwart them, and their dreams of a more perfect future.[36]

While the party can influence government policy during periods of authoritarian rule, it has not done well at the polls. The Jamiyat Ulema-i-Pakistan (JUP), a party representing Barelvi interests, and the Jamiyat Ulema-i-Islam (JUI), representing Deobandis, gained a larger share of the national vote than Jamaat-i-Islami in the 1970

[34] Emmanuel Sivan, *Radical Islam: Medieval Theology and Modern Politics* (New Haven and London: Yale University Press, 1985), pp. 22–3.
[35] Maulana Maududi was a consultant in 1960 when the syllabus for the new Madina University was drawn up — intended to rival Al-Azhar in Egypt; in 1962 he was elected a founder member of the World Islamic League at Mecca, intended to mobilise opinion against Nasser's Arab socialism. Maududi and one of his influential successors, Professor Khurshid Ahmad, were both recipients of the King Faisal International Prize for services to Islam (Maududi in 1979 and Ahmad in 1990).
[36] Lapidus, *op. cit.*, p. 890.

elections in Pakistan; none did particularly well, however, for between them they polled less than a quarter of the national vote.[37]

Mosque Formation and Community Consolidation in Bradford

Amongst the first Pakistanis to arrive in Bradford, as Dahya records, were a group of Mirpuri seamen who had been stranded in Hull and were sent to work in a local munitions factory in 1941.[38] However, not until 1959 was the city's first mosque opened in a terraced house in Howard Street. It was run by the Pakistani Muslim Association, and its trustees included both East and West Pakistanis, as well as members of several different sectarian traditions — reflecting the fact that the community was then in a "pioneering"[39] phase and at a stage of "fusion" (as Dahya puts it). But that initial unity did not last long. Over the next few years the Howard Street mosque came to be dominated by Pathans and Punjabis from Chhachh, the north-east corner of Attock District, while the appointment of a man trained in the Deobandi tradition, as its first full-time *'alim* in 1968 gave it a clear sectarian flavour.

But fission was proceeding apace. In 1961 the Bradford Muslim Welfare Society, most of whose members were Gujaratis from villages around Surat, established a mosque of their own — again in the Deobandi tradition — in a house in Thorncliffe Place. Soon afterwards Pir Maroof Hussain Shah from Mirpur District in Azad Kashmir formed the Association for the Preaching of Islam, and it was largely due to his efforts that Bradford's first Barelvi mosque was opened in 1966 in Southfield Square. Since then the number of mosques in Bradford has grown steadily: in 1969 there were six, in 1979 seventeen, and by 1989 no less than thirty-four, with nine supplementary schools teaching Islam but not functioning as centres of worship.

In sectarian terms, fifteen of these mosques and seven supplementary schools fall into the Barelvi tradition, while the Deobandis account for thirteen mosques and two supplementary schools. Of the smaller groups two mosques are within the Jamaat-i-Islami tradition, another belongs to Ahl-i-Hadith,[40] and two more are Shi'a. Finally

---

[37] These statistics are extrapolated from Anwar Syed, *Pakistan: Islam, Politics and National Solidarity* (Lahore: Vanguard Books, 1984) and S. Jamal Malik, "Islamization in Pakistan, 1977–1985: The Ulama and their places of learning", *Islamic Studies*, vol. 28, 1989, pp. 5–27.

[38] Dahya, *op. cit.*, p. 88.

[39] See Roger and Catherine Ballard, "The Sikhs: The Development of South Asian Settlements in Britain", in Watson, *op. cit.*.

[40] Ahl-i-hadith, the followers of the prophetic tradition, are a late nineteenth-century

there is a centre for the Ahmadiyya, whose continuing membership of the Muslim *'umma* has now become, as is discussed later, an exceedingly contentious issue.

It is striking that at present all these mosques and supplementary schools are still in inner-city wards. Only two are purpose-built, the rest being either in converted terraced houses, disused mills, cinemas or churches. In a sociological perspective, this confirms that the drift to the suburbs, so characteristic of other South Asian communities, has hardly begun among Bradford's 50,000 Muslims. Control of these institutions also provides a useful if rough-and-ready guide to the numerical strengths of the regional components of Bradford's Muslim population. In 1989 the Mirpuris dominated the management of fifteen mosques and seven supplementary schools; the Chhachhis seven mosques, and the Sylhetis from Bangladesh five; finally the Gujaratis were dominant in two mosques and a further two supplementary schools.[41] Regional loyalties have, however, intersected with questions of sectarian affiliation in some exceedingly complex ways. It is to these issues that we must now turn.

The Influence of Pir Maroof

Over the years no single person has had a greater impact on Muslims in Bradford than Pir Maroof Hussain Shah. Although he traces his saintly lineage back to Hajji Muhammad Naushah (1556–1654), his home was in Mirpur district. He first arrived in Britain in 1961, and spent the next quarter of a century working in textile mills. But at the same time he was a tireless organiser of religious activities: over and above his own role as a teacher, he had raised the funds (often by way of interest-free loans) needed to set up and run a whole series of mosques and supplementary schools.

Pir Maroof is in many ways a classic exemplar of the Barelvi tradition: drawn himself from a remote and economically undeveloped area, his Islam is essentially devotional, and focuses above all

---

Indian reformist sect. They accepted the genuineness of the classical collections of *hadith* and gave them a priority over the four schools of Islamic law, when the latter seemed at variance with the traditions. See Aziz Ahmad, *Islamic Modernism in India and Pakistan, 1857–1964* (London, Bombay and Karachi: Oxford University Press, 1967), pp. 113–22.

[41] Local Authority figures in 1989 suggest that the Muslim community numbers some 49,200, or 1 in 9 of the population of Bradford Metropolitan District. It is a young community and accounts for 23% of the district's school population. Probably in excess of 70% are from Azad Kashmir — usually referred to as Mirpuris; this is reflected in their dominance in local politics: in 1990, of the seven Muslim councillors six were from Azad Kashmir and the other from Punjab.

on the Prophet and his saints. The entire year is punctuated with religious festivals. The most important of these is the Prophet's birthday, which is the occasion for a public procession. The many saints are also celebrated with popular psalms and eulogies.

As the years have passed, Pir Maroof has become ever more heavily involved in religious activities. Only after the death of his elder brother in 1985, when he also became head of the Naushahi order, did he give up his job in the mill. Since then he has spent up to five months in each year visiting his devotees both in Pakistan and in the Pakistani diaspora in Western Europe, as well as taking responsibility for the construction of his two *madrasa* (schools for *'ulema*), one in his home village of Chakswari and the other at his family shrine at Dogah Shareef, Gujrat District.

Pir Maroof is also involved in a wider political and religious arena, for in 1973 he created the World Islamic Mission, an umbrella organisation for Barelvi *'ulema*, in association with Maulana Noorani, the leader of the Barelvi political party in Pakistan. Under the Mission's auspices, two of Ahmad Raza Khan's most important works have been translated into English: his Urdu translation of the Qur'an, and his well-known poem in praise of the Prophet, *The Salaam*, which is often read at the conclusion of Friday prayers in Barelvi mosques. The Mission is clearly intended as a counterweight to those whom the Barelvis dismiss scornfully as "Wahhabis",[42] whether Deobandis, Jamaat-i-Islami or Ahl-i-Hadith.

The issues dividing Barelvi and Wahhabi were made clear at a large gathering organised by the World Islamic Mission at the Wembley Conference Centre in May 1985. In the presence of a galaxy of dignitaries, including Pir Maroof and Maulana Noorani, the conference attracted more than 3,000 participants from all over Britain. Formal resolutions were passed condemning Saudi officials for confiscating and allegedly destroying Qur'ans translated into Urdu by Raza Khan; complaining about the draconian repression of Muslims in Madina and Mecca who had sought to celebrate the Prophet's birthday; seeking assurances that remaining sites associated with the Prophet, his companions and family would be respected and maintained; and objecting to the staffing of the World Muslim League, ostensibly intended to foster Muslim co-operation, almost entirely by Wahhabis, who represented only 2% of the Muslim community

---

[42] Muhammad, b. 'Abd al-Wahhab (1703–87), a Hanbalite preacher, committed himself to a return to the fundamental principles of the Qur'an and thus to cut away medieval accretions to the faith. To this end he sought to undercut the veneration of the saints, which he considered tantamount to polytheism. "With the conversion of Ibn Saud [in 1745] . . . Wahhabism became the religious ideology of tribal unification . . . [in] central Arabia." Lapidus, *op. cit.*, p. 673.

world-wide. The Saudi authorities, it is claimed, have not responded to these appeals.

Pir Maroof's myriad activities have, however, been bedevilled by personal and political rivalries, which in turn have brought the financial viability of many of them into question. One of his most ambitious projects was to build a large purpose-built mosque. The land for it had been purchased nearly twenty years earlier, but by 1990 he had been forced to cut his £8.5 million scheme, which had relied heavily on gaining Arab sponsorship, right back to £1 million, and even that was proving hard to raise at a time of economic recession.

Money was not the only problem. As early as 1974 his leadership was challenged by a rival Barelvi group, the Hanafia Association, many of whose members comprised devotees of another Mirpuri *pir*, Alauddin Siddiqui, and supporters of the Pakistan People's Party, antagonistic to Maulana Noorani's party in Pakistan. The Association thus announced plans to build another expensive purpose-built mosque close to Pir Maroof's chosen site. Mutual recriminations grew more vicious, and eventually came to a head in a stabbing incident.[43] Soon afterwards the Hanafia Association publicly announced that it refused to accept "the dictatorship of one man"[44] in the control of a planned Islamic Missionary College. Since then Pir Maroof's pre-eminent position has been further eroded with the establishment of two more large Barelvi mosques, each owing allegiance to other *pirs*.

Although his supporters still control many smaller mosques, limited resources have meant that Pir Maroof has had great problems keeping his best *'ulema*: Maulana Azmi left the Islamic Missionary College in 1979 after three years to join a mosque in Manchester, and Maulana Nishtar joined the rival Hanafia Association in 1982 after twelve years with Pir Maroof. Since they are rarely paid much more than £70 a week, a third of what might be earned in a mill, attracting and keeping able *'ulema* is a constant struggle. Of those currently employed in Pir Maroof's mosques, no less than eight are Gujaratis, a situation widely acknowledged to be less than ideal since most of the children they teach are native Punjabi- rather than Urdu-speakers, while the Gujaratis have little Punjabi.

The worst effect of intra-Barelvi rivalries has been the failure of Pir Maroof's vision to see the Islamic Missionary College, set up in 1974, develop into a fully-fledged Islamic seminary, capable of training a new generation of English-speaking *'ulema* and thereby freeing many mosques from the need to import personnel from South Asia. The strength of the Barelvi tradition is that it is not antagonistic to

---

[43] *Telegraph & Argus*, 27 Sept. 1979.
[44] *Telegraph & Argus*, 12 May 1979.

the need for youth provision. Maulana Azmi encouraged the creation of a Muslim youth group, al Falah, in 1979, and in 1989 another youth group was started by one of Pir Maroof's acolytes.

The Deobandis in Bradford

Bradford's thirteen Deobandi mosques have been rather more successful in maintaining organisational coherence, as well as coping with the inevitable tensions of regionalism and inter-personal rivalry. Thus although the management committees of seven of their mosques are controlled by Pathans and Punjabis from Chhachh in Pakistan, three by Sylhetis from Bangladesh and two by Suratis from Gujarat, their congregations are by no means so exclusively defined: many Punjabis and Mirpuris regularly worship at the large Bangladeshi mosque and at both the Gujarati mosques. Such interchanges are facilitated by the routine use of Urdu as a *lingua franca* by the Deobandis.

Deobandis have also reaped benefits from greater co-ordination and reduced inter-group competition. Thus rather than competing to set up seminaries of their own, most mosques have now sent students to one or other of the large and flourishing Deobandi seminaries set up at Bury and Dewsbury[45] in 1975 and 1982 respectively. Dewsbury is also the European headquarters of the revivalist movement, Tablighi Jamaat. The principal of Bury, Yusuf Motala, is a product of a Deobandi seminary at Saharanpur in India, the leading luminary of which, Maulana Zakariya (d. 1982), was one of the most influential figures in the revivalist movement.[46] It was Zakariya who directed his devotee, Motala, to establish a seminary in England.

Both seminaries are largely managed by Gujaratis and testify to the importance of this comparatively well-educated community, used to living as a small minority in the largely Hindu environment of India.[47] In the long run these seminaries will undoubtedly be of critical importance for the future of Deobandi Muslims in Britain. The Howard Street mosque appointed its first English-speaking *'alim*, a graduate of Bury, in the autumn of 1989; in the following autumn, another Bradford mosque appointed the first graduate from Dewsbury to be employed in Bradford. The availability of locally trained *'ulema*

---

[45] Bury is some 50 miles from Bradford, while Dewsbury is 10 miles away.
[46] Maulana Zakariya was one of Ilyas's nephews and a member of his inner circle, who advised him *inter alia* on the issue of succession — and was the author of the movement's manual of prescribed study, *Tablighi Nisab*. See Anwarul Haq, *op. cit.*
[47] According to the 1981 census of India, Gujarat has only 8.53% Muslims. See Raymond B. Williams, *Religions of Immigrants from India and Pakistan: New Threads in the American Tapestry* (Cambridge University Press, 1988), p. 88.

should free Deobandi mosques from their current dependence on recruits from overseas, many of whom are not closely attuned to the needs and concerns of British Muslims. However, the character and content of the education offered at these seminaries is not without its problems.

At present there are about 300 students at the Dewsbury seminary — 15% are from overseas — of whom about half are in the school section of 13–16 years old, while the remainder attend the more advanced *'alim* course, which takes seven years to complete. One of the few concessions made to the seminary's location in Britain is the exclusion of Persian from the syllabus; otherwise little has changed. The school section is slightly more flexible, to conform to legal requirements: the mornings are still devoted to the study of the Qur'an in Arabic and of Islamics through the medium of Urdu, while the English curriculum — which includes general science, maths, English and Urdu, all studied for G.C.S.E. — is studied in the afternoon. However, even then television and video are not allowed, since these are deemed to come within the Islamic prohibition against representations of living creatures.

What is evident, to this observer at least is that the students live in two unrelated intellectual worlds.[48] Different people teach the English and Islamic components of the course and there is little co-operation between them.[49] The Islamic dimension of the syllabus is taught by *'ulema* with a traditional training: in Dewsbury its central elements are Arabic, Qur'anic studies, Islamic (Hanafi) jurisprudence, the articles of belief and the six canonical collections of *Hadith*. Philosophy and theology are not taught, and historical studies are largely restricted to the lives of the four "rightly guided" Caliphs, the Prophet's immediate successors. The obvious question this poses is how far such a syllabus, which includes only a fraction of the rich storehouse of Muslim scholarship, and virtually excludes all contemporary discussion and debate, Muslim and non-Muslim, can provide a sufficient basis for the transmission of Islamic thought and practice in a British context.

[48] There is the real danger that these seminaries will duplicate the Pakistani experience. I.H. Qureshi (d. 1981), one of Pakistan's most distinguished historians and educationalists, observed that the leaders of the country's Islamic seminaries have "neglected modern knowledge to an extent that there is no scope for dialogue between those who have received a modern education and the graduates of the seminaries". Cited in Fazlur Rahman, *Islam and Modernity: Transformation of an Intellectual Tradition* (University of Chicago Press, 1982), p. 111.

[49] This was the judgement of the Muslim teacher who set up the school at Dewsbury and was a consultant at Bury. He regretted that there seemed little interest in introducing "A" levels or seeking validation from local universities for the Arabic and Islamic courses taught there.

The U.K. Islamic Mission

The transmission of a viable Islam in Britain does not simply depend on the activities of traditionalists, whether Barelvi or Deobandi. Members of the Jamaat-i-Islami movement have also been active and generated a number of institutions and organisations in Britain. Among these is the U.K. Islamic Mission, established in 1963 to organise and network study circles and mosques. The Islamic Foundation in Leicester, the movement's research and publishing house, has *inter alia* translated and printed many of Maulana Maududi's works along with educational materials for children. The Muslim Educational Trust and *Impact International*, a bi-weekly magazine, both reflect the same perspective. Leicester is also the headquarters of their youth movement, the Young Muslims U.K., founded in 1984, and of the National Association of Muslim Youth.

In South Asia Jamaat-i-Islami has always drawn the bulk of its support from the products of modernisation in the Muslim world, such as teachers, lawyers and engineers, amongst whom Maududi's scathing criticisms of the ignorance and obscurantism of traditional '*ulema* struck a resonant chord. Since most of the first generation of Muslim settlers in Bradford were of peasant origin, they provided little in the way of a natural constituency for Jamaat-i-Islami, people "for whom the ideological rigour of fundamentalism and studied rejection of Western ideas [was] attractive and popular".[50] So it was that the first U.K. Islamic Mission mosque in the city had to wait until 1981, to be followed four years later by another, run by its Bangladeshi equivalent the Dawa-tul-Islam.

The Dawa-tul-Islam mosque has proved highly successful: besides three full-time '*ulema* — one spent five years at Madina University, and his salary is still covered by the Saudi authorities — the mosque supports its own separate youth group to whom it offers some recreational facilities. In contrast, the U.K. Islamic Mission mosque, with a small constituency and limited funds, has run into all sorts of difficulties. It has been unable to find a permanent '*alim*, having hired four in five years. The situation was exacerbated by the Mission's failure to sustain a viable seminary in Manchester. Nevertheless, the Mission's youth wing, the Young Muslims U.K., has established a very active branch in Bradford.

Although their office and library were originally lodged in the U.K. Islamic Mission mosque, the Young Muslims have recently sought separate premises, thus giving themselves a more distinct identity. If Deobandi/Tablighi Jamaat remain within a clearly South Asian cultural milieu, this is not true of the Young Muslims. Although

[50] Modood, *op. cit.*, p. 150.

still conforming to Islamic codes of modesty, they dress in Western clothes, while their study circles — three for men and two for women — combine recreational activities with serious study. Their glossy magazine *Trends* includes an agony aunt column in which questions currently worrying Muslim youth are freely aired.

To be a member of the Young Muslims is to feel part of a global movement of Islamic renewal. At regional meetings and annual camps, speakers discuss Islamic struggles world-wide, in Afghanistan, Kashmir and elsewhere. Their library, which contains audio- and video-cassettes, gives access to debates and discussions throughout the Muslim world. Commitment to the Islamic mission, *da'wa*, is presented as a radical and all-encompassing alternative to uncaring and oppressive Western materialism. They attract members from all the ethnic groups and sectarian traditions in Bradford.

For the future it remains to be seen whether it can surmount some of the difficulties which led to the demise of the Islamic Youth Movement (IYM), which preceded it in Bradford between 1972 and 1980. The IYM depended on Jamaat-i-Islami personnel, imported from South Asia and sponsored by the Muslim Educational Trust, who taught Islam in Bradford schools where they recruited members for their élitist group. The hope was that such youngsters would provide the next generation's leadership for the U.K. Islamic Mission. IYM did not realise such hopes and folded when its members went on to further education or found themselves absorbed in earning a living. It is exciting to belong to an ideological movement when young and without responsibility, but when adulthood intervenes in a situation where one is a small minority within a minority, the rhetoric of Islamic revolution can soon appear utopian.

Beyond Sectarianism: The Struggle for Unity

Despite the vigour of all these developments, their sectarian character stands in sharp contradiction to the organisational unity most Muslims desire. What further steps have been taken to achieve this still elusive goal? Communities which feel themselves under attack tend to define and guard their boundaries with ever greater care against perceived enemies, within and without.

The Muslim sense of being a beleaguered minority was captured in an article by the director general of the Islamic Foundation in Leicester, when he asked, rhetorically:

Should . . . we accept to live as a grudgingly accepted minority sub-culture, always under siege, always struggling to retain the little niche it has been allowed to carve out for itself? That perhaps is the destiny to which most of us seem resigned . . . especially today the odds are . . . heavily stacked against [us] . . . Through institutions like omnipotent state, omnipresent media, compulsory school system, the tentacles of the dominant culture reach every heart and mind.[51]

This sense of perplexity and alienation felt by many elders, in combination with a desire to define boundaries with clarity, has produced some paradoxical results in Bradford. Before the *Satanic Verses* affair it was a common hostility to the heterodox Ahmadiyya sect which produced a measure of unity and shared action.

The Ahmadiyya movement was founded by Mirza Ghulam Ahmad (d. 1908) of Qadian in central Punjab. It began as a vehicle for Islamic regeneration and reform, and aimed amongst other things to defend Muslims from the increasingly vigorous assaults of Christian and Hindu missionaries. Before long, however, Ghulam Ahmad began to claim that he himself had received revelations directly from God, and was the promised Mahdi, the guided one who would appear in the last days to establish Islam. Many of his claims were understood to compromise the finality of Mohammed's prophethood and thus outraged the majority of Muslim leaders. The Ahmadiyya remain a small sect, but are socially influential given their members' high level of education. In all they are an ideal enemy within.

In 1953 Pakistan's Foreign Minister became the focus of violent anti-Ahmadiyya protests, which triggered the country's first period of martial law. In 1974 Prime Minister Bhutto, yielding to opposition, allowed the National Assembly to amend Pakistan's constitution to re-classify them as non-Muslims. When subjected to further physical and legal harassment,[52] the leader of the movement fled to Britain in 1984, where he established his headquarters. In Bradford the first Ahmadiyya centre for worship had been established in 1980.

In Pakistan it was the Deobandis who spearheaded the opposition to them, and this they have continued to do in Britain. So if the Barelvis met at Wembley to condemn the Wahhabis and their Saudi backers, the Deobandis regularly used the same arena to chastise the Ahmadiyyas. Resolutions passed at their fifth annual conference in October 1989 included demands that all remaining Ahmadiyyas be removed from influential positions in the federal and provincial governments of Pakistan, that their literature should be confiscated, and that the Islamic law on apostasy be enforced against converts to their movement.

[51] Murad Khurram, *Muslim Youth in the West: Towards a New Educational Strategy* (Islamic Foundation, 1986), pp. 6–7.
[52] Documented in harrowing detail in the report by an International Commission of Jurists, *Pakistan: Human Rights After Martial Law* (Karachi Study Circle, 1987), pp. 103–15.

If more of Bradford's civic and religious dignitaries had been aware of all this, they might have been more cautious in their response to an invitation from the Ahmadiyya Students' Association to attend a "Religious Founders Day" held in the city's central library in September 1986. The theme of the meeting — inter-religious understanding — seemed quite innocuous, as did their publicity material, in which the pious phrase 'Peace Be Upon Him' was appended to the names of Rama and Guru Nanak. But to local Muslims this was outrageous and heretical, since the phrase is only used of Islamic prophets. Faced with what they saw as the machinations of the enemy within, they organised a public demonstration. The result was anything but harmonious. Large numbers of people assembled, led by the representatives of the non-sectarian Council for Mosques, and in the ensuing melée the meeting was cancelled and seventeen protestors were arrested.[53]

In a rather different vein, an anti-Christian controversialist from South Africa, Ahmad Deedat, has also been the focus for shared concern. He takes up a long tradition of anti-Christian polemic, which can be traced back to a series of debates staged between Karl Pfander, a Christian missionary, and Maulana Rahmat Kairanawi in Agra, North India, in 1854.[54] Deedat claims to have been inspired by the latter's book *Izhar al Haq* (the Demonstration of Truth) in his attempt to counter "the insults . . . piled on Islam"[55] by Christians in South Africa. His organisation, the Islamic Propagation Centre International, now sells part of this work, newly translated into English.

Deedat has a considerable following. Having packed out the Albert Hall in 1985, his almost annual visits to Britain have always included engagements in Bradford. His last tour in the autumn of 1989 saw him entering the lists against *The Satanic Verses*. Video cassettes of his debates and lectures are widely circulated among English-speaking Muslims, and he has almost a cult following among many young people: his booklets and cassettes can be found in youth groups as different as the Barelvi al Falah and the Young Muslims U.K.

The Bradford Council for Mosques

While anti-Christian and anti-Ahmadiyya rhetoric has provided local Muslims with a sense of internal solidarity and identity, Bradford's

---

[53] *Telegraph & Argus*, 6 and 7 Oct. 1986.
[54] See A.A. Powell, "Maulana Rahmat Allah Kairanawi and Muslim-Christian Controversy in India in the Mid-19th Century", *Journal of the Royal Asiatic Society*, 1975/6, pp. 42–63.
[55] Ahmed Deedat, *Is the Bible God's Word?* (Birmingham: Islamic Propagation Centre, 1985), p. 62.

Council for Mosques — set up in 1981 in premises funded by a Local Authority grant — became an increasingly effective instrument during the 1980s for the articulation of the Muslim community's collective interests, and an institution with which Bradford Metropolitan Council and other public bodies could liaise and negotiate.

In the early 1980s the City Council was particularly receptive to such pressures. Having been subjected to severe criticism by a Commission for Racial Equality report in 1979 for its failure to face up to issues of equal opportunities and racial justice, its response — based on a remarkably frank Council report entitled *Turning Points*, published in 1981 — was very positive. The report, reviewing the history of immigration into Bradford, described the previous twenty years as "settlement by tiptoe": jobs, houses and schools in the inner-city areas had gradually been filled by South Asians, whose network of ethnic services had created a self-contained economic infrastructure and a separate cultural world. A dual society had emerged, whose members looked outward to mainstream British society for jobs, schools and services, but who still looked inward to preserve their own cultural values, especially in family life, religion and language. With economic recession beginning to bite, the report concluded that benign neglect was no longer an adequate basis for Council policy.

It was over educational issues that the Council for Mosques began to express its strongest concerns. As early as 1974, Pir Maroof's association had produced a booklet entitled *The Problem of Muslim Girls' Education in England*. Written in Urdu, it stressed the need for more provision for single-sex schools for girls — especially when they reached puberty — as well as sensitivity in the mainstream educational provision to the religious and cultural needs of Muslim pupils. In taking up issues of this kind, the Council for Mosques chalked up many successes during the 1980s. A proposal to amalgamate Belle Vue, one of Bradford's only two girls' schools, with an adjacent boys' school was halted. The Education Department was persuaded to issue a memorandum directing schools to allow modifications in uniforms, and to accommodate Muslim families' concern that their daughters should have access to single-sex arrangements for physical education and swimming. In another memorandum the Council agreed to provide *halal* food in schools, community languages began to be taught in upper schools, and a supplementary schools officer was appointed to seek to bridge the gap in provision between the supplementary and state schools. A new agreed religious education syllabus was finalised, and in 1986 a well-resourced Inter-Faith Education Centre was established.

Substantial though these advances were, they were not achieved without a struggle: indeed they were often bitterly contested. For example animal rights activists fought a long rearguard campaign against *halal* food. The Conservative chairman of the Education Committee also paid the price for supporting these measures, losing his seat in the 1984 elections. The Council for Mosques was one of a number of groups directly involved in the Ray Honeyford saga[56] which blew up in 1984 and was not resolved until December 1985. Thus throughout the 1980s the Council for Mosques was developing its confidence and expertise in conducting campaigns. So when Muslim anger at the publication of *The Satanic Verses* exploded in the autumn of 1988, Bradford was virtually unique in that it possessed an institution ready and able to channel the grievances of local Muslims, regardless of their sectarian differences, and on that basis to organise and sustain an extended campaign.

Although Bradford's Muslims — divided as they are by differences of caste, class, ethnicity and sect — by no means form a homogeneous mass, it is clear that these divisions are not so deep as to be unbridgeable. Once Muslim identity is brought into focus, many linkages can be seen to transcend them. Urdu, although the mother-tongue of only a small minority of Bradford Muslims, is widely used as a *lingua franca*; it is studied by Pushto-, Gujarati- and Punjabi-speakers in their mosques and understood by some Bangladeshis. Many of the *'ulema* themselves embody a transcultural identity, and despite the ever-present danger of fragmentation along sectarian lines, as happened in Birmingham,[57] the Bradford Council for Mosques has held together. Its success is due partly to its care in restricting itself to a specific and limited agenda, shared by many Muslims, and to the exclusion of the *'ulema* — except in a consultancy role — since their training has not, for the most part, equipped them to understand the demands of institutional life in Britain.

Worlds Apart: The Growing Linguistic Gap

Despite such expressions of Islamic solidarity, its consolidation is constantly threatened by the limited linguistic competence of many British-born youngsters, which makes many of them less able to gain access to the full range of Islamic resources. At Friday worship and in public processions to celebrate the Prophet's birthday the 16–25 age-group is heavily under-represented. One of the principal reasons

---

[56] See Mark Halstead, *Education, Justice and Cultural Diversity: An Examination of the Honeyford Affair, 1984–85* (London: Falmer Press, 1988).
[57] Danielle Joly, *Making a Place for Islam in British Society: Muslims in Birmingham* (Research Papers in Ethnic Relations no. 4, Centre for Research in Ethnic Relations, University of Warwick, 1987), p. 8.

for their absence is obvious: only a minority are sufficiently at ease in Urdu or Punjabi to understand sermons, addresses and devotional songs.

One of the richest worlds to which many young people now have only limited access is that of the *qawwali*, Sufi devotional music. For the past 600 years this tradition has provided consolation and spiritual nourishment for the faithful in a form accessible to all, lettered and unlettered alike.[58] Constantly asserting the superiority of *'ishq*, the passionate and overwhelming devotion of the believer to God, the Prophet and his saints, the *qawwalis* just as regularly mock the staid and bookish *'ulema*, accusing them of using their learning as a cover for hypocrisy. One of the most popular sources of such imagery is Waris Shah's classic poem *Hir Ranjha*, which is no less frequently alluded to in popular speech and in the cinema than by the *qawwalis* themselves. Throughout the poem — which is simultaneously a *Romeo and Juliet* love story and a complex Sufi allegory — the *'ulema* are pilloried for their iniquities, formalism and want of compassion. Ranjha inveighs against the *mullah*, accusing him of sitting "in the pulpit with the Quran in front of you, yet . . . you lead the village women astray; you are a bull among cows."[59] And if *qadis* (Islamic judges) regularly appear as villains, ready when bribed to dispossess Ranjha of his inheritance and to solemnise Hir's marriage against her will, then the tale's heroes are the *pirs*; it is they who are always ready to applaud and facilitate the consummation of the lovers' passion. In classic Sufi style such romances can be enjoyed both for themselves and as metaphors for the trials and tribulations encountered by devotees to God and his creation.

This devotional tradition is valued as a custodian of Islamic humanism, and valued by progressive writers in Pakistan as a vehicle for dissent. Typical of this perspective is an article in *Viewpoint*, a popular left-wing weekly, which cites the Punjabi Sufi writings of Bulleh Shah (d. 1750) as a "jihad against the tyranny of establishments",[60] both political and religious. Similarly, in his recent novel about the politics of racism and anti-racism in Bradford, Tariq Mehmood can still rehearse village banter at the *mullah*'s expense and refer to Hir Ranjha as the archetype of romantic love.[61]

As command of Urdu or Punjabi declines among young Muslims

---

[58] See Regula Burckhardt Qureshi, *Sufi Music of India and Pakistan: Sound, Context and Meaning in Qawwali* (Cambridge University Press, 1986).

[59] Charles Frederick Usborne, *The Adventures of Hir and Ranjha* (Karachi: Lion Art Press, 1966), p. 35.

[60] Nazir Ahmad, *Viewpoint*, 9 Aug. 1984, p. 18.

[61] Tariq Mehmood, *A Hand On The Sun* (Harmondsworth: Penguin Books, 1983), pp. 57 and 84.

in Bradford, and with it access to this devotional tradition, Muslims are now asking whether a viable, alternative tradition is being developed in English. The Bradford Muslim scholar Shabbir Akhtar has recently sought to address this issue. His study is a devastating indictment of an intellectual tradition. In his preface he refers to "the current intellectual paralysis [of Muslims] . . . an intellectual lethargy that has already lasted half a millennium". His plea is for "a critical Koranic scholarship" which connects with the concerns and worldview of modern man; the development of "a natural theology, responsive to the intellectual pressures and assumptions of a sceptical age". Akhtar feels the task is urgent since "the Koran is palpably becoming an irrelevance to our daily lives, to the mental travail of ordinary existence".[62]

Akhtar's analysis is echoed by Mohammad Raza, an *'alim* who has spent many years in Britain serving his community. Raza's study of the ethos, leadership and institutions of the Muslim communities in Britain paints an equally bleak picture. He contends that the Islamic institutions in Britain have not "even developed a critical view through which they can study their own heritage".[63] As for the Islamic academies and institutions in the West, the distinguished anthropologist Akbar Ahmed noted that they suffer from various structural defects: they usually centre on one individual and such people remain "somewhat isolated from each other . . . therefore, no schools or theoretical frames . . . are being developed; nor are young intellectuals, working under learned scholars, being groomed for scholarship."[64]

The Status and Function of the 'Ulema

Although the Islamic tradition accords great respect to its religious specialists, the *'ulema*,[65] such men are more appropriately identified as experts rather than as priests. Indeed since Islam draws no boundary analogous to that between clergy and laity in the Christian tradition, the status of such a specialist cannot be unambiguously identified, for in Pakistan as elsewhere in the Islamic world, while " . . . a man

---

[62] *A Faith For All Seasons: Islam and Western Modernity* (London: Bellew Publishing, 1990), pp. 66–7 and 112.

[63] Mohammed Raza, *op. cit.*, p. 63.

[64] *Discovering Islam Making Sense of Muslim History and Society* (London: Routledge and Kegan Paul, 1988), p. 205.

[65] There are many terms employed for such religious specialists: *mullah* is a Persian transformation of the Arabic *maula*, meaning a learned man; in South Asia it can have pejorative associations; *maulawi* and *maulana*, meaning "my master" and "our master" are more respectful; *imam* is a prayer leader.

of no religious learning who dressed like men of religious learning might well be ridiculed, there was no formal sense in which he could be defrocked."[66]

What then is the role, status and function of religious experts in Bradford? In Pakistani migrants' home villages, very few *imams* and *mullahs* had much learning, nor did they occupy a particularly elevated social status. As one commentator put it:

The *imam* leads prayers in the village mosque, performs marriage cere-monies . . . and recites the Quran to bless departed souls. He is usually semi-literate, and has some rudimentary knowledge of Islamic theology . . . The village community regards him as a low-ranking functionary equal to the barber, washerman, cobbler, or carpenter and compensates him partly in kind . . . The *imams*, and especially the *khatibs*, who deliver the Friday orations at the larger . . . mosques in cities, are more learned and command greater respect.[67]

Bradford's seventy *'ulema* vary no less in their levels of learning, and occupy positions right across this scale. The lowly *huffaz*, of whom there are about thirty, have rarely done much more than sup-plement their basic knowledge of Islam by learning the Qur'an off by heart, and their position is closely akin to that of the village *imam*. The remaining forty are more formally qualified, having completed courses of study in a seminary, and of these, nine have also obtained degrees from universities in Pakistan and Bangladesh, and five have tolerable English. Yet even a formally qualified *'alim* has but limited independence and little or no security of tenure; only three of Brad-ford's *'ulema* have formal contracts of employment.

Most of the rest, especially those who came as visitors to Britain and so must still renew their visas annually, are at the mercy of their mosque committee. Those who have acquired rights of domicile in Britain after five years' residence can, if they have acquired a reputa-tion as good speakers or have a talent for reciting the Qur'an or devotional songs, gain a little autonomy, since other mosques may well be keen to snap them up. Even so, the authority of even the most scholarly *'alim* is heavily circumscribed, and largely limited to the mosque itself. As Barton's study of one Bradford mosque made clear, the *imam* had "little experience of the life and work of most of the congregation: the pressures upon the factory worker and the school child are unknown to him . . . [thus] he has virtually no part to play in relations with the wider, multi-cultural society of Bradford."[68] Nor,

[66] Roy Mottahedeh, *The Mantle of the Prophet: Religion and Politics in Iran* (Harmondsworth: Penguin Books, 1985, 1987), p. 231.
[67] Anwar, *op. cit.*, pp. 221–2.
[68] Barton, *op. cit.*, p. 189.

indeed, are the *'ulema* expected to play a major role in articulating the community's political concerns. This is left to Bradford's Muslim councillors, unless the issue obviously falls within their remit, as it did with the *Satanic Verses* affair. Even then the Bradford Council for Mosques, which led the campaign, comprises the members of the mosque committees, the *'ulema*'s employers, rather than the *'ulema* themselves. Thus the *'ulema* do not command uncritical support, either in South Asia or Britain.

So, for example, a recent editorial in *Ujala*, a progressive Bradford-based Urdu monthly, contained a scathing attack on the religious and political leaders who stream into Bradford from Pakistan and Azad Kashmir. After rehearsing the common assertion that half the passengers on any plane from Pakistan are political or religious leaders, the editorial criticised them for their self-display of clan solidarity and their efforts to ridicule and humiliate their opponents, and concluded by telling them to go home and address the problems currently threatening to engulf Pakistan, rather than self-indulgently flying to Britain, where they did nothing but exhibit their "narrow-mindedness, illiberalism and cowardice".[69]

The 'Ulema in the Supplementary Schools

As long ago as 1979, Verity Saifullah Khan pointed to the problems emerging as a result of the differential participation by British-born Mirpuris and their parents in three distinct social arenas: the homeland, the Muslim communities in Bradford and the majority society.[70] Although more recent research has rightly insisted that these worlds are not hermetically sealed, and that many youngsters are therefore more at ease in the first two than is usually supposed,[71] many problems still remain, and nowhere more so than in the mosque and supplementary schools.

The inadequacies of many of the *'ulema* as teachers of the young continues to cause concern in many sections of the Muslim community. A distinguished local Muslim educationalist, in a paper to a national conference in Bradford, noted:

There are grave doubts expressed by almost everyone about the nature of supplementary provision, style of teaching, methods of instruction, disciplinary procedures . . . it may be said that they meet the needs of ritualistic

---

[69] *Ujala*, October 1989, p. 3.
[70] Verity Saifullah Khan, "Migration and Social Stress: Mirpuris in Bradford", in Saifullah Khan (ed.), *Minority Families in Britain: Support and Stress* (London: Macmillan Press, 1979), p. 51.
[71] See Shaw, *op. cit.*

self-identity . . . but one doubts whether the majority . . . come anywhere near meeting the spiritual and actual fulfilment of our . . . children.[72]

Classes are often large, even with as many as seventy children aged from 5 to 16. The teaching style is highly authoritarian, and the cane still used to keep discipline. The latter is supported by the Bradford Council for Mosques,[73] despite a ban on corporal punishment in Local Authority schools. In seeking to identify the reasons why so many young Muslims are adopting a "pop-cum-*bhangra*" lifestyle, far away from Qur'anic norms, Dr Butt, the leader of the Bradford branch of the Young Muslims, noted that "at the first opportunity [the boys] rebelled against a religion which has sometimes been literally beaten into them."[74] The text books used in many of the mosques and supplementary schools are also unattractive. Even those in English are often translations of old South Asian works, and reflect the world, imagery and concerns of a pre-industrial, agrarian society. One widely used book entitled *Lessons in Islam*, by Maulana Kifayat-ullah (d. 1952), devotes five pages to discussing which animals and substances make the water in a well unclean. The Islamic Foundation in Leicester and the Muslim Educational Trust produce professional material in English, but with so few *'ulema* competent in the language, it is not widely used.

Perhaps the most serious disadvantage of the traditional ethos of the mosque and supplementary school is that it leaves little or no space for questioning. Keen though the young may be to gain a better understanding of Islam, the intellectual framework with which they themselves are most familiar, and into which they will seek to integrate that knowledge, is a critical Western tradition. Thus unless their teachers have an understanding of that world, with its styles of argument and presentation, their efforts are unlikely to bear much fruit. Few do have such an understanding.

Many of the elders seem to have lost confidence in the *'ulema*. A study of a Bradford middle school, where over 90% of the parents are Muslims, found that all wanted some Islamic religious education in the syllabus. At the same time, "they were also unanimous in their . . . opinion that [the] *imam* should not be appointed in schools to teach religion but . . . qualified Muslim teachers . . . The parents have said that these *imams* inculcate the germs of anti-Western education . . . and their young children soon get trapped in their magical and . . . fantasy world."[75]

[72] Akram K. Cheema, "Education and the Muslims", *National Conference of British Muslims in Great Britain*, 29 April 1990, p. 5.
[73] *Telegraph & Argus*, 28 Aug. 1986.
[74] *Muslim News*, 15 Dec. 1989.
[75] Burhan ud-Din, "Asian Parents' views about their middle school children's educa-

Being Muslim and British: Making Space for the Young

Despite all these difficulties, young Muslims in Bradford are gradually establishing themselves on their own terms. In the late 1970s two youth organisations were formed: the Asian Youth Movement (AYM) and al Falah. AYM, established in 1978, sought to develop a unitary pan-Asian identity, which would bring together Hindus, Muslims and Sikhs to combat racism. Al Falah — an Arabic word meaning prosperity, which is included in the call to daily prayers — was set up in 1979 as a self-consciously Muslim youth group, intent on providing a secure environment in which youngsters could meet together, learn more about their faith, and enjoy recreational facilities. In 1983 the two groups found themselves on opposite sides in the public debate over the wisdom of separate Muslim schools. AYM objected to al Falah's advocacy of such schools, fearing that it would "automatically disadvantage Muslims".[76]

Although both groups have survived into the 1990s, AYM's attempt to develop a unitary Asian identity has made little headway. Inter-communal tensions in South Asia, along with the development of separate religious and community organisations in Bradford, has seen the consolidation of distinct communities. It is questionable whether any Muslim group, even the determinedly secular AYM, can provide a home for radical politics and anti-racism. By contrast one of al Falah's great strengths has been its preservation of links between Muslim youth and the religious tradition. Its patron, whose name adorns the plaque that commemorates the opening of its new building in 1985, is a Sufi saint from Pakistan, whose annual visits are celebrated with a programme of devotional songs.

If al Falah exemplifies the strengths of the Barelvi tradition, *Sultan*, a new Bradford magazine for 16-25-year-olds, further illustrates how aspects of the tradition continue to be congenial to youth. One issue carried an interview with the famous *qawwali* singer, Nusrat Fateh Ali Khan; as well as receiving pop-star treatment, he was also presented as a source of access to something deeper:

Bhangra is a combination of the East and West and I like it. We get loads of youngsters coming to our concerts and they dance bhangra music . . . with time I hope they will try to understand the depth of our music . . . Please remember our Indian/Pakistani culture even if it is through music.[77]

Other issues of the magazine provide an illuminating window into some of the current concerns of young Muslims. Many aspects of

---

tion" (M.A. thesis, Dept of Education, University of York), p. 77.
[76] *Telegraph & Argus*, 26 April 1983.
[77] *Sultan* 2, Sept.–Oct. 1989, p. 2.

South Asian culture, such as poetry and the *mehndi* ritual — which a feature article describes as playing an "essential part in the celebration of Hindu and Muslim ceremonies" — are affirmed; meanwhile abuses, such as those which have grown up around dowry and arranged marriages, are criticised on Islamic grounds. Similarly, Benazir Bhutto's accusations about her predecessor, General Zia, are repeated with approval, namely that he "tried to take away any form of democracy . . . by using Islam in a negative and degrading way. Zia was enforcing laws which . . . degraded women and insulted the Muslim religion. True Islam is a progressive and pure faith."[78] Many others echo such concerns. Dr Shabbir Akhtar in his recent book on the *Satanic Verses* affair insists on the need for "Muslim women . . . to interpret the sacred text and question the male bias that has patronised their oppression for so long". Likewise he distances himself from the persecution of the Ahmadiyya sect, arguing in favour of religious freedom, in sharp contrast to the position of virtually all *'ulema*.[79]

What we see in all these developments is what might be called a modernist impulse, that is a desire to project Islam in a more progressive way while still keeping faith with the tradition. Should such aspirations prove to be widely shared, the Deobandi/Tablighi Jamaat tendency is likely to have even greater difficulty in keeping the interest and commitment of the young; over and above the limited interest they show in youth work — on their own terms — their strictures against music, television and video often make them appear religious Luddites. Much will depend on how much space the rising generation of English-speaking trainees at the Dewsbury and Bury seminaries are allowed to question aspects of the received tradition, and thus to approach the concerns of the young with greater sympathy.

The final strand of Islamic resurgence — that associated with the Jamaat-i-Islami — is no less significant in Bradford. Its youth movement, the Young Muslims U.K., publishes *Trends*. Like *Sultan*, it provides a forum for the discussion of otherwise unaskable questions. Recent issues have explored such questions as: Is self-abuse, like fornication, a sin? Is watching films and TV against Islamic law? Are British clothes acceptable for Muslims? If a person wants to renounce Islam, can he? If not, why not? A lot of boys want to have girlfriends: could you give some good reasons to persuade them not to? However, the answers given differ significantly from the approach in *Sultan*, being more ideologically purist, and its critiques a good deal more

---

[78] *Sultan 3*, Nov.–Dec. 1989, pp. 19–20.
[79] Shabbir Akhtar, *Be Careful with Muhammad! The Salman Rushdie Affair* (London: Bellew Publishing, 1989), pp. 100 and 76.

rigorous. *Bhangra* music, for example, is rejected on the grounds that it encourages mixing of the sexes, and exposes Muslims to alcohol and sexual permissiveness. But although this might seem to place the Young Muslims in a very similar position to the trainees at Dewsbury and Bury, on other issues they are also critical of them. While both are committed to Islamic mission, *da'wa*, Young Muslims are critical of the minimalist interpretation of *da'wa* by Tablighi Jamaat, since it fails to engage in an "organised social, economic and political struggle to establish the Islamic way of life".[80]

In a recent editorial, *Trends* highlighted some pressing concerns with commendable clarity:

Recent events have shown the Muslims' desire to demand their rights. There have been vociferous calls for halal school meals, state-funded Muslim schools, introduction of Muslim family laws, the banning of a book . . . All these demands have their own merit [however] a neutral observer . . . sees Muslims, in a non-Muslim, secular, state, interested in only one thing: their rights . . . They don't seem interested in anyone else . . . where is the Muslim when it comes to voicing the worries of the elderly in society? . . . protesting against the destruction of the environment? What about the homeless and the jobless? The handicapped and the sick? What is required is for the Muslims to live in the spirit of Islam and give their duty precedence over their rights.[81]

These observations bring clearly into focus some of the major continuing challenges facing Muslims, locally and nationally. But it is not at all clear how, when, where and by whom these issues will be addressed. If most sects continue to import most of their religious teachers from South Asia — making them largely unfamiliar with the language and culture of British Muslims — how well equipped will they be to address this new agenda? And even though, locally, two seminaries within one sectarian tradition have been established, is their curriculum sufficiently flexible to accommodate these concerns? While few young Muslims in Bradford would identify themselves as other than Muslim, the precise nature of that identification in both the present and the future is still a very open question. Unless Islam in Britain gains the capacity to present itself in an intellectually intelligible and socially relevant way, it could become little more than a vehicle for the feelings of anger and bitterness generated by the exposure of the young to the chill winds of racial and ethnocentric exclusion.

---

[80] *Trends 2, issue 5*, 1989, p. 13.
[81] *Trends 3, issue 1*, 1989, p. 3.

DIFFERENTIATION AND DISJUNCTION AMONG THE SIKHS

Roger Ballard

A United Community?

Why focus on *disunity*, especially in a group which appears to out-siders to be a close-knit and coherent whole? It seems so unnecessary. More graphically than any other comparable group, the Sikhs — with their distinctive combination of beard and turban — are a classic example of a group whose members have used physical and cultural symbols to construct an ethnic boundary around themselves. Not only does their appearance mark them off unmistakably from all their neighbours in their native Punjab, elsewhere in India and throughout their global diaspora, but the Sikhs themselves invariably represent their community as homogeneous and particularly close-knit. Ideo-logically, they perceive themselves as members of a single corporate *panth*, who by definition are committed to co-operation, both politi-cally and economically as well as in religious and spiritual contexts.[1] Indeed their commitment to these ideals is directly expressed through their very symbols of distinctiveness. The adoption of the title Singh by all male Sikhs and of Kaur by all females sets them deliberately apart from all other communities, but also explicitly underlines an ideal of non-differentiation, while the beard and turban have exactly the same effect.

Nor is their commitment to unity and solidarity merely symbolic. Whether back home in Punjab, in the many settlements which Sikhs have established elsewhere in India, or in their large overseas dia-spora, they have been very successful in forming their own local networks. And so strong and resilient are the reciprocities thus gen-erated, that the Sikhs as a community are particularly well equipped to look after their own material interests. Thus despite the often severe adversities they have to encounter, as well as their need as emigrants to start from the bottom of the ladder, really poor Sikhs are hard to find. Even in the most hostile surroundings they have usually achieved at least a modest prosperity; and where circumstances were more favourable, they have generally done very well. Whether at home or

---

[1] W.H. McLeod, *Who is a Sikh?* (Oxford: Clarendon Press, 1989).

overseas, Sikhs have demonstrated a remarkable capacity to organise themselves.[2]

Yet such success has not been achieved without cost. Sikhs, like other similarly upwardly mobile minorities such as the Jews, have become uncomfortably aware that whenever an exclusive and highly visible group achieves some degree of prosperity, their neighbours are more likely to regard their success with envy and hostility than they are to admire it. In the face of such negative reactions, lying low is rarely an effective strategy, nor has it been the Sikhs' historically preferred solution. Thus their central response to the rising force of Hindu chauvinism in India — as to parallel forms of exclusionism which they are currently encountering elsewhere — has been to close ranks in defence of their collective interests, so further reinforcing their sense of corporateness and commonality. Hence it is hardly surprising that members of every localized body of Sikhs, whether in India or overseas, go out of their way to represent themselves as belonging to a community both tightly organised and homogeneous.

Yet as anyone with even fleeting experience of everyday life within such communities is aware, this simplistic vision flies sharply in the face of reality. Whether large or small, urban or rural, Punjab-based or migrant, every Sikh community finds itself riven by severe factional conflicts. However, the depth and bitterness of these conflicts is not necessarily immediately apparent to outsiders, since great efforts are usually made to conceal them; and when they do break surface, as they sometimes must, the fiction is still maintained. In such circumstances each side hastens to accuse the other of being a bunch of narrowly self-interested renegades unjustifiably and indefensibly undermining *panthic* unity. The ideal of commonality therefore remains unthreatened.

It is easy to see why discussion of this issue is likely to be avoided. Quite apart from the Sikhs' own concern to sustain their image of ethnic unity, outsiders generally find intricate details of apparently arcane factional disputes of little immediate interest. And in any case it is always tempting for academic analysts to produce generalisations about Sikhs at large — or at least about the members of any given local community — presenting them as if they formed a single homogeneous group. A straightforward description of a "community" and its "culture" — even if this is very much the analyst's own synthesis — is so much easier to present, and so much more accept-

---

[2] There is now a substantial literature on Sikhs both in Punjab and in the diaspora: see Khushwant Singh, *A History of the Sikhs* (Oxford, 1966); Gerald Barrier and Verne Dusenbery (eds), *The Sikh Diaspora* (Columbia, MO, 1989); and Joseph O'Connell (ed.), *Sikh History and Religion in the Twentieth Century* (Toronto, 1988).

able to external audiences who do not want to be bothered by apparently unnecessary complexities, than a carefully nuanced discussion of variation, differentiation and change. Moreover if the analyst is an outsider — as I am — avoiding these complexities has the additional advantage of obviating the need to wash what one's Sikh friends are likely to regard as dirty linen in public.

Yet however tempting it may be to succumb to these pressures, sanitised accounts which downplay, or worse still ignore, the extent of internal conflict will always be both analytically misleading and empirically inadequate. Not only are vital aspects of everyday reality glossed over, but discussion of the dynamics of social change is made virtually impossible. Hence I make no apologies for my focus on disunity. Not only is it a salient characteristic of every Sikh community I have encountered, but that very disunity is invariably the principal dynamic behind most processes of social and cultural change. In exploring the sources of differentiation amongst British Sikhs my aim is in no way to deny their many common characteristics, or to disparage their sense of collective *communitas*, but it is to insist that the forces of disjunction and differentiation within the group are of such significance that they demand comprehensive examination in their own right.

Foundations in the Punjab

Whatever contemporary ideologues may wish to believe, the presence of disjunctions within the Sikh *panth* is by no means a novel phenomenon. They are of long standing. To be sure, additional dimensions may have been added to these disjunctions as a result of Sikh settlers' British experiences, but they are by no means solely a product of their overseas residence. Most of their components can be traced back to the Punjab, and it is there that we must begin.

Perhaps the salient source of conflict amongst Sikhs — whether in Punjab or in the diaspora — is personal rivalry. This, of course, is by no means unique to them, but the immense enthusiasm with which they engage in factional disputes is perhaps best understood as an unfortunate negative consequence of their otherwise admirable commitment to egalitarianism. In a context where the ruling assumption is that every man is as good as the next, it follows that anyone who gets ahead and attains a position of leadership or even of public respect will start to overshadow all his close — and nominally equal — associates. With their honour and autonomy consequently threatened, all those with whom that person is involved may well be tempted to challenge rather than accept the leader's role, if only to preserve their own *izzat*. In such situations factional conflict soon follows — as can readily be observed in Sikh networks of all kinds, from the S.G.P.C. (the elected Central Management Committee for all the historic Sikh temples) right down to the local descent groups which form the basis of each village community.

Beyond personal rivalry, the next most significant cause of disunity is caste: for despite Guru Nanak's explicit disavowal of the whole idea, it cannot be denied that the caste system remains vigorously alive amongst the Sikhs. Thus while the superior position of the Brahmin is radically undermined, and the restrictions on commensality which are central to Hindu practice have been abandoned — most overtly through the adoption of the Sufi institution of the open *langar* (common kitchen) in which all devotees eat together — most other aspects of the caste system, notably the rules of endogamy and the hereditary ascription of occupation, have largely been left unchallenged. Kinship ties — which are critically important as the foundation for everyone's strongest and most binding mutually supportive relationships — remain overwhelmingly caste-specific to this day; moreover, because of the hereditary association with occupation, members of the same caste invariably have common class interests. And it is precisely the dialectics of these contradictory class interests — e.g. between merchants, peasant-farmers, craftsmen of various sorts, and landless labourers — which have sustained the Hindu caste system over the millennia.

The traditional form of many of these contradictions is, of course, being affected by contemporary technological changes, which are privileging the position of some while undermining that of others, while more and more villagers are now leaving the land and taking up urban employment. Yet this has not weakened the significance of caste. Given the intensity of competition for access to scarce resources in urban India, together with the routine personalization of nominally impersonal bureaucratic transactions, kinship ties (necessarily caste-specific) remain of immense importance, particularly when it comes to gaining access to material assets. Hence it is primarily through kin-based contacts and an "approach" that jobs, houses, electricity connection, school places, licences and permits to trade — indeed access to the whole paraphernalia of urban life — is best secured. So even though the traditional rural occupational contradictions are becoming steadily less significant, new forms of rivalry over access to scarce urban resources are simultaneously reinvigorating the strength of intra-caste reciprocities and inter-caste rivalries.

These disjunctions are further complicated by sectarian divisions. From the ten Gurus onwards, it is charismatic preachers who have always been responsible for maintaining the spiritual vitality of the Sikh faith. So even though orthodox Sikh theology may insist that

Nanak and his nine successors must be accorded a radically different status from all other teachers, the distinction in sociological terms is of little, if any, significance. In Punjab spiritual masters have always attracted a personal following, and their most ardent devotees mostly seek to promote their teacher to the highest possible rank, on an infinitely sliding scale which runs from the merely learned Gyani through the respected Sant to the divinely inspired Guru and on to the divine Sat Guru himself.

Few Sikhs with a strong commitment to the faith lack such a personal teacher to whom they give special veneration, and on whom they may bestow any of the above titles; and since teachers are many and their recommended practices diverse, there is ample scope for any of them to accuse others of wrong-headed deviance. Such charges are more likely to be made the further up the scale the teacher's title is pitched, especially when followers begin to show such devotion to their teacher that his very person begins to figure prominently in their daily worship. Those who follow other paths are then likely to argue that such practices put both the teacher and his followers beyond the pale of Sikh orthodoxy, but paradoxically those who press such charges with greatest force usually prove to be devotees of yet another saintly teacher to whom they show almost equal though differently structured respect. The bloody battles which took place between the Sant Nirankari Mandal (a sect with its own Sat Guru and its own distinctive interpretation of the Guru Granth Sahib) and the followers of Sant Jarnail Singh Bhindranwale during the early 1980s are a good example of this process. And although those involved in such disputes always assert that their motivation is entirely theological, one rarely has to look far to discover that other, much more secular contradictions lie close beneath the surface.

Whenever a teacher attracts a substantial following, those who gather round him begin to feel that they share social as well as spiritual characterisation in common. Such solidarity can be an effective base for corporate action, especially when — as is usually the case — those involved share material interests because of their common caste or class background. Sectarianism in this sense has long played a major role in the politics of the Punjab: indeed the *khalsa* itself had exactly such an origin. So although modern sects are usually regarded as unfortunate deviations from the ideal of a united *khalsa*, such divisions are nothing new in Sikhism. On the contrary, they can be traced back to the time of Guru Nanak himself.[3]

Even in the Punjab itself, a whole series of contradictions — arising primarily from the complex interplay between personal rivalry, caste,

[3] W.H. McLeod, *The Evolution of the Sikh Community* (Oxford, 1976).

class and sect — have long been present. Settlement in Britain has not so much created new disjunctions, but rather added a range of new dimensions to some long-standing processes of differentiation.

Sikhs in Britain — The Early Pioneers

Although mass migration did not begin until the 1950s, the pioneer founders of Britain's Sikh settlement had arrived much earlier. Details are scanty, but it seems probable that the earliest settlers were Sikh soldiers who had fought in France during the First World War, and stayed on in Britain instead of boarding the troopships back to India. In doing so they joined a number of other South Asian sojourners, most of whom were ex-seamen. Establishing a residential and occupational toe-hold in the midst of the great depression was far from easy, for in the face of high white unemployment all industrial work was effectively closed to them. So most of the early pioneers pursued a strategy already developed by the other ex-seamen: they worked as pedlars, selling clothes and household goods from door to door.

Most of these pioneers were members of the Jat (peasant farmer) caste, from which the Indian Army drew most of its recruits. But although their Army service may have enabled them to get to Europe, Jats had no prior experience as pedlars. However it was not long before they were joined by members of a very different caste, the Bhatras, whose traditional occupation was precisely that. In Punjab the Bhatras are such a small group that few outsiders have ever heard of them, but as Rose[4] reports in his invaluable compendium, their traditional occupation was as hawkers and fortune-tellers. Based in a few villages in Sialkot and Gurdaspur Districts, they ranged widely all over northern India in pursuit of trade. While their wandering lifestyle led to their being accorded a relatively low social status, theirs was nevertheless a skill with a considerable potential; and by the late 1920s, a few pioneers had made their way to Britain. Just how they did so is unclear. The Bhatras themselves tell a story of an earlier phase of settlement in Sri Lanka, whence they subsequently moved on to Britain;[5] and once they had discovered that they could profitably deploy their traditional skills within the British arena, more and more of their relatives gradually came to join them.

During the late 1930s a parallel process of chain migration also began to develop amongst the Jats, with kin and acquaintances joining men who had found a niche in Britain. But given the relative adversity

[4] H.A. Rose, *A Glossary of Tribes and Castes of the Punjab* (Lahore, 1883), vol. 2, pp. 93–4.
[5] Hindbalraj Singh, "Bhatra Sikhs in Bristol: The Development of an Ethnic Community" (unpublished M.Sc. dissertation, University of Bristol, 1977).

of British economic circumstances — at least compared to the opportunities available in Burma, Thailand, Hong Kong and East Africa
— the inflow into Britain was comparatively small.[6] Nevertheless
numbers grew steadily, and by the end of the 1930s most of Britain's
ports and many of its major industrial cities had small Sikh colonies.
Exactly how many people were involved is difficult to estimate, but
it is unlikely to have been more than a few thousand. In terms of
caste, the scale of the Jat and Bhatra presence was roughly equal, but
since overall numbers were so small, such differences were then of
less significance than they are today. Isolated in a foreign land, all
Punjabis — whether Hindu, Muslim or Sikh — tended to aggregate
together.

Mass Migration in the Post-war Period

Further immigration effectively halted between 1939 and 1945, but
was soon resumed once transport was available. At first most new
arrivals also became pedlars, but with the onset of the post-war
economic boom, the pattern of opportunities was transformed. Wage
rates and living standards rose fast, and large sections of British
industry suddenly found themselves acutely short of labour. In these
circumstances discriminatory practices were swiftly abandoned: employers wanted hands, no matter of what colour. Anyone willing to
work could soon find a job.

This shift from peddling to industrial employment began during
the war, but once it was clear that industrial jobs were still easy to
get, word quickly reached the Punjab. The result was an ever-increasing inflow of migrants, which lasted until the imposition of immigration controls in the mid-1960s. But although most of the newcomers
were adventurous young men looking for wider and better opportunities, they were by no means setting off into the blue. Thanks to
the presence of the early pioneers, most were reasonably well informed about the opportunities available, and had contacts from
whom they could expect help in finding both work and accommodation.[7] Migration therefore took the form of a cascading chain, in which
new arrivals invariably had a link with someone already settled in
Britain — usually kin but, failing that, acquaintance. Most were therefore drawn from the same villages and castes as the early pioneers.

With the Bhatras, the inflow remained tightly focused both socially
and geographically; and since theirs was such a close-knit and self-

---

[6] Tom Kessinger, *Vilayatpur, 1848–1968* (Berkeley: University of California Press,
1974).
[7] Gurdip Aurora, *The New Frontiersmen* (Bombay: Popular Prakashan, 1967).

contained community in the Punjab, chain migration scarcely stretched beyond the boundaries of the caste. But the pattern was rather different amongst the Jats. The Jullundur Doab — whence most Jat Sikhs in Britain originate — is one of the most densely populated parts of the Punjab. Poorer Jullunduri Jats have long looked for supplementary employment elsewhere. From soon after the imposition of the British Raj, many young men joined the Army. Others took advantage of opportunities in the Canal Colonies in West Punjab, as well as in British colonial possessions all around the Pacific and Indian oceans, and since the early 1950s they have provided the overwhelming majority of Sikh migrants to Britain.

There are now some 300,000 Sikhs living in Britain, and of these well over half are Jats. Given that many of the pre-war pioneers were Jats, and that they make up around half of the population in rural Jullundur, this is just what one might expect. But unlike the Bhatras, peasant-farmer Jats were far from being socially isolated. So although early settlers tended to give priority to assisting their caste fellows' emigration, fellow villagers with a range of other caste backgrounds — such as Ramgarhias, Ramdasias, Chhirs, Nais, Valmikis and so forth — soon found their way to Britain along the same routes, although the scale of emigration was less intense amongst the poorer non-landowning castes, above all because they often had difficulty raising the necessary finance. By contrast, as peasant farmers the Jats were much better placed: besides being rather better-off, they could, if necessary, mortgage land to raise cash. Hence by the early 1960s what can only be described as "migration fever" swept rural Jullundur. Apart from those with pressing family responsibilities, or with extensive property or business holdings to keep them occupied, there were hardly any young men who did not begin to dream of emigration, and until the imposition of immigration controls in 1962, they faced few difficulties in making their way to Britain.

Immigration Control and the Reunion of Families

Despite the introduction of work permits in 1962, the inflow of non-European migrant workers was not significantly reduced. Many industrial employers were still having difficulties in recruiting sufficient labour, and willingly facilitated the issue of vouchers: and as most were issued in favour of relatives and friends of existing employees, the whole process of chain migration was yet further reinforced. This window of opportunity did stay open long, however. Following some disastrous election results, the Labour Party reversed its earlier policy of hostility to immigration control. In 1965 the issue of vouchers was halted, and since then it has become steadily more difficult for Commonwealth citizens of non-European descent to settle in Britain.

Paradoxically, it was several years before these restrictions significantly reduced the inflow of Sikh settlers — although they did have an immediate impact on their age and gender. Before 1960 Sikh settlers were virtually all male. They saw their stay in Britain as temporary, since their principal aim was to earn and save as much money as possible, as quickly as possible before returning home. These sojourners saw little point in bringing over wives and children, for that would drastically reduce their capacity to save. But like so many migrants elsewhere, most stayed on much longer than they originally intended. Not only were they attracted by the prospect of continuing to earn good money, but they gradually felt more relaxed about the prospect of more permanent residence overseas. Yet the Britain about which they felt more comfortable was not an English Britain. As local Sikh colonies grew in size, many of the social and cultural styles, conventions and institutions of the Punjab began to be reproduced. Perhaps most importantly of all, Britain became an arena for status competition. With this it ceased to be a cultural and social no-man's-land, where all gratification was deferred against an eventual return, but was transformed into an arena for social interaction every bit as lively as the villages left behind. Almost unbeknownst to themselves, sojourners were being transformed into settlers.

This transformation also precipitated a radical change in migrants' domestic strategies.[8] While the early pioneers had been content to leave their wives and children at home, it now made greater sense to call them over to Britain or, if the man is unmarried, to fetch a bride from the Punjab. By the mid-1960s, swift family reunion had become the norm. Most newcomers waited no more than two or three years — during which they saved enough money to buy and furnish a house — before bringing their wives and children. Family reunion also had a major effect on settlers' lifestyles, for men soon felt the pressure, especially from their wives, to return to more orthodox ways. And once large parts of most settlers' kinship networks had been reconstituted in Britain, family rituals — particularly of birth and marriage — could at last be properly performed. Since then such events have been ever more elaborately celebrated, as a result of growing status competition between rival families.

[8] Excellent accounts of this period can be found in Arthur Helweg, *Sikhs in England* (Delhi, 1986), and in Alan James, *Sikh Children in Britain* (Oxford, 1976).

The East African Connection

By the end of the 1960s most families were reunited, and the volume of direct migration from Punjab declined sharply. Even so there was a continued inflow of Sikh settlers throughout the 1970s — primarily from East Africa. As several other chapters in this volume show, Punjabi migration to East Africa has an even longer history than that to Britain. It began in the closing years of the nineteenth century, when several thousand craftsmen, primarily Ramgarhia Sikhs from the Jullundur Doab, were recruited to work on the railway being driven up to Nairobi from the coast. Many stayed on to run the railway once it was complete, and as the colonial infrastructure grew, more and more Punjabis — the majority, thanks to chain migration, were Ramgarhias — also found their way to East Africa. Like their Gujarati peers, they occupied an intermediate position in the colonial social order: the European managerial élite occupied all the superior positions, while the broad mass of Africans, as peasants and labourers, were equally firmly their inferiors. But as a result of their position of relative privilege, Asian settlers were exposed when independence was finally granted, for the jobs they did and the businesses they ran were precisely those into which the Africans could most easily aspire to move. Once it became clear that there was little alternative to moving on, many took up the option of going to Britain: not only did they hold British passports, but many also had prior contacts with kin who had already settled there, having moved directly to Britain from Punjab. Yet despite these origins, East African Sikhs brought with them a distinctive set of attitudes, assets, experiences and expectations.[9]

Although by no means all East African Sikhs were wealthy, especially if they had only moved quite recently from India to Africa, the standard of living with which they had grown familiar differed sharply from that in Punjabi villages. European lifestyles were very much their goal. Yet although in some senses highly Westernised — most were well educated (and often professionally qualified) and fluent in English (as well as in Punjabi and Swahili), and often had at least some capital assets — the East African Sikhs were also used to the experience of living as a more or less excluded minority. Hence they had already developed a strong, and in many ways rather traditionalistic sense of ethnic consciousness. Thus East African settlers were not only better equipped to look after themselves economically — whether through business or employment — than direct migrants

---

[9] For a detailed account of the East African Sikhs, see Parminder Bhachu, *The Twice Migrants* (London: Tavistock, 1985).

from India, but they also formed, and certainly perceived themselves as forming, a distinctive social group.

Patterns of Settlement and Employment

In addition to disjunctions resulting from these differences in origin, further differentiation has been precipitated by the radical changes in the labour market in recent years, as well as by the differential impact of those changes in various parts of the country. Sikh settlements are thus far from identical and may indeed differ dramatically.

During the earliest phase of settlement, most Sikh pedlars based themselves in seaports such as Southampton, Bristol, Cardiff, Glasgow and Newcastle. And although the majority of those who arrived in subsequent phases of settlement moved into waged employment in major industrial cities further inland, most of those who stayed on in these seaport towns not only stuck to self-employment, but are also Bhatra by caste. Why should that be so? First, Bhatras tended to be rather less keen than Jats to abandon self-employment for wage labour, especially where the work on offer demanded considerable manual exertion. Secondly, the labour shortages which drew Sikhs — and especially Jat Sikhs — into industrial employment were most acute in outer West London, the industrial towns of the Midlands and, on a more limited scale, the textile towns of West Yorkshire: it was into these areas that the overwhelming majority of (largely non-Bhatra) Sikh migrants moved during the 1950s and '60s. But in cities such as Cardiff, Glasgow and Newcastle the post-war boom never took off. The growth of the Sikh population in these areas was therefore less explosive, and self-employment, rather than waged industrial work, has continued to be the principal source of income.

Nevertheless the scale and character of Bhatra entrepreneurial activities has changed greatly over the years. Although door-to-door selling remained their occupational mainstay until well into the late 1950s, as early as the late 1940s some of the more successful pedlars had begun to move up-market. Some became intermediate whole-salers, acting as stock-holders for their compatriots; others took stalls in the local markets, whilst the most successful of all opened permanent shops, usually in inner-city areas close to their now reasonably well established residential bases. Such enterprises required much greater capital resources than were needed to fill a pedlar's outsize suitcase with goods for sale, so this was a goal which it took some time to reach. However the very success of this strategy ensured that their success became a model for others. Today there appear to be no more Sikh pedlars. Those still trading are at least market stall-holders, and many former stall-holders have gone on to open a wide range of larger enterprises, including shops, supermarkets and whole-sale warehouses.

Such developments were not unique to the seaports, for there has always been a parallel self-employed sector within the Sikh colonies in the more industrially successful cities. However, in the long years of industrial boom the importance of this sector was largely over-shadowed by the sheer scale of industrial employment.

In the early days the jobs taken by Sikh migrants were all much of a kind: they were those in which native English workers were not interested, because they were hot, hard, heavy, inconvenient, and low-paid. But however unattractive to members of the indigenous working class, who were taking advantage of the boom to move upwards into easier and better paid slots in the labour market, doing such jobs was a major step forward for the newly arrived Punjabi settlers. The basic wage of a factory worker in Britain was higher than the salary paid to a senior official back in Punjab, and by working long hours — twelve-hour shifts six days or nights a week were soon virtually the norm — weekly take-home pay could be boosted still further.

As migrants began to use local rather than Punjabi standards of reference, however, their perceptions changed. They soon became aware that they were only given access to jobs that white workers did not want, and where wages were poor by local standards. So they began to look around for alternatives. As a result, the 1950s and '60s were periods of great geographical mobility. Most migrants were still unencumbered by their families, so men frequently moved from town to town in search of better opportunities, switching between foundries, textile mills, steelworks, bakeries and car assembly plants.

Some settlers thus achieved a fair degree of upward occupational mobility, but there were differences in the level of success of different groups. Relatively few of those who had come directly from Punjab villages got far beyond the semi-skilled level; many East Africans achieved rather more, not least because of their skills in bricklaying and carpentry. Having established a positive reputation for craftsman-ship, they had little difficulty in finding comparatively well-paid jobs in the building industry. Many such craftsmen subsequently moved on to start their own building companies.

Transport proved to be another area in which substantial occupa-tional mobility was possible, especially for those whose English was reasonably fluent, although once again migrants found their way into such jobs because of a lack of takers among the indigenous popula-tion. When the British economy began to stumble into recession in the late 1970s, unemployment rose inexorably, and before long even these opportunities dried up. Faced with both recession and routine racial exclusionism, an ever-increasing number of industrial workers reverted to the strategies developed by the earliest pioneers. Hence in recent years more and more people have stepped sideways into self-employment.[10]

The reasons for this seem straightforward. Even though Britain's white natives tend to be reluctant to offer jobs to members of the new minorities when suitably qualified white people are also available, they have shown little hesitation about entering straightforward commercial transactions across the ethnic boundary, especially when members of the otherwise stigmatised minority are prepared to offer sought-after goods and services at the right place, time and price. So although the recession has constricted all the conventional routes to upward mobility through the waged labour market, the Sikhs have — like members of many other new minorities — increasingly identified business and self-employment as the best means of getting on in the world. Moreover the Sikhs had a successful role model immediately to hand. Not only had many of the earliest settlers used the same strategy when they too faced inescapable exclusionism, but the most successful of them never took up waged employment at all, and concentrated instead on building up the range of business enterprises described earlier.

Recession and its Impact

During the 1980s this trend towards business and self-employment was strongly reinforced by severe industrial recession, to which the Sikhs, like most of the other groups described in this volume, found themselves disproportionately vulnerable. The reasons for this are simple. As a result of racial exclusionism, South Asian migrants' opportunities for employment were largely confined to unskilled jobs in traditional heavy industries — and it was those jobs which disappeared most rapidly in the recession. As a consequence of years of under-investment in plant and machinery, the arrival of new, capital-intensive but labour-saving technology, and ever-fiercer competition from overseas, many long-established companies, particularly in the textile and engineering sectors, collapsed so that by the mid-1980s as many as half of all middle-aged Asian industrial workers had lost their jobs. And with the recession being matched by ever-intensifying racial hostility, the prospect of their ever finding industrial employment again became remote, especially for those living in the Midlands or the Pennine region.

---

[10] Recent figures from the Labour Force Survey suggest that more than 20% of "Indian" men (Sikhs are not separately classified) are self-employed.

Faced by the collapse of the employment market on which they had come to rely, Sikh industrial workers had to find an alternative means of making a living. At the outset of the recession some of those who had been made redundant moved on to areas where industrial work could still be found: southeast England, for example, or even further afield in Germany. However as the recession intensified, alternative work became increasingly difficult to find, even for those prepared to move on elsewhere. In the face of these developments an ever-growing number of Sikhs have looked towards self-employment, both as a means of survival, and as a route to continued upward mobility despite the recession. Like migrants everywhere, they favoured activities which required a low initial capital outlay, but where success depended primarily on hard work. Hence market stalls, grocery stores, newspaper and tobacco shops, restaurants, garages and small building firms are much favoured, while the most successful have also begun to expand into larger and much more profitable enterprises, such as wholesale warehouses and supermarkets, and clothing and footwear manufacture.

While this relatively large-scale movement into self-employment, and beyond that into small-scale manufacturing was prompted primarily by the shrinkage of opportunities in the waged-labour market, such developments actually had much longer historical roots. As we have seen, many of the early pioneers made their living as self-employed pedlars, and from there moved on to become market traders and wholesalers, mostly specialising in cheap clothing. Before long these traders began to realise that it would be easy to sew up garments such as those they sold, since they had a relatively skilled labour force to hand in their own close female kin. Some of these businesses stayed small, but because a number of large and profitable manufacturing operations which now have multi-million pound turnovers began as tiny back-room enterprises, their success has spurred others to seek to emulate them. Hence what had previously been a steady trickle of people into small enterprises became a spate as the recession of the 1980s took hold.

However, these enterprises have not remained either very small or wholly informal. While at the outset they might rest on the labour power of three or four women, usually drawn from the entrepreneur's immediate family, they would be organised on a more formal basis once they grew in size. There was a shift of location from the back rooms of residential properties to regular industrial premises, and as more and more hands were employed, budding entrepreneurs no longer depended so much on the labour power of their own kinswomen.

Thus although the move into manufacturing continues apace, it is giving rise to new contradictions. Given the availability of cheap imports, as well as the growth of fierce competition between locally-based manufacturers — whose numbers have increased as more and more redundant Punjabi industrial workers have piled into the market — profit margins have been cut to the bone. To keep afloat, most Asian clothing manufacturers now only do the initial cutting and final packing on their own premises, and farm out the most labour-intensive work — the actual sewing of the garment — to women working on piece-rates at home. But there is now a clear social and communal disjunction between the entrepreneurs and the piece-working machinists, for while most of the former are either Sikhs or Muslims from central Punjab, the majority of home-working machinists are Mirpuri Muslim women. Besides the fact that they are reluctant to take up waged work outside the home, their husbands are now often amongst the long-term unemployed, so that even the pittance they earn as machinists is often a vital addition to the household resources.

One consequence of this is that there is now an increasingly marked divide, which includes ethnic and gender differentials as well as those of class, between the successful entrepreneurs — many of whom now live in expensive suburban houses and drive at least a Mercedes if not a Rolls Royce — and the myriad machinists, cutters and packers on whose labour their wealth depends. But although the underlying contradictions are obvious enough, they have not yet exploded into overt conflict.

The Emerging Second Generation

Apart from growing differentiation between sub-sections of the community, one of the most important developments in recent years has been the emergence of a second generation of British-born — and consequently wholly British-educated — Sikhs. While most Sikh parents of the first generation could be seen as "working-class", since the vast majority had moved into manual occupations on arrival in Britain, their aspirations for their children were much higher than those of their nominal peers amongst the indigenous working class. Thus in contrast to the latter, where several generations of proletarianization had confirmed them in the view that the best their children could hope for was to reproduce their parents' position in the social order, the least that Sikh parents expected was that theirs would abandon the manual work they themselves had been forced to accept, preferably in favour of a professional occupation. Medicine, the law, science and engineering were favoured goals.

On the whole Sikh parents have not been disappointed. Although their children often had to make do with the limited facilities available in relatively inferior inner-city schools, for the shift to the suburbs only began to take off during the 1980s, their educational achievements — in common with most of Britain's other South Asian communities — have been remarkable.[11] As compared with the white majority, a much higher proportion of young South Asians continue in full-time education and training beyond the age of sixteen, and their rate of enrolment on degree courses is nearly double the white norm.

However, formal educational qualifications provide no guarantee that one will gain access to professional employment. Thus even though young people follow their parents in taking a strongly instrumental view of education, so that Sikh students are overwhelmingly concentrated in technical subjects such as medicine, science and engineering, finding a suitable job proves far more difficult than for their white counterparts. While those who enter fields where skill shortages are acute — as in some aspects of software engineering, information technology and accountancy — may still get a job early, this is exceptional. As recession has advanced, supply exceeds demand in many of the professions for which young Sikhs have qualified themselves. Thus in science and engineering, and even in medicine, sufficient white candidates are generally available to fill most of the jobs on offer. So even though young British Sikhs are seeking openings at a different level in the labour market from their parents, their experiences are similar. Not only do they encounter much the same forms of exclusionism, but with increased competition exclusionism may be even more intense. Hence it is hardly surprising that young people's survival strategies are similar to those devised by their parents.

It is striking that among the younger people who have done especially well are those whose qualifications — as lawyers, pharmacists, accountants, dentists and doctors — enable them to set up in private professional practice. As their industrial-worker parents discovered long ago, even if the white natives are unwilling to give jobs to black people, they may still be prepared to do business with them, provided the terms and conditions are attractive. But moving into private practice is not an option available to all who go on to higher education. Chemistry graduates, for example, have little chance of working in their own field except as employees of a major manufacturing company — so those who fail to secure such a post soon after qualifying will have little opportunity of ever using their specialist education and gaining the experience needed to become independent consult-

[11] Roger Ballard and Selma Vellins, "South Asian Students in British Universities: A Comparative Note", *New Community*, vol. 12 (1984).

ants. Medical graduates can be trapped in the same way, for although
junior hospital jobs carry a "trainee" status, gaining an appointment
as a consultant or even being invited to join an established group of
general practioners is often uncertain.

Yet however depressing and dispiriting exposure to such exclusionism may be, relatively few young Sikhs have been overwhelmed
by the experience: instead they have fallen back on some of their
parents' strategies. One solution has been to re-emigrate across the
Atlantic, for all the indications are that in North America professionally qualified "East Indians" encounter less intense exclusionism than
do "Asians" in Britain. But although re-emigration has depleted the
ranks of those with internationally negotiable qualifications, especially in medicine, most of the second generation have stayed in Britain,
although many of the most enterprising have started business enterprises of one kind or another — ranging from market stalls through
insurance and estate agencies to small engineering workshops. Many
of these young entrepreneurs are university graduates who may feel
with some justice that they have been forced to take a step down in
the world. Even so their academic training is rarely wholly wasted.
As businessmen they tend to do well.

Thus Sikh settlers have made considerable upward progress
through the social order, for although the community's initial occupational centre of gravity lay firmly at the unskilled end of the industrial
working class, that is no longer so. The younger generation has made
a substantial shift towards professionalism and/or self-employment:
in a word, British Sikhs are as a group becoming steadily more
middle-class.

Changing Patterns of Co-operation and Competition

To return to our central concerns, it is against this backdrop of
economic and occupational change that Sikh settlers have been
engaged in ethnic colonisation. In doing so their trajectories of adaptation have varied, though they can also be seen exhibiting two
consistent but contrapuntal themes. Thus although there have been
constant efforts to enhance collective solidarity by closing ranks,
these have been accompanied by ever more vigorous internecine
factional squabbles.

The earliest pioneers had no alternative but to co-operate; it was
a matter of survival. Since single rooms were virtually impossible to
rent, pedlars usually lived together in a cheap terraced house which
they had either rented, or occasionally bought. Newcomers were
swiftly incorporated into these households. At the most basic level
this provided them with food and shelter; more important still, it gave

them access to survival strategies, since in addition to teaching new-comers how to sell on the doorstep, established pedlars also provided them with a suitcase full of goods with which to start business. Hence even if someone had entirely exhausted his savings in reaching Britain, the ethnic reciprocities of these pioneer households provided them with an instant safety net.

These relationships also contained some illuminating contradic-tions. At least in principle, such reciprocities were grounded in mutual co-operation, and indeed were always expressed in terms of quasi-kinship. Members of such all-male households behaved towards each other as if they were brothers; even so, it was not long before most such networks began to acquire a hierarchical dimension, with well-established entrepreneurs adopting the role of godfather-like patrons, who expected — and received — considerable social deference in return for their ability to arrange food, lodging and credit (and later waged employment) for less well-connected newcomers.

The underlying contradictions built into these networks between equality and hierarchy proved to be most important in the longer run. Thus, although the ability of patrons to provide support for new-comers helped to promote networks of reciprocity — and thus social cohesion — within the nascent community, this did not presage the emergence of social unity. Quite the contrary. Once patrons acquired positions of prestige, the logic of *izzat* came into operation. Rival patrons soon became competitors, with each constantly seeking to outshine the other.

Network-manipulation was crucial to the competitive process. While each patron sought to maximize his following both because that was prestigious in its own right and because it enhanced his ability to redistribute resources, the networks so generated were also extremely fissile. Where every man considers himself of equal worth to any other — an assumption close to the hearts of most Sikhs, especially Jat Sikhs — a leader's closest associates will by definition also be his greatest rivals, for however prestigious the association might be, it also necessarily places them in the patron's shadow. Hence Sikh networks and associations have been as prone to fac-tionalism in Britain as in the Punjab.

However the arenas within which such factional competition has been played out have not only differed significantly from those in Punjab, but also changed over time. While it was through the assis-tance they were able to offer pedlars that patrons initially rose to positions of influence, by the end of the 1950s their ability to operate on the shop floor had become far more crucial. Anyone who estab-lished a link with foremen or personnel managers in local factories was in a powerful position to assist newcomers, especially since jobs were hard, if not impossible to find without such a recommendation. Nor did the patronage process stop there. There was still the question of which job each person would be allocated, and who would be given access to the most valuable opportunity of all — overtime. Since many of the newcomers spoke little or no English, as well as being concentrated in organisationally peripheral and ethnically homogeneous work gangs, patrons had numerous opportunities to manipulate the whole situation to their own advantage.[12] Many, for example, demanded cash payments from those for whom they had arranged jobs or overtime. In the conventional British perspective this was simply bribery, but it is also possible to see it as part of a wider network of transactions in which migrants were engaged for their own reasons and on their own terms. Recompense for favours extended on the shop floor was by no means restricted to the industrial arena: reciprocation was often achieved elsewhere, and most neatly when clients were directed to assist each other, but on such terms that the patron could claim credit for helping them both.

Indian Workers' Associations and the Communist Party

Powerful though these networks of patronage soon became, it was not long before they were challenged by countervailing forces of a more egalitarian kind. Although Punjabi patrons always represent themselves as "helping" their clients, the recipients are always aware that the patron is doing well out of the deal himself. Thus while patronage networks eased newcomers' entry into the labour market, they also had a downside. Because they facilitated access only to those jobs which the white natives did not want, they not only locked migrants into an undesirable sector of the labour market, but also set them firmly apart from the institutions which white workers had developed to defend their industrial interests — the trades unions.

However, established trades union structures had little to offer them. As Punjabi workers soon realised, their exclusion from the better paid and more attractive jobs was often the outcome of collusion between management and the union, for shop stewards often had a decisive input to decisions about recruitment and promotion, especially to the more attractive jobs. But while they did so on a representative basis, in no way did they represent the interests of the entire labour force. Since it was the white branch membership which sustained the stewards in office, the latter were expected as a matter of course to look after the interests of white workers. Thus while the

[12] Dennis Brooks and Karamjit Singh, "Pivots and Presents: Asian Brokers in British Foundries" in S. Wallman (ed.), *Ethnicity at Work* (London: Macmillan, 1979).

Punjabis' own patronage networks certainly eased entry into industrial employment, they simply bypassed the alternative patronage structure through which exclusionism was institutionalised.

It was not long, however, before these patterns were subjected to radical challenge. Although most Sikh industrial workers were of peasant origin, they were far from politically naive. In the closing years of the Raj the Communist Party of India attracted much support amongst rural Jat Sikhs in Jullundur District, since it was perceived as offering a more vigorously articulated and militantly organised opposition to the British than the Hindu-dominated Congress. After independence in 1947 many idealistic young Sikh students joined the Party, so when migration took off during the 1950s and '60s, not a few of these "Comrades" found their way to Britain. Yet although they were better educated than most, their occupational fate was the same. They, too, had no alternative but to take unskilled industrial work. However their presence soon had a major impact on the shop floor: with a sophisticated political perspective and organisational experience, further reinforced by their education and idealism, they were swiftly pressed forward into positions of leadership, from which they challenged the old-style patrons' comfortably established hierarchies.

With their radical and egalitarian orientation, the Comrades and those inspired by them were soon promoting new and more critical forms of social and industrial solidarity, through the formation of Indian Workers' Associations. Despite the name, the I.W.A.s which sprang up in almost every industrial city during the late 1950s and early '60s were largely restricted to a Sikh — and especially Jat Sikh — membership.[13] The reasons are clear enough: besides the specific influence of the Comrades, who were themselves overwhelmingly Jat, in the early days of settlement the I.W.A.s were the only specifically Punjabi organisations which spread beyond migrants' immediate networks of kinship and patronage. At the most basic level they provided a vital arena for the organisation of mutual support outside the increasingly exploitative patronage networks. Once they were firmly established, the I.W.A.s became an effective vehicle for the articulation of Sikh workers' grievances, resulting in challenges not only to their own internal patronage networks, but also to the wider structures of exclusionism from which those patronage networks had previously buffered them. This led to a rash of activity on the shop floor, as Sikh workers began to take industrial action as a way of challenging their subordinate position in the labour market. While

---

[13] John DeWitt, *Indian Workers Associations in Great Britain* (Oxford University Press, 1969).

Comrades and/or I.W.A.s were involved in all these disputes, it is notable that the strikers' resolution was based at least as much on their commitment to Sikhism as to socialism. Thus although the I.W.A.s were nominally secular, local *gurdwaras* (then only in their infancy) provided strikers with not only a physical base but also financial support: appeals to the congregation for assistance invariably elicited generous contributions. Similarly the recitation of an *Ardas* — and if necessary Hindu and Muslim prayers as well — was widely used to reinforce collective solidarity.

Yet despite their great influence in the late 1960s and early '70s, thanks above all to their success in challenging the marginalisation of Punjabi workers on the shop floor, the significance of the I.W.A.s has steadily declined since then, so that by the 1990s they have become a distant historical memory. While factionalism was a contributory factor in this decline, especially after *izzat*-driven inter-personal rivalries became further exacerbated by the fragmentation of the Communist Party of India into pro-Moscow, pro-Peking and Naxalite segments in the late-1960s, it was paradoxically the growing impact of industrial recession that ultimately led to the demise of the I.W.A.s. This did not make things any easier for Punjabi industrial workers: while pressures on them intensified, the difficulties and dangers of taking industrial action — especially action that flew in the face of established union interests — escalated sharply. Hence despite real and increasing grievances, Punjabi workers have become less willing to take industrial action, aware that a worker who loses his job in an industrial dispute has little prospect of finding another.

However it is not just adverse conditions on the shop floor which have caused a decline in militancy. In recent years the number of Sikhs in manual industrial work has fallen precipitously, partly because of recession and consequent redundancy, but also because many of them had seen the writing on the wall long before the arrival of their redundancy notices. All those who could get out therefore did so well in advance, usually to start in business on their own.

As the industrial arena to which they were a response has declined in significance, so Britain's once thriving network of I.W.A.s has faded too, though it has not yet entirely disappeared. Some local I.W.A.s had substantial assets, such as the Dominion Cinema in Southall, which remained very profitable until the video revolution undermined the profitability of showing Hindi movies. For a while many I.W.A.s found a role as organisers of Republic Day and Independence Day celebrations, but by now the most significant role for most of them is to provide delegates to local Race Equality Councils.

The Rise of the Gurdwaras

Although Britain's first *gurdwara* was founded in the Shepherds Bush area of West London well before the end of the nineteenth century, thanks to the sponsorship of the Maharaja of Patiala, few of the early pioneers took much interest in religious practice: as young adventurers in a strange country their primary concerns were to save money and explore their strange new habitat.[14] Initially most took the view that Britain was best regarded as a social and cultural no-man's-land, in which moral and religious niceties could be left temporarily in abeyance. But as local Sikh settlements grew in size, with more complex networks of reciprocity, and as families began to be reunited, so more orthodox behavioural styles reasserted themselves. With these changing priorities religious concerns came to the fore, so that *gurdwaras* in which prayers could regularly and properly be said suddenly began to be established.

Most of the early ones were no more than ordinary houses in which one room was set aside for religious purposes. But given that Sikh religious practice is strongly congregational in character, involving the preparation and serving of food in the *langar*, as well as recitation from and teaching about the Guru Granth Sahib in the *Diwan*, each new temple soon became an active community centre, with a Sunday visit to the *gurdwara* being the norm even for those whose religious commitment was otherwise limited.

Once established, the *gurdwara* movement took on a dynamic of its own. Setting up each *gurdwara* was a major enterprise, for a considerable input of money and labour was needed to transform a cheap and run-down building into a suitably furnished and decorated *diwan* hall. Moreover the whole operation was often repeated several times in quick succession as the growing size of the local *sangat* forced successive moves from a small terraced house to a larger one, and from there into a disused church or chapel. Organising all this took much time and effort, and those who took on the task acquired prestige. Hence there was intense competition for seats on, and most especially the senior offices in, the Gurdwara Committee. Over the years that competition has not only intensified, but also reinforced the process of caste crystallization.

The Continuing Significance of Caste

Maximizing support in *gurdwara* elections is best achieved not so much by religious charisma or force of argument, as by mobilizing

---

[14] Gurdip Aurora, *The New Frontiersmen* (Bombay: Popular Prakashan, 1967).

networks of kin and clients. At the simplest level this promotes the emergence of caste-based voting blocs: for smaller groups this is the most effective way of articulating their interests. But it also promotes factionalism within the locally dominant caste, as contending leaders struggle to activate the maximum number of linkages within their own caste, complemented by the widest possible range of alliances with smaller local castes. Hence competition for places on the Gurdwara Committee, especially for such publicly prestigious roles as President and Secretary, is intense, and often precipitates factional disputes.

While the most vigorous of these disputes often erupt within the locally dominant caste, their force may lead to smaller castes having more influence than they might otherwise expect; their votes are worth courting, since candidates from their group may be added to each rival faction's slate. But the costs of such patronage are clear: although smaller castes may routinely be offered token representation, they will always be excluded from real power. This experience only reinforces pre-existing sentiments and solidarities. For example, in the few British towns where they are not in a majority, Jat settlers have tended to become resentful of their inability to exercise what many of them regard as their rightful role of leadership. Meanwhile in those cities where Jats are able to exercise that role, the consequential exclusion of non-Jats from positions of power and influence is a bitter reminder of the same state of affairs back in Punjab. Thus even though the division of labour which underpinned the caste hierarchy has virtually disappeared in Britain, caste remains a vitally important vehicle for community and religious organisation. Indeed inter-caste tension's have become so acute that a single *gurdwara* structure is rarely able to contain them. In most British towns with a significant Sikh population one finds a plethora of rival *gurdwaras*, each with a caste-specific management committee.

These relatively traditional inter-caste rivalries have been further supplemented by differences in the employment trajectories of each group, for even in Britain each caste has tended to develop a different occupational base. Before the recent recession decimated industrial opportunities, the (peasant) Jats were largely concentrated in physically demanding manual work and the Bhatras in small business and market trading, while many Ramgarhias had taken advantage of their traditional skills as blacksmiths and carpenters to become craftsmen in the building trade. So although the material interdependences which underpinned the caste system in rural Punjab were largely eradicated, the links between caste and occupation have not been wholly obliterated by the passage to Britain, although there has been at least one significant development: in their new environment some of the nominally "lower" castes have often grown wealthier than the Jats, and thus reversed the traditional hierarchy.

Thus, far from undermining caste disjunctions, the passage to Britain has, if anything, reinforced them. Bitter memories of entrenched patterns of status ascription in Punjab are still alive, as are the strategies long used to challenge them. This is clear in the case of the Ramgarhias who, thanks to their traditional craft skills and the additional boost to their skills and qualifications that many gained while resident in East Africa, are now the most affluent and successful British Sikhs. But they are also the most orthodox in religion and behaviour. In contrast to the Jats, they are more likely to avoid meat and alcohol, and to be more punctilious about leaving their hair uncut and wearing a turban; indeed they are best described as pursuing a Sikh version of Sanskritization. But if the Ramgarhias are thus in a position proudly to emphasise their religious orthodoxy, thus putting their more frequently clean-shaven Jat peers to shame, then the response of the latter has been equally conventional. Their counter-rhetoric seeks to dismiss the Tarkhans (as the Ramgarhias were formerly and less prestigiously known) as mere *nouveau riche* upstarts, and to rub in the insult they often dismiss the commitment to Sikhism of their former *kammi* (workers, dependants) as all show and no substance. In the face of such condescension, many Ramgarhias have become even more determined to steer clear of their "uncouth" Jat brethren.

The Bhatras, too, have been following their own distinctive social and cultural trajectories — partly for their own reasons and partly in response to pressures from non-Bhatra Sikhs, Jat and Ramgarhia alike, who tend to be all too ready to perceive the Bhatras as their social inferiors. The Bhatras exhibit many paradoxes. Although they are the longest established of Britain's Sikh communities, they are also the most conservative in their behaviour. Very few of the older women go out to work, and most families remain cautious about allowing their daughters to enter higher education; in no other section of the Sikh community are women expected to follow such strict rules of seclusion. And while the Bhatras can now be seen as being in the right place at the right time, since they were the group who first recognised that small business enterprise was the most effective means of evading white exclusionism, they have done little to capitalise on that advantage. By comparison with the Jats and the Ramgarhias, they have been left in a backwater. Although most Bhatra families live well above the poverty line, thanks to their almost universal involvement in small business, few have made it into the big time, since all Britain's biggest and most prosperous Sikh businesses are run by members of other castes. Nor is it only in business

that Bhatra progress has been less than spectacular: all the indications
are that their children achieve markedly less educational success than
those from Jat and Ramgarhia families. The reasons for these differences have yet to be fully explored.

Sectarian Divisions

Sectarian differences yet further compound these differences of caste.
Many Sikh sects now attract a following in Britain. They include such
established groups as the Nirankaris, Radhasoamis, Namdharis, Ramdasias and Valmikis (of whom the last three have a strongly caste-
specific membership) as well as newly emergent sectarian groups like
the followers of the charismatic preacher Sant Puran Singh Kariche-
wala. Sant Puran Singh, who died in June 1983, first started preaching
in East Africa, but acquired a following in Britain. His devotees have
established at least two *gurdwaras*, one in Birmingham and the other
in Leeds, in which worship is organised according to the Sant's
preferred styles. To some, these practices are unacceptably heterodox,
but since there has never been a clear consensus on how Sikh religious
rituals should be performed, each sectarian group and indeed each
local congregation has tended to develop its own conventions, based
on its interpretation of the Gurus' teaching. Hence rather than searching for some illusory orthodoxy, it is more illuminating to regard
religious practice as undergoing continuous change and adaptation,
no less overseas than in Punjab itself.

Religious activity in Britain is more intense than in most Punjabi
villages. This is so whether one looks to the scale of attendance at
regular *diwans* held every Sunday (as opposed to cursory attendance
on *sangrant*, the first day of the month, in most villages), or how
often noted *ragis* (singers) and *gyanis* (preachers) are invited to the
gurdwara and the size of the audiences they attract, or *paths* (recitations of the entire contents of the Guru Granth Sahib) are said, or the
enthusiasm with which *bhajans* and *kirtans* (singing of religious
songs) are organised by women. This intensification of religious
practice — partly the result of living in an ethnic colony, but also
parallel to similar developments caused by the politicization of religion in Punjab — has set off heated debates over the proper form
for religious practice. As arguments have grown fiercer, the easiest
way for Sikhs to discredit their opponents is to allege that practices
are "too Hindu". The leaders of most of Sikhism's many sects have
now climbed aboard this bandwagon, routinely dismissing their rivals
on these grounds.

These debates over proper Sikh practice were given an explosive
boosting in the 1980s by the rising influence of Sant Jarnail Singh

Bhindranwale, further underscored by his martyrdom in the Indian Army's bungled attack on the Akal Takht in June 1984.[15] Before his death, Bhindranwale's *jathedars* attracted little support in Britain, but the wave of revulsion following the assault on the Golden Temple was so great that British Sikhs were suddenly united as never before. In all sections of the community the new *shaheed* was regarded as a shining and faultless exemplar of religious steadfastness, and his chauvinistic teaching —᠆ that Sikhism differed utterly and comprehensively from degenerate Hinduism — suddenly became the new orthodoxy.

However, this did not last long. Once the emotive impact of the Indian Army's assault faded, and Punjab descended into ever deeper chaos as the intransigence and insensitivity of government policy was matched only by the violent impossiblism of a small number of Sikh militants, the intensity of these feelings waned, albeit to different degrees in various sectors of the community. The most enthusiastic support for Bhindranwale's position of chauvinistic fundamentalism, along with separatist demands for the creation of an independent state of Khalistan, has mostly been found among the Jats, while the East African Ramgarhias have been more sceptical. The whole debate has remained highly emotive, however, as pro- and anti-Khalistan factions have criticised one another ever more bitterly. Unity remains elusive. Despite Bhindranwale's martyrdom, the Sikhs as a community are now more bitterly divided than ever before.

Religion and the Younger Generation

For many younger British-born Sikhs recent developments are deeply bewildering. In Britain as in Punjab, religious teachers are moving in a steadily more conservative direction, so that even though their precise interpretations differ (often acrimoniously) all demand an ever greater commitment from their congregations. Young people thus find themselves under steadily rising pressure to conform, but although some of them have become religious enthusiasts in one or other of the new orthodoxies, most have remained more sceptical. This indicates not so much a declining commitment to Sikhism, as the deep inter-generational differences over what they should expect to draw from their religion and its associated traditions.

These differences have arisen for a variety of reasons, one of the most important being linguistic. While few British-born Sikhs have no Punjabi at all, most use it rarely, and then only in a restricted, mostly domestic range of contexts. Thus even when they become

---

[15] Roger Ballard, "The Bitter Drama of the Sikhs", *New Society*, 21 June 1984.

passionately interested in learning more about their religion and history, as many do at some point in adolescence, their limited linguistic ability is a profound handicap. Thus even though many may have spent long hours sitting in the *gurdwara*, most young people have only the most cursory understanding of Sikh history and theology.

Similar problems arise in many other contexts. Like the preachers at the *gurdwara*, Sikh parents often have little understanding of the kind of intellectual perspectives with which their children have become familiar as a result of exposure to the British educational system, and of the extent to which their lack of direct experience of rural Punjab weakens the effectiveness of graphic illustrations with which parents routinely seek to drive home the force of moralistic arguments.

Yet the rising generation of British-born Sikhs is not losing interest in its history and traditions. While a few may have turned away entirely from their roots, many more keenly sustain a sense of their own distinctive ethnicity, although in ever more complex and varied ways. For some, the maintenance of distinctiveness is simply a matter of pride: of boldly keeping a turban and beard in the face of British disapproval, thus making a continuous quiet protest against ethnic denigration. For others, Bhindranwale has become a romantic symbol of personal and social autonomy in another, potentially better world than racist Britain. And for still others, especially those of more intellectual bent, Sikhism is a conceptual system to be wrestled with and puzzled over, in an effort to match its teachings — to which young people have great difficulty gaining access, for the reasons mentioned — to their own personal experience, especially the secular and rational conceptual expectations provided by their British education.

There is little sign that the bitter experience of British exclusionism has enhanced organisational unity amongst the younger generation. Over and above the growing gulf between the educationally and professionally successful and those who have made less progress, caste continues to divide, not least because the personal reciprocities of friendship still flow more easily and smoothly along the pre-ordained channels of kinship. And last but not least, the range of ways of going about being a Sikh has now become so varied.

Varied though the options open to it are, the emergence of a generation whose experience has been wholly British is having a steadily increasing effect on the politics of local Sikh communities. Because of their British experience, younger people, especially those with advanced educational and professional qualifications, possess a wide range of skills. In particular they have an understanding of how the English managerial and financial system works, which the older generation largely lacks. Hence the idea of recruiting "young blood" on to the Gurdwara Committee often seems attractive to the community at large, while for young idealists it offers an opportunity to serve the community with which they identify, and to put their often radically reformist views into practice. Rarely, however, are such hopes fulfilled. The established elders find it hard to take the *kakas* (grandchildren) seriously. Indeed, the young professionals are often frustrated by the more traditional modes of factional politics in which underlying issues of principle are so easily swamped. Worse still, many of the *babas* (elders) feel they have all the time in the world to pursue their personal vendettas, which often causes young idealists to feel outflanked. With neither the time nor the energy for the struggle, many simply resign their posts in disgust.

So what are the prospects for unity? As a matter of principle Sikhs are strongly committed to the idea that they *ought* to form a closely knit, tightly organised and comprehensively unified community. Not only do the Gurus' teachings suggest that unity and equality form the core of what Sikhism is (or should be) all about, but more pragmatically this is also the best organisational strategy for achieving personal and collective security. Yet despite this commitment, few if any Sikh communities begin to match this ideal: all, down to the smallest, are deeply divided by factional disputes. Nor are these disjunctions fading away; if anything their scale and significance are growing.

Should we be surprised by this? From an analytical perspective the answer must be no. Though contemporary nationalists may scour the past for evidence to inspire and legitimise their current concerns, the truth is that even in Punjab the Sikhs have rarely if ever been fully united amongst themselves; more usually they have been bitterly divided, and once allowances are made for the change of context, disunity in Britain can be seen as having been caused by just the same forces. Contradictions of sect, caste, occupation, power and wealth, and above all personal rivalry, are endemic to Sikh (and Punjabi) society and have led to disunity. Yet they have also long been matched by countervailing forces: Sikhs have always been strongly committed to unity, no less for its pragmatic benefits than for ideological reasons. And it is when they have faced the most severe external threats (successively from the Mughals, the British, the Arya Samaj, the Muslims in the civil war following Partition, and now the rising forces of Hindu chauvinism) that internal contradictions have been most comprehensively glossed over, so allowing the Sikhs to move closer to their ideal condition of unity. Yet that condition was always uneasily constructed. Once the external threat has receded, the internal contradictions have always — so far at least — reasserted themselves.

Yet paradoxically it is this which holds them all together, and which accounts for their collective success. Despite, but also because of, their factionalism, the Sikhs' collective achievements have been both remarkable and substantial. Building rival gurdwaras within a few hundred yards of one another and installing taller and taller *nishan sahibs* (flagpoles) and larger and larger *langar* halls, marriage halls, sports halls, car parks and so forth would seem, on the face of it, to be a foolish waste of scarce resources. A single initiative would eliminate unnecessary duplication and bring about large economies of scale. But that is to miss the point. It is because of their vigorous pursuit of internal rivalries that Sikhs everywhere have made advances which are often the envy of other, less quarrelsome groups. Perhaps that is their secret.

VALMIKIS IN COVENTRY

THE REVIVAL AND RECONSTRUCTION OF
A COMMUNITY

Eleanor Nesbitt

Like all the other groups described in this volume, the Valmikis in Coventry form a tight-knit and mutually supportive community.[1] Though small in numbers — for the local settlement includes little more than 1,000 people — the Valmikis' distinctive experiences are far from insignificant, for they throw into dramatic relief many issues of much wider relevance. Hence this account is more than a descriptive ethnography. To understand the religious, social and cultural dynamics of the Valmiki movement, we have to explore how inequality is structured in Punjabi society, both in India and in the diaspora; also, how religion can be used as a means of countering the worst effects of prejudice and exclusion. In doing so we also challenge the widely-held assumption that Sikhism and Hinduism form distinct, homogeneous and wholly independent religious traditions. As we shall see, the Valmikis have followed their own unique religious and social course, and drawn freely and creatively on both traditions to construct their own distinctive synthesis.

It follows that neither the logic nor the dynamics of the Valmikis' adaptations to their new British environment can be fully understood without a careful consideration of their sub-continental roots. Nor are such issues relevant only to understanding the older generation of true migrants. A new generation of British-born Valmikis has now reached adulthood, and they too still regard their history — and especially other people's negative interpretations of their past — as a significant component of their current experience. How and why this should be so is the central theme of this chapter.

Who are the Valmikis?

Everywhere in the subcontinent the rural social order is marked by a

[1] The research on which this chapter is based was done under the auspices of the Department of Arts Education, University of Warwick. The Punjabi Hindu Nurture in Coventry Project was funded by the Leverhulme Trust and directed by Robert Jackson. The unstinting help of Rattan Chand and other members of the Valmiki community is gratefully acknowledged.

sharp division of labour, organised primarily on caste lines. Punjab is no exception, so the population of each village contains a number of hereditary and endogamous *zats*, each associated with a specific occupation; each is also ascribed a specific rank in the local caste hierarchy. But whatever merits higher-caste people may see in this system, those at the bottom regard it as a multiple unjustice, for despite their performance of a whole range of vital but "polluting" services, the lower-ranking *zats* receive few thanks for their labours. Their material rewards are meagre, and they are also the victims of gross social disparagement, which is almost impossible to escape, since a change of occupation has little or no impact on one's ascribed rank. Long-standing patterns of status-ascription are often sustained — particularly by members of a rival *zat* — even when a stigmatizing occupation has long been abandoned.

The Valmikis find themselves in just such a position. In the past most made a living as agricultural labourers working for higher-caste (usually Jat Sikh) peasant farmers. During the past century, and particularly since India's independence in 1947, the more enterprising members of the *zat* have, however, adopted a much wider range of occupations. In Punjab itself many have moved into urban industrial jobs, some have served as soldiers and yet others have sought their fortunes as migrants overseas. Even so, their *zat* is still inescapably linked, in the minds of most North Indians with a much more demeaning activity: sweeping up debris in the streets and the removal of household refuse. Like their close associates the Ravidasis, whose traditional occupations included the removal of dead cattle and tanning their hides to make leather, the Valmikis are conventionally regarded as *acchut*: "untouchable"[2] because "impure".

Thus despite their substantial contribution to the corporate welfare of the village community, members of these two *zat* have long been subjected to some particularly vicious social oppression. Excluded from owning land and forced to live on the outskirts of the village, they were also until very recently routinely prevented from entering most temples, *gurdwaras* and mosques, and even from sending their children to school. Nor have modern developments greatly improved their position. In view of the high principles most upper-caste people nominally espouse, one might expect that by now untouchability would have fallen into abeyance. All Punjab's major religious traditions — Islam, Sikhism and the Hindu-reformist Arya Samaj — are actively hostile, at least in principle, to the institution of caste. India's Constitution makes the exclusion of anyone from places of worship,

---

[2] The matter of physical contact is only one aspect of the progressively greater social distance between the most ritually pure and impure castes.

from employment or from education on grounds of untouchability a criminal offence, and a proportion of places in both the educational system and in government employment are now specifically reserved for members of the Scheduled Castes — as former untouchables are now officially known.[3] Nevertheless everyday practice still lags far behind these high principles, which have hitherto had little or no impact on popular attitudes. As the Valmikis are bitterly aware, the social stigma associated with their hereditarily ascribed occupation — in spite of its having long since been abandoned — is still very much alive. Even after the passage to Britain, higher-caste Punjabis remain as dismissive of the local Valmikis as ever. They normally take care to disguise their feelings, but when tempers are lost caution is thrown to the winds: abuse then becomes overt. Meanwhile, and at a more muted level, all sorts of backhanded insults still do the rounds. "Whom do the Valmikis get to read their scriptures?" I was asked by higher-caste Punjabis who knew of my interests. Taken charitably, the implication is that the community might, because it is relatively poverty-striken, have difficulty in finding literate priests. But the underlying message may be far more insulting: it suggests that Valmikis should not read, or even touch, the sacred scriptures because of their allegedly innate impurity.

What's in a Name?

Although Valmikis and the Ravidasis, who together form nearly a quarter of the population of many Punjabi villages, have long been subjected to systematic denigration, they have not taken their exclusion lying down: on the contrary they have always put up stiff resistance. To be sure their gains have so far been limited, given their small numbers and limited material resources; and precisely because of the weakness of their starting-point, their challenges to upper-caste chauvinism have been at least as much on an ideological as on an organisational plane.

As Jones[4] has shown, the imposition of British rule gave rise to a whole host of socio-religious reform movements among Hindus, Sikhs and Muslims alike, and the so-called Untouchables were no exceptions in this process. One of the most irksome burdens the Valmikis carried was the name by which they were conventionally known. Their *zat* title accurately identified the task they traditionally

---

[3] The use of the term Scheduled Caste to designate the most disadvantaged castes was begun in 1935. See Dilip Hiro, *The Untouchables of India* (London: Minority Rights Group, 1982).

[4] See Kenneth W. Jones, *Arya Dharm: Hindu Consciousness in 19th Century Punjab* (Berkeley: University of California Press, 1976).

performed, but by that very token it was also deeply stigmatizing. Hence as soon as they began to organise themselves and to demand greater economic, social and educational parity, one of their first acts was to renounce this stigmatic label and replace it with a much more prestigious title.

The name they chose — Valmiki[5] — was not an arbitrary selection, but rather a deliberate attempt to take advantage of history by associating the community more closely with Maharishi Valmik, the composer of that classic Hindu epic, the *Ramayana*. The revered Maharishi was, they insisted, a member of their *zat*, and as they rediscovered their roots it seemed wholly appropriate that they should rename themselves after their illustrious ancestor. According to Pandit Bakshi Ram, their own historian, this choice was further confirmed by Hazrat Mirza Ghulam Ahmed, founder of the Ahmadiyya movement, who had been hoping that they might adopt an Islamic identity.[6]

History is always a contentious issue, especially in contexts of social inequality. While dominant groups routinely use legendary accounts of their glorious past to legitimise their social superiority, marginalised communities find themselves treated in the opposite way, by being routinely excluded from established history as they are from social esteem. Hence those who seek to challenge exclusion find it useful to reclaim an alternative vision of their past. Besides being a powerful means of criticising conventional judgements, the very act of constructing an alternative history raises collective morale and allows the whole community to look forward to a prouder future. The Valmikis' own historiography thus offers an illuminating counterpoint to conventional understandings, underlining the extent to which these have been generated by — and still serve the interests of — Punjab's higher-caste majority.

The Valmikis in History

In the conventional origin myth, Punjab is presented as the very birthplace of Hindu civilization, and its higher-caste inhabitants as the descendants of the Aryan invaders who swept into the Indus valley from Central Asia nearly 4,000 years ago. However the Valmikis have a very different story to tell about these events: in their perspective the Aryans are not heroes but villains. According to Pandit Bakshi

---

[5] In Punjabi *b* and *v/w* are interchangeable, so their name can also be transliterated as *Balmiki*. Although this alternative spelling appears in some of the Valmikis' own writings, I have utilised the "*v*" form in accordance with the expressed preference of Valmiki community leaders in Coventry.

[6] See Pandit Bakshi Ram, *Balmiki Jati da Sankhep Itihas* (A Brief History of the Valmiki Community) (Ludhiana: Baba Farid Chand Nahar, 1969).

Ram, the Valmikis are the descendants of the Nags — the autoch-
thonous inhabitants of the Punjab whose civilisation was overrun by
the invading Aryans.[7] Hence their lowly status is not a consequence
of innate inferiority but rather of long-standing oppression, first initiated when the Aryan invaders deprived their ancestors of their
rightful inheritance.

Pandit Bakshi Ram also argues that the Valmikis' glorious past
can no longer be concealed. His researches reveal that Maharishi
Valmik was the tenth son of the Nag king, Pracheta, and an immediate
contemporary of both Rama and Krishna — a claim which he sub-
stantiates with numerous citations from ancient sources, including
Shakuntala, the *Bhagavata Purana* and the *Rig Veda* as well as the
Ramayana itself. But as a result of the Aryan invasion, the Nags were
pressed into servitude. Later, another account suggests, they were
forced to adopt even more stigmatising occupations by yet more
craven oppressors, as highlighted, for example, by Swami Dayanand
Saraswati's description of the way in which the devoted priests of
the Hindu temple at Somnath in Gujarat were forced to "grind corn,
cut grass and carry urine and faeces" following Mahmud of Ghazni's
invasion.[8] Set in this context, the Valmikis' recent social subordination can be seen as having honourable foundations.

While the Valmikis' vision of the past closely parallels that developed by the Ad Dharmis — a movement which attracted wide
support amongst Punjab's Untouchables early in the twentieth century[9] — such historical revisionism is not exclusively the preserve of
the lowest castes. To cite a parallel example, Punjab's Lohar and
Tarkhan *zats* (whose traditional occupation was as blacksmiths and
carpenters) have similarly renamed themselves: as Ramgarhias if
Sikh, and as Dhiman Brahmins if Hindu.[10] Renaming oneself in this

---

[7] See for example, H. Zimmer, *Myths and Symbols in Indian Art and Civilization*
(Pantheon Books, 1946), p. 63.
[8] Amritlal Nagar, "Adikavi Valmiki aur Shavpach Rishi Ki Santane" (The Children
of the First Poet Valmiki and the Rishi Shavpach) in Amritlal Nagar (ed.), *Sahitya
aur Sanskriti* (Delhi: Rajpal and Sons, 1986), p. 175, quoting Swami Dayanand
Saraswati, *Light of Truth*, an English translation of *Satyarth Prakash* (New Delhi:
Sarvadeshik Arya Pratinidhi Sabha, 1975), p. 391.
[9] A detailed account of this instance and of such historical revisionism in general
appears in Mark Juergensmeyer, *Religion as Social Vision: The Movement against Untouchability in 20th Century Punjab* (Berkeley: University of California Press, 1982).
[10] The first title is taken from Jassa Singh Ramgarhia, the noted eighteenth-century
misldar, who was himself a member of the Tarkhan *zat*. See W.H. McLeod, "Ah-
luwalias and Ramgarhias: Two Sikh Castes", *Journal of South Asian Studies*, vol. 4,
pp. 78–90. In choosing the title *Dhiman Brahmin* they were linking up with an
India-wide movement amongst members of skilled craftsman castes, and in this case
claiming descent from Maharishi Vishvakarma: architect, on Lord Brahma's behalf,
of the very universe itself.

way is far from being cosmetic, for one adopts at the same time equally far-reaching behavioural and religious changes.

The Valmikis have certainly been extremely active on this front, most strikingly through their sponsorship of a cult focused on the person of Maharishi Valmiki himself. His devotees identify him not only as *Jagat Guru* (World Teacher) but also as *Bhagvan* (God), and temples in which he can be so worshipped have been built by many Valmiki communities. But like the Lohars and Tarkhans who have split into Hindu and Sikh sections, not everyone has followed this particular path, for a significant proportion of *zat* members have turned instead to Christianity.[11] Missionaries have long been active in Punjab, though their converts have largely been drawn from the lower castes. If, as seems likely, many converts were attracted by the prospect of escaping from stigmatisation, they were disappointed: disparagement remains as intense as ever. But although conversion has introduced a new division within the *zat*, most Christian converts still feel a strong sense of loyalty to the community, even though many also feel that church membership requires them to distance themselves from all activities in the local Valmiki temple.[12] Yet despite the growth of this incipient divide, it is far from uncrossable, and marriages between Hindu, Sikh and Christian Valmikis are common. As among higher-caste Punjabis, religious boundaries are far more porous than those of the *zat*.

Conversion to Ambedkarite Buddhism is a further possible option. Like many Ravidasis, some Valmikis have followed the lead of Dr Ambedkar, the distinguished low-caste Marathi lawyer who framed India's constitution, and turned to Buddhism. The great merit of Buddhism, contended Ambedkar, was its anti-caste outlook and its roots — unlike those of Christianity — in India itself. Conversion to Sikhism also nominally offers a parallel, and an even more locally-rooted means of escape from the stigma of impurity: indeed the Sikh Gurus' powerfully articulated message of personal and social equality was one which many Valmikis have found most attractive. But as those who took those teachings at face value soon discovered, most higher-caste Sikhs were still as determined as ever to sustain established notions of social distance, whatever their Gurus may have taught. Until recently most rural *gurdwaras* were closed to lower-caste people. So although some Valmikis did indeed become en-

---

[11] See Maqbul Caleb, "Christian Sunday Worship in a Punjabi Village" in J.C.B. Webster (ed.), *Popular Religion in the Punjab Today* (Delhi: ISPCK, 1974).

[12] See Eleanor Nesbitt, "The Transmission of Christian Tradition in an Ethnically Diverse Society" in Rohit Barot (ed.), *Religion and Ethnicity: Minorities and Social Change in the Metropolis* (Kampen: Kok Pharos, 1993), for an account of cultural transmission in Coventry's Punjabi Christian community.

thusiastic followers of the Gurus' teaching, so earning themselves the sobriquet Mazhabi (literally "religious ones"), that very term indicates the patronizing irony with which most Sikhs viewed, and still view, the faith of lower-caste converts.[13]

The Ravidasi Parallel

The Valmikis are not alone in facing these dilemmas, however. The Ravidasis have gone through very similar experiences.[14] They too are an endogamous *zat* whose ascribed ancestral occupation as leather-workers resulted in their being treated as *achhut* by members of the higher castes. Like the Valmikis, they have achieved dramatically improved levels of education and wealth during the past century, and they too have rejected the demeaning occupational title of Chamar (literally "leatherworker") by which they were previously known, and instead named themselves after one of their most distinguished fore-bears — the fourteenth-century mystic Ravi Das.

While the Valmikis and the Ravidasis have often acted as allies, especially when confronting upper-caste chauvinism, this co-opera-tion has not spilled far into religious affairs or into the process of community formation. Although the Ravidasis arrived in Britain at the same time as the Valmikis, settled in the same areas and still live in very similar circumstances, they have formed their own separate and still strictly endogamous local community, and established their own temple. While in some senses they appear to be Sikhs — because, apart from the prominent position accorded Guru Ravi Das[15] in their *gurdwara*, little distinguishes their styles of worship from those of higher caste Sikhs — many still firmly identify themselves as Hindus. Indeed many of their traditions, such as observing *shraddh* and per-forming *havan*, are unmistakably Hindu.[16]

This syncretistic mixing of aspects of Sikh and Hindu traditions

[13] For a detailed account of the Mazhabi Sikhs, which claims their descent from Khatris, see Shamsher Singh Ashok, *Mazhabi Sikhan da Itihas* (History of the Mazhabi Sikhs) (Hounslow: K.S. Neiyyar, 1979–80).

[14] For a recent detailed account of the Ravidasis see Seva Singh Kalsi, *The Evolution of a Sikh Community in Britain* (Leeds: Department of Theology and Religious Studies, University of Leeds, 1992).

[15] For Ravi Das to be accorded honour in a *gurdwara* is in no sense unorthodox, since a selection of his verse is included in the *Guru Granth Sahib* itself. However the use of the word "guru" rather than "*bhagat*" (saint, mystic) is in opposition to the main-stream Sikh use of the word only for God, for the ten human Gurus beginning with Guru Nanak, and for the scriptural volume.

[16] *Shraddh* is an annual ritual in remembrance of a deceased relative. For one Valmiki girl's description see Eleanor Nesbitt, *"My Dad's Hindu, My Mum's Side are Sikh": Issues in Religious Identity* (Charlbury: National Foundation for Arts Education, 1991).

is far from being unique to the lowest castes, for close examination reveals that it is rarely possible to classify the religious practices of most Punjabi *zat* as wholly Sikh or wholly Hindu. This is not so much because communities muddle together elements of two wholly distinct traditions, but rather because they have drawn upon a common heritage of devotional practice. It is from that common heritage that reformist religious leaders have endeavoured to promote a Sikh code, purged — as they see it — of "illegitimate" Hindu accretions. From this point of view the projection of Sikhism as a distinctive system of religious and ritual practices — a process in which members of the Jat *zat* have played a leading role — has also involved a process of conscious selection which bears striking parallels to the strategies adopted by the Valmikis and Ravidasis.[17]

Overseas Migration

Like the majority of higher-caste Sikh and Hindu Punjabis, most Valmikis in Coventry originate from the Jullundur Doab, the densely populated triangle of land between the rivers Sutlej and Beas in East Punjab. The reasons why large numbers of peasant-farmers emigrated from this area are now well documented: with the fragmentation of their holdings, young men from expanding Jat families responded enthusiastically to every opportunity to earn money elsewhere.[18] Besides serving in the army and taking up land in the newly irrigated canal colonies in West Punjab, many set out overseas — to Singapore East Africa and ultimately Britain. By contrast little attention has been paid to the way in which landless families in the same area responded to these opportunities.

In 1896 the British authorities began to recruit craftsmen and labourers to work on the construction of a new railway in East Africa. While the majority of Punjabi recruits were skilled artisans belonging to the Ramgarhia *zat*, a number of Valmikis were also taken on, and thus found their way to East Africa. A Shree Valmiki Dharam Sabha was established in Nairobi in 1908, and the city's first Shree Valmiki *gurdwara* was opened two years later. A few years later a large temple was opened in Singapore by Valmiki soldiers serving in the British Indian Army, many of whom, having established this foothold, stayed

[17] For an analysis of this see Harjot Singh Oberoi, "From Ritual to Counter Ritual: Rethinking the Hindu-Sikh Question 1884-1915" in Joseph T. O'Connell, *et al.* (eds), *Sikh History and Religion in the Twentieth Century* (Centre for South Asian Studies, University of Toronto, 1988).
[18] See Arthur Helweg, *Sikhs in England: The Development of a Migrant Community* (Oxford University Press, 1979).

on there once they had completed their service. It was from these initial bases in Africa and Southeast Asia that Valmikis began to move to and establish themselves in Britain.

A Case Study

The story of Rattan Chand, one of the founders of the Valmiki community in England, exemplifies these processes. He was born in 1925 in Jandiala, a large village in Jullundur District, where his paternal grandfather earned a living as a tenant-farmer. His father and both paternal uncles both initially worked as agricultural labourers, but later switched to more lucrative jobs. Although he had never been to school and was taught to read and write Punjabi by a friend, Rattan Chand's father established himself as a lumberman, selling firewood, timber for furniture and the bark used by leatherworkers in the tanning process. In 1930 he gave up his business and went to Kenya with his younger brother. They settled in Eldorate where their maternal grandfather, who had gone to Kenya to work as a railway construction worker at the turn of the century, had already established a foothold. The pair made a reasonable living for themselves: Rattan Chand's father sold charcoal for cooking stoves, and his brother worked for the Eldorate municipality.

Conditions in Africa were far superior to those back in Punjab, where separate wells were set aside in the village for the Valmikis, the Ravidasis and the higher castes; the streets where the Valmikis lived were right on the outskirts of the village, and they were not allowed to enter either Hindu or Sikh temples. Instead they offered their devotions at home, although on Thursday evenings older men and women often lit a *diva* (a small oil-filled clay bowl containing a twist of raw cotton) at their own small shrine, for they had no temple. While most Valmikis were too poor to send their sons to school, Rattan Chand's grandfather had just enough to provide the necessary finance, and so from the age of seven Rattan Chand attended primary school in Jandiala. However, he and two or three other *"harijans"* had to sit in the back row separate from the other pupils.[19] Later he moved up to the Khalsa High School, and although allowed to sit alongside the other boys, he still had to drink water from a tap reserved specially for *"harijans"*.

In 1939, aged thirteen, Rattan Chand joined his father in Eldorate, where he continued his studies at the local school for Indian boys. Having joined the Indian Youth League, an affiliate of the Congress

[19] The term *harijan* popularised by Mahatma Gandhi means "child of God" but is now rejected by the castes to whom it was applied.

Party, he noticed that although local Africans were not regarded as untouchable, they still had to live as a separate underclass. In 1946 he made a brief visit to Punjab to get married, before returning to Kenya with his wife. For the next five years he worked in a tailor's shop, and although the clients for whom he hand-stitched clothes included the Aga Khan and the Prince of Wales, higher-caste Hindus were still sometimes upset by the prospect of an "Untouchable" measuring them and stitching their clothes. Still educationally ambitious, Rattan Chand attended evening classes in English and book-keeping, and in the midst of the Mau Mau uprising in 1952, joined the British Army. He continued his studies, gaining an honours certificate in Punjabi and the rank of accounts clerk in the East African Land Forces.

Rattan Chand had always dreamed of going to England for further studies, and had kept in touch with a friend from the tailor *zat* who had gone there. He had also been corresponding with two of his cousins, one of whom had moved to Britain from Singapore, and the other to Southall (in West London) from Nairobi. So when British passport-holders of Indian origin were given permission to enter Britain in 1961, Rattan Chand siezed his opportunity: while his wife and younger children returned to Punjab, he and his eldest son went to Coventry. Jobs were plentiful, and a Christian relative soon helped him to find work in a small engineering firm. In 1962 his second son joined him, and in 1964 his wife and daughters followed. The same year, needing better pay, he took a job as a labourer on the night shift at Herbert's machine-tool factory, and subsequently retrained as an overhead crane driver. He still attended evening classes in English and Education at the local College of Further Education, but his hopes of developing a professional career were dashed when he was told both that he was too old to become an articled clerk and that his overseas qualifications would not be recognised. He stayed on at Herbert's, and when the company closed down in 1978 he used his redundancy money to establish a drapery shop run by his wife and daughters, while he worked as a boilerhouse attendant in the University of Warwick. Here he worked and studied sociology as a part-time student until his final retirement in 1991.

Rattan Chand's sons and daughters, all of whom married within the Valmiki community, continue this pattern of upward mobility. His eldest son studied science at City University in London, worked as a chemist at Courtaulds until he was made redundant, and is now a qualified social worker. His second son is a psychology graduate, taught mathematics for eight years, and having taken his Master's degree in psychology, works as an educational psychologist. Rattan Chand's elder daughters have done both factory and community work, and his eldest daughter's eldest daughter has obtained a degree in accountancy.

The Valmikis in Britain

As with all other South Asian groups, it is difficult to estimate the size of the Valmiki community in Britain precisely. Since their surnames are not *zat*-specific, electoral registers cannot be used; hence the membership lists maintained by secretaries of Valmiki temples provide the best guide to numbers, and although these do not include details of Christian families, they do at least provide a good indication of where the majority of Valmikis have settled. On this basis it would appear that the largest Valmiki communities are in Birmingham, Bedford, Southall and Coventry, followed by Oxford and Wolverhampton. I was also told of lone families in Swansea, Glasgow, Bradford, Huddersfield, Derby, Gravesend and Hounslow.

Even in Coventry it is hard to estimate the size of the local Valmiki community: my informants' suggestions varied from less than 1,000 to over 2,000, but these may be on the high side. What is clear is that most Valmikis live in the northern parts of the city, especially in the Foleshill area, where a high proportion of the population are South Asian. Many families live close to the Jagat Guru Valmik Ji Maharaj temple in Fisher Road, which serves as a community centre as well as a place of congregational worship, while their Christian relatives — many of whom attend St Paul's Church, Foleshill — are clustered in the same area.

Institutionalisation of Valmiki Religious Life in Coventry

From this brief outline it might seem that thanks to hard work and high motivation, reinforced by strong family unity, Valmiki migrants in Britain have experienced an uncomplicated process of upward mobility. The reality has been more complex, for it also involved a deliberate social, political and religious consolidation of the community; these moves also continued processes already set in motion in Kenya and Singapore, as well as in Punjab itself. The Valmikis have organised themselves as a socio-religious group in response to the *double* exclusion to which they have been subjected. In addition to racial and ethnic disparagement from members of the surrounding white majority — to which other South Asian settlers were also exposed — Valmikis had to face the additional challenge of their higher-caste compatriots, especially their former masters the Jats, continuing to subject them to equally hurtful forms of exclusionism.

Back in Punjab most Valmikis made their living as agricultural labourers for Jat Sikh peasant-farmers, and it was precisely to escape this demeaning relationship that Valmikis were so keen to find jobs overseas. But while migration has brought them unprecedented wealth, it has by no means allowed them to escape the stigma of the past. In the eyes of most of their fellow-Punjabis they are still "untouchable" — as is clear in the processes which led them to establish their own separate temple.

The Establishment of the Valmiki Temple in Coventry

During the earliest years of settlement, networks of mutual support amongst migrants were largely unaffected by caste and sectarian affiliation. Whether new arrivals were Hindu or Sikh, high-caste or low-caste, all Punjabis sought to co-operate with each other. Valmikis therefore worked alongside their higher-caste peers on the shop floor, as well as making their presence felt in the trade unions, the Indian Overseas Congress, the Indian Workers' Association, the Community Relations Council, and so forth. They also worshipped with members of the much larger Jat community in Coventry's Sikh *gurdwara*. But tensions were building up. Besides being alarmed by the lack of interest shown by members of higher-ranking *zats* in their specific interests and concerns, Valmikis grew increasingly outraged by their treatment in the *gurdwara* itself. While Ravidasis, Valmikis and Mazhabis regularly worshipped alongside Jats in the *gurdwara*, the latter were most reluctant to allow them to use the cooking utensils in the *langar*, or to distribute *karah prashad*.[20] Though seldom explicitly spelled out, the message behind these exclusionary practices was clear enough: the very touch of such people was "polluting".

In the light of such treatment, it is hardly surprising that Valmikis in Coventry began to follow precedents already established in Punjab. Disassociating themselves from the upper-caste *gurdwaras*, they started raising funds for a separate temple of their own. This step towards separatism was a crucial move in their developing strategy of resistance. Besides providing a comfortable social arena beyond the reach of high-caste disparagement, establishing their own autonomous institutions not only boosted their corporate self-esteem but provided them with an opportunity to improve their image in the eyes of other Punjabi communities. Most important of all, it provided

---

[20] *Langar* is the vegetarian meal offered to all who attend the *gurdwara*. The word also denotes the area where this is cooked and eaten. *Karah prashad* is a sweet doughy mixture of wheat flour, sugar and clarified butter distributed to the congregation at the close of Sikh worship.

Valmikis with a forum within which the first generation could pass on to their offspring an assurance of self-worth which would be second to none.

These objectives could not be reached immediately for it took the Valmikis, like every other group of South Asian settlers, some time to gather the resources needed to create their own separate religious institution. So although they had little alternative to using the centres of worship established by higher-caste Punjabi Hindus and Sikhs during the early phase of settlement, as soon as inter-caste tensions surfaced they started to organise themselves on their own account. The earliest such initiative occurred in 1962, when a newcomer from Singapore began holding regular acts of worship — normally a Ramayana *path* (reading) — in his house. At the end of the proceedings he collected small sums of money towards that far-off day when the Valmikis would have their own temple. Meanwhile the first Valmiki marriage ceremony took place a few months later in the Foleshill Community Centre, under the supervision of a new arrival from Kenya.

During the early 1960s similar developments took place in a number of other cities, including Birmingham, Wolverhampton, Southall and Bedford, and Valmikis also began to organise themselves nationally. The most important event in their calendar is Valmik Jayanti, the Maharishi's birthday, and its celebration on a national level was first organised by the Balmik Adi Vir Maha Sabha (U.K.) in 1962.[21] For a few years Coventry's Valmikis travelled to Wolverhampton to attend these festivities, but in 1966 they set up their own local branch of the Sabha, and thus were able to celebrate the Maharishi's birthday on their own account for the first time that October, when a Ramayana *path* was held at the Bell Green Community Centre.

In the years that followed, they continued to hold their own religious celebrations, either in their own homes or in hired halls or community centres; a Mazhabi Sikh served as *granthi* (reader) and performed marriages. The next major step forward was made in 1978, when they bought a disused parcels office in Fisher Road, close to the centre of the densest area of Valmiki settlement, and it was here that Coventry's — and Britain's — first Valmiki temple was opened on 4 September 1978, just in time for the celebration of the Maharishi's birthday.[22] Since 1986 marriages have been registered

[21] The literal translation of this organisation's title is "Great Association of Valmik, the Primordial Hero".

[22] Britain's second Valmiki temple was later opened in Bedford, the third in Southall and the fourth in Birmingham, while in Oxford a school or community centre is still hired for Valmiki events. Unlike the Valmiki *sabhas* in Wolverhampton, Oxford, Bedford, Southall and Birmingham, the Coventry *sabha* is no longer affiliated to the

there, so obviating the need to go through a civil marriage at the
Register Office. Since its foundation the Jagat Guru Valmik Ji
Maharaj temple has been much extended; besides the main prayer
hall, it also includes a community centre, a kitchen and a dining area.
The community centre is used for marriage receptions, Hindi classes
and monthly lectures on topical subjects.

Religious and Ritual Practice in the Valmiki Temple

Valmiki religious identity has largely been forged as a means of
resistance to higher-caste Sikh and Hindu exclusionism, so it is hardly
surprising that contemporary Valmiki practice draws freely on both
those traditions, while adding some distinctive dimensions of its own.
These often take the form of alternative explanations for common
Punjabi customs. For example, in seeking to explain why some Valmiki men wear turbans over uncut hair (like *keshadhari* Sikhs) Rattan
Chand argued that both Maharishi Valmik and Tulsi Das had long
hair, while the turban is simply normal Punjabi dress. Valmiki traditions are still emergent and therefore practices vary greatly between
different temples — though in Coventry ritual practices tend much
more towards the Sikh than the Hindu end of the spectrum.

Thus while in some Valmiki temples a *murti* (image) of Maharishi
Valmik himself is the focus of attention, as in a Hindu *mandir*, the
focal point of the prayer hall in Coventry is more akin to that found
in any Sikh *gurdwara*. Beneath a colourfully decorated wooden canopy is the *manji* on which the sacred scriptures repose, and these are
covered in turn by vivid *rumalas* (cloths). To the left stands a covered
pan of *karah prashad*, while to the right the musical instruments
played by the *ragis* (musicians and singers) stand on a table. The
behavioural conventions followed by worshippers are also indistin-
guishable from those in any *gurdwara*. Having removed their shoes
before entering the main hall — a practice common to all Punjab's
religious traditions — the worshippers must also cover their heads.
Women pull their *chunis* over their hair, while men — except for the
small minority who follow orthodox Sikh practice and wear turbans—
use special white napkins with hem-wide tie-strings which are available at the door. On entering the hall men, women and children alike
file down the central aisle towards the scriptures beneath the canopy,
before which they kneel to touch the floor with their foreheads, a

central *sabha*, although cooperation continues at such times as the birthday of
Maharishi Valmik, when congregations join together for large-scale celebrations. On
the opening of Coventry's temple see "New Temple is First of Kind in West", *Coventry
Evening Telegraph*, 25 Sept. 1978.

form of obeisance known as *matha tekna*. Having paid their respects, a small offering — usually of money, milk, fruit or flowers, and perhaps even a *rumala* to mark a special occasion — is made, after which worshippers move back to sit cross-legged on the carpet in front of the dais, the men on the right of the hall and the women on the left.

Conventional though all this may seem to those familiar with standard Sikh practice, a closer look reveals that Coventry's Valmikis have reinterpreted the dominant idiom to create their own distinctive variations. For example they fly a flag outside their temple, just as a *nishan sahib* flies outside every Sikh *gurdwara*; but theirs is red, emblazoned with a silver bow and arrow, instead of the saffron-coloured Sikh pennant. In Punjab the Valmikis and the Ravidasis regard red as their sacred colour, while the bow and arrow recall the legend that Maharishi Valmik himself taught Lord Rama's sons Lav and Kush the skills of archery. Likewise the Valmikis' *nishan sahib* is not replaced at the spring festival of Baisakhi, as among the Sikhs, but on Maharishi Valmik Jayanti in mid-October.

Close examination of the pictures and the scriptures used in the temple reveals some even more significant departures from Sikh practice. In the main hall a large picture of Maharishi Valmiki — depicted as a venerable ascetic clad in a red robe — occupies a prominent position, facing the congregation from the wall behind the *manji*. And while the pictures of Sikh Gurus displayed elsewhere in the hall could be found in any *gurdwara*, other pictures explicitly celebrate the heroic activities of prominent Valmikis such as Bhai Jivan Singh, as well as of Maharishi Valmik himself.[23] Right at the rear of the hall — and thus directly in front of the scriptures — there are additional pictures of Guru Nanak, Guru Ravidas and Maharishi Valmik. While some Sikhs from local higher-caste *gurdwaras* suggest that this is inappropriate, Guru Ravidas's portrait has been placed in an identical position in the nearby Ravidasi *gurdwara*.

The choice and positioning of the scriptures highlights even more acutely the careful adjustments and compromises made to accommodate both Sikh and Hindu ritual modes, while also giving to both a distinctively Valmiki orientation. Although the *manji* on which the scriptures rest seems, at first sight, identical to that in any other *gurdwara*, in this case it is used to enshrine Valmiki's *Ramayana* in

---

[23] According to legend, it was Bhai Jivan Singh who courageously bore the severed head of the martyred Guru Tegh Bahadur to his successor, the tenth Guru Gobind Rai, for cremation. Before that incident Jivan Singh had been known as Jaita; but on receipt of his father's head the young Guru Gobind Rai is said to have uttered the words "*Ranghrete Guru ke bete*": the Ranghrete — an earlier name for the Valmikis — are the Guru's children. Thereafter the devoted Jaita was always known as Jivan Singh.

addition to the *Guru Granth Sahib*; indeed great care is taken to ensure
that both works are treated with equal honour.[24] This is not the only
available solution, however. In Southall, for example, the ritual idiom
is much more overtly Hindu in character. There a life-size *murti* of
Maharishi Valmik occupies pride of place, and is the principal focus
of worship; and while the *Guru Granth Sahib* finds no place in the
Southall temple, a copy of the *Ramayana* is always kept there, although it is not installed on a *manji* or made an explicit focus of ritual
activity. Similarly there is no requirement that those who enter the
hall of the Southall temple should cover their heads — a further
confirmation of the local preference for Hindu rather than Sikh ritual
and behavioural conventions.

These variations in practice and their eclecticism are not manifestations of religious uncertainty or confusion amongst the Valmikis.
On the contrary their imaginative reinterpretation of idioms drawn
from right across the range of established Punjabi religious traditions
is better understood as an indication of their devotional creativity. An
exploration of Valmiki liturgical practice yet further underlines the
extent to which this is so.

Sunday Worship in Coventry's Valmiki Temple

From about 10.30 in the morning families begin to arrive and, having
performed *matha tekna*, go to join the rest of the congregation sitting
on the carpeted floor in front of the *manji* for the *divan* proper. At
first sight the proceedings are virtually identical to those in any
gurdwara. Although the scriptures are the central focus of attention,
readings from them are relatively brief, the greater part of the *divan*
being taken up with homilies and hymns delivered by *gyanis*
(preachers) and *ragis* (singers). However it is the content of the hymns
and homilies which gives the proceedings a distinctively Valmiki
flavour, for while some pursue standard Sikh themes, others have a
much more overt sectarian character. Nowhere is this more manifest
than in their concluding prayers.

Here, once again, we see the Valmikis' creative syncretism, for
their liturgy brings together elements of Sikh and Hindu practice,
while also adding a distinctive flavour of their own. While the *divan*
in a *gurdwara* concludes with a recitation of the *ardas*, and proceedings in a Hindu *mandir* are completed with *arati*, concluding prayers

---

[24] The edition of the *Ramayana* used in the Valmiki temple is not Tulsi Das's Hindi
version, the *Ram Charit Manas*, which is read in other Hindu temples in Coventry,
or the Sanskrit composition attributed to Maharishi Valmik. Rather it is a Punjabi
translation of that text, printed — like the *Guru Granth Sahib* — in the Gurmukhi
script.

in the Valmiki temple draw simultaneously on both these sources.[25] Thus although an *arati* hymn is sung using the tune familiar to all Hindus, no lamps are waved, and the usual verse *Om jai jagdish hare* is replaced with a eulogy to Maharishi Valmiki:

> Praise to Valmik, praise to God Valmik,
> praise to Valmik, the true Guru.
> You are Lord of the whole creation,
> sustainer of the whole creation, giver of liberation.
> Praise to Guru Valmik, praise to Lord Valmik,
> praise to Valmik the true Guru.[26]

This hymn — which continues at some length in the same vein — is immediately followed by the recitation of a version of the *ardas*, which has also been recast so that its core theme is once again a hymn of praise to Maharishi Valmik, who, it is asserted, "is worshipped by the three worlds — heaven, earth and the nether regions: hence all the requests of those who believe in him will be fulfilled." Similarly it is the *Ramayana* rather than the *Guru Granth Sahib* which is praised as the most sacred text of all, with the assertion that "All who listen to the *Ramayana* will enjoy the bliss of pilgrimage to sacred places. By believing in Guru Valmik, everyone can achieve salvation."

Once the *ardas* is complete, slogans are called: one person recites the first part, and the congregation loudly completes the response. This parallels the calling of the deity's name in a *mandir*, and even more so the antiphonal Sikh war-cry

Jo bole so nihal   *sat sri akal*

The Valmikis borrow from both traditions when they cry:

Jo bole so nirbhai	*Valmik bhagvan ki jai.*
Valmik shakti	*amar rahe.*
Valmik jot	*jalti rahe.*
Jo bole so nirbhai	*Valmik bhagvan ki jai.*
The person is fearless who says	Praise to Valmik.
May Valmik's power	live forever.
May Valmik's light	keep burning.
The person is fearless who says	Praise to God Valmik.

---

[25] An *ardas* (literally "petition") always marks the conclusion of Sikh congregational worship, but the words of the Sikhs' *ardas* differ. See W.O. Cole and Piara Singh Sambhi, *The Sikhs: Their Religious Beliefs and Practices* (London: Routledge, 1977). *Arati* involves circling an oil lamp in front of the focus of one's devotion; the words sung while doing so differ depending upon the deity invoked.

[26] The words, which are printed in Gurmukhi on handouts available in the Coventry temple, are used by Valmikis elsewhere. The poem is said to have been composed by the Valmiki ascetic, Gyan Nath, whose *samadh* at Ram Tirath near Amritsar is much visited as a pilgrimage centre by members of the *zat*.

Finally *karah prashad* is distributed at the end of the proceedings, as it would be in any *gurdwara*.

Domestic Worship

As in most other Punjabi communities, Valmikis' domestic rituals are yet more diverse and draw even more eclectically on popular Sikh and Hindu practice. Thus while in one household domestic worship is performed before framed pictures of Shiva, Krishna and Lakshmi, housed together on a shelf in the living room; in another a picture of Charan Singh, the late Guru of the Radhasoami Satsang (Beas), dominates a living room in which pictures of Guru Tegh Bahadur, Guru Gobind Singh, Maharishi Valmik and Jathedar Baba Jivan Singh are also prominently displayed; while in yet another, framed pictures of Guru Nanak, Maharishi Valmik and Guru Gobind Singh hang side by side.

The Valmikis' life-cycle rites, especially those surrounding marriage, follow a similar eclectic pattern. Thus while all Valmikis use the traditional subsidiary rituals commonly associated with marriage, such as beautifying the bride and groom with turmeric paste before the marriage itself, and afterwards having them compete to extract a coin from a bowl of cloudy water, some prefer the central rite to be performed according to Hindu conventions, while others follow Sikh practice. In the former, known as *vedi viah*, the couple circumambulate a sacrificial fire under the supervision of a *pandit*, while in the latter they circle the *Guru Granth Sahib* instead, and this time in the presence of a Sikh *gyani*.[27]

To differing degrees families retain elements of widespread Punjabi Hindu custom and taboo. Many individuals refrain from eating meat on one day of the week; some girls still avoid washing their hair on a Tuesday or Thursday because if they do so their brothers may suffer harm;[28] and if someone in the family has measles or chicken pox, young girls may be regaled as *kanjakan*.[29] Likewise when a family moves to a new house it may be symbolically purified either with a *havan*, or by temporarily installing a copy of the *Guru Granth Sahib* in one room and sponsoring a complete reading or *path*.

[27] Details of the *anand karaj* can be found in Cole and Sambhi, *op. cit. Guide to Rules*, a booklet prepared by the Coventry Valmiki Association, includes the information that marriage may be performed according to either Sikh or Hindu rites.
[28] See Paul Hershman, "Hair, Sex and Dirt", *Man* (NS), 9, 1974, pp. 274–98.
[29] See Eleanor Nesbitt, *"My Dad's Hindu, My Mum's Side are Sikhs"*, *op. cit.*, p. 39.

Religious Festivals and the Second Generation

As we have seen, the central event in the Valmikis' calendar is the birthday of Maharishi Valmik, which falls a fortnight before Divali. While this is always elaborately celebrated in the temple, Valmikis have always celebrated all the other major festivals of North India, and are now also being drawn into the indigenous British festival cycle. As far as Valmiki children are concerned, Divali and Christmas are by far the most important festivals. Both events are marked in school, as well as being celebrated far beyond the Valmiki community. Divali is marked by visits to relatives, enjoying Indian sweets and letting off fireworks; but Christmas is also celebrated as a family reunion, accompanied by the giving of presents and the consumption of roast turkey. Likewise Mother's Day and Halloween are occasions which Valmiki children increasingly celebrate alongside their peers from other communities.

While such developments are an inevitable consequence of the passage to Britain, they also highlight a dilemma for Valmiki parents. For them, celebration of the annual festival cycle — which includes Holi, Lohri and Baisakhi, as well as Divali and Valmik Jayanti — provides a concrete reminder of life as it is lived back in Punjab, and of whose positive aspects they are deeply concerned to remind their children. For young people born and brought up in Coventry, however, most of these festivals, as well as that celebrating the Patron Saint of their own community, fade almost entirely before the intense build-up to Christmas: in this area as in so many others, parents' interests and concerns often seem quite irrelevant. Some more "traditional" festivals persist, however, notably Raksha Bandhan, which celebrates and reinforces the bond between siblings and cousins of the opposite sex. To this end girls tie a decorative thread around their brothers' and male cousins' wrists and receive a gift in return — a practice in which those who have grown up in Britain participate as enthusiastically as their elders.

Even so, many British-born Valmikis find aspects of their parental tradition boring and meaningless. How might this gulf be bridged? Surprisingly enough, the VCR is proving a very effective means of keeping them in touch with their roots. Since 1980 watching videos has played a significant role in the lives of South Asians in Britain, with the result that most Valmiki children are familiar with the Hindi movies produced by the film studios of Bombay.[30] Like millions of

---

[30] For the increasing and significant role of video viewing in the lives of children of South Asian origin in Britain see M. Gillespie, "Technology and Tradition: Audio-Visual Culture among South Asian Families in West London", *Cultural Studies*, vol. 2 (2 May 1989), pp. 226–39.

other South Asians of all ages in all parts of the world, they participate
in a common fantasy world which strongly influences their taste in
music and clothes. There can be little doubt, either, that many hours
of film-watching, in a genre of entertainment wholly unfamiliar to
their non-Asian contemporaries, strongly reinforces their distinctive
sense of identity.

Such videos may well also strengthen children's acceptance of
supernatural phenomena which they might otherwise dismiss as irrelevant or untrue. Thus a Valmiki teenager described a "massive
snake, a *nagin* with a gold thing between its eyes" which is said to
live in her mother's village near Jullundur.[31] As we saw earlier, Nags
have a special place in Valmiki history, and although most young
people are only hazily aware of the details, several popular Hindi
films — of which *Nagin* is the best known — have emphasised the
special status of Nags, while also lending credibility to the belief,
widespread in India, that snakes can turn into human beings.

In addition to commercial movies, home-made videos also promote a distinctive sense of Valmiki identity. Family events, especially
weddings, are now routinely recorded on tape, not just in Britain, but
in India as well, so allowing virtual participation in the widest possible
family circle. But perhaps the most important event of all — at least
for the Valmikis — was the broadcasting of an epic version of the
Ramayana in nearly 100 episodes on Indian television in 1988, and
its subsequent re-transmission in Britain in 1991 and 1992. The fact
that Valmikis in India threatened to go on strike if the televised serial
omitted the scenes showing Valmik with Rama's sons Lav and Kush,
indicates the intensity of their feelings about the ancient epic, and the
significance they attached to its appearance on television. Even before
this, many Valmikis in Coventry already had videos recounting the
story of Valmik, Sita, Lav and Kush, but the public broadcasts have
redoubled their interest.

The Self-perception of Valmiki Children in Coventry

The way Valmiki children currently perceive themselves is clearly
pertinent to the future of the Valmiki community in Coventry, and
interviews with fourteen children between the ages of eight and
fourteen offer some illuminating pointers in this direction. First, all
the interviewees identified themselves primarily as "Indian" rather
than as "British". Thus nine-year-old Rena, who had never visited
India and whose Singapore-born mother also grew up locally, was

---

[31] According to Zimmer (*op. cit.*, p. 63), Nagas are Genii superior to men who carry
a precious jewel on their heads.

still adamant that she was Indian, insisting "I come from India, our family came from Delhi." And while many were rather uncertain how to identify themselves in the face of the sectarian divide between Hindus and Sikhs, most wisely perceived it as more of a continuum than a disjunction. As one girl put it, "I know what culture I am, Hindu, but it's not as if we're restricted to Hindu because we believe in Sikhism as well, it's just one thing really." And again: "I say to myself I'm a Sikh but really I'm a Hindu Punjabi. I do many things that Sikhs do. We go to a *mandir* but I call it a *gurdwara.*"

At the same time, most Valmiki children felt that the parental pressures on them were much less strict than those on many of their peers, be they "proper Sikh", Muslim or Jehovah's Witness. As one girl put it: "If I was a Sikh I wouldn't have this short hair; and I wouldn't be wearing a skirt if I was a Muslim." To quote another:

I don't really believe that you must do this, mustn't do that, like some Sikh families say, "God says you mustn't cut your hair, you mustn't eat meat, you can't show your legs". Some Sikhs wrote letters saying that they should stop the show because their daughters go and it's against their religion to dance. I think that's a load of rubbish.

All this suggests not only that the growing generation of British-born Valmikis identify strongly with India, but also that they view the religious practices of their community positively and as less restrictive than those to which their contemporaries in other South Asian communities are subjected.

In other spheres, however, Valmiki children's experience is much more painful, since double exclusionism on grounds of both caste and race is deeply wounding. It leaves no sanctuary whatsoever. Thus one young Valmiki whose family had moved into one of the smartest areas in Coventry found himself abused — a common experience amongst children of upwardly mobile Asian families — for being a "Paki", and had stones thrown at him in the street by other children in the neighbourhood. But while children of upper-caste families do at least have the solidarity of their own Gujarati or Punjabi communities on which to fall back, Valmiki children may also be disparaged by their Asian peers. Those who remain within the relative safety of Asian-majority areas can expect to avoid the worst forms of racial abuse, though that offers no protection against abuse from other Punjabi children still familiar with the disparaging terminology from which older Valmikis have been fighting so hard to escape. As a fourteen-year-old Valmiki girl reported: "There's a lot of fighting in school over religion, and mainly about caste. Some people go round saying, 'What caste are you? You're lower caste!' because of what their parents have told them." Casteism has survived the passage of a generation as well as the passage to Britain. Apologists for all this, of whom there are many among Britain's higher-caste Punjabis, can and do argue that all children are called names in the playground, that such verbal abuse is insignificant compared to the centuries of oppression suffered by the Scheduled Castes in India, and that in any case caste differences are as nothing compared with the viciousness of racism. But for Valmikis casteist insults are the more hurtful because they emanate from those whom they might have expected to be their allies in battles against racism. Nothing is more likely to sustain the Valmikis' vitality and solidarity than their bitter experience of double exclusion.

Indications for the Future

While it can be expected that the British-born second generation will be as keen as their parents to sustain a distinctive social, cultural and religious identity, it is clear that as the new generation reaches adulthood, the whole character of these collective activities will begin to change. In particular the temple could become less significant as a social arena. A further threat to communal solidarity arises from straightforward geographical and social mobility. As more and more Valmikis gain professional qualifications, enabling them to move out of the areas of densest South Asian population in which their parents were more or less obliged to settle, the corporate unity of the Valmik Sabha could well decline. But there is also force in the contrary hypothesis, that because of their exposure to double exclusionism, Valmikis will value their communal ties all the more keenly. But while their sense of pride in belonging to a large, warm and united community, and of sharing a unique heritage of pride and pain, is unlikely to be lightly abandoned, just what the future holds has become the subject of much dispute and discussion — focussing, amongst other things, on the exact nature of that heritage and how it can best be developed in Britain.

Differences of opinion about these issues lie at the heart of the debate which erupted after a community centre was built immediately next-door to the Valmiki temple, having been designed in such a way that all activities in the community centre are clearly visible to worshippers in the prayer hall. That might seem innocuous enough, but arguments about the consequences directly highlight the contradictory social pressures on British Valmikis, caught as they are between the norms and expectations of the wider society and those of higher-caste Punjabi Hindus and Sikhs.

As we have already seen, the Valmikis' own behavioural conventions are often much more relaxed than those followed by upper-caste

Punjabis — or which they at least claim to follow. As a community the Valmikis are less hypocritical, for they have never regarded (or even pretended to regard) the consumption of either meat or alcohol as taboo. Yet in adapting to life in Britain, they have found themselves caught in a curious dilemma. While any moves they might make towards the adoption of Western social and cultural conventions — which might be regarded as "modern" and "progressive" in any other South Asian community — tend, in their case, to be read in precisely the opposite way. For most upper-caste Punjabis such "loose" behaviour by Valmikis simply confirms their age-old assumptions about the ingrained inability of the lower social orders to behave with propriety. Valmiki elders are well aware of the negative judgements that other Punjabis would make about the consumption of meat and alcohol in the community centre, let alone the holding of Western-style parties in which women might both drink and dance, and therefore strongly oppose its use for these purposes. Yet if the elders succeed in imposing strict rules to hold upper-caste prejudices at bay, they may severely undermine the centre's potential as a unifying point for the community. If so restricted, the younger generation may feel it more appropriate to centre their social activities elsewhere.

Unlike their Indian- (or at least overseas-) reared parents, the rising generation do not feel linguistically isolated from the wider British society, while in Punjabi contexts they do not necessarily feel that the Valmik Sabha is the best, or even the most appropriate, platform from which to articulate their views. For them, a rhetorical strategy stressing the centrality and indispensability of Maharishi Valmik to Hinduism and of Bhai Jivan Singh to Sikhism is largely irrelevant as a means of confronting the social stigma of so-called untouchability. They would rather confront the issue head-on.

Here again, recent developments in technology and fashions in entertainment are a pointer to one source of increased self-esteem. The huge popularity of modern adaptations of *bhangra*, the exuberant folk music and dance of Punjab, is increasing the solidarity of the younger generation, both with other Valmikis and with Punjabis and South Asians generally.[32] As one young man who plays in a widely acclaimed local *bhangra* group said, "I've gone a bit more closer to my religion, yes, because a couple of years back I just didn't like

---

[32] See Sabita Banerji and Gerd Baumann, "Bhangra 1984–8: Fusion and Professionalisation: A Genre of South Asian Dance Music", in P. Oliver (ed.), *Black Music in Britain: Essays on the Afro-Asian Contribution to Popular Music*, Open University, pp. 137–52, and Gerd Baumann, "The Re-invention of Bhangra: Social Change and Aesthetic Shifts in a Punjabi Music in Britain", *The World of Music: Journal of the International Institute for Comparative Music Studies and Documentation* (Berlin), XXXII (1990), 2, pp. 81–97.

being an Indian because we used to get picked on . . . we used to be called 'Paki'. But now I've gone closer to it because now Indian music is coming out." Enthusiastic references to *bhangra* at weddings and parties recur in the conversation of teenagers, and although this helps to offset the negative associations of being "Asian" in Britain, it also marks off one generation from another. Many elders are irritated by what they see as the ugly raucousness of many *bhangra* lyrics.

The issue of marriage is also crucial to the future structural cohesion of the community, for *zat* boundaries have long been maintained through endogamous marriage. But already a number of young Valmikis have contracted non-arranged "love" marriages, either with non-Asians or with higher-caste South Asian partners. While in the latter case the spouse is likely to be cut off from his or her family, young Valmikis also risk parental displeasure for marrying "wrongly". At present most marriages are still arranged — within the caste, of course — but even this can pose problems. By time honoured convention a couple cannot marry if there is an overlap between their own, their parents' or their grandparents' *got* (a local descent group, whose name is frequently adopted as surname), but because of the small size of the Valmiki settlement in Britain compliance with this rule has become more difficult. Yet any relaxation of these rules would invite severe criticism from the higher castes, which are only too happy to rub in any suggestion that the Valmikis lack familiarity with the proper forms of behaviour.

Like every other group of South Asian settlers, the Valmikis face many dilemmas as they seek to work out how best to sustain a sense of religious and cultural identity. Like all the rest, they are split between the need to conserve the resources of their traditional heritage as a source of confidence, solidarity and collective mobilization in the face of uncertainty and exclusionism; but they are equally aware that tradition may need modification if its relevance is to be sustained to a new environment. This is especially true of the interests and concerns of the rising British-born generation who are usually only dimly aware of the issues facing their community in the subcontinent. But while Valmikis share much with their peers as they puzzle their way through their dilemmas in search of a viable strategy of resistance, they differ in one crucial respect: because of the cruel legacy of caste exclusionism, religious and cultural reconstruction is even more difficult for them.

Rattan Chand exhorts his grandchildren to have confidence in themselves, and believe that their capacity to achieve is as great as that of members of any other *zat*. He also urges them to tell people that they are Valmikis, for to do otherwise would suggest that their identity is something to be ashamed of. One Valmiki teenager said: "I say I'm no caste. I'm Hindu Punjabi. I don't believe in caste." Such defensiveness shows how hard it can be to put such advice into practice in front of one's Punjabi peers.

That Valmiki strategies of adaptation run parallel to those of their higher-caste peers is clear enough. They, too, use the resources of their cultural heritage to build themselves a prouder, more successful and more secure future. Yet for the Valmikis that heritage is rent with deeper contradictions than most. They are no less active than their higher-caste peers who are now so heavily involved in rebuilding a mainline Hindu, Sikh or Muslim heritage, yet they — like all ex-Untouchables — also face the task of developing a critical perspective towards that mainline heritage. For them cultural reconstruction is not simply about resisting racial exclusionism, but also about mounting a parallel challenge to *caste* exclusionism.

In challenging racial exclusionism, South Asian settlers have the immense advantage of being able to draw on a range of values, images and understandings largely beyond the ken of their excluders. But in mounting a parallel challenge to caste exclusionism the Valmikis are much more circumscribed. In conditions of severe and long-standing adversity, the only cultural materials out of which such strategies of resistance can be built are those developed by the dominators; this is why Valmikis have twisted and turned their way right across the religious and cultural environment of the Punjab, appearing variously as Hindus, Sikhs, Muslims and Christians — but in their moments of greatest confidence they appear as followers of a unique religion whose roots long predate all these mainline traditions.

Being a Valmiki has many dimensions, and although this has given rise to diversity, it is not an indication of social, cultural, historical or religious confusion. Rather it can more appropriately be regarded as evidence of the immense creativity of the Valmikis' resistance to the double exclusionism to which they are still so unjustly subjected.

"I'M BENGALI, I'M ASIAN, AND I'M LIVING HERE"

THE CHANGING IDENTITY OF BRITISH BENGALIS

Katy Gardner and Abdus Shukur

In the summer holidays of 1988, Tariq Ali, or Terry to his London friends,[1] took time out from his sixth form college to visit his father's village in Bangladesh. Both he and his family had been looking forward to the visit for many months. Tariq had arrived in Britain at the age of two, and throughout his childhood he had cherished the image of Sylhet as a land of lush beauty, wonderful food, and trees laden with exotic fruit. Thus, although he had no real memory of his family's village, he had always thought of it as home. Yet the reality of rural Bangladesh came as a painful shock. Terry was wholly unprepared for village life: the absence of electricity and running water, the lack of privacy, the insects and (in the middle of the monsoon) the mud. He was horrified by the poverty of his distant relatives, their village ways, and the expectations they had of him. He longed for London; he wanted his mates, his car, and the TV. If this was what it meant to be Bangladeshi he would rather call himself British.

Terry's experience provides a useful starting-point for the central theme of this chapter. Through his experiences, as well as those of his family, we aim to show that conventional understandings of the character of Britain's South Asian populations need careful reassessment. Until recently, anthropological accounts have tended to highlight the cultural insularity of South Asian communities and their fundamental social and cultural institutions, rather than the relations between different groups and mainstream British culture.[2] Particular emphasis has also been placed upon the creation and maintenance of ethnic boundaries, and the enduring nature of settlers' links with home.

Such perspectives remain pertinent within the specific historical

---

[1] Although their names have been changed, the individuals mentioned in this paper are all based on real people.

[2] See for example Verity Khan, *Minority Families in Britain* (Basingstoke: Macmillan, 1979), and James Watson, *Between Two Cultures* (Basil Blackwell, 1977).

context of primary migration; earlier accounts of South Asians in Britain, although many more focus on Pakistanis than on Bangladeshis, are still relevant to the lives and aspirations of older members of Terry's family.[3] These men migrated to Britain between 1940 and 1960, having left their wives and children in Bangladesh. With their dependents at home, ties with their villages of origin invariably remained strong. Most men returned home every few years, were closely involved with national and local Bangladeshi affairs, and continued to feel a local identity.[4] But since then the picture has radically changed. The behaviour and attitudes of most British Bengalis are now primarily a product of their local experience. To set these issues in context, we begin by considering the history of overseas emigration from Bangladesh.

Bangladesh: The Historical Context

Bangladesh is a small but densely populated country; its 110 million inhabitants squeezed into an area no larger than England and Wales. Most of the country is low-lying, and occupies much of the delta formed by the Ganges and Brahmaputra rivers. The population are mainly rural, the majority relying upon subsistence rice production. The country is predominantly Muslim, and although Bengali Islam traditionally leaned towards Sufism, there has recently been a revival of strongly puritanical reformist tendencies. But despite calls from some quarters for Bangladesh to become an Islamic state, religious freedom and pluralism survive; the population still includes some 20 million Hindus, and rather smaller numbers of Christians, Buddhists and followers of tribal religions.

Bangladesh has only been an independent state since 1971. When India gained independence from British rule in 1947, the country formed the Eastern wing of Pakistan, from which it broke loose in 1971 after a bloody civil war. Since then it has had a tumultuous history. Notorious internationally for its poverty and natural disasters, it was caricatured as an "international basket-case" by Henry Kissinger, and since then the label has stuck. This image is also closely related to the country's heavy dependence on foreign aid. Unable to survive without huge inflows of international assistance, it has little real independence or autonomy.[5]

[3] For example Badr Dahya, "Pakistanis in Britain: Transients or Settlers?", *Race* 14 (1973), and Caroline Adams, *Across Seven Seas and Thirteen Rivers* (London: Tower Hamlets Arts Project, 1987).
[4] John Eade, *The Politics of Community: The Bangladeshi Community in East London* (Aldershot: Gower, 1990).
[5] Rehman Sobhan, *The Crisis of External Dependency* (Dhaka, 1982), and Rehman Sobhan, "Bangladesh and the World Economic System" in Harris and Alavi (eds),

Dependence is not solely the result of international aid, for Bangladesh also relies heavily on remittances from international emigration. Between 1976 and 1983 nearly $US 2 billion was remitted annually by overseas Bengalis. The Gulf War, with the consequent loss of remittances from nationals working in Kuwait and Iraq, contributed to a national economic slump and further exacerbated political insecurity.

Whilst the movement of single men to Saudi Arabia and the Persian Gulf is comparatively recent, having been triggered off mainly by the oil boom in the 1970s and '80s, such movements represent only the most recent stage of the region's involvement in international migration. As elsewhere in South Asia, overseas migration has a much longer history. To understand the specific characteristics of the movement to Britain, we must look at one particular district: Sylhet.

Sylhet: A Land of Saints and Migrants

Tucked away in the north-east corner of Bangladesh, close to the hills of Assam, Sylhet has always had a distinctive regional identity. This is partly a result of geography. Although much of the region is flat, it is one of the few parts of Bangladesh where there are also small hills. Its distance from the Bay of Bengal and the deltaic landscape of the south means that cyclones are not such an imminent danger as in other districts, although Sylhet is as prone to floods as the rest of the country. During the wet season rivers frequently overflow and take with them great chunks of land, causing crops to be lost and homes ruined: both land and lives are as insecure here as elsewhere in Bangladesh.

Sylhet's special identity is, however, more cultural than physical. In addition to its distinctive local dialect and culinary traditions, the recent history of Sylhet has also taken it on a different path from the rest of the region. Like the rest of Bengal, Sylhet's fate was determined by foreign powers for many hundreds of years. Once the Mughals seized power in 1622, wholly indigenous rule was not re-established until 1971. Islam arrived in Sylhet long before the Mughals, thanks to the efforts of the renowned Sufi saint Shah Jalal, who led an army of Yemenis into the area and overthrew the Hindu Raja in 1384. Shah Jalal is still revered: his shrine in Sylhet town is a major pilgrimage centre, and his presence confirms the District's distinctiveness. Many local farmers proudly insist that the burial of the saint and his many disciples in its soil accounts for the prosperity and fertility of their *desh*.

The Sociology of Developing Societies: South Asia (London: Macmillan, 1989).

Bengal remained subject to Mughal rule up till the arrival of the British East India Company in 1765. One of the principal aims of the Company was to gain control of the region's production of high-quality cotton textiles. Sylhet played only a limited role in textile manufacture, and its new rulers tended to regard it in much the same way as their Mughal predecessors had done: as a potentially trouble-some frontier region. This reputation was largely a result of the district's geographical position, hard up against the hills of the eastern frontier; in contrast, the lowland population of rice farmers rarely proved politically troublesome.

Whilst the imposition of British rule had a devastating impact on the textile producing areas, in Sylhet the introduction of tea as a cash crop most affected the local economy. The hillier parts of the district proved ideal for its cultivation, and it quickly proved profitable for the British plantation owners. For the local population, however, wages in the plantations were abysmally low, and few Sylhetis took jobs on the new estates; labour was therefore imported from other parts of India, especially Orissa and the North-East. The descendants of these original immigrants still form the bulk of Sylhet's contemporary tea-plantation labour force.

A further crucial development was the British decision in 1874 to separate Sylhet from the rest of Bengal and incorporate it administratively into Assam; Sylhet only re-joined Bengal again in 1947. The new administrative arrangements were to have a huge impact on local land tenure, and these in turn influenced the Sylhetis' propensity to migrate. In Bengal proper, the British made a land revenue settlement with a small number of *zamindars*, thus effectively conferring rights of ownership on them. Those fortunate enough to acquire these *zamindari* rights soon gained positions of immense wealth and power; their tenants, who often numbered hundreds even thousands, were correspondingly impoverished. In Assam, however, the potential claims of large *zamindars* were largely overlooked; instead the settlement was made as far as possible with the actual cultivators of the soil, who paid their revenue direct to the British authorities. Cutting out the *zamindar* intermediaries and creating a vast number of small tenancies made for administrative complexity. It also deeply affected the rural social structure. While few peasant farmers were particularly rich, they avoided social and political subordination to a *zamindar*. There was no rent to pay, and given their direct title to their holdings, they could sell them if they wished. Thus instead of being mere tenants, subordinate to a small élite of landlords (as was, and still is, the case in much of Bengal), the majority of Sylhet's farmers became owner-cultivators.

As in Punjab, Sylheti families who owned the land they worked developed a reputation for pride; family status depended upon their ability to control their own property, and not sell their labour. Even today many Sylheti villagers declare with pride that they were always *taluk dar* (independent tenure holders paying rents direct to the British) rather than *raiyats* (tenants). Such owner-occupiers formed a distinct rural class, and when the opportunities for overseas migration appeared, they were in a better position to raise the capital outlay for their fares, if necessary by mortgaging their land. In sharp contrast to landless families where every pair of hands was vital for day-to-day production either through subsistence agriculture or wage-earning, landowning households could often spare the labour of one or even two of its young men. Their greater financial independence also meant that they were more accustomed to thinking of long-term investment, enterprise and profit than their landless neighbours.

Thus while Bangladesh is the poorest part of the subcontinent from which large-scale emigration to Britain has taken place, abject poverty has not been the main cause of departure. Rather, Sylhetis' propensity to migrate has been largely driven by the pulls of profit and adventure, to which they had both the confidence and resources to respond enthusiastically. Almost identical characteristics have been observed in every other part of South Asia where there have been high levels of overseas migration. Like these too, Sylhet also has a long history of emigration.

From Ships to Restaurants: The History of Sylheti Emigration

The first links in the chain of Sylheti emigration were forged before the end of the nineteenth century. By the end of the eighteenth century, Bengali seamen (known as *lascars*) were being employed on British merchant navy ships. They were hired to do the most unpleasant jobs for wages that were usually only a small fraction of those offered to white seamen. Even so, these were sufficient to draw in an ever-increasing number of enterprising and able-bodied young men to the dockside in Calcutta from as far away as Sylhet.[6] Finding work was far from easy; without the assistance of a broker who could arrange the papers, provide accommodation and effect the necessary introductions, it was virtually impossible. By the beginning of the twentieth century many Sylhetis had gained enough experience to become brokers themselves. Other districts, such as Noakali and Chittagong were also well represented among the *lascars*, but it was the Sylhetis who soon almost monopolised the jobs of being "fire stokers".

The dockside brokers in Calcutta were in a position of power, for

6 Caroline Adams, *op. cit.*

they determined just who would be recruited by the shipping companies. Sylhet's near-monopoly was thus partly the result of a handful of powerful brokers who invariably favoured their own kinsmen and fellow-villagers. A well-worn path was thus soon established between various villages and the dockside in Calcutta. Even today large-scale emigration to Britain is largely restricted to a few *thanas* (administrative districts); within these specific clusters of *"Londoni"* villages from which many inhabitants have moved to Britain can also be identified.

Sylheti villages are not nucleated settlements, but consist of dispersed clusters of patrilineally-linked households grouped into homesteads. Although the households are economically independent, they remain socially linked by their common ancestry, and are usually physically close together. Once a homestead becomes too large it splits, so that a group of brothers or patrilineal cousins moves off to another site, usually nearby. Many villages are therefore often inhabited by only a handful of "core" lineages, each of which has split into a multitude of different homesteads and households. And since overseas migration has been strongly socially channelled, with kin helping each other to migrate, close links have developed between Britain and particular lineages, which are in turn rooted in specific villages.

For many men, working at sea was only the first stage in their travels; they sailed all over the world, to the Far East and Australia, America, Europe, and Britain. Once in dock, particularly in London and New York, many illicitly slipped ashore, knowing that their fellow-countrymen would help them find work and accommodation. As Adams (1987) has recorded, a few early settlers provided just such a base in London, enabling them to take advantage of the higher wages available in Britain. After a few years of hard grind, these young entrepreneurs of the global labour market would seek out another ship to take them back to Calcutta, *en route* to Sylhet.

Until the mid-1950s a steady trickle of Sylheti men entered Britain in this way. Networks were well established; new arrivals were drawn into London's small but thriving Bengali community, then (as now) mainly concentrated in and around Spitalfields in East London. These early pioneers were mostly drawn from middle-income rural families with access to sufficient capital to launch them in the initial phase of migration. Few, if any, envisaged staying permanently in Britain, for far from being "pushed" into migration by rural poverty, it was the attraction of high foreign earnings which had "pulled" them there. As older migrants stress today, their primary aim was to earn money to send home. Their remittances were then invested in Sylhet, mostly in land and housing.

During the late 1950s and early '60s the pattern of migration changed dramatically, largely due to the rapid growth in demand for unskilled labour in the industrial cities of northern England. The several hundred or so early pioneers in London were consequently joined by thousands of additional settlers, almost all of whom arrived through the by now well-established chain. Many went directly from their villages to textile factories in the north, with only brief diversions through Dhaka and Heathrow airport. There they became industrial workers, clocking up as much overtime as possible to send home as much money as possible.

It may seem ironic that a rural class which despises labouring in one context was keen to embrace it in another. One returned migrant in Sylhet explains: "Us farmers find factory work easy. Heavy labour — it's all the same, isn't it?" More to the point, the factory wages were high enough to outweigh the stigma attached to such work; although it was unpleasant and still involved social subordination, the latter was at least to an alien (and therefore socially irrelevant) British management, not to their Bengali peers. Nevertheless, factory work was seen as little more than an unpleasant necessity. Once they had accumulated some capital, or been made redundant, many British Sylhetis soon moved on to other enterprises, working in restaurants or small clothing factories.

Migration during the 1960s was further reinforced by changes in immigration law. Under the provisions of the 1962 Commonwealth Immigration Act, labour migrants could only enter Britain if they held a "voucher" from an employer indicating that they had a job to go to. Given their wholly correct judgement that the system would not last long, most Sylhetis working in Britain promptly set about obtaining vouchers for their friends and kinsmen. The "chain" effect was thus reinforced; younger men whose senior kin had previously worked as seamen took advantage of their contacts to come to Britain and take the factory jobs which their sponsors had arranged for them. Many settled around Spitalfields, but others ventured to cities such as Birmingham, Bradford and Manchester.

The experience of Terry's senior kinsmen typify that of the early pioneers. By the Second World War a few members of their village, including his father's paternal uncle Abdul Hossain, had already established the first links. With a cousin and a few friends from other middle-income families in the village, they found work in Calcutta, became seamen, and after several years at sea slipped ashore in Britain. Although Abdul Hossain regarded himself as a sojourner with no intentions of settling permanently, he nevertheless spent most of the next twenty years in Britain, although he also returned to his village every couple of years and regularly remitted money to his wife and children. Like most men of his generation, his social commitments and loyalties remained primarily grounded in Sylhet, where he has now retired.

In the early 1960s, however, he was working hard, sending money home to support his immediate family and buy land, and also saving some for British-based investments. When the "vouchers" became available, he was able to obtain the documents needed to enable both his eldest son and his nephew (Terry's father) to enter Britain; he could also pay for their tickets. As young men in their twenties, both were eminently employable. Initially they worked in a Birmingham foundry, but after a few years moved to Oldham. Meanwhile Abdul Hossain, now at the centre of an increasingly large network of kinsmen and fellow-villagers, moved back to London. In partnership with three friends he bought a small café in Spitalfields, where he started a restaurant business.

Terry's father worked in Oldham throughout the 1960s. During this period he returned to Bangladesh twice: once to get married — when he stayed for two months — and then a year later to see the son his wife had produced. He tried to return every few years, but as the recession of the early 1970s set in, this became increasingly difficult. Eventually he was made redundant, and for the next couple of years was unemployed. This was the first time he had had such an experience. Realising that the prospect of finding permanent work in Lancashire was remote, he decided to move to London, where Abdul Hossain was by now well-established in the restaurant trade. Terry's father has worked in the restaurant business ever since. Soon after his arrival in London he had saved enough to bring his wife to Britain, and since his cousin was also reuniting his family, the two bought a large house in Hackney (East London).

The Sylheti Context of Migration

While the first generation of migrants were establishing a foothold in Britain, all sorts of changes were occurring back in Sylhet. By the mid-1970s, the social and economic standing of most families fortunate enough to have sent a migrant to Britain had changed substantially. Nearly all had increased their land holdings and many had built smart new homes. In the parts of Sylhet where there has been extensive emigration, "*Londoni*" homesteads stand in stark contrast to those of their non-migrant neighbours. Beside the traditional mud and thatch homes, "*Londoni*" houses are instantly recognisable. They are built of brick and concrete, two and sometimes three storeys high. Some are surrounded by imposing walls, and nearly all are brightly painted, their verandahs decorated with pictures of flowers, the names

of their owners and Arabic inscriptions. Some have vivid representations of aeroplanes painted on their walls. No one can doubt the
success and prosperity of those who live there.

It is not simply individual households which have benefited. The
inflow of remittances has brought the whole area a short-term economic boom. The building of *pukka* (brick-built) homesteads, together with investment in shops and hotels in the local towns, has
directly increased regional prosperity. But although Sylhet's remit-
tance economy has indeed encouraged a temporary building boom,
there have been other less positive effects. Land prices have risen, so
that only those with considerable capital (acquired through foreign
earnings) can afford to buy it. The prices of basic commodities and
labour have also risen. Meanwhile lavish conspicuous consumption
has become the order of the day, and families compete through it for
status. Communities marked by high levels of emigration have thus
become increasingly polarised. Those with access to remittances can
afford to buy land and live in relative comfort, while those without
bideshi links — who were more likely to be landless and poor in the
first place — have seen local economic differentiation increase still
further.

The Changing Character of Sylheti Settlement: Restaurants and Businesses

The Sylhetis who arrived in Britain during the 1950s and '60s were
overwhelmingly male, and if married, their wives and children usually
stayed in Bangladesh. Those who arrived in their teens in the early
'60s always returned to Sylhet to marry, but inevitably came back to
work in Britain soon afterwards. Thereafter they became what Ballard
has described as 'inter-continental commuters', dividing their lives
between work in Britain and the domestic and familial world of their
villages, to which they returned for extended visits every few years.

By the early 1970s this pattern began to change. New legislation
had made movement back and forth between the two countries increasingly difficult, and many migrants had begun to fear that unless
they claimed British nationality and brought their dependants to join
them, their rights of free movement might evaporate altogether. The
whole character of migration swiftly altered: new arrivals were now
most likely to be the wives and children of earlier settlers, entering
officially as dependants. By the mid-1980s the British Bengali population had grown to around 100,000 people. At the same time, the
pattern of employment had also shifted. Although industrial employment was becoming increasingly scarce, few Sylhetis stayed un-

employed for long. They turned their entrepreneurial skills in another direction: to the restaurant trade.

Whatever the style of cuisine or location of the restaurant, Sylhetis virtually monopolise the "Indian" restaurant business in Britain. Few British towns lack an "Indian" restaurant, and over 90% of these businesses are owned and run by Sylhetis. The origins of the trade can be traced to the nineteenth century when they worked as galley-hands. When they jumped ship, they established cafés and tea-houses close to the docks for their fellow-travellers to find familiar food. Adam's account of Sylheti migration to Britain recounts the early history of these establishments in some detail.

The number of cafés (mainly Sylheti, but some Punjabi- or Gujarati-owned) expanded considerably in the 1960s and '70s, especially in areas where large communities of Bangladeshis, Pakistanis and Indians were developing. The original clientele were largely single South Asian men who lived and worked locally. The majority of British people had yet to discover the delights of South Asian food. As one of the earliest café-owners points out:

"Nowadays almost everyone eats curry; you can even buy curried crisps. But when I first opened my café shop on the Commercial Road in 1962, things were different. We had to sell egg and chips and other things to start with. The customers took a long time before they started trying curry — even then we would have to add milk to it to make it mild for them. At first they would always have chips with their curry, never rice. Once I had a man who wanted to fight me because he found a bay-leaf in his curry. I had to explain that we added bay-leaf to give it flavouring."

Indian restaurants have come a long way since then. Through a mixture of clever marketing, good timing and changing national tastes, they have become a national institution. Many of the earliest establishments have changed beyond recognition — their decor, their cuisine and the availability of alcohol all indicating that the target clientele is now middle-class and white. This trend is particularly obvious in chic and expensive establishments such as the Last Days of the Raj and the Rickshaw in Covent Garden, and the Bombay Brasserie in Kensington. These initiatives have been one of the business success-stories of the last few decades. Besides providing employment for many Sylhetis, they have helped to establish them as an entrepreneurially successful group.

These few top entrepreneurs owe their wealth largely to the labour of large numbers of men working for long hours and low pay as waiters and cooks. Nearly all are Sylheti and have gained their jobs through the networks which still bind Britain's Bengali communities closely together socially as well as economically. But while the restaurants are nearly always Sylheti-run, by no means all Sylhetis have stayed in the trade. Young men who have grown up locally are often less than enthusiastic about entering the low-paid jobs in catering, heavy industry and the clothing business which their parents were compelled to take, and have begun to seek out other options: in recent years ever-increasing numbers have thus entered higher education. studying subjects ranging from electronics to community care.

Parental perceptions are changing too. Higher education is increasingly identified as a route for both greater earning potential and social mobility. Younger British Bengali women are also pressing forward in the same direction though, given the strength of parental fears, rather more slowly. Even so, an ever-increasing number are continuing into higher education after school, and are employed in sectors ranging from business to the social services. Those from more conservative families are more likely to work at home, often as piece-workers in the clothing industry.

These changes are illustrated by developments in Terry's family. Although Abdul Hossain has returned to Sylhet, where he has recently purchased a town house, Terry's father and uncle co-own and manage a restaurant in the East London district of Bethnal Green, purchased through savings and the sale of Abdul Hossain's Spitalfields establishment. While Terry's eldest brother Iqbal and one of his cousins work there, he himself studies management at a local college. Terry's younger sister too plans to go on to higher education, although the hurdle of her "A" levels still lies ahead. Another cousin has expanded into computing. Meanwhile Terry's peers have a wide selection of jobs, all broadly of a white-collar kind; none of them is a factory labourer or 'sweat-shop' employee. But while it was Abdul Hossain's hard work and shrewd investment which made these leaps possible, the family's rapid transition from being factory workers, the rewards of whose labour could only be reaped in Bangladesh, to businessmen with rapidly diversifying interests makes it far less likely that their younger members will ever settle back in Bangladesh.

However, one should avoid over-wide generalisation. Many families have been less successful, with most of their members still doing low-status and low-paid jobs and living in the relative poverty of East London tenements or squalid bed-and-breakfasts. There are many possible explanations for the growing differences between individual families. Whilst it is true that most Sylhetis were small 'owner-occupier' farmers before their arrival, this conceals considerable heterogeneity in wealth, skill and education. Also, once they have arrived in Britain, further influences such as employment opportunities, shrewdness of investment and stages in the family's life-cycle have come into play. Families who quickly reunited themselves in Britain during the 1970s rather than waiting until the mid-1980s may also have been in a more advantageous position. They were spared the high costs of "international commuting" between Bangladesh and Britain, and benefit from the economic contributions of children who could find work as soon as they left school, and from wives able to do piece-work at home. As Ballard has pointed out, the different timings of family reunions amongst Mirpuri Pakistanis and Punjabi Sikhs has had a substantial effect on the subsequent history of these various groups.[7] Variations within these wider "communities" may be just as extensive; some British Bengalis have now reached their third generation in Britain, while others, especially newly married women, have still only just arrived.

From Sojourners to Settlers: The Changing Nature of Migration

It is clear then, that migrant strategies and expectations are in constant flux. Sylhetis have long been entrepreneurs, taking advantage of whatever opportunities they could find to enhance their rural earnings. They have also responded to ever-changing external conditions, such as the rise and decline of the British Merchant Navy, the rise and subsequent disappearance of a demand for their labour in British industry, and the tightening of British immigration law. These have been paralleled by changes back home which have further affected the strategies and perspectives of *Londoni* migrants.

The men who arrived to work in Britain during the 1950s and '60s viewed themselves essentially as sojourners, for their wives and children stayed in Bangladesh and their overseas earnings were still regarded as contributions to the joint household economy. Hence it was to this domestic arena that migrants returned as often as possible. Such behaviour closely parallels that found in the early phases of most other South Asian settlements in Britain, and gave rise to assumptions which were graphically dubbed the "Myth of Return" — the belief that their stay in Britain was only temporary.[8]

Among the older generation of Sylhetis such ideas are still very much alive; their links with Bangladesh remain crucially important and many devote much energy to maintaining economic and kinship relations there. Some, like Abdul Hossain, have returned more or less permanently to Bangladesh, and while others still live in Britain, many hope to retire to Sylhet. There are older men who have never been

---

[7] Roger Ballard, "Migration and kinship", in C. Clarke *et al.*, *South Asians Overseas* (Cambridge University Press, 1990).

[8] Mohammed Anwar, *The Myth of Return* (London: Heinemann, 1979).

joined by their wives, and still remit most of their earnings back home. Thus despite the reconstitution of kinship networks in Britain, most families maintain close economic and social links with Bangladesh, with the result that social arenas in Bangladesh and Britain are woven together by an elaborate series of reciprocities. Whilst the inhabitants of *Londoni* villages remain dependent upon money sent from Britain, their kin in Britain receive goods and services from Sylhet which help them to reconstruct Sylhet in a Western setting. The strength of this relationship is graphically illustrated by the funerals of men and women who have died in Britain. Very often their bodies are flown back to Sylhet, so that their relatives can see them one last time, and then buried in the home village in land acquired as a result of their labours overseas.

However, the character of these reciprocities is changing rapidly. Although the older generation are still deeply involved in such commitments, current changes are undermining younger people's commitment to them. Whilst the latter may still pay lip-service to the notion of return to the "homeland", their lives are centred in Britain, and their links with kin and land back in Sylhet are weakening. Thus although the ties still exist, many younger people now regard themselves as British rather than as Bangladeshi: the people to whom they are most committed live in Britain, not Sylhet.

Once the original male migrants had brought their wives and children to Britain, the need to return regularly to their villages was reduced. As one village woman, whose cousins had left for Britain six years earlier, commented: "My *chacha* [uncle] used to come back every year or so, but now that everyone's gone to London, we haven't seen him for over five years." There are many reasons for this. Airfares for a whole family are prohibitively expensive. Work and school commitments in Britain are a further constraint, and couples with young children often find visits to Bangladesh a problem: their children are unused to the climate and diet, and lacking immunity to tropical illnesses, often fall sick. Many young families now set off equipped with British-bought baby food and medicines. Others have sent their children to Bangladesh for schooling, in the hope that they will learn to speak good Bangla and benefit from direct exposure to Bengali culture, only to find that they are trailing behind in an entirely different system of education. These changes in domestic and familial contexts have been paralleled by major developments in two arenas which had hitherto played a key role in keeping the links intact: the ownership of land, and marriage.

Land Ownership and its Consequences

Over the years, economic links between Sylhet and Britain have primarily revolved around the acquisition and upkeep of land. Since property was collectively owned by joint families, if one or more brothers migrated, another would stay at home to look after both the land and the wives and children of the absent migrants. Those overseas regularly remitted their savings and any surplus was used to buy more land. Emigrants returned regularly both to see their families and to negotiate land business.

Migration has had a major impact on the dynamics of household organisation, particularly on inheritance and the division of landed property. Traditionally, property was divided equally amongst brothers after their parents' death: the joint family then split into separate units, and while still living in the same homestead, each had a separate hearth. When brothers are working abroad, however, this division may be only partial, and sometimes never takes place. The mutual dependence between the different components of the extended family is simply too great: brothers in Bangladesh need the remittances, while those in Britain rely upon their kin back home to look after their fields and families.

Such arrangements can only easily be sustained if migrants return regularly. But once wives and children go to Britain, the need for return visits is drastically reduced, and the financial relationships between Britain and village-based kin groups become increasingly complex. Whatever relatives in Bangladesh may expect, British residents are no longer able to remit on the scale they once did. Their primary economic responsibility is now to dependants in Britain, and they may also have invested in British homes and businesses: although they notionally share the rice and the profits from village land, those based in Britain are in no position to enjoy their formal rights. Jointness is thus increasingly theoretical rather than practical. In these circumstances resentments can easily build up on all sides, as one person begins to feel that others are failing in their obligations.

It is the younger generation's relationship to land which has changed most radically. With no experience of rural life, fields thousands of miles away hold little interest for them. Meanwhile, kinsmen tending the land as sharecroppers may increasingly treat it as their own; Bangladeshi law allows tenants to claim ownership of holdings after a certain number of years, and British owners may find it difficult to sustain their rights, given their physical distance and their unfamiliarity with land law. As actual control of holdings shifts in favour of Bangladesh-based kin, the importance of the landed connection declines.

Marriage

Marriage has been a central link between British Bengalis and their rural roots. Because for many years male migrants far outnumbered women, most marriages were between *Londoni* men and Sylhet-based women. These unions reinforced social solidarity in several ways. New brides brought a fresh infusion of Sylheti culture and language, which was then passed on to their British-born children. Matches between cousins have bonded extended families more closely, whilst those between unrelated families created new affinal links between Britain and Sylhet. Marriage also has implications for migration: while senior men usually left their wives in Bangladesh, young British–Bengali men who marry in Bangladesh nearly always bring their wives back with them. Sylhetis who arrange their sons' and daughters' marriages with *Londonis* expect their offspring to go to Britain, provided that they can make their way around the formidable obstacle of the British immigration laws. Marrying is one thing; gaining permission to live with one's partner in Britain, especially for Bangladesh-based husbands, is quite another.

Many young British–Bengali men still return to Sylhet to find wives whom they will eventually bring to Britain, and while some *Londoni* women marry village men, this is less frequent. Their 'Britishness' — in education and outlook — is a constraint on the arrangement of marriages with village men, both for the brides and for their prospective grooms. It is also harder for husbands to gain entry to Britain: the immigration authorities suspect that the 'primary purpose' of such marriages is entry to Britain, and argue that since patrilocal residence is the Sylheti norm, wives should join their husbands in Bangladesh and not *vice versa*. Meanwhile in Sylhet both brides and grooms from Britain are eagerly sought as partners because they offer the prospect of entry into Britain.

Despite this, an increasing number of matches are now made within Britain. This is partly a result of demographic change: Britain's Bengali population no longer has an excess of males as it did up till about 1980. It also reflects shifting aspirations and attitudes. As the local community has become more self-sufficient, arranging marriages within Britain has become easier, obviating the need to go to Bangladesh to find a spouse. While marriages between British-Bengalis may not reinforce links with kin back in Sylhet, they do offer an opportunity to strengthen ties with British-resident kin, or to construct firmer bonds with non-relatives with whom the parents share business concerns. These British links are coming to be seen as more important than those with kin back in Sylhet.

There has also been a change of attitude among would-be partners.

Young people brought up in Britain and widely exposed to Western notions of love and marriage put greater emphasis on sharing common interests with their spouses. The tension between parental notions of an ideal partner, based in traditional ideas of kinship and the status hierarchy, and new ideas of self-chosen romantic love deserves a chapter in itself. It is also an issue which remains unresolved for many young British Bengalis. For them the idea of marriage to someone of whom they have no prior knowledge, who has been selected for them by village kin, and who has had no experience of British life, is an increasingly unacceptable prospect. Against this must be set feelings of obligation and loyalty to their parents, their positive commitment to their roots, and the difficulty of finding a suitable partner in Britain. As long as this difficulty continues, so will marriages with Sylheti-based spouses. Two recent marriages indicate the degree to which the model now varies.

Iqbal's case is typical of the newer style. Now in his late twenties, he has lived in Britain since he was ten, although he returned to his natal village for a year in his teens. His reactions to Bangladesh are far more positive than those of his younger brothers, although he too now identifies strongly with Britain. All the same, when his family first raised the question of marriage, he was horrified at the thought of marrying a village girl with whom he feared he would have nothing in common. Family rows continued for many months until he was eventually formally introduced to a young London Bengali woman by one of his cousins. Like him, she spoke better English than Bengali, and she also had a job. Having agreed to marry, they saw each other for several months before the marriage took place, and now live with the family in Hackney. Such a marriage is in many ways a compromise between the traditional arranged form, and the Western-style relationship. Since their marriage this couple have not been to Bangladesh; they feel no need to do so, since all their immediate kin live in Britain.

A cousin who arrived in Britain at the same time as Iqbal had a different experience. Having returned to Sylhet a year ago, ostensibly for a visit, his family put him under great pressure to get married. Initially he resisted, but the concerted force of his village-based family and his parents (who had returned with him) finally persuaded him to at least "view" a few girls: his greater freedom of choice in selecting a bride was a concession to the changing mores of the younger *Londoni* generation. A suitably attractive and well-connected young woman, introduced through family links, was eventually found, and they were soon married. Having returned to Britain, he was awaiting at the time of writing the clearance of her immigration papers and her arrival in London.

While both marriages illustrate the ways in which the relationship with Bangladesh is changing, they also demonstrate that change is taking a variety of forms. Most British-Bengali families retain substantial links with Bangladesh, and the nature and intensity of these links is increasingly influenced by British circumstances.

The New British Bengalis

What are the implications of these changes for the next generation of British-born Bengalis? As we have seen, their attitudes and lives often differ radically from those of their parents and grandparents. This is hardly surprising in view of the far-reaching social changes in Britain over recent decades, the altered pattern of migration from Sylhet, and changes in their parents' villages. In such a context, we need to examine the changing nature of British-Bengali identity, people's shifting attitudes to Bangladesh, and their new ways of dealing with life in Britain. These are far from homogeneous, as they depend upon a range of factors from class, age and sex through to individual leanings. The blanket category 'Bangladeshi' is increasingly obsolete.

While links with Sylhet remain of central importance to those born and brought up there, their offspring born and raised in Britain often have different attitudes and priorities. Thus many of the children and grandchildren of the original migrants are aghast when confronted, like Terry, with the reality of rural Bangladesh. In sharp contrast to their parents, this is *not* the source of their personal and social identity. So even though Bangladesh and their Bengali-ness are still crucially important to almost all young British Bengalis, the country itself is a largely alien world. Paradoxically, nothing underlines the British-ness of their personal and social identities more strongly than a visit to Bangladesh.

For first-generation migrants the myth of return was a crucial means of denying that migration implied fundamental changes; however well-settled they might actually be, the myth allowed them to see themselves as sojourners. But their children face a very different reality. They may be British, but they are aware of how unwilling the white natives are to accept them as such. For them, therefore, Bangladesh is an ideal land where they are accepted. Constructed by those who have never lived in Bangladesh, or at least not since infancy, the new myth is concerned less with the prospect of return than with an image of Bangladesh as a beautiful and peaceful land where life is easy, honest and straightforward. Ironically, this is an almost exact replica of the image of Britain which Bangladeshis who have never been there have of it. From the other side however, Bangladesh is "home", where one's roots belong, and its image is elaborated from stories told by relatives, photographs and, for some, wishful thinking. As Eickelman and Piscatori (1990) point out, "home", the fixed point of return, is subject to constant re-imaginings by travellers; their dreams and longed-for reality always exist elsewhere. Given their limited experience of Bangladesh, this ideal image provides a psychological escape-route in the face of disparagement and adversity. Like all those excluded by a dominant culture, most young British Bengalis attach great importance to identifying their roots and cultural heritage. But when they "return" to Bangladesh, many find their myth exploded as the extent of their separation from Bangladesh is thrown into relief.

But let us return to Terry, for his experience has also been shared by several of his friends, although in varying degrees of intensity. Iqbal, who left Sylhet at the age of ten, has different feelings. He has more direct memories of village life, and still has friends there. For him, the idea of one day returning, especially to Sylhet town, and starting a business is a realistic possibility. For Terry, however, "home" came as a shock. Staying with his parents and siblings in their usually deserted quarters in the family homestead, hastily made habitable for their visit, his first month was spent in adolescent rebellion. He spoke English whenever he could, insisted on wearing shorts and a T-shirt, spurning the very thought of a *lunghi*, and sat sullenly when relatives came to visit. Left to himself, he listened to his Walkman and read thrillers.

The message which Terry was intent on conveying was that he had nothing to do with village life, and that his culture was Western. Whilst his Bangladeshi origins had provided a niche and particular identity in Britain, here in a Sylheti village he stressed his British identity. His radical switch is not exceptional, for as numerous anthropological analyses have shown, ethnicity is context-dependent and apt to be unconsciously manipulated according to needs or adversity. However, Terry's temporary rejection of all things Bangladeshi was somewhat extreme, and many young Bengalis react less violently, visiting Sylhet several times and enjoying the experience. Nevertheless, their experience remains the same: their identity is not wholly based in rural Sylhet. Such feelings of alienation may be harder for young women to cope with. Although their brothers face similar pressures to conform to Bangladeshi and Muslim norms, they can at least enjoy the higher status and greater freedom accruing to being male. Among young women non-conformity is far more shocking, and some may find that from a relatively "liberated" life in Britain, where they attended mixed schools, had English friends and may even have been allowed to go to parties and discos, they are now expected to behave like village women. They shock their relatives intensely when they fail to act in a suitably "modest" and obedient way.

The way in which young British Bengalis form identities differing substantially from those of their parents is illustrated by the following examples. They are not particularly typical, but reveal variety in experience and identity. Joyoti is twenty-four, and has lived in Britain since she was four years old. As a secretary in a City office with a flat of her own, she readily agrees that her life-style does not conform to the usual stereotype. Such young women are still relatively rare. Many Bengali parents are still uneasy at the prospect of their daughters working outside the home — hardly surprising given the strictness with which the conventions of *purdah* are interpreted in Sylhet — and for unmarried women to live apart from their parents is even more unusual. But customs are changing. Pressure from daughters to continue in education, the need for their wages and, if they have "white-collar" work, the novel experience of their employment being prestigious rather than shameful, all mean that within the next few decades more and more Bengali women will join the employment market. This goes together with the growing acceptance amongst younger men that their wives should go out to work.

Joyoti has no intention of ever returning permanently to Bangladesh. As she says: "I think all the poverty would really get me down. It puts me off a bit. I just go there for holidays." But this does not imply comprehensive anglicization, for as she also emphasises: "I know lots about Bengali culture and religion. We know our roots, but we're westernised, no doubt about that. But at the end of the day, you're brown aren't you?"

This last remark is important. For many British Bengalis, their experience of white racism provides a central component of their self-definition. Reactions to the experience vary, but even the most cursory exploration soon reveals the extent to which the preferred cultural and political expressions of almost all young British Bengalis have been powerfully moulded by their exposure to the forces of racial exclusionism. All ultimately face the same dilemma. Deeply ambiguous though their location in British society may be, it is Britain alone which provides them with their ultimate frame of reference. To illustrate these points, we close by exploring two very different forms of cultural and ethnic expression, both of which are creative responses to circumstances in Britain.

Joi Bangla

In Bengal, *Joi Bangla* — "Long live Bengal" — has long been a popular slogan for the articulation of nationalist challenges to oppression, whether British or Pakistani. But in Britain it has gained new resonance. After a British Bengali pop group used it as its name, the term became associated with the fashionable, moderately rebellious and highly politicised sub-culture of large numbers of young Bengalis. In common with many other youth sub-cultures, they identify themselves by following a particular type of music; theirs is "Bangla", a locally generated mix of rap, electronic pop and traditional Bengali folk-music. There are now many Bangla bands in Britain, and their music, itself a creative response to a wide variety of influences, effectively sums up the multi-faceted social identities of both its performers and its fans.

Joi Bangla originated from a youth group in the East London borough of Tower Hamlets whose central aim was to generate a more positive awareness of Bengali culture amongst British-born Bengalis. Both the group and the sound of *Joi Bangla* now have a considerable following. Frequently performed at local gigs and community festivals, their songs mostly have a political content, and deal with subjects ranging from community politics in East London and inner-city life, to Bengali nationalism. As a backing singer with the group explains: "I rap in Bengali and English. I rap on everything from love to politics. I've always been into rapping . . . it was rebellious, the lyrics were sensational. I could relate to that, I could identify with it. Like living in the ghetto and all that . . ." And the message? "It's coming from the heart. It's: 'I'm Bengali, I'm an Asian, I'm a woman, and I'm living here.'"

In many ways *Joi Bangla* parallel developments in the rest of British youth culture, where difference from accepted norms of mainstream adult ways is always highly valued. Thus whilst identifying themselves as Bengali, and so placing their experiences within a political framework, their concerns and forms of expression are easily accessible to non-Bengalis. In the context of conventional Bengali culture *Joi Bangla* may seem highly non-conformist, but within the more general context of British youth culture its activities are unexceptional.

Islam: The New Reformists

Another expression of cultural identity and distinctiveness in sharp contrast to *Joi Bangla* has also emerged: support for Islam, especially in its more militant forms. On the face of it, commitment to Islam would seem thoroughly 'traditional'; it is explicitly separate from mainstream white culture, has the direct aim of returning its followers to their Bengali Muslim cultural roots and norms, and is quite separate from the blending of Western and Bengali influences so manifest in *Joi Bangla*. But the traditionalist label can be misleading, because increasing commitment to Islamic values, which is manifest amongst many sections of British Bengali youth, is by no means a return to old traditions. Rather it is born from contemporary circumstances.[9] Like Bangla music, it is a response to the experience of racial and ethnic exclusionism, but in this case espousing the language of cultural separation rather than of creative borrowing.

Care must be taken in identifying the nature of this new commitment to Islam. Among members of Britain's white majority there is a widespread assumption that all Muslims are "fundamentalists" who enthusiastically advocate the burning of books and the assassination of Salman Rushdie. While clearly articulated arguments developed in an Islamic perspective do indeed appear far more threatening to mainstream white society than the usual stereotypes of Asians and of Bengalis in particular, who are generally perceived as passive, insulated and non-confrontational, popular images of these new developments still radically misinterpret what is really going on. Certainly commitment to the maintenance of Islamic values has increased since the early 1980s, and recent developments have shown British Muslims to have a much greater capacity to be vocal and politically proactive than white liberals previously imagined. But like all stereotypes, the image of Muslims as "fundamentalists" misses out great chunks of the truth. British Muslims subscribe to a wide range of beliefs and behaviour, and only a small minority can properly be described as militant. Undeniably, however, Islam is an increasingly important vehicle for the articulation of their interests and concerns.

Reactions to the *Satanic Verses* affair and the coverage of Muslim issues in the media have brought all this to a head. However much they may seek to identify themselves as British, young Bengalis regularly find that others assume them to be first and foremost Muslim. As Terry's seventeen-year-old friend Shibli explains:

"During the Rushdie affair, both me and my friend Dev [a Hindu of Indian origin] were constantly asked by other people at work to defend the Islamic fundamentalist position. This was only because both of us are brown. It didn't matter what religious opinions we held, whether or not we were fundamentalists, or even if we were Muslims at all . . . "

Yet however stereotypical the majority's images of Muslim fundamentalism may be, they have not appeared from a void. Strident commitment to Islamic beliefs and values is indeed increasing amongst many British Bengalis, especially the younger generation — a development of central importance to our discussion.

Anthropologists have often emphasised how religiosity can provide excluded groups with a convenient and effective means of ar-

[9] See Eade, *ibid.*

ticulating their collective economic and political interests. One does not need to be a social scientist, however, to recognise that British Muslims' increasing commitment to Islam is linked to their ascribed social status. Their new allegiances are both a reaction to, and a defence against, the experience of racial exclusionism; and while this was something which their parents also had to face, the rising British-rooted generation is no longer prepared to tolerate explicit denigration. Thus while the older generation were easily intimidated by the threat of 'Paki-bashing', their children and grandchildren are determined to fight back. Their "fundamentalism" is therefore largely a result of their *British* experience, especially their exposure to racism. As another friend of Terry's puts it:

"I'd always considered myself to be British, because I was born in this country, and grew up in this country. That all changed one day when a white friend and I were waiting to get into a club and when it came to our turn the doorman said to my friend, it's OK for you to come in, but not the Paki. That incident really made me think, no matter what we do and how westernised we have become, the one thing we cannot do is change the colour of our skins. For that reason I became very much interested about finding out about my culture and religion."

Islam provides both a positive identity, in which solidarity can be found, together with an escape from the oppressive tedium of being constantly identified in negative terms. Even more important, Islamic rhetoric not only condones fighting for one's rights and acting in collective defence of a Muslim brotherhood, but explicitly encourages it. The ideal of collectivity is not however confined only to Britain. More than any other faith, Islam is a world religion; hence a heightened commitment to Islam allows those involved both to express their frustrations with mainstream British society and to join a worldwide trend which links them politically and financially to the global *umma* in other Muslim countries.

More and more young Bengalis now identify themselves first and foremost as Muslim rather than as Bengali or Bangladeshi. Their parents and grandparents are of course Muslims too, but for them it was not Islam, but rather their origins in Bengal, in Sylhet, or more likely in their localised *desh* through which they expressed their social and cultural identity. The adoption of a Muslim identity does not preclude some degree of allegiance to Bangladesh; rather it reinforces it, for it also implies rejection of Western culture. In the ideal of a global community joining together Muslims from all over the world, the specifics of Bengali culture are often seen as a distraction.

It is easy and convenient for outsiders to talk of "Bangladeshis", but the label is becoming increasingly inappropriate. Locally born and bred children of Sylheti descent, fluent in English and educated in British schools, are first and foremost British. Their links with Bangladesh and the stereotypic identities which outsiders still all too often seek to impose on them are dissolving into new formations. It is not that young British Bengalis are, as Watson suggested, 'between two cultures'.[10] Rather, they have constructed new and varied lifestyles of their own. While it has long been recognised that migration is a process, the ways in which migrants and their offspring adapt re-adapt and continually re-interpret their values and lifestyles in their new settings have been little studied. We hope that in a small way this discussion of the changing nature of the Bangladeshi presence in Britain and the dynamic nature of British Bengali identity begins to fill the gap.

[10] James Watson, *Between Two Cultures*, *op. cit.*; see also page 30 above.

CASTE, RELIGION AND SECT IN GUJARAT

FOLLOWERS OF VALLABHACHARYA AND SWAMINARAYAN

Rachel Dwyer

Britain's Gujarati population now numbers over half a million people. As a group they are widely regarded as being among the most affluent and successful of Britain's South Asian settlers, and as having achieved their wealth through a combination of entrepreneurial skill and sheer hard work. While many Gujaratis are highly educated, having gained professional qualifications in such fields as technology, science, medicine, economics, business, management and law, there is nevertheless a stereotype of the Gujarati family as running a newsagent and tobacconist shop from which it has made a great deal of money by combining long working hours with clever business practices. This is as common in the South Asian community as among the white majority. Indeed a similar image is promoted by the Gujaratis themselves. Most take great pride in their mercantile traditions, as well as the presence of many millionaires within their ranks, despite their having only recently arrived in Britain.

Yet apart from business enterprise and their highly developed and distinctive cuisine, Gujaratis are also known for another great love: religion. For most, religious practice is an important dimension their everyday life, and this now has clear consequences at an organisational level. No longer content with converting disused Christian churches into their places of worship, most of the huge diversity of sects and caste-based communities into which the Gujaratis are divided have raised the money needed to construct purpose-built temples — some on a spectacular scale. While their spires and flags have brought new forms of architecture to many British cities, the rituals and festivities performed there now reproduce almost the entire range of Hindu belief and practice.

There is no space here to discuss the totality of Gujarati religious practice, or to examine in detail all the many different sects and castes. Instead this chapter outlines the history of Gujarat and the region's longstanding tradition of overseas emigration. It then explores the origins and development of two Vaishnava sects: first the followers of Vallabhacharya (also known as Pushtimargis) and secondly the followers of Swaminarayan. A large proportion of Hindu emigrants from Gujarat are involved in one or other of these groups.[1]

The Environment and Economy of Gujarat

The modern state of Gujarat lies north of Bombay, and is bounded by the Indian Ocean to the west, Pakistan to the north, and the states of Rajasthan, Madhya Pradesh and Maharashtra to the east and south. The historical core of Gujarat proper is north and east of the Gulf of Khambat, but Gujarat today includes the Saurashtra peninsula (also known as Kathiawar), as well as the marshy and sparsely populated Kachchh further to the northwest. It is a region of plains and low hills, but its climate is extreme: temperatures vary from sub-zero in winter to a scorching 48° in summer. Nearly all the rain falls during the short summer monsoon, ranging from a substantial 1500 mm. in the south to under 25 mm. in Kachchh.

The region has an ancient tradition of commercial, financial and industrial activity. Thanks to its long coastline and many good harbours, it has always been an ideal take-off point for overseas trade to the Middle East, and for inland trade northwards to the Indo-Gangetic heartlands; indeed archaeological excavations at the great Harappan port of Lothal provide evidence of such trade with Mesopotamia dating back to the second millennium BCE. During later periods of Buddhist, Hindu and Muslim domination, there are many references to Gujarat as a centre of trade and commerce, and these patterns have continued right through to the present. In this atmosphere local traditions which place great emphasis on hard work and frugal living have flourished, and have thus provided an ideal ethic for entrepreneurial success.

Yet despite Gujarat's well-deserved reputation for trade and commerce, agriculture has always been the mainstay of the local economy and today employs two-thirds of the population. The region has also long been involved in textile manufacturing; by the sixteenth century, Gujarati merchants were supplying large amounts of high-quality cotton cloth both to the Middle East and to Europe. The growth of the Lancashire cotton industry under imperial protection during the nineteenth century was a major setback to local weavers and merchants alike, but by the early twentieth century, mechanised textile

[1] The research on which this chapter is based could not have been completed without the assistance I received from a large number of members of both Pushtimarg and the Swaminarayan movement. However, I owe particular thanks to the families of Amitaben Lalitchandra Patel in Vadodara, and of N.C. and B.M. Patel in Bombay, Vadodara, Ahmadabad and London.

mills were being established in Gujarat itself. The industry flourished despite British opposition, and today the region supports manufacturing enterprises ranging from traditional textiles to petrochemicals, which in turn have spawned an active service sector in such areas as banking, money-lending and jewel trading.

History

Although Gujarat's distinctive social and religious characteristics are firmly rooted in Hinduism, other influences have been far from insignificant. Buddhism and Jainism have had a profound effect on local beliefs and practices since ancient times, as has Islam during the past millennium. The period of the Solanki dynasty, which ruled Gujarat immediately before the establishment of Muslim rule towards the end of the eleventh century CE, represents for many Gujarati Hindus a golden age when the region was independent and Hinduism and Jainism were the dominant ideologies, even though Muslims were active in the region. Muslims from the Middle East were trading in Gujarati ports as early as the seventh century, and by the ninth century most major cities included a Muslim quarter. However, the whole character of Hindu–Muslim relations changed radically in 1026, when Mahmud of Ghazni swept down into Gujarat from Afghanistan to sack and plunder the great Hindu temple at Somnath. Petty raids continued for some time, but eventually Gujarat came under the rule of the Tughluq Sultans of Delhi. Their control of the province was far from absolute, and therefore as the Delhi sultanate was weakened by the depredations of Timur Leng, Zafar Khan, a Rajput convert to Islam who was ruling the province as a tributary of Delhi, broke away from his feudal overlords in 1407 to establish the autonomous Sultanate of Ahmadabad. The dynasty remained independent from Delhi for just over a century and a half, until Akbar, the great Mughal, reimposed central control.

Although Islam informed the ideology of the ruling élite, Muslim rule was not a hegemonic theocracy. The Sultans struggled to maintain control against local threats and against the Marathas, who invaded sporadically, until the area came under British control early in the eighteenth century. The British ruled some of the area directly, but much of it was administered through its agents in the princely states.

The lengthy experience of Muslim rule had a major impact on the local social order, weakening the role of the Rajputs or Kshatriyas, the traditional Hindu ruling classes. The traditional competition for status between Kshatriyas and Brahmins, seen elsewhere in India, was replaced in Gujarat by a struggle for ideological dominance between the Brahmins and the merchant and trading castes, known as Banias.[2] The wealth of the Banias derived mainly from overseas trade, and the prestige acquired by their ritually pure practices, have allowed them far more social influence than they have achieved elsewhere in India. Since the Banias so comprehensively overshadow the few remaining Kshatriyas, it is the local merchant élite, rather than the warrior Rajputs or priestly Brahmins whom upwardly-mobile peasant groups have sought to emulate.

Conversion to Islam

Not all of Gujarat's merchant communities are Hindu, however. A significant minority converted to Islam, in both the Sunni and the Shi'a traditions, the latter divided into numerous sectarian sub-groups. Among the merchants, the most important Muslim groups are the Shi'ite Bohras and Khojas (who include the Aga Khanis and Isna Asharis) and the Hanafite Sunni Memons.

As elsewhere, conversion to Islam usually occurred among entire social groups, rather than individuals. In contrast to North India, where upper-class Muslims often claim descent from Afghan, Turkish or Persian invaders, most Gujarati Muslims freely acknowledge their Hindu origins. Thus the Khojas acknowledge that they were originally Lohanas (peasant-farmers) by caste: their name is a Gujarati form of Persian *khwaja* 'lord', itself a translation of the Lohana caste title, *thakur*. Among the Khojas the largest and best-known group are the Nizari Ismailis,[3] who trace the succession back to the seventh Imam, Ismail, and recognise the authority of a living and visible Imam, the Aga Khan. As hereditary Imam, the Aga Khan has absolute authority over his followers in religious and social matters; under his guidance they have moved in directions regarded as highly unorthodox by most other Muslims, for they are no longer required to perform *namaz* (daily prayers), to observe the Ramadan fast, or even to undertake the *hajj* (pilgrimage to Mecca).

Late in the eighteenth century some 2,000 Ismailis, then known only as Khojas, migrated from Kachchh and Saurashtra to Bombay, where they soon became wealthy, well educated and highly influential as merchants and shipowners. Before the Aga Khan's arrival in Bombay from Central Asia in 1843, the Khojas had acted outwardly as Sunnis (*taqiyya*), but when a lengthy dispute in the British-run

---

[2] These groups are referred to by the compound name "*vaniya-brahmin*" as the groups to be emulated.

[3] For a brief outline see the introduction to C. Shackle and Z. Moir, *Ismaili hymns from South Asia* (London: School of Oriental and African Studies, 1992).

courts was resolved in 1882, most agreed to accept his authority. The Khojas who refused to do this defected to the closely-related Isna Asharia sect, who are "Twelvers": that is, they assert that when the twelfth Imam disappeared in 873 CE he simply went into hiding and will remain concealed until he reappears to herald the Day of Judgment.

By contrast the Mustalian Ismailis, more commonly known as Bohras,[4] believe that although God's messenger remains hidden he is to be found at all times on earth, where he lives and dies as an ordinary man and names his own successor. The Bohras include several sub-groups, including the Daudis, the Suleimanis, the Alavis and the Atba-e-Malik. The Memons, who are Sunnis rather than Shi'as and before their conversion were also Lohanas, had their original homes in Sindh and Kachchh but were among the first groups to move to the new European trading centres, first in Surat and then in Bombay.

Given their active involvement in trade and other mercantile activities, each of these groups has established a substantial overseas diaspora. Ismaili[5] and Bohra merchants established themselves in East Africa during the colonial period, and from there members of these two communities have moved to Britain, the United States and Canada. By contrast the Memons' initial overseas bridgehead was in South Africa, where their descendants remain. Finally, many families from all three communities moved north to Karachi when Pakistan separated from India in 1947.

Caste amongst the Gujarati Hindus

If sectarian divisions amongst Gujarati Muslims seem intricate — and we have only been considering those of the merchants — then the caste divisions of the Hindu majority are more complex still. Indeed the local caste hierarchy has several notable features. Not only has it given rise to a set of sub-divisions even more elaborate than those seen elsewhere in India;[6] but at a politico-economic level the Vaishyas are dominant over the Kshatriyas and even in ritual hierar-

---

[4] Asghar Ali Engineer, *The Bohras* (New Delhi: Vikas, 1980).
[5] Although the Bohras are technically Ismaili Shi'as, the term "Ismaili" is used here in its popular usage to refer to followers of the Aga Khan.
[6] H.S. Morris, *The Indians in Uganda* (London: Weidenfeld and Nicolson, 1968), p. 45. The major caste structures in Gujarat are *varna* (class), *nat-jat* (*jati*, caste, an endogamous and commensal group) and *atak* (exogamous group within the *nat-jat*). After the *nat-jat*, *gam* (village) is important, followed by *kutumb* (family). See Rohit Barot, "*Varna, nat-jat* and *atak* amongst Kampala Hindu" (*New Community*, 1974, pp. 59–66)..

chy the nominal superiority of the Kshatriyas is questioned by many
Vaishya. Since traders and financiers are socially more prominent
than administrators, landowners and chiefs, it is not surprising that
business acumen is more highly valued and respected in Gujarat than
in any other area of India. Indeed Gujarati and Marwari Banias (the
latter from slightly further north) are commonly stereotyped as *the*
businessmen of India, in the subcontinent and beyond.

The Gujarati Banias[7] share many features, such as their hereditary
occupational specialisms, and so are best understood in this context
as a *caste-category*, for many distinct castes are so identified. Apart
from the considerable number of Jains, most are Vaishnavas, and
many too are followers of the Pushtimarg; as a group they have a
reputation for ritual purity, and for practising strict vegetarianism.
While only those *vaishya* groups with a long history of mercantile
activity are regarded as "true" Banias, several prominent trading
castes not of Bania origin virtually acquired Bania status by adopting
these forms of behaviour. For example, the Bhatias were originally
Rajputs, but having become successful traders in Saurashtra and
Kachchh, they adopted Vaishnavism and vegetarianism during the
fifteenth century. Their prosperity increased further when they migrated to Bombay from the early nineteenth century, where they were
soon involved in the Middle Eastern trade. Few now question their
status as fully incorporated Banias.

Two further closely connected castes, the Lohanas and the Bhansalis, have similar origins and have followed similar paths. They too
achieved considerable economic success in nineteenth-century Bombay, the Lohanas as grain-dealers and shopkeepers and the Bhansalis
as general traders. Most members of both groups are enthusiastic
Vaishnavas, and besides their involvement in Pushtimarg, many are
also devotees of the Lohana saint Jalaram.[8]

Another group who have risen rapidly in social status are the
Patidars (many of whose members use the surname Patel), who have
only gained their prominence during the twentieth century. They were
originally Kanbis, who form Gujarat's largest and most widespread
agricultural caste, emerging from among the Leuwa Kanbis of the
fertile Kheda district, where they form the politically and economically dominant caste. As Pocock[9] argues, the term "Patidar" is best
understood as an ideal — one must endeavour to *become* a true Patidar, and in pursuit of it the upwardly-mobile Kanbis not only began

---

[7] In Gujarati the term for a merchant is *vaniya*, but since the same word is pronounced
Bania both in Hindi and in Indian English, that spelling is used here.
[8] Rachel Dwyer, "Jalaram" in J.R. Hinnells (ed.), *Who's Who of World Religion*
(London: Macmillan, 1991).

to emulate the Banias' concern for ritual purity, but also became heavily involved in Vaishnava Bhakti. Today most Patidars are members either of the Pushtimarg or of the Swaminarayan movement, and many now accept their claim to be Banias.

Certain differences between the Patidars and other Banias remain. Although their entrepreneurial aspirations are as strong as those of all other Banias, they do not wear the sacred thread and, perhaps as a result of their own rapid rise in status, they remain acutely concerned about relative status amongst themselves, particularly over marriage. While Patidar villages are exogamous, groups of villages are also organised into "marriage circles" within which all marriages should, in principle, take place. However both the marriage circles themselves and the descent groups of which they are composed are ranked hierarchically, so that arranged marriages, invariably accompanied by large dowry payments, are the essence of Patidar status-competition.

The Sectarian Dimensions of Gujarati Hinduism

Although Gujarat experienced many centuries of Muslim rule, only about 10% of its population converted to Islam; apart from even smaller Jain and Zoroastrian minorities, the remainder are Hindu, practising a wide range of sectarian traditions. While the great majority follow one or another form of Vaishnavism, there is also a significant Shaivite minority, mostly Brahmins by caste. Amongst the Vaishnavas, a majority offer their devotions to Vishnu in the form of his incarnation as Rama, while the remainder worship him as Krishna. Within the last category are two major sects, Pushtimargis (often identified simply as "Vaishnavas") and the followers of Swaminarayan.

Although these two sects include only a minority of local Hindus, the Pushtimarg has had a far-reaching impact on Gujarati culture since its introduction to the area during the sixteenth century. So too has the Swaminarayan movement, even though its emergence has been more recent. Their impact has been large for two reasons: first because they have attracted the enthusiastic support of many wealthy merchants, and secondly because they have been vehicles for Sankritisation, especially those wishing to convert new-found wealth into higher social status. It is thus hardly surprising that both movements have been popular among overseas migrants, especially those in both East Africa and Britain.

[9] David Pocock, *Kanbi and Patidar* (Oxford: Clarendon Press, 1972).

The Pushtimarg

One of the most important developments in North Indian Hinduism during the sixteenth century was the rise of devotional *bhakti* movements within a strongly Vaishnava framework. Two outstanding leaders emerged: the Bengali Chaitanya (1485–1533), whose teachings had a profound influence throughout North and East India, and the Telugu Brahmin Vallabhacharya (1479–1531), who attracted a large following in North India and in Gujarat. The philosophical basis of Vallabhacharya's teaching is called *shuddhadvaita vedanta*, "pure non-dualism".[10] This holds that since there is nothing other than Brahman, all the multitudinous components of the existent world are real and part of Brahman, and are differentiated by having various aspects of their cosmic essence manifested or concealed. Since he followed the path of devotion (*bhaktimarg*) rather than knowledge (*jnanmarg*), Vallabhacharya urged his followers to experience the divine through the nine forms of devotional worship or *bhakti* — listening, singing, remembering, worshipping, serving, praising, servitude, companionship and finally self-surrender to Lord Krishna. Although Vallabhacharya made several lengthy pilgrimages around India, he lived as a householder rather than as a *sannyasi* or ascetic. Hence his sect contains no monastic order and attaches little importance to asceticism, austerity or meditation.

After his death, Vallabhacharya was succeeded by his elder son Gopinath (1512–33) and then by his younger son Vitthalnath (1516–48) who is regarded as having made a contribution second only to Vallabhacharya in the founding of the Pushtimarg. His major contributions were to the institutionalisation of the cult and the organisation of its leadership. He brought the sect firmly under family control by his teaching that Pushtimargis should take Vallabhacharya's male descendants as their gurus. Vitthalnath married twice, and six of his sons by his first wife and one by his second survived him. After his death the leadership of the movement was divided between them, and each became the founder of one of the seven major branches, known as *gaddis* or 'thrones'; these are still occupied by male descendants of Vallabhacharya, known as Maharajas.

Only the Maharajas may give initiation into the sect. Initiates should ideally be children aged between two and five, and in addition to being given the eight-syllable mantra *Shri Krishna sharanam mama*, 'Lord Krishna is my refuge', they put on a *tulsi* wood necklace. This is followed by a second ceremony around the age of twelve for

---

[10] See R.K. Barz, *The Bhakti Sect of Vallabhåcårya* (Faridabad: Thomson Press, 1976). For a detailed discussion of Vallabhacharya theology see J.D. Redington, *Vallabhåcårya on the Love Games of Krishna* (Delhi: Motilal Banarsidas, 1983).

boys, and just before marriage for girls. A *tulsi* leaf is placed in the hand of the candidate, who repeats the formula dedicating mind, body and wealth (*man, tan* and *dhan*) to Krishna.

Vitthalnath confirmed the authority of each of his sons shortly before his death by presenting them with an image of Krishna. In the Pushtimarg these are identified not just as a *murti* ('image') but as a *svarup* ('true representation') of the deity himself. For Pushtimargis, the most important of these *svarups* is that of Shri Nathji, who was discovered by Vallabhacharya on Govardhan hill in the Braj area; his status as a real form of Krishna rather than a mere representation of him was reinforced by his being housed in a *haveli* (mansion) rather than in a *mandir* (temple). Since 1669 he has been housed at Nathdwara near Udaipur in Rajasthan, which has become India's second richest centre of worship after Tirupati. Shri Nathji has been passed down by primogeniture through Vitthalnath's sons, and his custodian is regarded as Tilkayat or head of the sect. The *svarups* which Vitthalnath gave his sons are still treated with great respect by most Pushtimargis, although some of their leaders — notably H.H. Shyam Goswami — now argue that these were intended for private worship within the family and so make their initiates vow never to visit *havelis*.

However, most followers of the Pushtimarg regularly visit a *haveli* housing a *svarup* which has been worshipped by a male descendant of Vallabhacharya, since it is believed that the *svarup* absorbs and reflects the devotion it is given. The way in which the *svarup* is worshipped yet further underlines the distinctiveness of the Pushtimarg. Such worship is described not as *puja* "worship", but as *seva* "service". In their sectarian perspective *puja* is regarded as a selfish act carried out in hope of obtaining a reward.

Daily *seva* by Brahmin priests of a temple-based *svarup* is divided into eight periods: the deity is woken, served breakfast, dressed, seen off to his cow-herding duties, given his main meal, put to rest, woken, given a snack, served an evening meal, and finally put to sleep for the night. Devotees are permitted to enter the temple only during these periods of *darshan*, each of which lasts about fifteen minutes. Since the temple is considered Krishna's private dwelling, to enter it outside these appointed times would violate his privacy. Worship is congregational and is accompanied by music called *haveli-sangeet*, and once the *darshan* is complete, food which has been offered to the deity is returned to the worshippers as *prasad*. There are no age, caste or sex restrictions, although non-Hindus are not usually allowed into the presence of the major image.

As a focus for their domestic worship, devotees receive a specially consecrated *svarup* called "Thakorji" ("Lord") from one of the Maharajas. Such a *svarup* never loses its sacredness, so if a devotee finds it impossible to care for it properly, it must be returned to the Maharaja who may then give it to another devotee. Once the *svarup* has been made *pushti* ("fit to be worshipped"), service to it must never be delayed or interrupted: just as a child suffers if maternal nourishment and affection are withdrawn, so the *svarup* would suffer if similarly neglected. In each family the *svarup* is handed down from father to son, and worshipped by all household members. It is regarded as an active participant in the real world, so Pushtimargis are expected to focus their devotions overwhelmingly and exclusively on serving Krishna's real presence; one attends to all the various needs of the *svarup*, just as one would with one's own child: hence the *svarup* must be kept washed, fed and entertained, as well as being wrapped up in warm clothes during the winter. A simplified observance of the pattern of public worship is also followed.

Most families also perform *seva* either in a room specially set aside for it or, failing that, in the corner of a room used for other purposes, where the Thakorji as well as pictures of Shri Nathji, the founders of the sect and the family's own guru are kept. Their first act on rising is to repeat the deity's name, bathe him and serve him food, for nothing may be eaten without first having been offered to him. Another common feature of Vaishnava households is the presence of a *tulsi* (sacred basil) plant, which the women circumambulate and water before placing a lamp before it every morning and evening. Many other rituals are also observed, including a large number of fasts, while food restrictions demand not only a strictly vegetarian diet but also the avoidance of "strong" and over-stimulating food such as onions and garlic.

Recruitment to Pushtimarg

The Pushtimarg has always been patronised by the urban rich, be they princes and kings or wealthy merchants. It sought and received the patronage of three Mughal emperors as well as the personal devotion of the Maharanas of Mewar, but its recruitment has largely been restricted to the mercantile communities of Gujarat and Rajasthan (and hence the areas to which members of these castes have subsequently migrated) with a small following in Braj. Like his father, Vitthalnath went on a number of lengthy pilgrimages, several of which took him to Gujarat. A regular visitor to Ahmadabad and many of the region's other towns, he established the sect's major geographical centres in the area. As early as the seventeenth century, the sect had attracted many followers in Gujarat, especially amongst the mercantile communities whose members had enormously increased their wealth as a result of increasing overseas trade. Most were therefore Banias, Bhatias or Lohanas, although the movement also gained some followers among artisan groups such as the Patidars, Suthars (carpenters) and Luhars (blacksmiths), together with a few Brahmins, Jains and Muslims.

It seems that there was deliberate recruitment amongst the wealthier sections of the population during the sect's early history, since it brought prestige and offered a means of financing its expensive rituals. There are several reasons for the sect's appeal to wealthy merchants. While devotees must in principle dedicate all their possessions to God, it follows that, the larger one's offering (albeit symbolic), the greater Krishna's favour is likely to be. Secondly, the ritual complexity of *seva* allows the rich ample opportunity to display their wealth publicly, while also earning admiration and religious virtue. Finally, since merchants, in particular those who travel, are in constant contact with potential sources of pollution, the sect's concept of ridding the soul of impurities at initiation enabled traders to sustain their ritual purity despite such occupational hazards. These factors also appealed to the lower castes: sect membership enabled them to embark on a process of Sanskritisation without abandoning their polluting occupations.[11]

The Swaminarayan Movement

One of the last sects to arise from North India's sixteenth-century Vaishnava renaissance was the Swaminarayan movement. Founded by Sahajanand Swami (1781–1830), this sect has also been extremely influential, and it is estimated that around 5 million Gujaratis have affiliated themselves to it.[12] Swaminarayan devotees are drawn from a wide range of castes, including Brahmins, Banias, Sonis, Kanbis, Suthars, Rajputs and Luhars. Also the sect has recently made inroads in the worldwide Gujarati diaspora and is now expanding rapidly. Since it, too, is grounded in Vaishnava devotionalism, many followers of Swaminarayan regard the movement as a reformed version of the Pushtimarg. The two sects do indeed have much in common, and many families which follow the Pushtimarg include devotees of Swaminarayan. However, there are significant differences between the two sects, which can lead to antagonism.

The movement's founder Sahajanand Swami, later known as

[11] R.J. Cohen, "Sectarian Vaishnavism: the Vallabha Sampradāya", in P. Gaeffke and D. Utz (eds), *Identity and Division in Cults and Sects in South Asia* (Philadelphia: University of Pennsylvania Press, 1984).

[12] R.B. Williams, *A New Face of Hinduism: The Swaminarayan Religion* (Cambridge University Press, 1984).

Swaminarayan, was born near Ayodhya in what is now Uttar Pradesh. As a teacher he did not develop a new philosophical system, although he was influenced by Ramanuja, one of the most renowned of the early Vaishnava philosophers, and by his own teacher, Ramanand Swami. He urged his followers to give their primary devotional allegiance to Narayan or Krishna, but he also permitted worship of all the main Smarta deities such as Vishnu, Shiva, Ganpati, Parvati and Surya, unlike the Pushtimarg's exclusive devotion to Krishna. Swaminarayan made a number of pilgrimages to Gujarat, and eventually settled in Bhavnagar. There he came to be regarded as an incarnation of Lord Krishna himself, and during his lifetime six major temples were built in his honour at Ahmadabad, Bhuj, Vadtal, Junagadh, Dholera and Gadhada.

The sect's doctrine, ritual and organisation are established in three works — one in Gujarati and two in Sanskrit. Of these the *Shikshapatra*, written by Swaminarayan himself, is the most important; the *Vacanamrutam*, which is also the first work in modern Gujarati prose, is a collection of his sermons, while the *Satsangijivanam* is a hagiography by Shatananda Muni. In his teaching Swaminarayan emphasised social reforms and the need for charitable work, although broadly the sect can also be described as puritanical, with moral rectitude and the maintenance of ritual purity being accorded great importance. And since Swaminarayan was an ascetic who observed strict celibacy, the sect contains an ascetic order, and austerity is highly valued — again in sharp contrast to the Pushtimarg.

Followers of Swaminarayan are divided into four main classes: *brahmacharis* (ascetic priests) who may only be Brahmins; *sadhus* (ascetics, some of whom are also priests) who may not be from a lower caste than the Kanbi, and from whose ranks the *mahants* (chief ascetics) and *kotharis* (temple managers) are drawn; *palas* (temple servants); and finally the *satsangis* (laity), who make up the majority of the movement. Since the *satsangis* are not ascetics, they may mix with women and participate in ordinary commercial affairs, from which they are expected to contribute an annual tithe of 10–20% of their income.

Although Swaminarayan was an unmarried ascetic who headed the movement during his own lifetime, he adopted one son of each of his two brothers shortly before his death. By devolving his spiritual authority within his own family, he thus ensured that a hereditary line of householder-*acharyas* would succeed him and established a household and an ascetic division of the sect. He also laid the foundation for the movement to be split into two "dioceses": one based in Ahmadabad, covering the area north of a line between Calcutta, Dwarka, Vadodara and Rajkot, while the second is based in Vadtal and covers the entire area south of this line. Hence the Vadtal "diocese" includes both the Junagadh temple and the Swaminarayan *gurukul*, where the main image of Lakshmi-Narayan is to be found.

There have been further schisms within the sect, mostly around the question of whether the ascetics, rather than the descendants of Swaminarayan, should lead the sect. One of the most important of these break-away movements is the Akshar Purushottam Sanstha, a large and rapidly growing group now over one million strong. It split away from Vadtal in 1906, under the leadership of an ascetic called Shastri Maharaja, and its current leader is Pramukh Swami, a Patidar from Chansad in Vadodara District. Because of the stress on asceticism, leadership in the Sanstha is much more a matter of spiritual merit than hereditary descent. As a result its leaders have been drawn from a wide range of castes, which has undoubtedly contributed to its popularity. In a similar fashion, although status-maintaining ritual purity remains important, the Sanstha accepts members of all castes (excluding Dalits, formerly called 'Untouchables') as *sadhus*, not restricting recruitment to this role solely to Brahmins, as do the other Swaminarayan sects. Sex segregation is rigorously imposed: ascetics have no contact whatsoever with female devotees, and letters from women have to be read out to them by a member of the laity. Nevertheless, Pramukh Swami and the other ascetics are active as teachers, and travel regularly overseas, maintaining close links with Gujarat and the lay community, attracting many wealthy followers.

Whatever their precise sectarian affiliation, temple worship is of great importance to followers of Swaminarayan, of whom many spend Saturday and Sunday evenings at the temple. Here the basic rituals are similar to those followed in the Pushtimarg — since Swaminarayan prescribed the same eight *darshan* periods laid down by Vitthalnath — but these are supplemented by talks and discussions, and meals are provided. Many followers also keep Thakorji at home, along with an image of Swaminarayan and perhaps of their own personal guru. Many of the images and symbols in these domestic shrines are virtually identical to those used by the Pushtimargis, and likewise all food is first offered to the deity; however, ritual care rarely approaches the degree of elaboration found in Pushtimarg.

The Followers of Swaminarayan

Since its founding at the beginning of the nineteenth century, the Swaminarayan movement has expanded rapidly, both in Gujarat and even more in the overseas Gujarati communities of East Africa, Britain and North America. It has tended to attract a much higher proportion of devotees from amongst the non-Bania castes than has the Pushtimarg, such as the Kadwa and Leuwa Kanbis, Rajputs, Kolis and Kathis in both Saurashtra and Gujarat proper. Although the movement accepts recruits from all castes, including the Untouch-ables, this does not mean that caste distinctions are wholly irrelevant within it. Most are observed, and indeed there is still a separate shrine for Untouchables at Chhani near Vadodara. In the Akshar Purushot-tam Sanstha, however, Pramukh Swami has taken steps to avoid these distinctions by giving full initiation to both tribals and Untouchables. Hence, despite opening its membership to castes which are clearly outside the Bania élite, the movement's strong commitment to as-ceticism and its careful maintenance of the rules of ritual purity have ensured that this has not been achieved at the cost of a lowered status. Indeed in popular perception the Swaminarayan movement is a highly prestigious social institution, so that joining it is likely to be associated with upward social mobility.

The Patidars (otherwise known as the Leuwa Patels) provide a clear example of just such a process, since many members of this caste have risen to greater prominence after joining the sect. It is not hard to see why. First, its puritanical ideals offer an excellent foun-dation for business success, not least because the adoption of a simple lifestyle facilitates the accumulation of wealth. In addition, member-ship of the Swaminarayan movement also brings direct social ad-vantages, for as well as the religious prestige arising from the sect's reputation for purity, it is often suggested that the sect operates like the Freemasons by providing a forum for establishing and providing a guarantee for business contacts. If Swaminarayan is described as a sect of emerging commercial farmers and capitalist entrepreneurs,[13] most of its members take that appellation as a compliment.

But it is not just the quest for prestige and prosperity which lies behind the movement's rapid increase in membership, for a large number of converts have also been drawn in as a result of visits to the villages by the movement's leaders, and of the many social programmes they have set up. Swaminarayan himself pioneered the sect's work in this sphere, and even today devotees often point to building projects on which he himself laboured. Impressive and well-maintained temples and guest-houses constructed in this way can be seen throughout Gujarat, as constant reminders of the movement's affluence and prestige. In 1992, the Akshar Purushottam Sanstha built an impressive new temple in Gandhinagar and provided a state-of-the-art audio-visual display to accompany it. Through widespread

[13] D. Hardiman, "Class base of Swaminarayan sect", *Economic and Political Weekly*, 10 Sept. 1988.

press coverage and word of mouth, this brought home the prestige of the sect to a wide audience.

Settlement in East Africa

Merchants of Gujarati origin have traded in spices, ivory and textiles in East Africa for almost 2,000 years. Although few of them took up permanent residence until quite recently, these traders were a routine feature of the prosperous coastal cities founded by the Arabs from the seventh century onwards. Their prosperity began to be undermined when the Portuguese took control of the trade routes across the Indian Ocean during the sixteenth century; and when advances in navigation allowed much longer ocean passages and the East African cities ceased to be important ports of call, they declined still further. They revived somewhat early in the nineteenth century when the Sultan of Muscat moved his capital from Oman to Zanzibar, which soon became a major slave market. Finally the British arrived in the mid-nineteenth century, ostensibly to suppress slavery, and soon began to trade in rubber and ivory, gradually extending their operations into the East African interior.

The increase in trade, together with the building of a railway from Mombasa to Uganda between 1896 and 1931, led to the recruitment of over 30,000 indentured labourers from India, mostly Punjabis, to build the railway, but of these only about a quarter stayed on to help run it. More significant from the Gujarati point of view, however, were the commercial opportunities opening up, both in the remote interior and in the new cities being built along the railway such as Nairobi, Nakuru and Kisumu in Kenya, and Kampala, Jinja and Tororo in Uganda.

By 1901, 35,000 Indians were living in Britain's East African protectorates, of whom some 80% were Gujaratis, three-quarters of those being Hindus while the rest were mostly Ismaili Muslims.[14] As the local economy expanded, there was a shortage of skilled craftsmen, clerks and, above all, small traders to distribute manufactured goods imported by the major British trading houses among the African population. Further immigration from South Asia seemed an ideal means of filling this gap. Meanwhile the pressure to emigrate was being fuelled by conditions in Gujarat. Plague struck in 1899–1902 and again in 1916–18, an influenza epidemic raged in 1918–19, and there was famine (1899–1900). There were also the perennial problems of land shortage and unemployment, exacerbated by the

---

[14] Hugh Tinker, *The Banyan Tree: Overseas Emigrants from India, Pakistan and Bangladesh* (Oxford University Press, 1977).

decline in the local textile industry in the face of competition from the Lancashire mills. The geographical proximity of East Africa, and its longstanding links with Gujarat, caused the volume of emigration to increase, and by 1950 over 190,000 people of Indian origin were living in Kenya, Uganda, Tanganyika and Zanzibar.

By then a tripartite form of social stratification had emerged throughout the region. Europeans ran the administration and practised large-scale agriculture, the Indians ran the cotton, sugar and clove industries, and controlled almost all the small-scale trade and much at a higher level too, while most of the Africans were firmly at the bottom of the pile, scraping a living either as subsistence farmers or as unskilled labourers. But despite their exclusion from the upper echelons of the East African social order, many Indian settlers had begun to put down firm roots in the territory. While in the past most migrants had not only been born and educated in India, but had returned there to get married and aimed to retire there once their sons were old enough to take over the business, all this changed during the Second World War. Since it was virtually impossible to travel back to India, children began to be educated through to secondary level in East Africa rather than being sent back to India, and marriages were also arranged within the settlement, provided always that a spouse of the right caste could be found.

While the basic features of the caste system were maintained in this as in many other spheres, the full caste hierarchy was by no means fully re-established in East Africa. Not only did the precise details of *jati*-ranking vary in the different areas from which they came, but migrants were drawn from only a small number of castes — most were either merchants, peasant-farmers or artisans. Nor did many of them continue to practise their traditional occupations: the vast majority ran their own businesses. All this led to fragmentation, and only when the Ismaili Muslims emerged as an integrated group, capable of exercising social and political power on behalf of its members, did the Hindus first appreciate the benefits of closer unity. Then they, too, organised themselves, and a large number of caste and sectarian communities gradually "crystallised".[15]

Citizenship

When India and Pakistan gained Independence in 1947, their populations acquired separate nationalities in their own right, though still within the broad framework of Commonwealth citizenship. The position of South Asian settlers in East Africa was different, since they

[15] H.S. Morris, *op. cit.*

remained direct subjects of the Crown and therefore entitled to British passports. Thus although they were also entitled to apply for Indian citizenship on grounds of descent, the Government of India advised all East African Asians to take British rather than Indian citizenship, and to identify not with India but with Africa.[16] At the same time India gave strong support to African aspirations for greater economic and political advance, while tending to view the activities of the Asians as economically exploitative.

Most of the Indian migrants, however, hoped to stay in Africa permanently. Certainly, many older people still returned to India once they retired, but the attitudes of the younger generation were different. They had achieved considerable prosperity in East Africa, and enjoyed living there. For them Britain appeared an over-permissive society, while India was perceived as economically backward: they perceived themselves afresh as "East African Asians".

As the East African territories began to win independence in the early 1960s, the whole situation changed. The new governments' policies of "Africanisation" made the East African Asians' position increasingly untenable: they realised that they would have to look to a future elsewhere. But where would that be? Some returned to India; others, especially those with professional qualifications, left for North America; but the vast majority concluded that their best option was to move to Britain. Almost all were entitled to British travel documents of one kind or another. Anyone born in India before August 1947 was entitled to British citizenship, as were those born in most of Kenya, although those born in the coastal strip which formed the Kenya Protectorate and anywhere in the Uganda Protectorate were technically not British citizens but British-protected persons. In the past such details had mattered little, since travel documents were issued freely, and those (relatively few) who wished to use them to enter Britain had few if any difficulties.

However, as the volume of direct migration from India and Pakistan increased, so did hostility to their arrival, with the result that ever stricter immigration controls were introduced by the British government. At first these applied only to citizens of other Commonwealth countries, such as India and Pakistan, but as the pressures towards Africanisation built up, and with it an awareness that several hundred thousand British-passport-holding East African Asians might consequently seek to exercise their right to enter Britain, the ultimate indignity took place. The British passport itself was devalued, above all by the introduction of the concept of partiality in the 1968 Im-

---

[16] Hugh Tinker, *Separate and Unequal: India and Indians in the British Commonwealth 1920–1950* (London: C. Hurst, 1975).

migration Act. Henceforth only British "patrials" (i.e. those with a parent or grandparent who had actually been born within the British Isles) were fully British, and so entitled to enter the country without hindrance; but the Act stripped those who were not patrials, i.e. most East African Asians, of all such rights, despite their apparently valid passports. The aim was clear: to prevent this category of British passport-holders from exercising their right to settle in Britain.

This change had dire consequences for East African Asians who thereby became stateless. They were now equally unwelcome (though for widely differing reasons) in their country of residence, their country of ancestry *and* the country which issued their passports. However in the longer run Britain found it impossible to avoid its responsibilities under international law, for these people were indubitably holders of British passports. Eventually, almost all who so wished were permitted to enter Britain.

Gujarati Settlement in Britain

Thus, it is hardly surprising that out of around half a million Gujaratis in Britain, about half have strong East African connections. At some levels there are big differences between the direct migrants and those who came by way of East Africa: broadly the latter tend to be better educated, have greater fluency in English, be more likely to come from a mercantile background and, except for refugees from Uganda, to have arrived in Britain with at least some capital to found new businesses. Yet although most East African Gujaratis have rapidly achieved at least moderate prosperity since arriving in Britain (a few have prospered greatly), and although they tend to be more socially progressive than their direct-migrant peers, especially over issues of gender and marriage, in religion they tend towards a village-like conservatism, even if they have never been to India.

One must not overestimate the difference between the once- and twice-migrants. Members of both groups have similar and often identical regional, caste and sectarian origins in Gujarat, and it is this, rather than the contingencies of residence at one point or another in the diaspora, that is the principal foundation of their most important social networks. So even though the East Africans may have arrived in Britain with rather more sophisticated survival skills than their direct-migrant peers, there is no reason why members of the latter group should not acquire exactly the same skills themselves. Most have indeed already done so.

There have, however, been substantial differences between the two groups' patterns of settlement. Thus while most of the East Africans arrived in Britain after the traumas of Africanisation in the late 1960s and early '70s, and came as complete families including all ages from tiny children to elderly grandparents, the direct migrants followed the same course as those described in most other chapters in this book. The pioneers, virtually all male, arrived during the early 1950s; numbers increased rapidly until the early '60s, when immigration controls became a major obstacle to further settlement. Finally the settlement began to be consolidated through the reunion of families, although the Gujaratis moved more swiftly than many other South Asians: even for the direct migrants, family reunion was largely complete by the early 1970s.

At first, most Gujarati migrants, like other South Asians, took low-paid jobs in industries which were acutely short of labour. As in other groups, village-kin ties were often used to gain access to jobs, and this led to their becoming heavily concentrated in certain parts of North London, in the Midlands (especially in Leicester), and rather less in northern cities such as Leeds, Bradford and Preston, patterns which have continued to this day.

From the outset, many Gujarati settlers were keen to set up their own businesses. Thus some of the earliest entrepreneurs set up as grocers, supplying their fellow migrants with rice, flour, vegetables and spices, but always using their village-kin ties to get the enterprise off the ground.[17] Since then Gujarati businesses have flourished, and by no means restricted themselves to the ethnic market. Many of the proverbial corner-shops, in particular the confectioners/newsagents/ tobacconists, are now run by once-migrant Gujarati families, while the well-honed mercantile and commercial skills of the East Africans have often allowed them to be even more successful. One of the most successful retailers is Nareshbhai Patel, a prominent member of the Swaminarayan sect, who started by washing dishes and is now chairman of both Europa Foods and Colorama Photographic Laboratories. While business and self-employment are still highly regarded within the community, many younger Gujaratis are now entering the professions, particularly medicine and pharmacy, the law, accountancy, banking and management.

There can be little doubt that the Gujaratis now make up the most prosperous part of Britain's South Asian population, and there are said to be over 100 Gujarati millionaires living in Britain.

Caste divisions among Gujaratis in Britain

As we have seen above, the Gujarati social order is highly differentiated by caste, and the same is true of the Gujarati settlement in

---

[17] R. Desai, *Indian Immigrants in Britain* (Oxford University Press, 1963).

Britain. Castes also vary greatly in size. In Britain, the Patidars, who number around 100,000 are the largest group by far. Most have the surname Patel, although Desai and Amin are used by certain sub-groups. While about half of Britain's Patidars came by way of East Africa and the other half directly from India, they differ from most other Gujarati communities in that they have not established a single national caste organisation, despite being very conscious of their common Patidar identity. Their *jati* contains a number of sub-divisions, the most important being the marriage circles; at this level they are well organised, maintaining associations and directories, to facilitate amongst other things the operation of their marriage system, complete with its complex hierarchy of ranked villages.[18] Even though firmly rooted overseas, many Patidar families still keep strong links with their villages of origin through these marriage circles. Though they may spend little time in their ancestral villages, they may nevertheless renew and restore those links by choosing brides from them, and by giving cash donations for charitable projects, which sustain the family's prestige.

The next largest community are the Lohanas, who are probably between 30,000 and 35,000 strong, with more than two-thirds in North London and about a quarter in Leicester. Nearly all are of Saurashtran origin, and almost all are twice-migrants — nearly every family has a link with East, Central or even South Africa.[19] While the Lohanas thus have weaker ties with the subcontinent than the Patidars (they no longer look for brides in India), they nevertheless remain very conscious of their status as true Banias, and maintain a particularly strong caste association. They are virtually all Vaishnavas, and al-though strong sectarian allegiances are uncommon, they include a number of followers of the Pushtimarg as well as of Jalaram, a specifically Lohana saint. Other high-caste groups include a small number of Soni Jati Banias (goldsmiths), several hundred Modh Bania families, some Bhatia families and a few hundred Brahmins. Of these communities some are followers of the Pushtimarg or Swaminarayan, while others are Shaivites.

There are smaller numbers of non-mercantile castes, including several thousand Kanbis (agricultural labourers, peasant farmers) of various sub-castes, the most numerous being the Kadva Kanbi Patels of Surat District[20] and the Leuwa Kanbi Patels from Bhuj (Kachchh),

---

[18] H. Tambs-Lyche, *London Patidars: A Study in Urban Ethnicity* (London: Routledge, 1980) and M. Michaelson, "Domestic Hinduism in a Gujarati Trading Caste" in R. Burghart (ed.), *Hinduism in Great Britain* (London: Tavistock, 1979).

[19] Michaelson, *op. cit.*, p. 33.

[20] M. Michaelson, "The Relevance of Caste among East African Gujaratis in Britain", *New Community*, 7, 3 (1979), pp. 350–60.

who are followers of the Maninagar branch of the Swaminarayan movement. The Prajapatis (see Warrier's chapter, below), who were traditionally potters, have become closely linked with two castes of carpenters, the Mistrys and the Suthars. In Bradford the Shri Prajapati Association has its own temple, which is also used by Hindus of many other castes. It appears that while most Prajapatis are non-sectarian, many Mistrys are followers of the Pushtimarg and Swaminarayan. Finally there are a number of low-caste groups such as the Mandhata Patels, who were originally Kolis (fishermen and peasants) from Surat District, as well as a significant number of Mochis, traditionally leather-workers (see Knott's chapter, below). By the early twentieth century, some Mochis had become members of the Swaminarayan sect.

Political and Politico-religious Links

While the political sympathies of Gujaratis, like the majority of other migrants, were at first strongly in favour of the Labour Party, many of the more affluent settlers have recently become enthusiastic supporters of the Conservatives, by whom they have been equally actively cultivated. In 1991 John Major marked his first year in office as Prime Minister by hosting a dinner attended entirely by Asians, where the guest-list included the film star Amitabh Bachchan and prominent businessmen such as the Hinduja brothers. However, involvement in British politics in no way precludes involvement in Indian, and particularly Gujarati, politics. Many settlers sustain links with Indian political parties, especially the Hindu revivalist Bharatiya Janata Party.

In Britain, one of the largest and most active revivalist organisations is the Vishva Hindu Parishad, or World Hindu Union. Founded in India in 1964, the VHP is now active in eighty countries and has close links with temples and religious groups throughout Britain. VHP members already provide support and information at many community functions, and the long-term aim of the organisation is to articulate the collective views of Hindus in Britain, in much the same way as the Board of Deputies represents the Jewish community. Indeed it has already moved a considerable way in that direction, as was evident at the Virat Hindu Sammelan (Great Hindu Congress) which it organised in 1989. Drawing together all Britain's major Hindu organisations, the meeting — held in the "new town" of Milton Keynes — was attended by at least 55,000 people.

In organising such a large function, care was taken to draw in the widest possible range of religious groups. Hence the leaders of all the most important local Gujarati sects shared the stage, with the exception of Pramukh Swami of the Akshar Purushottam Sanstha: though invited to attend as chief guest, it was clear that he would have to turn down the honour since women would be present. However the meeting had an equally specific political agenda. Not only did leaders of the VHP and the BJP play an important part in the meeting, but its central theme was Hindu unity — in India quite as much as in Britain. So, for example, the printed programme was dedicated to Dr Hegdewar, founder of the militantly revivalist Rashtriya Swaymsevak Sangh (RSS), and included articles supporting a *Hindutva* ("Hindu-ness") perspective on Indian politics, and the building of a Ram Janmabhoomi temple in Ayodhya on the spot then still occupied by the Babri Masjid; the programme included messages of support from Buckingham Palace, Lambeth Palace (seat of the Archbishop of Canterbury) and 10 Downing Street.

Even so, the precise nature of the links between politico-religious groups such as the VHP, the BJP, the RSS and their allies, on the one hand, and the Vaishnava sects on the other is far from clear. While the Pushtimarg is organised in such a way that it provides few opportunities for close links with such organisations, the Swaminarayan Hindu Mission in Neasden appears to follow the VHP programme closely, although overt connections with the party are invariably denied. Even so, the organisation provides a platform for the VHP, helping both the sale of its propaganda and its efforts to raise funds. Moreover Pramukh Swami himself has made clear his enthusiasm for the building of a temple in Ayodhya.

Sect

This section explores the role of sect among British Gujaratis, concentrating on the Swaminarayan movement and the Pushtimarg. The aim is to show how they have adapted to a British context, to contrast the role which caste and sect play in the lives of devotees and to consider how their current status and organisation are likely to affect their future development.

Although many British Gujaratis have never been to India, and so have had all their sacred rituals performed in either Britain or East Africa, many still hope to return there to scatter the funeral ashes of their parents or spouses, have their marriages performed, have *darshan* of their guru or go on pilgrimage. In the midst of this, both sects have made a number of adaptations to life in Britain, so although still closely focused on India they have developed a new set of relationships with their sacred land.

In the Pushtimarg the Maharajas, male descendants of Vallabhacharya, play a crucial role, since they are regarded as gurus by their devotees. Yet although a few Goswamis make regular visits to Britain, where their week-long performances of readings and preaching from the sacred texts (usually the *Bhagavata Purana*) attract large congregations, only one Pushtimarg Maharaja is resident in Britain at the time of writing. But given that the sect has no ascetic order, and that priestly rituals are of little significance, it is around the family's own specific Maharaja that Pushtimarg religious practice tends to focus. As a result, regular visits to India have become an inescapable necessity for the most committed devotees, so much so that all the most important aspects of the sect's religious practice still tend to be focused on India and to occur there.

As we have seen, Pushtimarg worship in India is performed mainly on a caste and family basis, with paramount emphasis on the development of an intense, immediate and intimate relationship between the devotee and the object of his or her own devotions. Devotees enjoy communal worship of their *svarup* in a *haveli*, and can take great aesthetic pleasure in music, painting and all the other arts that are deployed in that context. In Britain, however, all this is much attenuated, for none of the *havelis* so far established yet enjoys a fully orthodox status. In Leicester, for example, the *haveli* contains only pictures and not a *svarup*, and while the one in Leyton (East London) does house a consecrated *svarup*, there is some doubt about its status. It was installed by Goswami Indirabetiji, an important figure to many Pushtimargis since she is a direct descendant of Vallabhacharya, but as a woman, she is considered by many of the more orthodox followers of Pushtimarg to have no right to perform the ceremony of consecration.

These *havelis* do not regard the organisation of cultural or youth events as any part of their role, nor are they seen as prestigious centres for religious practice by other Hindus: indeed their devotional styles differ so much from those followed by others that their *havelis* are rarely visited by non-sectarian Hindus. Nor are they the centre of the sect's most active religious practices, for among themselves communal worship is more likely to consist of *satsang* (meetings of devotees who gather to sing and pray together) in private houses. In Leicester a typical group of this kind meets on a Friday night; the *satsang* begins by reading texts of the sect, goes on to discuss them, and then finally and at some length moves on to singing devotional songs. Besides organising visits to pilgrimage sites associated with the sect in India, such groups are also the basis of a number of local and national Pushtimargi associations.

For the younger generation a major obstacle to their wholehearted participation in sectarian activities is that most of its ritual proceedings are conducted in Sanskrit and Braj Bhasha (a dialect of Hindi). The

Sanskrit is usually glossed in Hindi or Gujarati, but even so many young people cannot read either of these scripts, while Braj Bhasha and even Gujarati songs often remain incomprehensible to the younger generation because of their extensive use of an archaic and religiously specialised vocabulary. Hence their only access to the tradition and its texts is through listening to their oral performance. But since their opportunity to do so is largely confined to domestic shrines, and since their problems of comprehension are exacerbated by linguistic difficulties, many have little or no understanding either of the liturgy or the songs. Nor are there any other easily accessible sources of information about Pushtimarg for those who are unable to read either Gujarati or Hindi. Indeed since young people know so little of the tradition into which they were born, the very survival of Pushtimarg in Britain may be endangered unless long-term action is taken soon.

By contrast the Swaminarayan movement has been able to adapt to local conditions much more positively, and to compromise its essential beliefs and practices much less than the Pushtimarg — as it also did in East Africa. One great advantage is that followers are expected to pay the movement a tithe (nominally of 10–20%) on their income; and although many hand over much less, the obligation nevertheless generates a substantial cash-flow. Not only have local Swaminarayan groups found it easy to purchase and convert redundant old buildings into places of worship, but the sect was also responsible for the erection in Willesden (North-west London) of the first purpose-built temple in Britain. Among other things this has led the followers of the Swaminarayan Hindu Mission, who currently meet in a school in nearby Neasden, to embark on plans to build an enormous temple of their own.

The Swaminarayan Hindu Mission is indeed extremely active. Its congregation meets every weekend, with the largest gathering on Sunday evenings, when food is provided for everyone after all the talks and *bhajans* have been completed. Should Pramukh Swami be visiting London, thousands will come to hear his sermons. Swaminarayan is now very much a global movement, so the sect's leaders are constantly on the move between India and every part of the Gujarati diaspora, while celebrations of the leaders' birthdays, as well as pilgrimages to places associated with Swaminarayan, draw the laity constantly back to Gujarat. In contrast to Pushtimarg, ascetics play an important role in the Swaminarayan movement, and although they currently receive their training in Gujarat, plans are afoot to establish the ascetic order in Britain, thus yet further strengthening the movement's local roots. Thus while the sect maintains close links with Gujarat, it delegates a great deal of authority to local leaders.

Nevertheless the movement has also sustained a tight organisational structure amongst the laity, which draws members into a plethora of sub-groups such as the women's group, and a variety of specialist committees. Since all these ultimately report back to the leaders in India, the sect has developed a tight framework of responsibility and cooperation into which to draw its members.

It also succeeds in making an effective appeal right across the generations. Thus while proceedings in the temple are enthusiastically supported both by the very young and the old — as is to be expected — there is also a strikingly large attendance amongst those aged between 18 and 30. As members of the sect's youth group, these are likely to be the sect's future organisers. In their regular meetings they are already acquiring administrative skills by organising anti-smoking and anti-drinking campaigns amongst the adults, as well as competitive recitations of songs and sectarian texts by the children. These young adult activists are highly regarded within the sect and are thus given great encouragement.

Swaminarayan liturgical and devotional practices are much more accessible linguistically than are those of the Pushtimarg. English translations of many of the movement's most important texts are freely available, but in any case the language of both the liturgy and the texts is straightforward modern Gujarati, rather than classical Sanskrit or archaic Braj; not only does this make it relatively accessible to the younger generation, but the movement actively encourages young people to improve their linguistic competence by attending the Gujarati classes which are provided at most temples. In the wider scene, the Mission was responsible for setting up Britain's first Hindu primary school, and it was planned to open a secondary school in the autumn of 1993. However their attitudes to education are far from parochial: in most subjects the syllabus will follow the National Curriculum although, as might be expected, religious instruction will be concerned mainly (although not exclusively) with the teachings of Swaminarayan.

The Swaminarayan movement is also active and visible in the Gujarati community at large. Its members played a pivotal role in the Virat Hindu Sammelan in 1989, and they arranged the Swaminarayan Cultural Festival of India held in Alexandra Palace in 1985. The sect's leaders are constantly on the move around the global Gujarati diaspora, making frequent visits to Britain. When Pramukh Swami himself makes a visit, he travels extensively to meet his followers, and puts in an appearance at a large number of non-sectarian Hindu functions, as long as his strict rules about avoiding the proximity of women are comprehensively observed. Details of Pramukh Swami's visits are publicised weeks in advance in the local Gujarati press, which also provides detailed coverage of his speeches and other activities.

As a result the Swaminarayan movement attracts an ever-larger membership, and draws in converts from other Gujarati communities, particularly from amongst the Oshwal Jains. This process of conversion probably began in East Africa, where the movement has long been regarded as highly prestigious, and has clearly continued in Britain. The broad reasons for the movement's success are not hard to identify. First, its beliefs and practices are closely congruent with Hindu orthodoxy, although with a rather firmer emphasis on asceticism and moral purity. Its temples provide an exclusively Gujarati meeting place, where women are encouraged to wear traditional clothes, Gujarati food is provided and Gujarati is the language of both devotion and communication. Thirdly, and perhaps most important of all, it has been able to show flexibility without appearing to compromise either its religious or its ethical principles. Indeed its success has been so great that the Swaminarayan movement has come to represent in Britain the dominant form of Gujarati Vaishnavism — and even of Hinduism.

GUJARATI PRAJAPATIS IN LONDON

FAMILY ROLES AND SOCIABILITY NETWORKS

Shrikala Warrier

This chapter seeks a narrow focus in two complementary ways: first, it examines the experiences of a specific caste group — Hindu Gujarati Prajapatis;[1] and secondly it highlights the active roles played by Prajapati women in the whole process of migration and resettlement. More specifically still, it aims to explore the structure of family roles and sociability networks amongst those settled in London. Here we have to examine the consequences of the large-scale entry of women into paid employment on the ideology of family and kinship, and the impact of this post-migration development both on patterns of relationships within the family and on the wider networks of kinship and friendship.

Until recently, most studies of South Asian communities in Britain viewed the world from a male perspective.[2] Great emphasis was placed on the force and continuity of structures of patriarchal authority, and on the maintenance of traditional patterns of reciprocity between male-dominated kin groups. In consequence, women have often been presented as occupying essentially subordinate positions in the social and domestic order. Given the assumption that South Asian women are — and always have been — a muted group, a "social problem" perspective has almost always been adopted in analyses of their behaviour. This pathologising tendency is particularly striking whenever the new roles and strategies devised by such women have led them either to challenge, or to re-negotiate traditional conventions. This account, by focusing on women as *active participants* in the migration-settlement process, seeks to restore women to their proper place at the centre of family life.

---

[1] This chapter draws on fieldwork in 1980–5 for a Ph.D. thesis entitled "Family Roles and Sociability Networks in a Gujarati Community in London", submitted to the University of London.
[2] Notable exceptions to this tendency can be found in the work of V. Saifullah Khan, "Purdah in the British Situation" in Barker and Allen (eds), *Dependence and Exploitation in Work and Marriage* (London: Longman, 1976), A. Wilson, *Finding a Voice* (London: Virago, 1978) and P. Werbner, *The Migration Process* (London: Berg, 1991).

Prajapatis in their Gujarati Context

While large and prosperous landowning and trading castes such as
the Patidars, Lohanas and Oswals have received much attention in
anthropological accounts of Gujarati society, the Prajapati *jati* —
whose members' traditional occupation was as *kumbhars* or potters
— has been almost overlooked. Given the specialist nature of their
traditional occupation, Prajapatis form only a small proportion of the
population of rural Gujarat. Theirs is also a very scattered community,
for although a few Prajapati families can be found in most villages
in the region, in none do they cluster together to form a numerically
significant proportion of the local population. And most crucial for
their social status, in the pre-migration period few, if any, Prajapatis
owned and cultivated arable land.

Like the providers of other specialist craft services, the Prajapatis
occupied a lowly position in the caste hierarchy, since they owned
no land and lacked the wealth of the more successful trading castes.
However, theirs was a position of solid respectability — their specialist occupation was in no sense polluting. Like many other castes
in a similar position, the Prajapatis assert that their "real" status is
much higher than that to which they are usually ascribed. Numerous
myths are cited to validate this claim, one of the most common being
that they, like most other artisan castes, had once been princely
Kshatriyas but were forced to change their occupations — and so
hide their true caste affiliation — to escape the vengeful wrath of the
sage Parasurama.[3] An alternative explanation invokes the glories of
the distant epic past, referring to a legend related in the *Brahmavaivar-
ta Purana*, whereby potters are the descendants of one of the nine
illegitimate sons of Viswakarma, Architect of the Universe on behalf
of Lord Brahma himself.

Within the structure of the village economy, Prajapati craftsmen
traditionally supplied the earthenware pots which everyone needed
for cooking and eating, as well as for storing water and grain; and as
elsewhere in India the Prajapatis played a crucial ritual role in all
higher-caste life-cycle ceremonies, being responsible for the provision of ritually pure pots.[4] Like all other craft specialists, these roles

---

[3] According to a legend with wide currency in India, the sage Parasurama, regarded
as the sixth *avatar* of Lord Vishnu, vowed to kill all Kshatriyas to avenge the death
of his father.

[4] A column of seven pots of diminishing size is arranged in each of the four corners
of the wedding *mandap*, the platform on which the rites are solemnized. It was also
customary for the female members of the bride's family to perform *puja* at the potter's
wheel before the start of the wedding rituals. In reward for his involvement, the potter
usually received a gift worth much more than the pots he supplied. The only pot

were fulfilled in the context of a hereditary *jajmani* relationship: in return for the services they rendered, their patrons rewarded them with a small share of their crop after each harvest. Some were provided with small plots of land to cultivate on their own account.

As Pocock has pointed out, potters are the one artisan group for whose services there has been no increase in demand as their patrons grow more wealthy. As rural Gujarat has grown more affluent, vessels made of brass and other metals have become more widely available for both cooking and storage. Hence apart from what is required for ritual purposes, there has been a sharp decline in the demand for kiln-fired pottery. Even so, many Prajapatis have been able to use their skills to find new avenues to prosperity — for example, by applying their knowledge of kiln-baking to the manufacture of bricks and tiles. However they have invariably sold these products to their customers strictly for cash, so extracting themselves from the hierarchical implications of the *jajmani* system. More recently still, many have moved into such trades as carpentry and stonemasonry, both of which are proving quite lucrative in the contemporary economy.

In Gujarat as elsewhere in India, caste status is largely determined by the roles of its male members in the division of labour — and in this case pottery, brick-making and carpentry are all regarded as essentially male occupations. The ability to keep women in seclusion and so remove them from economic activity is a further indicator of rank within high-status groups. However, this does not hold lower down the caste hierarchy, where women regularly participate in productive processes both inside and outside the immediate domestic economy.

Prajapati women were no exception. Besides their immediate domestic tasks they were responsible for bringing suitable clay from outlying areas of the village, for firing the kilns, and for selling the finished products. Some women from poorer Prajapati families supplemented household income by working as domestic servants or even as agricultural labourers for more affluent — and invariably higher-caste — families. Moreover, since pottery ceased to provide a viable source of income, it has above all been Prajapati women who have kept the caste's traditional craft skills alive.

The Prajapatis are endogamous: in other words, they expect both partners to a marriage to belong to the same caste. Hence in their case the boundaries of the caste define the universe within which all meaningful social relationships are conducted. Unlike the higher-caste Patidars with their hierarchically arranged marriage circles, the

---

supplied with no expectation of a return was that used to wash a dead body before cremation.

Prajapatis do not subscribe to any scheme of differential ranking amongst themselves. Hypergamy plays no part in Prajapati marriages, and although marriage may not take place between those with whom a kinship link can be traced according to the customary rules of *sapinda*[5] exogamy, there is no objection to families establishing reciprocal marriage alliances, as when a pair of brothers marry two sisters, or a brother and sister are married to another sibling pair. Marriage itself is normally viri-local, and set within the context of a patrilineally extended family. Once married, a woman therefore expects to join her husband in a village some distance away from the one in which her natal family live.

Although the Prajapatis pride themselves on the simplicity of their marriage ceremonies and the absence of elaborate dowry payments — at least by contrast with the crippling level of conspicuous consumption characteristic of the higher-ranking Gujarati castes — both betrothal (*sagai*) and marriage (*vivah*) are marked by extensive gift-giving. The bride's parents, assisted by her maternal uncle, are expected to provide her with clothes and jewellery and to defray all the expenses of the wedding. Apart from the dowry, the bridegroom, his parents and the other relatives who accompany him to the wedding ceremony also receive gifts. These are never reciprocally exchanged, but flow asymmetrically from the bride's side to that of the groom. Thus, while marriages are invariably arranged between families of more or less equal social and financial status, the flow of gifts and prestations associated with marriage has the effect — as is commonplace in North India — of emphasising the social superiority of the bride receivers.

This uneven flow of gifts is sustained for many years after the marriage, for a woman's parents are expected to give her clothes and jewellery on all important ceremonial occasions, and her brothers to display elaborate benevolence towards all her children. The relationship between affines also tends to be rather formal and restrained: if the proper role of the husband's family is to be the recipient of gifts and gestures of respect from his wife's family, they, by contrast, should be exceedingly hesitant about accepting even the most basic hospitality from those to whom they have given a daughter in marriage.

In other spheres of domestic activity, however, the influence of higher caste norms is much less marked. So, for example, the

---

[5] Among the Prajapatis, marriage is prohibited between those who share a common ancestor to the seventh inclusive generation on the male side, and to the fifth on the female side. Nevertheless these limits are frequently transgressed in practice, since relationships beyond the third or fourth generation on either side can rarely be recalled.

Prajapatis accept the legitimacy of both divorce and widow-remarriage, both of which are shunned by higher-caste Gujaratis as violations of Brahmanical codes of morality.

Migration to East Africa

As the nineteenth century progressed, technological change and the gradual introduction of a money economy had a major impact upon the fabric of village life throughout India, especially in Gujarat. Traditional caste occupations began to be abandoned in favour of more lucrative alternatives, and people from all backgrounds began to move away from their villages into nearby towns and cities in search of better opportunities. This migratory tendency was reinforced by a series of natural disasters — including famine and plague — which hit Gujarat in the late nineteenth century.

However, migration in Gujarat was not confined to local movements, nor was it solely a product of nineteenth- and twentieth-century change. Merchants from Gujarat had been involved in overseas trade for almost four millennia, and had already established a foothold on the coast of East Africa long before European colonial expansion transformed the economy of the whole region. For the Gujaratis one of the most important of these developments was the British push into the interior of East Africa during the late nineteenth century. As news of the opportunities thus becoming available filtered through to the towns and villages of Gujarat, Prajapatis were soon amongst those who decided to seek their fortunes across the seas. As skilled craftsmen, they were well placed to take advantage of the colonial construction boom, and to continue to do so as the East African economy expanded.

It was men alone who took part in the initial stages of migration to East Africa, where they lived a bachelor life between periodic visits to their wives and families in their native villages. Although a small number of men did bring their wives and children to join them in the early days of settlement, family reunion only became normal after the end of the Second World War. Once women and children arrived, more or less settled South Asian communities sprang up in all the major towns in Kenya, Uganda and Tanzania. The Prajapatis were involved in this process, but because of their small numbers and lack of political and economic influence — at least by comparison with large and powerful groups such as the Patidars and Lohanas — little attention has been paid to them by the chroniclers of East African Asian society: if they are mentioned at all, it is as part of the catch-all category of "*choti-jat*", literally "little castes".

While there was little need for Indian immigrants to restrict themselves to their hereditarily ascribed occupations once they reached East Africa, members of those *choti-jat* who had directly marketable skills often continued to use them — so, for example, many of the earliest Prajapati settlers were initially employed as carpenters, masons, construction supervisors and so forth.[6] Later their preferences changed, and many moved into clerical jobs, a few became skilled manual workers — motor mechanics, for example — and a small number acquired advanced educational qualifications and entered the professions. However in contrast to higher-caste Gujarati settlers, for whom trade and commerce was by far the most popular and prestigious way of making a living, few Prajapatis moved into this sector of the economy.

Though few, if any, Prajapati settlers fully emulated the commercial successes of their higher-caste fellow migrants, they have nevertheless made considerable economic progress, at least by Gujarati standards. There was thus a steady inflow of new arrivals, and the Prajapati settlement in East Africa grew steadily both in size and self-sufficiency, but even so, close contact was sustained with India. Brides were sought from there once young male migrants had established themselves economically, and elderly people often returned to their natal villages once they had retired. As soon as families began to be reunited, schools were established in East Africa; however, sons were often sent back to India for higher education. Few if any Prajapati families were in a position to send their offspring to study in England, as members of the more affluent castes often managed to do. But it was through marriage that the most important links with India were maintained. Prajapati brides were often brought over to be married to East African grooms, while East African Prajapati girls for whom no suitable local groom could be found would return to Gujarat as brides.

The Growth of the Prajapati Settlement in Britain

As in East Africa, most British Prajapatis hail originally from Surat District in southern Gujarat, particularly the region around the town of Navsari. And while a small proportion made their way directly to Britain from Gujarat, the vast majority arrived by way of East Africa. Like many migrant families originally drawn from humble backgrounds in Gujarat and who became relatively prosperous during their East African sojourn, their wealth was not matched by a strong

---

[6] The title "Mistry" (a common surname among Prajapatis) can be translated as "foreman of a building site". It is also used as a generic term by Gujarati, Punjabi and Hindi speakers to describe skilled craftsmen of all kinds, but particularly carpenters, joiners and masons.

political base; thus when nationalist movements gained momentum in newly-independent Kenya, Uganda and Tanzania, the Indian community came under ever-increasing pressure from the upwardly-mobile aspirations of the local Africans. They found themselves being encouraged to quit Government employment, and it became increasingly difficult to pursue commercial activities.

In response to these pressures the major exodus of Prajapatis to Britain was from 1967 onwards, with a further boost after the expulsion of the South Asian population of Uganda in 1972. There was, of course, much hostility to their arrival from members of Britain's white population. However, unlike direct migrants from the Indian subcontinent, the great majority of East African Asians held British passports and were thus exercising their legal rights to residence — rights explicitly confirmed by a previous Colonial Secretary — when they chose to settle in Britain.

British Prajapatis are fairly widely scattered; the largest communities are in the north of England, the Midlands and the Greater London area — particularly in Harrow, Wembley and the boroughs of Brent and Barnet, with smaller settlements in Hounslow, Norwood, Balham and Tooting. Home-ownership among the Prajapatis is common. Most families live in pleasant neighbourhoods, often those with a high proportion of residents from South Asia. Shops in these areas cater to ethnically-specialist demand, and include Asian grocery stores and sari and video shops where the latest Bombay film releases can be hired. Homes are generally well-maintained and equipped with colour televisions, VCRs and a range of labour-saving gadgets. While the decor is usually a mix of European and Indian styles, African handicrafts are often prominently displayed on the walls or in showcases. If a family shrine has been set up in a corner of the living room, the atmosphere is filled with the fragrance of lighted incense sticks.

Male Experience in the British Employment Market

Like other East African Asians, many Prajapati men found it hard to deploy their skills successfully in the British employment market, so even former white-collar employees were often forced to take jobs of a much lower status. Those who settled in the Midlands and the north of England became skilled and semi-skilled manual workers in manufacturing industry; in London, more moved into the building trade and into white-collar employment. Since their arrival, most of the older generation have found occupational mobility hard to achieve, and have been badly affected by the recession of the late 1980s and early '90s. By contrast younger men are pursuing opportunities in a wide variety of sectors, and taking advantage of government-sponsored training schemes. Education is highly regarded as a means of achieving upward mobility, and many school-leavers opt for professional training in engineering, electronics, accountancy, business studies, pharmacology and computer science.

Although Prajapatis repeatedly point out that theirs is not a business community, it is evident that "merchant ideology"[7] is by no means wholly absent from their psychological makeup. Though there are still only few Prajapati professionals, most are self-employed; meanwhile many non-professionals — especially those who experienced discrimination at work, or felt their jobs were under threat from the recession — hope to set up businesses of their own.

Women and Work in Britain

The experience of Prajapati women has been rather different from that of Prajapati men. Before their arrival in Britain few, if any, had any experience of working for wages outside the home, but since then they have entered formal employment in ever-increasing numbers. This has transformed their functions within the household, as their role now includes resource procurement along with the long-established one of resource management; and while the transformation is due to a combination of factors, both negative and positive, and entailing both compulsion and choice, they have weakened — though not eliminated — the traditional division of labour between the sexes.

Like all other Asian women, the Prajapatis were catapulted into a society where women's participation in waged employment was rapidly increasing. The growth of mass production, and even more the expansion of the service sector, created many jobs for women, although these rarely required either skills or vocational training. As has often been noted, the urban labour market is sharply divided into "masculine" and "feminine" jobs with women workers tending to be concentrated in jobs with low pay, low status and little opportunity for advancement. This is true of most South Asian women, who have been thrust into a working class that is sharply stratified by skill and gender, and even more so by race: perceived as a cheap and flexible source of labour, they are markedly over-represented in semi-skilled and unskilled manual jobs.[8]

Of my Prajapati informants only one was professionally qualified, and she was self-employed. Few of the women aged between forty and sixty had formal educational qualifications, and most had only a

[7] H. Tambs-Lyche, *London Patidars: a Study in Urban Ethnicity* (London: Routledge, 1980).

[8] P. Bhacha and S. Westwood, *Enterprising Women* (London: Routledge, 1988).

limited grasp of English. And although most were employed, they were confined to a range of occupations — as machinists, packers and finishers in food-processing, clothing and light engineering industries, or in semi- or unskilled jobs in the service sector. However, most women aged between twenty-five and forty tended both to be better qualified and much more accomplished in English. Almost all had had at least some of their education in Britain, and were striking out in all sorts of new directions, to become computer programmers, opticians and pharmacists, as well as the more humdrum staple of clerical and secretarial work in banks and offices. Many were also entering youth or adult training schemes to acquire more marketable skills.

In the development of the Prajapati community, the routine involvement of women in the labour market was both a novel and very much a *British* phenomenon, and most still felt the need to justify their behaviour. Economic need was regularly cited as their principal motivator, although there is a distinction between working out of absolute financial necessity and doing so to enhance the family's standard of living. Generally, the sharp increase in Prajapati women's economic activity after arriving in Britain was a strategic response which families adopted to cope with the problem of settlement in an unfamiliar and often hostile environment. However, much has changed since the early days. With high inflation, falling real incomes and rising male unemployment, accompanied by a perceived need to maintain a "decent" standard of living, many Prajapati families have come to rely increasingly on female earning capacity. Against this backdrop it is noteworthy that while neither career prospects nor the intrinsic interest of the job itself emerged as influential in making older women decide to seek paid employment, the need to escape from boredom and loneliness at home was mentioned by most of them.

Amongst Britain's white majority, nation-wide surveys have shown that labour force participation rates reach two peaks: in the early years before childbearing, and after the youngest child in the family has become self-sufficient. By contrast it appears that many Prajapati women — and almost certainly the women in other South Asian communities — enter the labour market at the stage in the family life-cycle when domestic responsibilities and expenses are at their heaviest. Most were caught between two contradictory pressures: the perceived need, on the one hand, for access to more than one income to support a reasonably comfortable life-style; and on the other the pressing logistical problem of fulfilling their obligations both at work and at home, particularly caring for their children.

Women's employment patterns thus appeared greatly influenced by the number and age of their dependent children, as well as by the availability of traditional support structures. While many older women worked full-time, most mothers of pre-school children were only able to do so when they lived in joint family households, where responsibility for child-care could be entrusted to grandmothers. By contrast those who lived in nuclear households often found access to suitable daycare for their children difficult. Thus women with at least one child below the age of ten, and lacking the support of a co-resident extended family, were much less likely to work full-time. If financial pressures became severe, younger children were left in the care of older siblings both after school and during school holidays, so enabling the mother to take a full-time job. Sometimes neighbours also helped out in the care of school-age children — and, as the case below shows, these arrangements did not necessarily involve a cash transaction, but rather recompense in the context of a more elaborate exchange of mutual aid.

A Case Study: Premlal Mistri and Sitaben

At the time of interview Premlal Mistri, his wife Sitaben and their six-year-old daughter had recently moved out of Premlal's parents' house to one of their own. The mortgage repayments on the new house were high, and in order to cover them Sita decided to go to work, provided suitable child-care arrangements could be made for their daughter. They hoped, at first, that Sita would only need to work part-time, but she had such difficulty finding anything which fitted in with school timings that she had little option but to take up a full-time job. They could not afford expensive child-care services, so they turned to their English neighbours — whose child went to the same school — for help. It was arranged that the neighbours would look after the Mistris' daughter between the end of the school day and Sita's return from work at 5 p.m., and that in return Sita would babysit for the neighbours whenever they wanted to go out in the evenings. In addition the Mistris also looked after their neighbours' cat when they went away on holiday. Longer school holidays posed a major problem, however. Sometimes each parent arranged to take time off from work so that either one or the other would be at home with the child; sometimes Premlal's parents helped out, and sometimes the neighbours. However they were most reluctant to use the services of a professional childminder because these tended to be very expensive. They preferred, instead, to reinforce their relationship with their neighbours by giving expensive gifts on birthdays and at Christmas.

The Structure of the Domestic Group

As Sitaben's experiences show, the household structure in which married women find themselves is a major constraint on their economic activities: thus we should now look at the impact of this crucial variable for Gujarati Hindus in general and Prajapatis in particular. For Gujaratis, the ideal-typical household or *ghar* is a joint family — a multi-functional unit where members of three or more generations live together under one roof, holding property in common and pooling their incomes to meet their collective expenses from a single common fund. Ideologically the jointness of such a household is symbolised by their use of a single common hearth or kitchen, the collective participation of all group members in ritual and ceremonial activities, and their acceptance of the ultimate authority of their eldest male member. The expected kinship structure of such an ideal-typical household results from the cultural norms of post-marital residence: married sons are expected to live with their parents, and brothers to continue living together after the death of their parents.

Nevertheless few, if any, Prajapati households in London conform fully to this ideal. Some do so in a modified form, as when a household includes an elderly couple who live with one of their married sons and his wife and offspring; but most Prajapati households encountered were essentially nuclear units, consisting of parents and their unmarried children. This might be taken as evidence that the Prajapatis are adapting to their new socio-economic context by assuming the moral values of the surrounding British society. However, careful examination revealed that no one model of household structure could be identified as "normal". Most domestic groups had passed rapidly through a number of phases, and had been both "joint" and "nuclear" at different points, depending on how they adapted to their generally rather poor economic circumstances.

So while the great majority of these Prajapati households had a nuclear structure, almost all had at one time included additional relatives since their arrival in Britain; however these had invariably been the husbands' kin, recruited in accordance with the strongly patrilateral emphasis of Gujarati kinship.

Likewise major changes in households were largely cast in a "traditional" pattern. In one case a nuclear household became extended after an eldest son brought his newly-married wife to live with him in his parents' household. In the other a complex joint household nominally split into two elementary units after a married son with his wife and children moved out of his parents' household — which also included his still unmarried younger brothers and sisters — into a house of their own. But the resultant division was hardly a gulf. The son's new house was just down the street, everyone still met daily and usually ate their evening meal together, and during the day the children (one of pre-school age) were usually looked after by their grandparents while their own parents went out to work. In this case residential separation for the participants was largely nominal. Buying an additional house was primarily a means for a growing family to ease the pressure on its accommodation, as well as acquiring a valuable material asset which would benefit everyone. Meanwhile daily interaction, above all at meals, directly symbolised the jointness of the two ostensibly separate households.

Also, in several instances, a household's nominally nuclear core was temporarily supplemented by the husband's elderly parents. Though in principle only "visitors", their expected length of stay was unspecified: indeed the existence of such "mobile grandparents", often in permanent global transit between the households of all their offspring, clearly illustrates the inappropriateness of drawing simplistic conclusions about household structure from its physical membership at any given time. The household in the sense of a *ghar* has much more a conceptual than a physical reality: it is the quality of its members' *relationships* that matters most.

Nevertheless when an elderly father is in residence, patterns of behaviour alter: household members try to conform, albeit temporarily, to the ideal type of a patrilineally-extended joint family. However, when the elderly visitor is a widowed mother, the impact is rather different. Although her presence often has a somewhat conservative influence on domestic behaviour, she may also contribute crucially to the household economy, especially if she takes care of the children while her daughter-in-law goes out to work.

Most young couples live for the first few years of marriage in the husband's parental home. Cultural values notwithstanding, practical considerations also make joint living both necessary and desirable. Few young couples have the resources to buy a house immediately after marriage, and despite the personal adjustments that have to be made — particularly by women — to cope with the inevitable strains of joint living, most young people are well aware of the advantages, particularly the economies of scale. This initial phase of joint living is also often seen as a period of domestic apprenticeship for the young bride, when she is initiated into the ways of her husband's family, such as their dietary preferences and culinary practices, as well as their ceremonial and ritual observances. A very positive value is ascribed to those women who manage to live amicably for several years with their in-laws, and they earn considerable respect amongst both their kin and the wider caste-community.

Such arrangements are rarely permanent, unless the husband is his parents' only son, for the marriage of a younger brother almost always leads to the establishment of separate households — with the need to reduce overcrowding being cited as the reason. However, as we have just seen, the significance of such developments is far from transparent. Numerous instances of daily interaction and taking meals together make it clear that the uncritical use of numerical data about residential patterns can be misleading. To suggest that South Asian households are coming to have an increasing physical resemblance to native English households — so that they are in that sense "nuclear" — is accurate enough, but their members' relationships are not therefore becoming more like those majority norms.

Decision-making and the Division of Labour in Joint Households

Overtly, the Prajapatis represent themselves as strongly committed to the traditional model of the Hindu joint family, in which power is hierarchically distributed by age and sex. Hence they are also committed to the view that all family members should accept the authority of the eldest male; women, at least in theory, are therefore subordinate to men, while younger people of both sexes should remain subject to the authority and control of their elders.

Yet although these ideas provided the broad framework within which families operated, it was obvious that in practice the process of decision-making, as well as the domestic division of labour, is affected by other factors: the number, age, and marital status of the sons living within the parental unit; the economic activities of all its members of both sexes; and, last but not least, the specific contribution of each member to the total household resources.

Whether he is economically active or retired, the eldest male's formal position as the head of the household is rarely, if ever, challenged, and major decisions are never taken without first seeking his views. That does not mean that elderly heads of household are necessarily involved in decision-making itself. Since the ultimate strategic objective of most families is to maximise their economic self-sufficiency and stability, greater importance than ever before is now attached to formal education, professional competence and social and linguistic skills — the very qualities that elderly family heads are likely to lack. Thus younger family members often influence decisions about such things as property purchase and investment, even though great care is always taken to submit what is in fact a *fait accompli* to the head of the family for his formal seal of approval.

The position of women is even more complex. Apart from the nominally subordinate position of all women, wives enter their husbands' families as "outsiders" and thus rarely participate directly in important family decisions. But that does not mean they are wholly powerless: most seek to have a subtle influence over their husbands as the *ex-officio* representatives of each conjugal unit in the wider patricentric household.[9]

Most important of all, a woman's relationship to the household's authority structure changes according to its stage in the developmental cycle, and the number of married sons still living within the parental unit. Other things being equal, a daughter-in-law's influence is greatest in households where elderly and economically inactive parents live with one married son and his gainfully employed wife, and least among newly-married wives of younger sons in large, multi-generational households.

Even so, further paradoxes lie buried in such contexts. In a household with only one daughter-in-law, all her earnings from employment are likely to form her contribution to the family's common fund. In large multi-generational households with several earning members, it is unusual for an employed daughter-in-law to do this, but although she may keep her own money, she will also be barred from using her wage-earning capacity to obtain greater influence in family affairs. This does not mean that her earning power is without significance; it is actually a vital potential resource, especially when a married couple feel that their interests are not being served by the family as a whole, for it may then form the core of capital they will need to strike out semi-autonomously on their own account.

Decision-making and the Division of Labour in Nuclear Households

Relationships in households containing only a single married couple tend to be more flexible than those in larger and more complex domestic groups.[10] The conjugal partnership is then often much closer and more intense, for in the absence of other kin the couple tend to become more dependent on each other for support and companionship. Moreover, wives in nuclear households are usually less

---

[9] Several studies of South Asian families, e.g. R. Ballard, "South Asian Families" in Fogerty (ed.), *Families in Britain* (London: Routledge, 1982) and P. Bhachu, "Apni Marzi Kardi" in *Enterprising Women* (London: Routledge, 1988), have shown that changes in the position of women within the household can be related to their enhanced earning power. My own research suggests a qualification to this view, since it shows the insufficiency of seeking to assess the impact of a daughter-in-law on joint family decisions merely because of her earning capacity.

[10] S. Vatuk, *Kinship and Urbanization* (Berkeley: University of California Press, 1972) and Bhachu, *op. cit.*

restricted by the age- and gender-based hierarchies in the distribution of power which are so prominent in extended families. So whether or not they are gainfully employed and so able to contribute directly to the domestic economy, wives in nuclear households invariably exercise much more control over the family's resources, as well as playing a greater role in decision-making.

This is not to suggest that marital relationships are egalitarian: indeed the idea that a husband and wife might routinely participate as equals in decision-making and similarly share all domestic and child-care responsibilities is explicitly rejected. Many couples treat such a prospect as synonymous with "Women's Lib", which they regard as a wholly undesirable ideology and thus to be rejected out of hand. They prefer the term "complementary" to define their ideal of conjugal roles and relations.

Certainly both husbands and wives expect to have clearly differentiated areas of responsibility, based on their own personal knowledge and competence as well as on culturally-specific understandings of the proper form of gender roles. Thus decisions about investments and long-term financial planning are nearly always left to the husband, not only because he is usually the principal breadwinner but because "men usually know more about such matters". Men also appear to have the final say on such issues as children's education and whether or not their wives would go out to work. On the other hand all decisions about child-care within the home, the day-to-day running of the household and, most critical of all for the family's public standing, the exchange of gifts with kin are regarded as belonging to the wife. Though some husbands have been known to refer somewhat facetiously to their partners as their "home minister", control of the home sphere clearly brings women considerable power and influence.

Such influence can only be acquired, however, at the cost of much hard work. In line with their expectation that the domestic division of labour should be based on complementarity rather than equivalence, most couples take it for granted that men should pay bills, the mortgage and for household repairs, and perhaps occasionally help with the shopping, while it is up to their wives to cook, clean and care for the children. However women's move into paid employment has put great pressure on such conventional expectations. Thus while working wives tend to receive more assistance than full-time housewives from their husbands, most women actually find themselves working a double or treble shift — doing some housework before leaving for work, and resuming it on their return. Male participation in child-care and domestic work varies a great deal, depending, among other things, on whether the wife is working full- or part-time, whether the husband does shift-work or overtime, and whether professional and/or community commitments cause him to be out of the house for long periods and thus unavailable to offer assistance.

Age is important too. Most younger men accept in principle the idea of a more "joint" pattern of role sharing, particularly since the absence of female kin and the high cost of hired domestic help has clearly deprived women in nuclear households of many of their traditional sources of support and aid; they also accept that sharing responsibility for getting things done is essential if the household is to function efficiently. Nevertheless many older couples and some younger ones seem caught in a hiatus between practical realities and the strength of early socialization. So despite all the pressures on them, many people find it hard to break away from conventionally established gender-role expectations.

All this is further complicated by the stage the household has reached in its developmental cycle. When it includes grown-up off-spring, for example, husbands tend to contribute less to domestic activities. Conversely, young women with pre-school children but based in nuclear households can generally negotiate much more help from husbands.

The Organisation of Extra-familial Sociability Networks

Besides the intra-domestic activities discussed so far, the Prajapatis also maintain a wide range of relationships extending far beyond the boundaries of their own immediate household. Relationships in this external network fall into two distinct categories: those involving kin, and those with a much broader and more amorphous body of friends, neighbours, workmates and fellow caste members.

In general, individuals and families expect to be able to draw both material assistance and emotional support from their immediate kin when they need it, and therefore great value is attached to making kinship networks as strong as possible. However the resultant inter-changes are neither uniform nor comprehensively egalitarian, not least because of the inbuilt asymmetry of affinal ties.

As noted earlier, Gujarati kinship is strongly patrilateral, one result being that couples in nuclear households tend to maintain much closer contact with the husband's kin than the wife's. Traditionally a man's relationship with his wife's kin is expected to be rather formal and subject to all sorts of restrictions. While visiting a father-in-law's house, sons-in-law are treated with elaborate respect and courtesy which they are under no obligation to reciprocate, for the parents and older siblings of a married woman would not normally accept hosp-itality — "not even a glass of water", as the saying goes — from her husband and his kin. This is why men are reluctant to stay too long at their father-in-law's house, for fear of earning the dubious reputation of being a scrounging *ghar-jamai* or resident son-in-law.[11]

Nevertheless these particular traditional rules are slowly changing. If a wife's parents and siblings also live in London, they are frequently visited. Moreover there are at least two occasions in the year — the festivals of Raksha-Bandhan and Bhaibij — when an exchange of visits between a married woman and her brothers is virtually obligatory.[12] By contrast interaction between married sisters is much more a matter of "structured chance", and usually occur either during the celebration of life-cycle rituals (to which large numbers of guests are invited) or when sisters' visits to the parental home coincide. It is this primary kinship network that provides the arena for the most active sociability, within which financial aid and services of various kinds are routinely exchanged.

Beyond this immediate circle of close kin, geography as much as genealogy determines the frequency of face-to-face contacts, as well as the exchange content of each relationship. So although instances exist of uncles lending money to nephews to buy a house, and cousins setting up small businesses together, relationships between secondary kin tend to be governed by compatibility of interests and personal friendship.

Given their position as "twice migrants", the primary kinship network of most Prajapati families normally spans at least three continents. But while such separation alters the quality of relationships, they are by no means falling into abeyance. Everyone seeks to keep in touch through regular letters and phone calls, and the vitality of the network is reinforced by visits to and by parents and siblings living elsewhere in the world. Contact with more distant kin is selective, and largely sustained by older people.

In the immediate British context, however, kin and non-kin networks frequently merge into a single social entity, with the emotional bonds of close friendship regularly being expressed in an idiom of kinship. While close friendships are, as always, based on shared interests, attitudes and values, they also tend to be with "one's own kind"; hence "best friends" are often other Gujarati Hindus from East Africa.

---

[11] A *ghar-jamai* earns the pity of others since it implies being in a state of dependence more appropriate to a daughter-in-law.

[12] At the festival of Raksha-Bandhan, usually in July or August, sisters tie a *rakhi* around their brothers' wrists to safeguard them from harm. In return, brothers pledge to protect their sisters and safeguard the welfare of their children. The festival of Bhaibij falls on the day after Diwali, which itself marks the commencement of the New Year. At Bhaibij, women formally invite their brothers to come and eat a meal, in return for which they are presented with a gift.

Such relationships are rarely established at an individual level; here married couples act as a single unit, with husbands having the greater say in the choice of friends, and determining the frequency and nature of contacts. The comparative absence of female friendship networks is significant, and seems to result from working womens' multiple responsibilities, which leave them little time to be involved themselves in active female-centred networks of non-employed Prajapati women. And although many Prajapati women strike up friendships with their colleagues at work, these rarely have much impact on the effective network of most married couples. Given the strength of male domination at home, friendships amongst women are very vulnerable; if the husbands of a pair of women friends fail to get on, their own relationship is unlikely to flourish.

By contrast the social contacts of younger Prajapatis are much more likely to cut across ethnic boundaries, and are anything but linguistically or culturally isolated. Most young people speak to their friends in English — with a pronounced local accent — and this is often spiced with Gujarati and Swahili words and phrases. Their leisure interests are equally eclectic. Thus while they may well follow the progress of their favourite pop groups and go to rock concerts at Wembley Arena with their friends, they are equally enthusiastic about dressing up and going to *garbha* dances[13] during the Navratri festival, or simply visiting the Bhajia House, a well-known snack bar on Ealing Road. Yet despite this eclecticism, the great majority of those whom younger people identify as "close friends" turn out to be fellow Gujaratis — even if not of the same caste or sect.

The Shree Prajapati Samaj

Many Prajapatis are also heavily involved in the activities of their caste association, the Shree Prajapati Samaj UK, which is an important feature of their social life. As in all other caste associations, membership is restricted to Prajapatis, and its purpose is to preserve and defend the collective interests of the Prajapati *jati*. Established in 1975, the Samaj has grown into a thriving national organisation, with branches in twelve towns and cities outside London, an annually elected council, and both a well-defined constitution and a formal set of procedural rules. Despite widespread concern about the Prajapatis' position as a small and exposed minority in an often hostile British society, the Samaj has adopted a firmly "non-political" agenda, and

[13] Throughout the ten days of the Dassera festival, Gujarati Hindus celebrate with traditional folk-dancing such as the *garbha-ras*. The dancers move round in a circle, clapping their hands or beating two sticks together in time to music. Both sexes participate.

makes little or no effort to address external English power structures, either locally or nationally. Its arena is much more parochial. If it seeks to organise and articulate the distinctive interests of the Prajapati *jati*, then it does so primarily in relation to the many other *jatis* of the local Gujarati community. Rivalry between castes is intense, and each has formed its own separate caste association to organise and articulate its members' collective interests.

As well as publishing a newsletter, the Samaj organises a wide range of social and cultural events which enable fellow *jati* members to gather and exchange news, renew contact with kin and friends, and explore potential affinal links. And while formal links have not yet been established between the Shree Prajapati Samaj UK and its counterparts in India or East Africa, it has sometimes cooperated with other South Asian organisations to provide services from which all sections of the Gujarati Hindu community might benefit. Thus, in Coventry the local Samaj has set up a weekend supplementary school to teach children Gujarati; and in Bradford it was the Prajapatis who were largely responsible for establishing a Hindu temple, which is used by all local Hindus regardless of *jati* affiliation.[14]

By contrast no formal contacts are maintained between the Samaj and any of the majority community's organisations and institutions, although regional branches have occasionally contributed to local charities. Thus although many individual Prajapatis are personally involved in social transactions which cross ethnic boundaries, the Samaj — which nominally represents the "collective will" of *jati* members — is much more inward-looking.[15]

Certainly the Samaj has this inward focus — as is manifested in the use of Gujarati as the principal medium of debate and discussion, and in the fact that its goals are both derived from and articulated in terms of a Gujarati folk tradition. However, it also sees itself as providing a bridge between one social universe and another, particularly for the younger British-born generation. Thus, while parents are encouraged to bring children to all the Samaj's social events, there is widespread concern that the younger generation may have difficulty retaining a sense of "Prajapatiness". The Samaj has therefore set up

[14] In 1980, the Prajapatis in Bradford bought a disused chapel and converted it into a *Mandir*. While regular daily *pujas* are performed by members of the caste on a rota, a Brahmin priest is called in to officiate for major festivals. Though primarily run by Prajapatis, the temple is open to all Hindus.

[15] Even though writing about ethnic boundary maintenance in a very different context, Haaland suggests that it involves "a categorical dichotomisation of people who are like oneself, with whom one may have relations covering all sections of activity, and people who are different from oneself, having different evaluations, with whom one interacts in a limited number of capacities". This neatly and succinctly sums up the quality of Prajapatis' interaction with the society which encompasses them.

a separate Youth Wing to provide a range of social, cultural, recreational and educational activities for children and adolescents — including discos with both Western and Indian pop music, sporting events, and seminars on topics of particular concern to young people.

Meanwhile in an effort to encourage women to take part more often, and be more active in the affairs of the Samaj, a women's group or "Mahila Mandal" was set up in 1979. Those involved in it were expected to assist in the organisation of religious ceremonies such as *satsangs* (gatherings to sing devotional hymns), and organise catering for the Samaj's major annual rituals. This they indeed do, but even so women's participation in community affairs remains limited: meetings of the Mahila Mandal are poorly attended, since many women can not spare the time; meanwhile leadership roles in the Mahila Mandal still largely reflect the status of members' husbands, rather than their own autonomous aspirations.[16]

The decision to settle in Britain was a momentous one. As all Prajapati families were well aware, it was bound to affect many crucial aspects of their lives. Yet despite a strong commitment to keeping the most vital aspects of their cultural heritage alive, they also took the view that flexibility was essential. So they set about devising new norms and points of reference in their daily interaction with a society organised according to the socio-cultural assumptions of the dominant English majority. Much has changed through those interactions, not least women's role and status in the home and in the community at large.

While migration to Britain was mainly motivated by a search for material success, it had particularly dramatic consequences for Prajapati women, since their entry into the labour market in large numbers was one of the strategies their families adopted to help achieve their economic goals. But when one attempts to make sense of the complex relationship between female wage-earning, gender roles and the structure and ideology of the family, it appears that the impact of migration cannot be interpreted only as a one-way process in which change is a simple unambiguous consequence.

---

[16] The Prajapati Samaj UK has a complex organisational structure. Each local branch has a large committee with numerous office-bearers, including a President, Vice-President, Treasurer, Assistant Treasurer, Auditors and several Area Secretaries. A National or Central Committee, the Madhya Sanstha, unites all the local Associations. During the course of my fieldwork no women sat on the Central Committee, and only one who functioned as an Area Secretary — although jointly with her husband. In the North West London Mahila Mandal the majority of Committee members were wives of office-bearers in the local branch of the Samaj proper.

Migrant communities, perhaps more than most, constantly create and re-create their systems of cultural meaning as they seek to cope creatively with changed social relations and life-styles caused by their new socio-economic environment. Yet despite much experimentation with new norms and modes of action, the process of cultural re-interpretation clearly takes place around a core of well-established values which, precisely through their link with the past, provide those who use them with emotional security and psychological support.

So although working for wages has been a novel experience for most Prajapati women, the money they earn has been used in a broadly "traditional" way: it has brought tangible material benefits for the entire family while also enhancing women's bargaining power as against their husbands, and the strength of the conjugal partnership *vis-à-vis* other kin in the husband's extended family. But despite these real gains, not all women succeed in negotiating a more effective position in the domestic power structure. Their experience of work and their recognition of the significance of wage-earning tend to be specifically in accordance with Prajapati definitions of a woman's proper role both in the family and in the public domain.

The greatest crisis facing Prajapati families comes from factors beyond their own control. The sharp reduction in Britain's rate of wealth generation in the wake of inflation and high interest rates has led to unprecedentedly high unemployment, to which members of the ethnic minorities — women as well as men — are particularly vulnerable.

But paradoxically, these very adversities have also begun to cause some creative responses amongst many of the new minorities. High unemployment and discriminatory recruitment practices have helped to generate what can best be described as a "culture of entrepreneurship" in Britain's South Asian community. Many Prajapati men, particularly in the younger age groups, have broken out of waged employment to set up small businesses. They are also bringing about a redefinition of the relationship between minorities and the dominant majority. At least they offer an escape from the under-class and the state of deprivation and dependence hitherto synonymous with membership of an ethnic minority.

However, the effect of these changes on the internal structure of the family and on the position of women within it is more problematic. While few Prajapati women have found paid employment a particularly liberating experience, it has nevertheless made them more aware of their rights as workers — inside as well as outside the family. But as paid employment has become less attractive as well as harder to secure, moving over to contribute to the family business makes good economic sense. But what of the consequences? Access to wages earned on their own account and by their own efforts has undoubtedly given Prajapati women the chance of greater power in the home, though this has to be qualified by the many other factors discussed in this chapter. With further growth in entrepreneurship, and with women becoming ever more comprehensively involved in increasingly family businesses of growing prosperity, will their autonomy increase further, or will they be pressed back into more "traditional" forms of dependence? Time alone will tell.

THE GUJARATI MOCHIS IN LEEDS

FROM LEATHER STOCKINGS TO SURGICAL BOOTS AND BEYOND

Kim Knott

Although the Mochis are a small and little-known caste who make up only a tiny fraction of the Gujarati presence in Britain, nearly half the Hindus in Leeds belong to the Mochi community. In Gujarat itself local Mochi communities are rarely very large, with the result that the settlers who have congregated in Leeds trace their origins to a large number of small towns and villages in Gujarat; most families also spent some time in East Africa before settling in Britain.

Like the members of most other Gujarati castes, the Mochis of Leeds see and refer to themselves as a "community". Reciprocities within the group are strong, for beyond the extended family it is to the community of caste that most people feel their primary allegiance. As a caste, the Mochis can be seen as one amongst a number of endogamous, hereditary and occupationally linked groups, although in their case their once-stigmatising ancestral skills as leather-workers have led to their being ascribed a relatively low position in the caste hierarchy, both in India and in Britain. However, caste as a system has now undergone considerable change, both in Gujarat and in the diaspora. Thus while parts of a once comprehensive system still exist — as in the rules of endogamy — the system as a whole is now greatly attenuated. Following emigration to environments with much more varied and open occupational opportunities, the complex web of interdependences which once bound castes together has withered; so where castes of low, middle and high rank were once linked by a complex exchange of goods and services, each now tends to go its own separate way — or so the theory goes.[1]

Yet how far does this accurately represent the experience and social location of the Mochis? How far have they found themselves on a par with other higher-ranking Gujarati communities in ability to obtain access to resources and social status? How distinctive has the Mochis' communal experience been in the course of their migratory journey from Gujarat to East Africa and then to Leeds?

[1] In "Division and Hierarchy: An Overview of Caste in Gujarat", *Contributions to Indian Sociology* (NS), vol. 16, 1957, pp. 1–33, A.M. Shah laments the absence of studies of small castes in Gujarat.

In answering these questions, it is valuable to reflect on the experience of a small, low-ranking and relatively powerless caste. New circumstances have undoubtedly brought many changes, so that the lives of its members are now very different from what they were in the past. However those changes cannot be understood without carefully considering the Mochis' collective memory of political and social disadvantage.

Mochis in Gujarat

The Mochis are one of a number of *choti jati* or small castes[2] whose existence has attracted less attention than have Gujarat's larger and more affluent groups such as the Leva Kanbi Patidars, the Lohanas and various Vania groups.[3] If mentioned at all in the literature, references to them tend to be buried in regional caste profiles, or in some of the early general accounts of Gujarati caste and tribal life;[4] in studies of Indians in East Africa and Britain, they appear only as one caste among many.[5]

This treatment is neither surprising nor wholly unjustified, since the number of *choti jati* residents in most towns and villages is usually small. Occupationally, members of these castes were skilled artisans: Darjis — tailors; Suthars — carpenters; Kumbhars or Prajapatis — potters; Mochis — shoemakers. They are found scattered throughout the State of Gujarat, but since only a few families from each caste live in any one town or village, they do not form large local communities. Several sociological studies have shown this to be true of the Mochis. An account of Olpad region in south Gujarat refers to three Mochi families out of 793; in that area the locally-dominant

---

[2] Bharati, *The Asians in East Africa.* (Chicago: Nelson Hall, 1972).

[3] Studies of more populous castes include David F. Pocock, *Kanbi and Patidar* (Oxford: Clarendon Press, 1972); Harald Tambs-Lyche, *London Patidars* (London: Routledge & Kegan Paul, 1980); Rohit Barot, "Caste and Sect in the Swaminarayan Movement", in R. Burghart (ed.), *Hinduism in Great Britain: The Perpetuation of Religion in an Alien Cultural Milieu* (London: Tavistock, 1987); Maureen Michaelson, "The Relevance of Caste among East African Gujaratis in Britain", *New Community*, vol. 7, no. 3 (1979), pp. 350–60; Maureen Michaelson, "Caste, Kinship and Marriage: A Study of Two Gujarati Trading Castes in England", unpublished Ph.D. thesis, University of London, 1983.

[4] S.V. Mukerjea (ed.), "Baroda District", in *Census of India 1931*, vol. xix, 1931; R.E. Enthoven, *The Tribes and Castes of Bombay* (Central Government Press, 1920).

[5] H.S. Morris, *The Indians in Uganda* (London: Weidenfeld and Nicolson, 1968); Bharati, *The Asians in East Africa*; Michaelson, "Caste, Kinship and Marriage"; Kim Knott, *Hinduism in Leeds: A Study of Religious Practice in the Indian Hindu Community and in Hindu-Related Groups* (Community Religions Project, University of Leeds, 1986); David Bowen, "The Evolution of Gujarati Hindu Organisations in Bradford", in Burghart, *Hinduism in Great Britain.*

group were Kolis.[6] At Haria near Bulsar in south Gujarat there were two Mochi families out of 299, the majority being Anavils and Dublas,[7] and at Mahi village in central Gujarat there were four Mochis in a total adult population of 1,972, the major groups being Patidars and Kolis.[8] The same is true for Mochis throughout the State, with each town or village supporting several families.[9]

With no detailed study focusing primarily on the Mochis available, the two most informative accounts are those of Enthoven and Mukerjea, both of which provide a brief statistical and descriptive portrait.[10] In 1931, there were nearly 27,000 Mochis living in the area now officially known as Gujarat, and the caste was divided into three exogamous sections, the Ahmedabadis from central Gujarat, the Khambatis from the west (generally known as Kathiawadis) and the Surtis from south Gujarat. The Khambatis were the largest section, numbering about 13,500. The Ahmedabadi section were about 7,500, and the Surtis about 6,000.[11] The Mochis were mostly Hindu, though some had converted to Islam and a few were Jains.

Like many other low-caste groups, they laid claim to prestigious origins in the distant and legendary past:

According to their own account they were Rajputs living near Champaner, who got their present name because one of them made a pair of stockings or *moju* out of a tiger's skin. Traces of their Rajput descent appear in their tribal surnames: Chohan, Chudasma, Dabhi, Gohel, Jhala, Makwana, Maru, Parmar, Rathod, Solanki and Vaghela.[12]

However through misfortune in war Mochis were forced to take up the lowly occupation of leather-worker. Thus in common with many other skilled artisan caste groups in Gujarat, they claim descent from princely Kshatriyas and regard themselves as "fallen Rajputs".[13]

[6] C.N. Shukla, *Life and Labour in a Gujarat Taluka* (Bombay: Longmans, Green, 1937).

[7] V.H. Joshi, "Economic Development and Social Change in a South Gujarat Village" (unpubl. MS., University of Baroda, 1966).

[8] Panchanadikar and Panchanadikar, "Social Stratification and Institutional Change in a Gujarat Village", *Sociological Bulletin*, vol. 25, no. 2 (1976), pp. 225–40.

[9] The caste association directory for Mochis in Leeds, *Pragati Mandal Directory* (Leeds: Pragati Mandal, 1980), shows that those settled in the city came originally from sixty different villages, towns and cities.

[10] Enthoven, *The Tribes and Castes of Bombay*; Mukerjea, "Baroda District".

[11] To establish these figures I have reworked the statistics provided in volumes 8, 10 and 19 of the 1931 *Census of India* ("Baroda District" [vol. XIX], "Western India States Agency" [vol. X], "Bombay Presidency" [vol. VIII]). The area which is now Gujarat was previously divided into political divisions which bore no relation to current patterns of regional organisation and association.

[12] Mukerjea, "Baroda District", p. 451.

[13] *Ibid.*, p. 435. Claims to Kshatriya or Rajput status by other Gujarati communities are mentioned in Pocock, *Kanbi and Patidar*, *op. cit.*; A.M. Shah and R.G. Shroff,

Elsewhere in India those whose traditional occupation brought them into direct contact with leather are normally regarded as *acchut* — "untouchable". But in Gujarat the position is more complex, for there are two leather-working castes: the Khalpas — skinners and tanners; and the Mochis — who used prepared leather to make items such as saddles or shoes. In traditional estimation only the former were explicitly designated as untouchable. Thus although they are of low status, the Mochis are formally regarded as belonging to the Sudra Varna, as do all other skilled artisans. So in sharp contrast to the North Indian Mochis, who form a subsection of the leather-working Chamar caste and are thus held to be untouchable,[14] Mochis in Gujarat are not seen in this way, nor were they so designated in the 1931 Census:

The Mochi holds a low position in social scale, and though he does not touch Khalpas, Dheds or other depressed classes, a high caste Hindu formerly considered the touch of a Mochi a pollution . . . the use of flesh and liquor has grown less and in some places has ceased. For this reason, and also on account of the advance of the caste in education, the Mochi has lost his "untouchable" character in Gujarat, unlike other provinces, and is freely admitted to schools etc., and mingle without restraint with other classes.[15]

Older Mochis in Britain, when speaking of life in Gujarat, recall that the Khalpas were seen as being potentially polluting and hence of inferior status. However they also recall that they themselves were the victims of similar prejudices, and that from 1935 up to 1962 the Mochis were classified, along with the Khalpas, as amongst the "Backward Classes" of Gujarat.[16] While this did not alter their rank

---

"The Vahivanca Barots of Gujarat: A Caste of Genealogists and Mythographers", in Milton Singer (ed.), *Traditional India: Structure and Change* (Austin: University of Texas, 1959); Michaelson, "Caste, Kinship and Marriage"; Banks, "On the Srawacs or Jains". The Chamars of North India, as distinct from so many groups in the West, claim Brahmin origins: G.W. Briggs, *The Chamars* (Delhi: B.R. Publishing Corporation, 1975 [1920]).

[14] In Leeds, the anniversary of Ravidas, a revered and respected North Indian Chamar from the sixteenth century, is celebrated. Ravidas provides an exemplar for some Mochis in Leeds who have become vegetarian and pride themselves on their hard work in the Hindu temple.

[15] Mukerjea, "Baroda District", p. 451.

[16] The "Backward Classes" comprised the Scheduled Castes, the Scheduled Tribes and the Other Backward Classes. The Khalpas were a Scheduled Caste; the Mochis one of the Other Backward Classes. In 1962 this situation changed, and only the first two categories continued to be singled out for protective discrimination: André Beteille, *Castes: Old and New* (London: Asia Publishing House, 1969); J.M. Mahar (ed.), *The Untouchables of Contemporary India* (Tucson: University of Arizona Press, 1972). In a detailed study of untouchability in rural Gujarat, Desai found that there was some improvement in the economic and social welfare conditions of untouch-

in the ritual hierarchy, it did entitle both to certain advantages on the grounds of their social deprivation.

Mochis in East Africa and Britain

The Mochis, like members of other Gujarati communities, migrated to East Africa in the colonial and post-colonial period, but on arrival they remained a small and relatively powerless minority. Many continued to work as makers or sellers of shoes, but in Uganda they were a tiny minority in trading circles: only 1% of trading licenses went to them, while 70% were held by Patidars, Lohanas and Ismailis.[17] Also, while trade was the goal of most East African migrants, many members of the *choti jati* continued to rely on their caste occupations to make a living,[18] for two reasons: first, these artisan trades continued to be economically lucrative in East Africa, and secondly members of higher *jatis* still refused to engage in polluting occupations.[19] Thus in contrast to the trading castes for whom endogamy became the only remaining feature of caste practice, the *choti jati* "have preserved trade-exclusiveness as a structural criterion".[20] This is similar to the available evidence about the Mochis and all the other artisan castes in Gujarat, most of which have similarly maintained their long-standing specialisms. A further important factor is the pride in their own skills found in all the *choti jatis*, particularly amongst the Mochis. The saying "Even if sawn in two a Mochi remains a Mochi"[21] neatly sums up their attitudes.

Of the Mochis in Britain, around three-quarters arrived by way of East Africa.[22] The exodus from the region began in the mid-1960s with families coming first from Tanzania, then Kenya and finally, in 1972, Uganda, largely as a result of Africanisation policies. In the same period a number of Mochi families also arrived from Fiji. There are no formal statistics for the number of Mochis in Britain, but it seems likely that they amount to 6-7,000 people. The largest populations are in Birmingham, Leicester and London, followed by Leeds, Coventry, Wellingborough and Luton, with smaller numbers in Bradford, Preston and Maidstone.

---

ables, particularly in the south, though cultural changes were very slow: I.P. Desai, *Untouchability in Rural Gujarat* (Bombay: Popular Prakashan, 1976).
[17] Morris, *The Indians in Uganda*, pp. 91, 184–5.
[18] Bharati, *The Asians in East Africa*, p. 35.
[19] *Ibid.*
[20] *Ibid.*, p. 64.
[21] Mukerjea, "Baroda District", pp. 451–2.
[22] Leeds Pragati Mandal, *Pragati Mandal Directory; Directory 1983* (Bradford: Kshatriya Sudharak Mandal, 1983).

The Mochis of Leeds

The Mochis are the largest Gujarati group in Leeds. Amongst Hindus, they are slightly outnumbered by the Punjabi Khatris, and the city's population also includes rather larger communities of Sikh Ramgarhias and Jats, also of Punjabi origin. Just under half of Leeds's Gujaratis are Mochis, and a further third are Patidars, while the remainder are drawn from a range of other castes such as Suthars, Lohanas and Brahmins. In 1979, the local Hindu population numbered about 2,500, of whom about two-thirds were Gujarati. There are no reliable figures for the growth of the Hindu population since then, but numbers will undoubtedly have risen. Given the high proportion of young people, births substantially outnumber deaths.

In 1980 the Pragati Mandal (the Leeds Mochi Association) produced a directory listing all its adult male members, which showed there were a total of 143 Mochi households in the Leeds area, suggesting a total head-count of about 650 persons.[23] Compared with other higher-caste Gujarati groups in Leicester, London and Birmingham, this is a very small figure; nevertheless, the Mochis substantially outnumber all other Gujarati castes in Leeds, a factor of some relevance in patterns of cross-caste organisation and socio-political relations in Leeds.

But despite their small numbers, Leeds Mochis are far from being comprehensively united. Even the Pragati Mandal contains several significant sources of tension. First, it serves to unite two distinct regional groups, the Kathiawadis and the Surtis, although the latter group is the much greater force, since only nine of the 143 households are Kathiawadis. Secondly, it represents an amalgam of Mochis who migrated directly from the subcontinent and their caste-fellows who arrived from East Africa.

In the early 1980s, all the Kathiawadi Mochi families lived in Harehills, an inner-city area popular amongst Punjabis and Pakistanis. Three households (each from a different *kutumb* or patrilineal descent group) lived in one street, and another two households (both from the same *kutumb*) lived around the corner from one another. However the majority of Surti Mochis lived in Burley and South Headingley, an area several miles away settled predominantly by Gujarati families and university students. In recent years, a number of extended families have begun to move out to other areas of Leeds, buying houses and small businesses in more suburban areas. Mochis now live in Armley, Alwoodley, Far Headingley, Adel and Horsforth as well as in the key areas of Burley and South Headingley.

---

[23] Leeds Pragati Mandal, *Pragati Mandal Directory*.

At that time, there were complex settlement arrangements among the Surti Mochis. For instance one man, originally from Anaval in South Gujarat, but more recently resident in Nairobi, had settled in a house in South Headingley with two of his sons and their families, while two other sons lived nearby with their own wives and children, as did yet another extended family from Anaval via Nairobi. There were many similar cases involving tight-knit patterns of settlement, although it was clear that educational or employment opportunities and changing values had caused families to be more scattered.

The most powerful bond is the *kutumb*, with the result that brothers and cousins usually follow the same migration pattern. Families arriving in Leeds via the same African city, often hailing from the same town or village in Gujarat may well also choose houses within easy reach of one another. In Britain, as in India, it is the women who are expected to move away from their natal homes on marriage, so in being transformed from daughters into wives they also move from one *kutumb* to another. Nowadays, however, it is not unusual for young couples to set up nuclear units some way away from the husband's family home, thanks, amongst other things, to the addition of the woman's wages to the family purse.

Mochi settlement in Leeds began in the late 1950s. By then the once thriving local leather and footwear industry was in decline,[24] but tanneries and boot and shoemakers were still in evidence in the city. The first Mochi to settle in the city was an educated and ambitious young man from Bulsar in south Gujarat who found work as an assistant foreman at Gibsons, a local tannery. In 1959, after a short stay in Birmingham, his cousin Trikumlal came up to live with him in Leeds, and took a job in the same tannery.[25] These two men were the first Gujarati Hindus to settle in Leeds, although a Patidar had lived in nearby Batley for a year or so before their arrival.

Within a year of arriving in Leeds, Trikumlal Bulsara had bought a house in South Headingley[26] which provided shelter for other

[24] In 1870, there were thirty-four tanneries, 700 shoemakers and 100 boot and shoe manufacturers; by 1893 the industry had grown still further, supporting 11,500 workers. At that time, "as an immigrant occupation, footwear ranked second only to tailoring" (p. 121) with a large number of Jewish workers: Joseph Buckman, *Immigrants and the Class Struggle: The Jewish Immigrant in Leeds, 1880–1914* (Manchester University Press, 1983). By 1959–60 the number of factories had been reduced to fifteen tanners and carriers, fifteen boot and shoe manufacturers and two surgical boot-makers.

[25] There were also three or four households, containing several Mochi males, in London at this time.

[26] Trikumlal Bulsara, a founder member of the Pragati Mandal and an official in the Hindu Temple management committee, was an extremely active community member until his death in 1985. He was of great assistance in providing information for this study.

Mochis from the subcontinent and East Africa then beginning to arrive. Trikumlal bought another, bigger house in 1962, and around the same time he and some of his friends obtained work at H.W. Poole, a surgical boot- and shoemaker. Two years later these men founded a community association, the Pragati Mandal, the first Gujarati organisation in Leeds and indeed the first Mochi caste association anywhere in Britain;[27] its aims were to maintain links with the subcontinent, foster ties amongst settlers in Britain, offer cultural and educational support to its members, and send money back to be used by and distributed through the parent association in south Gujarat. Its formation proved timely, as a year later a substantial number of Mochi families began to arrive in Leeds from Tanzania and Kenya.[28] Four years later, a similar organisation was formed to serve Mochi families in nearby Bradford.

Further organisations were set up in Leeds during the mid-1960s. The Hindu Cultural Society was formed in 1966, largely by Punjabi Hindus, although some Gujarati Mochis and Patidars were involved. The following year, the Society established a Hindu Charitable Trust and in 1970 it bought a large house in Burley for use as a temple and cultural centre. Until 1988, when the Sanatan Hindu temple was opened in Chapeltown by the West Yorkshire Bengali Hindu population, this was the sole non-sectarian religious meeting-place for the Leeds Hindus.[29] Yet despite their involvement in cross-caste religio-cultural ventures, Mochis remained committed to their own separate organisations. In 1969, the Mahila Mandal, a women's section of the Pragati Mandal was set up, and in the mid-1970s many young Mochis became involved in a boys' youth club affiliated to the Hindu Swayamsevak Sangh; it specialised in sporting activities, and its leader was a local Mochi.[30]

---

[27] In nearby Bradford a Gujarati association, the Bhartiya Mandal, had been formed as early as 1957. It served all caste and religious groups, including the few Mochis resident in Bradford at that time: Rashmi Desai, *Indian Immigrants in Britain* (London: Oxford University Press, 1963); Bowen, "The Evolution of Gujarati Hindu Organisations in Bradford".

[28] The settlement pattern of most Hindu migrants — including Gujarati Mochis — has been rather different to that proposed by Roger and Catherine Ballard for the Sikhs: "The Sikhs: The Development of South Asian Settlements in Britain", in James Watson (ed.), *Between Two Cultures: Migrants and Minorities in Britain* (Oxford: Basil Blackwell, 1977). Theirs has been a later settlement, characterised particularly by their arrival from East Africa as whole families, often with useful skills and knowledge gained from their previous migration experience.

[29] Members of the Sathya Sai Baba Movement and the Swaminarayan Hindu Mission have met in the homes of members.

[30] As Bowen says ("The Evolution of Gujarati Hindu Organisations in Bradford"), the right-wing political overtones of the Indian Hindu Swayamsevak Sangh, to a large extent, were neutralised in its British counterpart.

This was part of a more general pattern. The 1960s, and early '70s witnessed the founding a wide range of religious and cultural facilities.[31] Some of these sought to involve whole the Hindu population, but many of the larger castes formed representative organisations of their own, on a national and sometimes even an international basis. Both kinds of initiative — the first generally Hindu, and the second more caste-specific — developed at the same time, and often involved the same people. As a result the relationship between the Mochi community and other sections of the local Hindu population is complex. While the Mochis are internally divided by regional origins and settlement history, they invariably seek when representing their interests to outsiders to operate as a single unit. Thus while the Pragati Mandal is of great formal significance — for it allows Mochis to present themselves as a united and effective community — it matters less within their own social arena, where it does no more than organise an annual dinner and about four committee meetings a year. Kinship is still the primary vehicle for everyday social relationships, so local structures are essentially informal. Hence it is in external contexts that the Pragati Mandal comes into its own.

National and International Links

Together with nine other *choti jat* caste associations, the Pragati Mandal is affiliated to the Gujarati Arya Kshatriya Mahasabha UK. The Mahasabha organises an annual cricket league and a bi-annual *garaba* (folk dance) competition in Birmingham, the latter maintaining at least a semblance of cultural homogeneity and allowing kinship ties to be underlined by a more formal organisational structure. Parallel Mahasabhas have been established in Fiji, Kenya and a number of other African countries, and all are affiliated to the Surat and Bulsar District Mochi Parishad. Besides coordinating its offshoots in the diaspora, this last body also provides a focus for charitable work in south Gujarat: to this day rural Mochis still seek help from their local caste *panch* with financial and marital problems, and if these cannot be resolved locally, they are referred upwards to the *taluka panch*.

A further vital role of the Parishad is its sponsorship of the quarterly magazine *Hitechu*, a vital source of news and information about developments in Gujarat, especially for those who came to Britain directly from India. Such news tends, however, to be much less

[31] Robert Jackson, "The Shree Krishna Temple and the Gujarati Hindu Community in Coventry", in David G. Bowen (ed.), *Hinduism in England* (Bradford: Bradford College, 1981); David G. Bowen, "The Hindu Community in Bradford" in Bowen, *Hinduism in England*; Bowen, "The Evolution of Gujarati Hindu Organisations in Bradford".

significant to those in the second generation of overseas residence, most of whose immediate kin are now settled either in Britain or Africa. To some, then, the geographical span of Mochi caste relations is wide; to others, the connection with Gujarat has become symbolic, since Britain is now the most significant active arena for caste-based relationships. Indeed many Mochis with a long history of overseas residence now feel socially superior to their caste-fellows back in Gujarat, one result being that few marriages are now contracted with partners from India.

Established family relationships and potential marriage ties are the grounds for keeping in touch with Mochis in other British cities. Compared to the Patidars' complex system of village marriage circles and exogamous clans, the Mochis' marriage rules are straightforward. By tradition Surti, Ahmedabadi and Kathiawadi Mochis should not intermarry, although "wrong" marriages do occasionally occur. Within these exogamous divisions marriage is restricted only by the *sapinda* rules, which forbid marriage between those who can trace descent from a common ancestor within five generations. However the *atak* — an exogamous unit which refers variously to *gotra*, occupation or place of origin, and from which surnames are sometimes derived — has little significance for Mochis. When asked to which *atak* they belong, most state their surname, e.g. "Parmar", "Solanki" or "Chauhan". However those who share such a name are not affected by rules of exogamy.

Mochis only began to use surnames early in the twentieth century, particularly in connection with the registration of property rights. Most adopted prestigious Rajput clan names, but some chose place names (Bulsara, Surti), deity names (Ramji), or occupational names (Tailor) instead. In Leeds nearly all Mochis use the name Parmar, but this does not restrict marriage choices. Position within the caste is more meaningfully identified by the *kutumb* name of one's father or husband, or on one's original *gam* or village, although more probing questions are asked if the object is to ascertain whether a particular person might be suitable as a marriage partner.

Most Mochis vehemently deny practising hypergamy and dowry-giving, saying "Only Patels do that!", but a small number of wealthy families do engage in elaborate and cripplingly expensive gift-giving. In most families, however, marriage is accompanied by little more than the exchange of symbolic gifts: while jewellery is sent with the bride at the time of her wedding, the groom's family provides her with new clothes as well as the *mangala-sutra* or wedding necklace.

Employment

Barring a few elderly women and those affected by recession, most Leeds Mochi women go out to work before and after marriage and have done so ever since the earliest phase of settlement.[32] At the outset most found jobs in the clothing industry, where many are still seamstresses or pressers. Some do other manual jobs such as cleaning, and others are self-employed and work from home, producing food or items of clothing, or selling cosmetics. Younger women have begun to move into office work as secretaries, and many are training through day release or night classes for banking or bookkeeping qualifications. In common with their contemporaries of other castes, a growing number of young Mochis of both sexes study engineering, accountancy and a range of other science-based subjects at university or college. Law is frequently mentioned when girls are asked about their future career plans.

These changes will obviously take the community far from its traditional occupation of leather-working. Some Mochis, like the early settlers, are still employed in Leeds's tanneries and in the boot and shoe industry, but the contraction of manufacturing cost many their jobs, leading to high unemployment. Over the years there has been a steady growth in the number of small businesses run by the Leeds Mochis: Trikumlal Bulsara's household goods shop was the first of many such businesses, which now include off-licenses, small grocers, newsagents and video shops, not to mention a motor repair garage, a watchmaker, a tailor, a chiropodist, an insurance broker and a Gujarati vegetarian restaurant. In 1984 there were sixteen small businesses among a population of about 650, and although their number has since increased, it still lags far behind the figure for the smaller Patidar community. In 1984 around 450 Leeds Patidars owned some forty small businesses, and now they include three medical practitioners, several solicitors, a pharmacy, a petrol station and a launderette as well as many licensed grocers and newsagents.

As more young people achieve success in education and move into clerical or professional jobs, the Mochis may begin to catch up. Their slow progress by Gujarati standards reflects their social and occupational heritage as a poor artisan group with little or no earlier experience as traders. So although the "merchant ideology" of most other Gujaratis affects the Mochis, they have not yet developed its

---

[32] For accounts of Gujarati women in Britain and work, see Sallie Westwood, "Workers and Wives: Continuities and Discontinuities in the Lives of Gujarati Women", and Shrikala Warrier, "Marriage, Maternity and Female Economic Activity", in Sallie Westwood and Parminder Bhachu (eds), *Enterprising Women: Ethnicity, Economy and Gender Relations* (London: Routledge, 1988).

potential very far. Despite radical change in their social and geographical environment, Leeds Mochis are still a predominantly working-class community, thus controlling fewer resources and wielding
less power than their Patidar neighbours.

However, the community's caste and class position is defined by
its relationship with other South Asians of differing caste and ethnic
backgrounds, particularly in the public domain of religious practice.
In Leeds, as we saw earlier, this has been organised collectively,
drawing in Hindus from right across the city regardless of caste and
sectarian affiliation.

Social Interaction through Religion

Until 1983, Leeds was the home of a well-known Mochi holy woman,
Prabhadevi Chauhan.[33] Born and brought up in south Gujarat, Deviji
came to Britain from Nairobi in the early 1960s, and there she soon
attracted a constant stream of visitors. As well as Mochis, Patidars
and other Gujarati Hindus from the Leeds and Bradford area, they
included Bengalis, Punjabi Sikhs and Pakistani Muslims. In an interview in 1982, she explained that she had been devoutly religious since
1947, getting up at 4 a.m. and praying for two hours each day: "Every
day I pray the Gita, and some prayer for Mataji, also *arti*, and the
beads, the 108 beads."[34]

Local opinion about Prabhadevi varied. Some said that when she
first came to Leeds she had the power to work magic, *jadu*, but only
used her talents privately. Others alleged that her powers were used
initially in black magic, but that she stopped praying to the goddess
Kali, turning instead to the goddess Ambamata to help people with
their personal worries and problems. When people consulted her, it
was said that "*Mataji ave*" (the Goddess comes): Prabhadevi was said
to be possessed by Ambamata, who was able by using her as a medium
to heal sickness, bring good fortune to those without work, make
infertile women pregnant, cause sons to be born in families without
them, and so on. Prabhadevi usually gave her clients a tonic of rice
or lemon and in return they gave her money and gifts. Sometimes,
she contacted the dead on their behalf by going into a trance. Of this
she said:

One woman came to me at home and said, "My father has died three months
ago: I want to find out why he has died and what his end is, but he won't

---

[33] John Bowker, *Worlds of Faith: Religious Belief and Practice in Britain Today*
(London: Ariel Books/BBC, 1983); Knott, *Hinduism in Leeds, op. cit.*
[34] Bowker, *Worlds of Faith*, p. 72.

talk to me". So I take the three hours of prayer, and I find out what her father won't say, then I give exactly the answer.[35]

Such powers are said to run in families, and within such families Shakti — the divine, female creative power — can turn to good or bad, or lie dormant.[36] Rumours abound. In Leeds, for example, several Mochi women are said by others to serve the dark goddess, Kali.[37] One was said to have caused considerable fear and anxiety not only in the Mochi Community but among Gujarati Hindus at large by conspiring with Kali to subjugate her husband. The whole family was viewed with deep suspicion, and a young woman who had married one of her sons and then left him lived in constant fear of reprisal. When anything untoward happened — to a young baby, a successful businessman, a pregnant mother or a happy child — it would be said that *"dakane kare lu che"*, the witch has made it happen. This particular *dakan* was thought to cast spells at home or use the power of the evil eye to produce evil effects on people. One woman was so fearful that she spent much of her pregnancy behind locked doors, but if they did meet in the street, it was of the utmost importance that the *dakan* be treated with great respect for fear of provoking her wrath.

Several other Mochi women in Leeds were also said to be mediums for Ambamata (another manifestation of Shakti) particularly at the time of the festival of Navratri. The nine night festival is closely associated with worship of the goddess, and its celebration is popular amongst Gujaratis because of the opportunity it provides for folk dancing. In many cities the festival is celebrated along caste lines, and in Leeds the Kathiawadis have sometimes met separately from Surti Mochis to dance the *garaba* and *ras*, the two dances at the heart of the festival.

Since for Gujaratis Navratri focuses on the worship of the goddess Ambamata, women play important roles in its celebration.[38] This is also the time when those women who are mediums become entranced by the goddess, though usually only in the company of their own immediate relatives and friends. In this sense they differ from women like those described above whose reputations not only extend beyond

[35] *Ibid.*, p. 105.
[36] A number of people take a more academic interest in the beliefs and practices related to magic. One family I visited owned a Gujarati book, *Jadu Mantra Tantra Prakash*, containing pictures of both Ambamata and Kali, as well as complex spells addressed to both.
[37] Knott, *Hinduism in Leeds*, pp. 173–5.
[38] Penny Logan, "Practising Religion: British Hindu Children and the Navratri Festival", *British Journal of Religious Education*, vol. 10, no. 3 (1988), pp. 160–9; Merryle McDonald, "Rituals of Motherhood among Gujarati Women of East London" in Burghart (ed.), *Hinduism in Great Britain*, *op. cit.*, pp. 50–66.

the caste boundary, but who operate beyond it as well, whether for
good, as with Prabhadevi, or ill (by rumour at least), as with the
dakan. But in both cases inter-caste divisions evaporate: in the face
of such mystical powers every Gujarati is both a potential client and
a potential victim.

Because her clients came to visit Prabhadevi in her own house, it
eventually became known as "*Mataji Mandir*", and a meeting place
for all of them regardless of their caste; and despite her own low-caste
status, Deviji's charisma and spiritual power drew in large numbers
of higher-caste supplicants. They entered her house and received food
blessed by the goddess, *prasad*, from her hands; and although some
questioned her authenticity, her social status was never a matter of
dispute.

However it was not only at "*Mataji Mandir*" that Hindus of all
castes found their paths crossing. They had much the same experience
at the nearby temple run by the Hindu Charitable Trust. This, as we
saw earlier, was deliberately established by and run for all Leeds'
Hindus, and although its management committee has at different
times been all-Gujarati and all-Punjabi, a balance has more often been
struck between the two. In 1984, for example, it consisted of two
Punjabis, two Gujarati Mochis and a Patidar, all of whom were
seriously committed to improving facilities for non-sectarian worship
(*sanatan dharma*) and fostering cross-caste cooperation.

The majority of Mochis are members of the Leeds temple, and
together make up around two-thirds of its membership. Most visit at
least for the major festivals of Navratri, Mahasivratri, Holi and Jana-
mastami, but some attend much more regularly — a few even doing
so daily. Indeed during the early 1980s, when no Brahman priest was
in residence, some devout Mochis decided in the absence of an
appropriate ritual specialist that there was no alternative to performing
daily *puja* and *arti* themselves.[39] Worship now proceeds in a rather
more orthodox way, but it still regularly brings Mochis, Patidars,
Punjabi Khatris and Brahmans together in the same place. More
informal friendships and associations tend, except amongst committee members and a few more westernised families, to be caste-
specific; there is little sign of overt prejudice, but most people find
it easier to mix with those with whom they already have a relationship.

Despite their involvement in the temple, Mochis often refer to
themselves as a community which is largely uninterested in religious
matters. Naturally, there are individuals for whom this is far from the

[39] Only members of the Brahmin caste are of sufficient ritual purity to conduct temple
rituals. There are those in low or untouchable castes in India who have some special
religious powers (particularly to conduct services to or become possessed by spirits
of various kinds), but these never extend to temple rites.

truth: some older men and women are renowned for leading a devout life focused on domestic worship and prayer.[40] However one particular characteristic of the Leeds Mochis is their lack of participation in sectarian movements.[41] Thus while many Gujarati Hindus in Britain are strenuously involved in the Swaminarayan movement, the Sathya Sai Baba fellowship, Pushti Marg and the Hare Krishna Movement, the Mochis are noticeably disinterested. A few profess devotion to Shirdi Sai Baba, Jalaram Bapa or the goddess Santoshi Ma, but no formal groupings focused on these figures have yet emerged in Leeds.

Caste and Class among the Mochis

In Leeds, as in some other British cities, Mochis have congregated together in sufficiently large numbers to form a majority of the local Hindu population. This is in sharp contrast to rural Gujarat, where they were thinly spread as isolated family units. In Leeds, as in Gujarat, many initially worked as shoemakers — indeed some deliberately chose the city as a settlement base because of its traditional, though by then declining leather-working industry. Yet despite pride in their artisan tradition, many have since abandoned it. While some of the older generation saw shoemaking as a means to make enough money to set up their own business, many of their British-born offspring set their sights on quite different goals. Thus while the "merchant ideology" so characteristic of Gujarat is still influential amongst the first generation, it is being replaced by a "professional ideology" in the second generation, who often speak of the "DEAD" — Doctors, Engineers, Accountants and Dentists. In seeking to pursue such careers Mochis and most other British Gujaratis are following parallel paths.

Even so, their experiences are not identical with those of the Patidars and Lohanas. More Mochis are factory workers; most Mochi women go out to work to supplement the family income; and because they lack experience of trade and capital acquisition as part of their caste heritage, rather fewer have set up their own businesses. Thus despite their strong commitment to *pragati* (progress), they are still a disadvantaged group in Gujarati terms. Nevertheless they maintain a considerable amount of corporate caste activity, notably through endogamous marriage, active maintenance of a caste association, and continued involvement in shoemaking and related occupations. How-

---

[40] For more information on the religious life of the Leeds Mochi community see Knott, *Hinduism in Leeds*.

[41] Bharati reached much the same conclusion in his account of Hinduism in East Africa, for he reports that "most *choti jat* people identify with the more conservative, *sanatani* type of Hinduism" (*The Asians in East Africa*, p. 67).

ever, this is not indicative of a *systematic* maintenance of caste relations; Mochis no longer make shoes for members of other Gujarati castes, and those still involved with leather-related activities work in factories producing goods for the open market. Hence their relationship to their nominally hereditary occupation has became increasingly peripheral, while they have also developed much the same structures, and pursue much the same goals, as do other Gujarati castes in Britain.[42]

A further feature of Mochi experience in Britain is that while first — generation women and men tell many stories of the prejudice once shown towards them by higher-caste people back in Gujarat because of their involvement with leather, few such stories are told about inter-caste relations in Britain. While one pandit from the Hindu temple refused to accept water offered to him in their homes, Mochis have been extremely active in local religious life, to the point of conducting *puja* in the temple in the absence of a Brahmin. Likewise they routinely eat alongside members of higher castes: prejudice on the basis of potential pollution seems largely to have disappeared from inter-caste transactions. Had Mochis felt ostracised either in Britain or in East Africa through their work with leather, they might have felt the need to abandon their specialism, but instead many continued with it. It is the decline in the local shoemaking industry, together with the pursuit of self-employment and professional qualifications by the second generation, which has finally begun to sever the community's links with its ancestral craft.

Women and Resistance[43]

We have examined the role of the caste association and kinship networks in maintaining of caste differentiation, and the way in which the community relates to others in religious contexts. But one also has to remember that the Mochis themselves are not internally homogeneous — some aspects of that diversity, as between the Kathiawadis and Surtis, have been already been mentioned — and as the Mochi presence in Britain has grown steadily over the past thirty-five years, new issues have come to the fore and new demarcation lines have been drawn. Women's activities, which became increasingly important after the first wives and wives-to-be arrived in the early 1960s,

---

[42] Tambs-Lyche, *London Patidars*; Michaelson, "Caste, Kinship and Marriage"; Michaelson, "The Relevance of Caste among East African Gujaratis".

[43] Parmar discusses the issue of Indian women whose resistance is expressed in labour disputes in P. Parmar, "Gender, Race and Class: Asian Women in Resistance", in *The Empire Strikes Back* (London: Centre for Contemporary Cultural Studies/Hutchinson, 1982).

now extend well beyond the spheres of work and religion. So, for example, while women have had their own "Mahila" sub-section in the Pragati Mandal since 1969, they were not entitled to stand for election to the full committee, membership of which is restricted to heads of households. But since some households are now headed by women, calls have been made — so far without success — for them to be allowed to join it. While there is some support from both sexes for this innovation, the majority view is still that women should be content with membership of the Mahila section.

Perhaps unwittingly, a further group of women has been led to challenge the caste's established principles — those who have taken the decision, for whatever reason, to leave their husbands. When marriages break down an effort to resolve the couple's differences is invariably made by other caste members, who urge the woman to return and try again. Those who fail to renegotiate the relationship and decide to live separately often feel rejected by the community and isolated from it: single women with children find it particularly hard to gain acceptance and to escape the taint of continuous gossip and scandal.

Likewise many young women who have not yet entered the trials of marriage and householdership are privately vociferous about their experiences, especially the issue of gossip. They are aware that these matters often come to a head at weddings and festivals, when their elders have the opportunity to discuss the behaviour of others, swap stories and spread rumours. One girl spoke of her experience at the festival of Navratri: "I know quite a lot of Gujarati lads from school, just to talk to. I see them go by. I talk to them, you know, when you're doing the stick dance, but, I mean, if anyone sees you, that's it. They'd just start talking. Even if you just say 'Hi. How are you?'" From the adults' viewpoint, criticism of such behaviour is justified; it reflects general concern for the good name of the family, and the difficulties that any blemish might bring when they seek to establish a respectable marriage in the future. Most young people cannot come to terms with the operation of caste, and fail to understand its complexities. To many it is simply iniquitous:

"What I don't really like about religion is all the castes and everything. That's what really gets me, you know. One's higher than the other. I don't really believe in that. You're a person. Everybody's the same. I mean, my father, he believes that you can't get married to another Indian unless he's a Shoemaker . . . I got really angry because he said, 'If you get married to somebody else who is Indian but not a Shoemaker, I'll disown you'. This is what I think: as long as he's Indian, you know, he's still human."

Another young woman took up the same theme:

"I think we're all one as it is. All we've been given is different castes and religions. Underneath that we're all the same. That's what I believe. It doesn't matter to me what religion you are and what caste you are. You should be able to see who you want when you want, and marry who you want."

But she also recognised the boundary-maintaining function of caste, particularly in courtship and marriage. So although she wished it were possible to take home a Mistry boy and tell her parents "This is just someone I'm seeing at the moment", she also recognised that for the time being this was just a dream. As for herself, she is convinced, like most of her peers, that caste is both restrictive and unjust.

Nevertheless there have been cases where young people have felt sufficiently confident to oppose their parents' choice of partner, and marry outside the caste. Although there is usually consultation over such decisions, this is an area where what one thinks and feels about the issue is very different from what one actually does. Yet most still see family loyalty as necessarily taking precedence over personal views and attachments. So when young women marry outside the caste and thus contradict their parents' wishes, they invariably suffer hostility and isolation.

In such complex circumstances resistance is neither easy nor straightforward. Yet, as we have seen, women have often been at the forefront, especially where they found themselves at odds with the prevailing values of established caste practice.

Some men may also take up positions of resistance to caste, but for them it is tends to have a different meaning. Women are just as bound by caste as men; indeed they are often its most wholehearted upholders. But how far are they wholly members of it? Women are responsible for preserving the purity and honour of the family, and play a key role in maintaining kinship relationships through marriage arrangements and gift exchange. They can also contribute to the economic well-being of the caste — and hence to its status in relation to others — both through their wages and through the nature of their work occupation, whether office or manual work, participating in the family business or training for a professional qualification. Nevertheless women's participation in the affairs of the caste is often channelled into women-only networks and family gatherings and thus largely hidden from view.

Women's voices often resonate with feelings of isolation, and with the pressure of the norms and expectations by which they feel bound. These voices, and many others yet unheard, are also part of the Leeds Mochis' story.

JAIN WAYS OF BEING

Marcus Banks

This chapter explores the ways in which the Gujarati Jains living in Leicester have set about maintaining and expressing their corporate identity.[1] Although they belong to two different *jatis* — one of which is discussed in far more detail than the other — both use much the same cultural dialectic to organise their corporate behaviour. At one level this proceeds as a closed set of negotiations between the two *jatis*: indeed the differences in meaning and cultural direction to which these give rise are a major theme of this chapter. However their discourse is simultaneously conducted on several further levels, for both groups are equally heavily involved in a wider set of negotiations about their location within Britain's wider South Asian community. On the discourse between the two *jatis* — and hence within contexts largely congruent with the religious structure and organization of the Jain religion — I seek to show that Jainism regularly renews and maintains itself through working out of inbuilt tensions, so that its followers experience repeated cycles of cohesion and fracture. And although such cycles can also be observed amongst Jain populations in India and East Africa, I am primarily concerned here with tracing these processes of coming together and drawing apart amongst the Jains of Leicester.[2]

Jains in Britain

About 17,000 people living in Britain are followers of the Jain faith.

[1] I did fieldwork in Leicester and Gujarat State, India, in 1982–3, and made several later visits to both locations, so the "ethnographic present" of this chapter is located in the mid-1980s. I am grateful to the (then) Social Science Research Council and to the Smuts Memorial Fund, Cambridge, for their financial assistance.

[2] In many ways the discussion in this chapter parallels that developed in my paper "Competing to Give, Competing to Get: Gujarati Jains in Britain" in Anwar and Werbner's *Black and Ethnic Leaderships in Britain* (Routledge, 1991), which examines the financial and leadership strategies of the Leicester Jains; to a rather lesser extent parallel arguments may also be found in my chapter entitled "Orthodoxy and Dissent: Varieties of Religious Belief among Immigrant Gujarati Jains in Britain" in Carrithers and Humphrey (eds), *The Assembly of Listeners: Jains in Society* (Cambridge University Press, 1991), which is concerned with aspects of religious belief among Leicester Jains. The parallelism is deliberate: while all three papers reach similar conclusions, they employ very different kinds of data.

While the vast majority are of Gujarati origin, most arrived in England after a period of residence in East Africa, mostly in Kenya. Few came to England before the early 1960s. Almost all belong to one of two *jatis*: the Visa Srimalis and Halari Visa Oswals — identified hereafter as the Srimalis and the Oswals.[3] In India both groups claim Rajput origin, and fall broadly within the middle-ranking trading castes (*vania jatis*) of Gujarat.[4] Although there are references to the Oswals, my main concern is with the Srimalis. Nevertheless comparison of the organization and activities of the two groups is illuminating. In particular it soon becomes clear that common features occur not so much because of the common logic of their shared religious tradition, but rather because members of both *jatis* have a similar capacity to draw upon — or reject — the resources and potentialities of Jainism in developing their cultural strategies.

Back in Gujarat the two groups differ somewhat in origin: the Oswals' background is primarily as farmers, while the Srimalis' forefathers are more likely to have been traders and shopkeepers, mostly in small urban centres. Amongst Jains in Britain, members of both groups trace their recent origins to the town and district of Jamnagar, on the north coast of the Saurashtran peninsula in the western part of Gujarat State, an area formerly known as Kathiawad. In the Oswals' case the link is exclusive and total: every adult Oswal in Britain knows the name of his or her village of origin, and probably has close kin living there. The Srimalis are less homogeneous in their origins: many trace their ancestry to a variety of regions in Saurashtra, while a minority come from elsewhere in Gujarat and would not normally marry Saurashtrans. But the contrast in the experiences of the Oswals and the Srimalis forms a key element in understanding the courses of their differing cultural, political and economic lives.

Literature on the Srimalis and Oswals, and indeed on Jains in general, is sparse, and the few accounts of the Jain presence in Britain are almost exclusively concerned with the Oswals.[5] There are almost

[3] Some of the Srimalis are in fact Dasa and not Visa Srimali. The Visa-Dasa division is found in many of the trading *jatis* of western India, and is said to refer to the degree of "purity" of the group's descent from the original ancestor. While this distinction is still important in India, it became blurred during the Srimalis' sojourn in Africa, so most now consider themselves Visa. But although both Srimalis and Oswals tend to refer to themselves as such, the latter often identify themselves as "Oswal" too, while the term "Srimali" is rarely heard. The Oswals refer to the Srimalis as "Dasas" and the Srimalis to the Oswals as "Mahajans".

[4] As noted by Arvind M. Shah and Ramesh G. Shroff, "The Vahivancana Barots of Gujarat: A caste of genealogists and mythographers" in Milton Singer (ed.), *Traditional India: Structure and Change* (Philadelphia: The American Folklore Society, 1959, p. 63), in Gujarat the *vaishya* or trading category occupies second place in the *varna* hierarchy, taking precedence over the *kshatriya* (warrior or Rajput) *varna*.

[5] See for example Maureen Michaelson, "Caste, Kinship and Marriage: A study of

as few detailed accounts of other Gujarati groups in Britain, with the result that the dynamics of caste and sect have remained largely undocumented,[6] and that Jains have been either overlooked or lumped casually with the mass of Gujarati Hindus. All this in the face of a large literature in which the crucial importance of religious and caste groups in the formation and maintenance of social structures in India in general and Gujarat in particular is emphasised.

Yet this gap in British Asian studies also reflects confusion amongst Leicester Jains themselves, particularly amongst the Srimalis. How are they best identified — as a *jati* or as a religious group? Before we get to grips with this issue, the content of one of the least known of the world's ancient textual religions will be briefly outlined.[7]

The Religion of the Jina[8]

Jainism (from *jina*, conqueror) is of similar antiquity to Buddhism: both religions are the only surviving remnants of the post-Vedic *sramana* (renunciatory) movements. Its main spokesman was the Kshatriya prince Vardhaman, popularly known as Mahavira (great hero), who taught that extreme asceticism was the most effective means of enlightenment and thus of release from the cycle of rebirth. Mahavira and the later codifiers of Jainism stressed the principle of *ahimsa* (avoidance of violence) as a means of self-discipline: to cause harm to any living thing was said to show violence (and hence worldly attachment or concern) in the soul of the perpetrator, which would in

---

two Gujarati trading castes in England" (unpublished Ph.D. thesis, University of London, 1983) and S. Shah, "Who are the Jains?", *New Community*, vol. 7 (1979), pp. 369–75.

[6] One of the few examples is Maureen Michaelson, "The relevance of caste among East African Gujaratis in Britain", *New Community*, vol. 7 (1979), pp. 350–60.

[7] Jainism does appear in some works — usually intended for theology students or religious education teachers (e.g. Kenneth Folkert, "The Jainas", in C.J. Adams (ed.), *A Reader's Guide to the Great Religions* (New York: Free Press, 1977)) — as a world or "great tradition" religion. However, Jainism seems never to have spread beyond the boundaries of present-day India, and, overseas emigrants apart, its 3.5 million present-day followers are largely confined to four states in western and central India.

[8] Fuller details of the origins of Jainism, its history and the textual structure of its belief (which does not necessarily bear a direct relation to the beliefs and practices of contemporary Jains) can be found in several works, of which the most comprehensive and dispassionate is probably Padmanath S. Jaini, *The Jaina Path of Purification* (Berkeley: University of California Press, 1979). Paul Dundas's recent book (*The Jains*, London: Routledge, 1992) incorporates anthropological perspectives on contemporary Indian Jain belief and practice, while my own *Organising Jainism in India and England* (Oxford: Clarendon Press, 1992) gives much detail on the lives of Jains in both Jamnagar and Leicester.

turn prevent that soul from detaching itself from worldly existence. Although the principle of *ahimsa* can be expressed in many ways, one of its most prominent manifestations is the practice of strict vegetarianism. At its most extreme this can mean avoiding root vegetables and green leaves, because they either contain or harbour large numbers of microscopic life-forms.[9]

If one assumes that the "aim" of any religion (as experienced by its devotees) is to translate worldly problems into the supernatural realm in such a way that they can be dealt with by a supra-human power, Jains find themselves in something of a quandary. While their scriptures acknowledge the existence of deities, these are considered to be as much bound by the passions in their souls as all other forms of existence — including human beings. Hence the only beings considered omnipotent (and thus able to solve the human predicament) are those who have achieved enlightenment; but by that same token such beings must also have severed all ties with the affairs of humankind and the world. Consequently all that Jains can do in search of salvation is revere these heroic beings, hoping to emulate their path. Among these enlightened souls twenty-four, who remained on earth for some time after enlightenment to preach their message, are considered specially important. Mahavira was the last of these teachers — known as *tirthankaras* (ford builders), or *jinas* (conquerors). Modern Jains follow a synthesis of Mahavira's teachings, together with their associated commentaries. In India, the religious tradition is maintained by professional ascetics — *sadhus* (monks) and *sadhvis* (nuns) — but in Britain, which currently supports no such ascetics, religious matters are located firmly in the hands of the laity. Most Jains I have met in Britain (and many in India) not only believe in the power of the *tirthankaras* to offer them aid or blessings, but see no contradiction in making parallel demands on Hindu deities.[10]

Like most other major religious traditions, the Jains are divided into numerous sects and schools. Of these only two are represented in any numbers in England. While the great majority of Oswals and about half the Srimalis are Deravasis (temple dwellers) whose worship may be conducted in temples, the remaining Srimalis are Sthanakavasis (dwellers in halls) who dispense with images and instead meditate in bare halls. Behavioural differences are much less significant than these theological differences. Most British-based

[9] Most Jains in Britain today however follow the normal pattern of Gujarati vegetarianism, which avoids flesh and eggs and which treats certain items such as garlic and onion with suspicion largely because of their reputed aphrodisiac qualities.
[10] Jain religiosity is discussed much more fully in Marcus Banks, "Orthodoxy and Dissent".

Sthanakavasis practise some form of image-focused worship, and the temple remains the principal focus of worship in the Srimali community.

From India to East Africa

Of the many *jatis* in India which are either exclusively Jain or have Jain members, only the Srimalis and the Oswals moved to East Africa in any numbers. Why emigration was restricted to members of only these two *jatis* is not clear, although this is a problem with all migrants' precise social origins. Although it appears easy to show that a certain combination of structural factors precipitated migration, it is far from easy to explain the *non*-migration of those apparently in almost identical circumstances. With the Srimalis and Oswals, the most important factor seems to be that they were the two largest Jain groups in the Saurashtra-Gujarat region. Hence the initial outflow can be explained as the outcome of their ability to "spare" emigrants without compromising their landholding and trade monopoly, while the ongoing process of chain migration ensured that movement would continue to be organised along *jati* lines.

For example, one of my Leicester informants described how many Srimalis from the small town of Lalpur, about 35 km. south of his own home in Jamnagar, emigrated to Uganda around about the turn of the century. In the late 1960s some had moved on to Manchester, where most of the rest joined them after the 1972 expulsion. (By contrast this informant and his brother chose for a variety of reasons to settle in Leicester instead.)

Those analysts who have sought to identify the earliest "push" factor behind emigration from Gujarat often point to the great famine and crop failure in Saurashtra between 1899 and 1901.[11] Yet many of my older informants (all born at least twenty years later) took a different view. They claimed that movement from India to East Africa was primarily driven by a spirit of commercial enterprise; and at least one author takes the view that, for Oswals at least, push factors were soon replaced by pull, for "Word would get around that conditions in Africa were good: other people would emigrate."[12]

Oswal migrants were drawn exclusively from the *bavangami*, a group of fifty-four villages around Jamnagar, although some migrants may also have spent some time away from home either in Bombay or in Jamnagar itself. By contrast, Srimalis tend to come from Jamnagar and its surrounding villages, or from other places in the east

---

[11] See, for example, J. Zarwan, "The social and economic network of an Indian family business in Kenya, 1920–1970", *Kroniek van Africa*, vol. 3 (1975), p. 221.

[12] Zarwan, "The social and economic network", p. 222.

and south of Saurashtra such as Wankaner, Rajkot, Junaghad, Bhanvad, or from towns and villages yet further east such as Ahmedabad and Valsad. On the other hand they were *not* drawn from Kutch, or from northern and eastern parts of Gujarat.

While the Oswals form an endogamous group within which there are few limitations on marriage other than the rules of surname exogamy, the Srimali population, in East Africa as in Britain, were more heterogeneous in origin, for the *jati* was somewhat artificially constituted from a number previously-endogamous sub-*jatis*. Nevertheless they soon developed a strong sense of solidarity amongst themselves. Even in 1982 most Leicester Srimalis of Saurashtran origin emphasised that they would much prefer to marry their children with fellow Saurashtrans, and would thus seek to avoid matches with the small number of Ahmedabadi Srimalis who had also settled in the city.

Since it defines their *jati* identity, the Oswals' link with Halar, the area around Jamnagar, cannot be overstated; this area has also been heavily involved in overseas migration. There were two Jain (probably Oswal) customs officers in Mombasa as early as 1826,[13] but large-scale emigration from Halar began during the last two decades of the nineteenth century, reaching a peak between the world wars.[14] My own informants in Leicester and Jamnagar confirmed that while Srimali emigration from this area followed a similar timetable to that of the Oswals, their destinations were somewhat different: Srimalis settled in all three East African territories, but the Oswals mostly confined themselves to Kenya. Until 1940 there were only two or three Oswal families in Tanzania, though their numbers increased to around twenty in as many years; there were never more than a handful of Oswals in Uganda.

Table 8.1. ESTIMATED SIZE OF THE JAIN POPULATION
IN POST-WAR EAST AFRICA[15]

		Estimated Jain population	Proportion of local South Asian population (%)
Kenya	1948	6,000	6
Uganda	1948	400	1
Tanzania	1957	1,000	1

[13] Shah, "Who are the Jains?", p. 371.
[14] Zarwan, "The social and economic network", p. 222.
[15] The figures are extracted from J.S. Mangat, *A History of the Asians in East Africa, 1886–1945* (Oxford: Clarendon Press, 1969), p. 142.

Jains were a very small minority of the South Asian population of East Africa, as Table 8.1 shows, although these figures may be underestimates: in India some Jains are known to have reported themselves to be Hindus in the census,[16] and some may have made the same public presentation of themselves in East Africa, where censuses made no record of *jati* affiliation. However it seems reasonable to assume that most of Kenya's 6,000 Jains were Oswals, while the great majority of those in Uganda and Tanzania were Srimalis.[17]

Once they had arrived in East Africa, the Oswals — most of whom had previously made a living as farmers and landholders — moved swiftly into trading and mercantile activities. Indeed they are a classic example of a "crystallized community",[18] due partly to their numerical strength and partly to the strength and continuity of their links with Saurashtra. For the Srimalis the position is less clear. They were not so numerous, and being drawn from a much wider geographical area, they did not form an endogamous group. Hence their commitment to reconstituting the Navnat — a loose federation of trading *jatis* — in order to compete more effectively with larger *jatis* like the Oswals, who had little difficulty in organizing themselves autonomously.

In a further contrast with the Oswals, the Srimalis in East Africa put a high premium on acquiring greater literacy and managerial skills, so although many sought to establish businesses, the majority actually entered government service.[19] While such jobs were secure and moderately well-paid, they provided few opportunities for large-scale economic advancement and capital reinvestment. Indeed this occupational difference is almost certainly the principal reason why Oswals settled exclusively in Kenya, where they were able to develop a network of business contacts and information exchange, while the Srimalis became more spatially scattered as they took up government jobs wherever they arose.

It was during the stay in East Africa that the Oswals appear to

---

[16] Vilas A. Saugave, *Jaina Community: A social survey* (2nd edn) (Bombay: Popular Prakashan), p. 291.

[17] Zarwan, *op. cit.*, p. 223.

[18] H. Stephen Morris, *The Indians in Uganda: Caste and sect in a plural society* (London: Weidenfeld and Nicolson), p. 34.

[19] Quite why the Srimalis did not have such an entrepreneurial success as the Oswals is hard to estimate and probably results from a combination of factors: the Oswals' success was perhaps not as great as it seems — Zarwan, for example chose a single, highly successful Oswal "business family" for his study, which is probably not representative; the Srimalis had the skills for other forms of employment which the Oswals lacked (agriculture being neither a desirable, nor a possible activity in East Africa); additionally, the Oswals' much greater numerical strength meant that greater potential resources for capital investment could be drawn upon.

have developed a stronger and more self-conscious interest in Jainism, even though were of course "Jains by birth". Oswals in both Leicester and India freely admitted this, a point corroborated by Michaelson;[20] more concretely, their construction of large and impressive temples in Nairobi in 1926, in Mombasa in 1963, and again in Nairobi in 1984 testifies not only to this awakened interest, but also to the importance of demonstrating piety and wealth though charitable giving and patronage.

The Srimali community developed along rather different lines. In 1916 a Srimali established a temple in a private house in Mombasa, which was used by both Oswals and Srimalis. Five years later a house was bought specifically for religious purposes, after the formation of the Mombasa Jain Swetambara Derasar Sangh, an organisation in which both Oswals and Srimalis were involved. Especially in the early days, these temples were focal points of the community, so as well as their being centres of worship, men gathered there in the evenings to gossip and play cards.

A further consequence of the move to East Africa was that the many Jain sects and sub-sects gradually began to consolidate into two major groupings: the image-worshipping Deravasis and the image-less Sthanakavasis. This development has had very different consequences for the Oswals and the Srimalis. Since the vast majority of Oswals are Deravasis, this bi-partite consolidation has had little impact on their own collective solidarity; however the Srimalis—as many as half of whom are Sthanakavasi — were yet further divided by it. In Kenya the Srimalis were strong enough numerically be able to establish separate Deravasi and Sthanakavasi meeting halls and temples; but in Tanzania and Uganda the largely Sthanakavasi Srimalis felt they had little alternative but to co-operate with local Deravasi Oswals and build joint meeting halls. Though nominally image-less, these halls could also be made to serve as temples since all the necessary religious paraphernalia was normally kept in side rooms.[21]

Even so, there is no evidence that the Srimalis and Oswals ever contemplated a full *jati* merger, for inter-marriage remained rare. In their own eyes at least, the Srimalis ranked higher than the Oswals, and although the latter sought to translate their entrepreneurial success into higher status, not least through extensive patronage of religious

[20] Michaelson, *Caste, Kinship and Marriage*, p. 131.
[21] The fact that the Srimalis in Uganda were largely Sthanakavasi is a consequence the chain-migration of kin (sectarian affiliation being ascriptive) from small regions of Saurashtra. Doubtless the same is true for Tanzania, though I have less evidence for this.

institutions and activities,[22] the gap was never closed, and the two groups remained distinct. Since the Oswals had active ties in India, they ultimately felt no need to rely on Srimalis to endorse the legitimacy of their claims, just as the Srimalis' alliance with other small trading *jatis* in the Navnat federation, which replicated structures found in India before emigration, allowed them autonomy from the Oswals.

By the mid-1960s, however, all the developments generated in the more or less comfortable context of colonial East Africa began to be transformed. In 1962 Uganda gained its independence, followed soon afterwards by Kenya and Tanzania (the product of a merger between Zanzibar and Tanganyika). Four years later the withdrawal of settlement rights from British passport holders of South Asian descent precipitated the first "panic" exodus of East African Asians to Britain, which was followed by the mass expulsion of all Uganda's Asians in 1972. In the midst of these processes there seems to have been nothing very distinctive about the Oswals' and Srimalis' movement to Britain. Like most other East African Asians, they largely ignored the efforts of the Uganda Resettlement Board to distribute them neatly around the country. Those who arrived with investment capital often chose to settle in London or Manchester, while those with little or nothing mostly made for Leicester. Employment was quite easy to find there, and support could be expected from the already thriving local Gujarati community.

Jains in Leicester

The earliest Jain settlers — mostly Oswals — arrived in Britain in the early 1960s. Most of the early pioneers arrived directly from India, although some had also been sent from East Africa, either to open businesses or to study. Emigration from Kenya gradually boosted numbers, and an Oswal Association was established in 1968; by the early 1980s it included around 4,000 families, probably representing some 15,000 people. The Srimalis moved slightly more slowly since they only arrived in Britain in significant numbers after the African crises. They came in close association with other members of the

22 All Jains in India are thought — by themselves and others — to be traders and businessmen, regardless of their actual occupation. These Oswals (confusingly, there are other groups in the Jamnagar region with a similar name but whose members were not involved in emigration: see *Organizing Jainism*, chapter 2) did not have a mercantile background before their emigration and there is little evidence of religious expenditure on their part in the Jamnagar region before the twentieth century. They could, however, lay claim to their Jain identity once mercantile activity began and temples were built by them in India as well as in East Africa.

Navnat, and at present there are three or four Navnat-type associations in Britain, with some 3,500 members of whom about 2,000 are Srimali Jains.

So far, however, Jain groups have only bought three properties in Britain. The first is a large country house north of London, bought by the Oswals around 1980 and still being renovated at the time of writing. The second is a house in Birmingham bought in the late 1970s by a group of local Jains (mostly Navnatis, but also including some non-Gujarati Jains) in collaboration with an American Jain organization, itself consisting of a few Indian Jains and some white converts; at the time of my study this initiative appeared moribund. The third property is the Leicester Jain Centre, which is discussed in detail below. Finally there is an (unconsecrated) image of Mahavira in a Hindu temple in Wellingborough, and several Hindu temples in Leicester (and probably elsewhere) have lithographs of Mahavira or of other *tirthankaras* displayed as icons on their walls.

Yet although Leicester's local newspaper has carried occasional articles about events at the Jain Centre, the Jain presence in Britain has otherwise been virtually ignored by the media, as by most academic researchers. While the small size of the community may be part of the explanation, their lack of a public profile may also be due to contradictions inherent in the character of Jain identity itself. As many Oswals readily admit, their interest in their religion — and especially awareness of their distinctive character — only developed while they were in East Africa, though this process coincided with a resurgence of boundary-drawing in India itself.

The middle to late nineteenth century was a low period for Jainism in North-west India, and its resurgence can be traced, paradoxically, to the impact of British attitudes and assumptions.[23] While the British initially regarded the Jains as a wholly discrete group, they later came to view them as a component of the Hindu social universe; later still, when the uniqueness of the Jains' philosophical and theological positions gradually came to be appreciated, the Jains and their social institutions were castigated by their Western admirers for their apparent "capitulation" to the Hindu society in which they were encompassed, while the religious and philosophical perspectives enshrined in their ancient texts were elevated to the status of a major world religion.

Most contemporary Jains in both India and Britain therefore draw on a range of often contradictory elements to construct their social identity. These include the traditional pattern of "inherited" Jainism,

---

[23] Marcus Banks, "Defining division: An historical overview of Jain social organisation", *Modern Asian Studies*, vol. 20 (1986), pp. 447–60.

which is inextricably linked to notions of identity and behaviour appropriate to the trading castes of Saurashtra; and the textual religion of Jainism with its stress on the inner, not the outer person, much advocated by Jain ascetics (both monks and nuns) and by many (lay) leaders in India. To all this some further, novel patterns of belief and practice have recently been added, thanks primarily to the teachings of a number of Jain ascetics who have travelled to the United States, and have sought to use the ancient textual religion to address the problems of contemporary post-industrial society. While this latter form of Jainism is rather more popular in the United States (where some white Americans have become converts) than in Britain, it is nevertheless a further pool of inspiration for the construction of a Jain identity in Britain.

The Srimalis in Leicester

Srimalis arrived in Leicester in significant numbers after the Kenyan and Ugandan crises of 1967–8 and 1972 and during the subsequent exodus from Tanzania. The majority of household heads seem to have arrived from Kenya, followed by Tanzania and Uganda, with only very few — usually ageing parents — coming directly from India.

For the reasons given earlier, most of Leicester's Srimalis are of Saurashtran origin, either from the Jamnagar-Rajkot area in the north of Saurashtra or from around Junaghad and Porbandar in the south. However, their direct connection with India is usually distant: even older people were often born, or at least had been brought up, in East Africa, although a number of older women had been brought over from India as brides in their late teens or early twenties. Though the link often has to be traced back over several generations, most Leicester Srimalis originate from small towns rather than big cities or little villages; before emigration they (or more usually their ancestors) were mostly shopkeepers, although many had a supplementary income from smallholdings worked by either hired help or tenant farmers.

In 1982 there were about 100 Srimali households in Leicester, containing perhaps 500 individuals. By comparison there were only about eighty Oswal households in the city: even though the Oswals are the most numerous Jain group nationwide, they are outnumbered locally by the Srimalis. The latter have not formed a cluster in any one area of the city, and instead follow the same broad pattern of distribution which applies to Gujarati Hindus as a whole. Like most other local Gujarati communities, the Srimalis are moderately prosperous; they too are following the outward movement from their original settlement in Highfields.[24] There has also been a parallel shift from the Belgrave Road area north of the city centre towards the newer Rushey Mead estate, further north. While a small number of Leicester Srimalis have become very wealthy and several more are in high-status occupations such as medicine and law, the community as a whole is best described as lower middle-class. Its members live in a devalued though not socially-stigmatised housing environment, and most are employed either in manual or in clerical jobs.

Table 8.2 PATTERNS OF EMPLOYMENT AMONG SRIMALIS IN LEICESTER

Type of occupation	No. of persons
Doctor	3
Other medical	1
Accountant	2
Own business (shop etc.)	16
Service and clerical worker	
skilled[25]	6
unskilled	10
Factory worker	17
Unemployed[26]	6
Retired[27]	15
No information	29

My informants often suggested that Leicester had attracted a poorer class of Asians, particularly people who had not managed to transfer their savings out of Africa before their expulsion. Those with capital to invest usually settled in London or Manchester, while younger people with professional qualifications had moved to the United States or Canada. Leicester's only attraction was that it offered relatively easy access to employment. Although some settlers had managed to start a business — usually a shop or light industrial concern

[24] Deborah Phillips, "The social and spatial segregation of Asians in Leicester" in P. Jackson and S.J. Smith (eds), *Social Interaction and Ethnic Segregation* (London: Academic Press, 1981), p. 107.

[25] This includes three salesmen — two selling insurance and one clothing.

[26] The distinction between 'Unemployed' and 'Retired' has been made purely on the basis of age, except in two cases where the retired household head is less than sixty-five but is unable to work through ill-health.

[27] This category includes two female heads of household who are supported by their children.

— by the early 1980s, the majority of Srimalis in waged employment were still in service occupations (see Table 8.2).

Apart from their religious affiliation, there is little that overtly distinguishes the Srimalis from other Gujarati Hindus in Leicester. Their diet, clothing, language, aspirations for their children and so forth are similar to those of other much larger groups such as the Lohanas and the Patidars, and just as varied. Some Srimalis are conservative, others liberal; some enjoy Western food (usually, but not always, vegetarian), while others spend much of their household budget on vegetables imported from India or Africa. Some women stick resolutely to saris after marriage, while others wear Western blouses and skirts, especially since some factories forbid the wearing of saris for safety reasons. Thus the Leicester Srimalis — in their patterns of housing, occupational and educational mobility, household structure and composition etc. — can be seen as close to other local Gujarati communities. For the key to Srimali identity we have to look at the institution to which they all belong: the Jain Samaj.

The Jain Samaj (Europe), Leicester

The Samaj was founded in 1973, as both a social and a religious organization, by the Oswals and the Srimalis jointly. Much of the initial impetus came from the Srimalis, because the Oswals had already set up a national organization to serve their social purposes if not yet their religious needs. Before the establishment of the Samaj, Leicester Srimalis had of course maintained informal contacts with each other, based primarily on relationships established in East Africa, if not in India. Young couples with children went out in small groups to have picnics at local beauty spots, and older retired or unemployed men met in the afternoons to play cards. Some of my informants spoke nostalgically of those early days — not so very long before — much as their English counterparts might fondly remember the days of home entertainment before television. Now, they said, everything was organised through the Jain Samaj, which brought together large numbers of people in big functions. Informal activities still continued, but with only limited free time available, it was usually easier to attend the large pre-arranged functions.

The founding of the Samaj was a major innovation, being the first joint collective venture in which the Srimalis and the Oswals had ever formally cooperated.[28] But the alliance was always uneasy, given the

---

[28] Informal arrangements had operated in East Africa, particularly in Uganda where the Oswals had been few. Although there are no joint religious projects in Jamnagar — or, to my knowledge, in the region — there are members of the two *jatis* who do cooperate in business ventures.

rivalry between the two *jatis* in both India and East Africa, and indeed it collapsed amid bitter recriminations after four years. According to my Srimali informants, the arguments that led to disintegration erupted — ironically — during the Swami Vatsalyan Bhojan, an annual "feast of affection" held at the close of Paryushan, the principal Jain festival. The dispute focused on some *ladus* (sweet balls) which had been provided by the Oswals but been criticised as sub-standard by some prominent Srimalis. This was obviously a stock scenario: in Jamnagar I was told stories about similar arguments breaking out between Srimalis and Oswals in the midst of joint feasts.

While the alliance lasted, however, the common religious identity shared and perceived by both groups provided an effective focus for unity. In an annual cycle which reached a high point in the period of confession and forgiveness known as *Paryushan*, religious functions were held in hired halls, and a religious school for young people was also established. The school was set up by one of the Samaj's Srimali founders working closely with a prominent Oswal, and it ran for two hours each Sunday morning. As in India, where religious education classes like this are held daily in towns with a Jain population, the children who attended were taught to memorise basic Jain *mantras* and recitations, and given simple explanations of their meaning.

Yet tensions were never far from the surface. Even while the alliance held, the Samaj's very constitution was challenged by some members of the Navnat. They argued that although some of the federation's constituent *jatis* had Jain members, of whom one or two had become members of the Samaj, the Srimalis' commitment to an exclusive body such as the Jain Samaj was socially divisive. This argument was reinforced by the resentment felt by many non-Srimali members of the Navnat (who were not only "true" *vanias*, but included some of the most affluent members of the group) towards the Srimalis for having allied themselves with the equally affluent but non-*vania* Oswals. Eventually a new Navnat-type organization (the Midland Vanik Association) was formed; and although the Srimalis eventually affiliated the Jain Samaj to the Association, they did so only after the Samaj had ceased to include Oswals.

The Jains are far from unique in having religious organizations which cut across caste divisions; in Leicester Muslims and Sikhs routinely organise themselves in this way, while many Hindu temples attract a cross-caste attendance. However, the problems which caused tension between the Srimalis, the Oswals and the Navnatis within the Jain Samaj can be much more specifically identified. First, while the Samaj allied only two *jatis*, this had little meaning except in contexts where their shared religious identity was emphasised; secondly, whatever they themselves might say, their religion functions with an exclusive and largely ascriptive membership. Thus while Jains can (and regularly do) attend Hindu temples in Leicester, their own functions are both much smaller and sufficiently esoteric to discourage casual visitors.

This last point is equally true of local Muslim groups, and rather less so of the Sikhs. However these groups are in no sense Hindu, nor are they necessarily Gujarati. By contrast Jains *are* thought to be Hindus of some kind, both by other Hindus and to some extent by the Jains themselves, for their organisational strategies have run parallel to, and often meshed closely with, those adopted by other Hindu *jatis* in East Africa. Thus the Srimalis were involved with the East African Navnat association, while the Oswals had their own association which was closely analogous to those formed by virtually every other Hindu *jati* in East Africa.

A list of all the Asian organizations in the city was compiled by Leicester City Council in 1978,[29] and though undoubtedly incomplete, this reveals some interesting trends which help to "place" the Jains. Of the seventy-nine groups listed, no less than fifty-six are Gujarati Hindu organizations, if that category includes the Jain Samaj and the local branch of the Oswal Association. Of the remainder, eleven are Muslim, nine Sikh and three Bangladeshi. But of the fifty-six Hindu organizations at least thirty-one are *jati*-specific; indeed some *jatis* are represented several times over. For example the Limbachias and the Lohanas each have their own "welfare" organizations as well as the regular *jati* body; similarly a number of closely associated *jatis* are sometimes represented by a single organization, such as the Prajapati Samaj. But apart from these specifically *jati*-based organizations, ten groups (mostly temple committees and worship circles) could be classified as religious, and a further fifteen (such as the Indian Art Circle and the Old Asian People's Association) as broadly cultural in character. While recruitment to and management of these non-*jati* groups may or may not be along *jati* lines — it is often difficult to tell — what is clear is that *jati* solidarity remains one of the most important vehicles for group organization among Leicester's Hindus.

By contrast, Leicester's eleven Muslim groups appear exclusively religious, as are six of its nine Sikh organizations. There may be other lines of division within these communities, e.g. those based on regional and linguistic specificities, but from a Gujarati Hindu view-

---

[29] My only acquaintance with this list was a rather tattered and much amended copy kept under the desk at the public library; for this reason I do not give a bibliographic reference. The list gave only the name of the organization and the local contact — the discussion, therefore, is based on my own interpretation, supplemented by the local knowledge of several informants.

point these are relatively invisible: informants regularly referred to Muslims and Sikhs as if they belonged to monolithic entities whose members are wholly united by religion. Given its exclusivity and organizational coherence, the Jain Samaj was also perceived as a religious body analogous to those formed by Sikhs and Muslims, and thus as not comparable with Hindu religious groups.

After the withdrawal of the Oswals from the Jain Samaj, the Srimalis were left in the curious position of being able to "choose" the character of their corporate identity. They had inherited the Samaj's name and had begun a fund-raising drive (which soon involved the Leicester City Council, the Manpower Services Commission and the Inner Area Programme) to buy a property for a religious centre; but they could not honestly claim to represent all Leicester's Jains, given the Samaj's now-exclusive association with a single *jati*.[30] Faced with this dilemma, certain elements within the Srimali community, particularly the leader-figures of the Samaj, decided to continue stressing a religious identity; their commitment to Jainism transcended their *jati* identity. Several factors underpinned this development. First, given the general apathy of the rest of the Srimalis, the leaders' religious belief and dedication became a driving force for the whole community.[31] Secondly, while their common religion had not been strong enough to bridge the Srimali/Oswal divide, it did prove able to unite the local Srimalis despite their differences of occupation, education and regional origins. Thirdly, and on a different plane, an apparently religious organisation was judged more likely to attract external funding than was a nominally more parochial and exclusivistic *jati* (i.e. caste) group.

This was only one view, however. Despite their use of some ritual practices which suggest that they are followers of an exclusive religion, and the widespread conviction amongst non-Jain Gujaratis that this is so, many Jains take a very different position. For example, a report which appeared in the local newspaper in 1973 when the Jain Samaj had just been formed referred to the group as a "sect", and quoted a spokesman as having stated that its aims were "to promote good relations between its members and other communities".[32] But four years later, after the split with the Oswals, another spokesman took a very different position, saying that "Jainism is not a sect or just one more conflicting ideology. It is a way of thinking and

---

[30] The split between the Oswals and the Srimalis was not quite as absolute as I may have made it sound, for some Oswals remain members of the Samaj and occasionally attend religious functions. However all of them are also active members of the Leicester Oswal Association.

[31] See Morris, *op. cit.*, p. 40.

[32] *Leicester Mercury*, 12 Nov. 1973.

living".[33] In the first statement the Srimali-Oswal alliance is viewed as creating a bounded community, albeit of a religious character, whereas the second suggests a more "open" position, thus allowing the (by then) almost exclusively Srimali membership of the group to be pushed into the background.

In 1978 the Samaj bought a disused Congregational chapel in the centre of Leicester, and this eventually became the Jain Centre.[34] From the start it was used both for religious events such as wedding receptions and for social functions such as dance competitions; it was also available for hire, although non-members were charged considerably more than members. Finance for the project was raised both through membership subscriptions and through patronage. Donations were received from Jains living in other parts of England as well as in Leicester itself, and these were supplemented by successful grant applications to various local and central government bodies.

Two years later the Samaj embarked on an even more ambitious project, which involved a partial reconciliation of the Oswals and Srimalis. A number of leading Oswals and Srimalis met in London and decided, after some argument, that the Leicester Jain Centre should become a place of meeting for all Jains, irrespective of *jati*, origin or residence, and to reflect this the name of the organization was changed to "Jain Samaj (Europe), Leicester". For the Srimalis (or at least their leaders) this was a "success", and it was primarily due to their being the only Jain group in Britain with any viable property. Yet although the Samaj had also proved remarkably successful in raising finance, due largely to the tireless efforts of its president, a further consequence of the initiative was that the Srimali leadership had to promise to effect a reconciliation with Leicester's Oswals. As one might expect, this task is proceeding only very slowly.

The new image and direction which the Samaj sought to adopt was expressed through a new journal, *The Jain*. Its predecessor, *Jain News*, had appeared since 1977 as a cyclostyled news-sheet largely in Gujarati. In sharp contrast, *The Jain* was professionally printed, included an English-language section which was often longer than that in Gujarati, and contained book reviews, glossaries of Jain technical words in Prakrit and Sanskrit, and a generally more academic content. The extra production costs were met through advertising.

At much the same time plans were made to transform the Centre itself by gutting the chapel almost completely in order to construct an elaborate sandstone and marble temple within it in a "traditional"

---

[33] *Leicester Mercury*, 17 Sept. 1977.
[34] I discuss the details of this purchase and other financial aspects of the Leicester Jain Samaj more fully in "Competing to give".

North Indian style — at a cost of at least £500,000. By the time of writing reconstruction was largely complete, and the temple had been inaugurated. Further plans for the future had begun to circulate, including building up a library, making the place a centre for the international study of Jainism, and employing a full-time worker to give short courses in Jainism and meditation — plans that clearly assume a clientele far beyond the small Leicester Srimali community.

At the beginning of this chapter I suggested that tensions, internal and external to its tradition, allow Jainism to create a dynamic which serves to draw its followers together and to pull them apart again. Little of this is unique to the Jains, not least because this pattern is cross-cut by similar processes of drawing together and apart as between the generations, and to which migration has given a further dynamic twist. It is also worth emphasising that both elements are necessarily complementary to each other, so although my discussion here has primarily been concerned with moving apart, the idea of unity has by no means been entirely absent. At the outset the Srimalis worked cooperatively alongside the Oswals, and despite the split between them, they are now working towards unity once again through their plans for the Jain Centre.

In grasping the dynamics of this process, the thrust of my argument in this chapter is that Jainism — the cultural factor that serves to unite the Srimalis and the Oswals — is best regarded not so much as a textually-fixed entity but rather as a pool of values, ideas and legitimating strategies which are constantly available as an inspirational resource. The trajectories of cultural development expressed in the Srimalis' and Oswals' varied but interdependent adaptations to their new environment offer a clear demonstration of just how this may occur.

As far as the Srimali community in Leicester is concerned, my outline of the history of the Jain Samaj suggests a simple three-phase process of development. During the first phase the Srimali-Oswal alliance was articulated primarily through a common 'religious' identity. In the first part of the second phase, in 1977–8, the Srimalis had no alliance and no property, and during this period their religious and *jati* identities were equally strong. The next two years saw the purchase of the Centre — initially for use by the Srimalis alone but soon "opened" to all Jains — and the emergence of a modified alliance between the Srimalis and the (London) Oswals, leading to the creation of Jain Samaj (Europe), Leicester. These developments in turn initiated a third phase, which was once again predicated on a religious identity but, this time, around the identification of Jainism as a world religion, rather than just a source of common ground between two Gujarati *jatis*.

Reality has, of course, been much more complex than this simplistic analysis may suggest. Even if they were familiar with all the information presented here, by no means all Srimalis who provided information would necessarily agree with the assessment given here of their recent history, for many might well choose to emphasise other perspectives. Secondly, while the maximum use was made of all documentary source, and as many people as possible were consulted, our version of history is itself a synthesis of other stories, and perhaps of myths: some of the most crucial events in this account (like the argument over the *ladus*) appear in other local Jain mythologies which I have collected in India. Thirdly, the Srimali community itself is by no means monolithic: "leaders" acquire their leadership role for all sorts of different reasons, and it is a grave mistake to assume that they necessarily represent the views and wishes of the main body of the community. Indeed the third phase which we have identified is by far the least representative of the desires and aspirations of the relatively silent majority, for most of the non-leaders are still firmly rooted in the second phase, where the possibility of switching back and forth between a religious and a *jati* identity is still quite open.

For most Srimalis Jainism is still primarily a function of being Srimali, for in both India and Africa it was this which marked them off from members of other Vania *jatis*. Although it is often suggested that sects in India regularly become castes, with the Lingayats of South India regularly cited as an example, this view is much too facile, not least because the Jains of Gujarat have apparently managed to retain discrete *jati* and *varna* identities over several hundred years. Nevertheless, Srimalis in both Leicester and Jamnagar often suggested that Oswals were Jains "of a different kind", and evidence can indeed be cited to support this view. Largely as a result of past rivalries, Oswals and Srimalis in the Jamnagar region adhere to slightly different sectarian traditions, manifest not so much in terms of differences in belief, but rather in practice. Each group follows a slightly different religious calendar, and uses slightly differing rituals.

In Jamnagar, the Srimalis function as a *jati* group through their property ownership. They own — as do other local *jatis* — two *vadis*, "*jati* halls", in which *jati*-specific social and religious functions take place.[35] In the same way, Jain temples and various other kinds of specifically religious property are owned not by sects or by the Jains as a whole, but by *jati* groups and sub-groups. Hence the purchase of the Jain Centre, together with the withdrawal of the Oswals from the Samaj, led many Srimalis to believe that the Centre was to function

---

[35] See Banks, *Organizing Jainism in India and England*, chapter 4, for a discussion of Jamnagar Jain property relations.

as a modified *vadi* — as a place specifically associated with the religious and social functions of the *jati*. Thus the initiation of the third phase disoriented many Srimalis. During fieldwork in 1982 as well as on subsequent visits, I encountered a good deal of puzzlement and even of resentment at the direction the Samaj was taking. Many felt they were being left behind, that the leadership was out of touch with their feelings, and that the temple project was too ambitious. There was particular concern that the money might run out half way through the project, leaving them with nothing but the empty shell of a building.

More recent visits have, however, convinced me that the Centre is thriving; while it may have excluded or permanently alienated some people, it has attracted far more. It can also be seen as a social and organisational success, combining traditional conceptual frameworks and their associated modes of authority with modern bureaucratic methods. Thus although the Jain Samaj (Europe), Leicester has assumed its current structure largely as a result of local historical and cultural particularities, it would be wrong to limit our analytical vision solely to this context. The conventional view of migrants as standing "between two cultures" implies that they are subject to a series of structural, behavioural and psychological transformations as they move from one fixed pole to another. By contrast I prefer to view these transformations as features inherent in the cultural process itself. Hence the Leicester Jains' organisational transformations are better understood as taking place on — and as having repercussions for — many different levels. And there is nothing new about these developments. Rather they are as old as Jainism itself. On the one hand they offer a further rehearsal of arguments and discourses about mercantile strategy which have developed in one small region of Gujarat during the last four and a half centuries, while on the other they also incorporate all sorts of contemporary inter- and intra-ethnic dialogues of both a religious and secular kind, and which are the outcome of their new British context. No discussion of migrant groups in Britain will ever be complete without such a sense of ideological historicity.

PARSI ZOROASTRIANS IN LONDON[*]

John R. Hinnells

Although the Parsis are one of the smallest of the South Asian communities in Britain, they can also claim to have the longest historical roots there, since a Parsi Association was founded in London in 1861. So despite their small numbers, the dilemmas the Parsis have faced, and the processes of change and adaptation they have passed through, often seem to parallel — though in microcosm and over a much longer period — the experiences of larger groups of South Asian settlers who have arrived in Britain during the past half-century.

The term "Parsi" is generally used to denote the people from Pars, Persia, who settled on the north-west coast of India in the tenth century of the Christian era. Not all left for India, however, and those co-religionists of the Parsis who remained in Iran normally identify themselves as Zoroastrians — and sometimes also as "true Iranians" in contrast to the "Arab invaders" who subsequently brought Islam into the region. Although Iranian Zoroastrians are sometimes referred to as "Parsis" by members of the Indian community, the Iranians feel such an "Indian" label to be inappropriate; most Zoroastrians in India are generally proud to assert a Parsi identity, thus emphasising the strength of their conscious difference from other local groups and communities. Thus while most recent emigrants from India and Iran are content with the names by which they were known before migration — i.e. either as Parsis or Zoroastrians — many of their overseas-born offspring prefer to be identified either by the religious title "Zoroastrian", or more generally as "Persians". This second choice may be due either to a sense of secular ethnicity or to their awareness of most British people's ignorance of the very existence of Zoroastrianism. All these labels serve to emphasise their ancient heritage,

[*] I should be explicit about the perspective in which this chapter is written, for I am neither a sociologist nor an anthropologist, but rather a historian specialising in the development of the Zoroastrian tradition. This account is very much a report on research in progress, and is part of a global study of the contemporary Parsi and Zoroastrian diaspora in India, Pakistan, China, East Africa, Britain, America, Canada and Australia. The Parsis are a highly literate group, and I have therefore drawn heavily on the community's own archival material. This has been further supplemented by the results of a global questionnaire survey which elicited almost 1,700 responses, as well as by 242 in-depth interviews conducted in Britain.

while enabling them to distance themselves from negative images of Islamic fundamentalism. Hence although this chapter is concerned primarily with Parsi emigrants from the Indian subcontinent and their offspring, recent migrants from Iran now form a small though far from insignificant component of the local Zoroastrian community.[1]

Zoroastrians in India

The Zoroastrian religion traces its origins back to the teaching of its founder prophet Zarathushtra, or, as he has commonly been known in the West from the times of the Greeks, Zoroaster. The prophet lived in north-east Iran in approximately 1,200 BCE, and in the sixth century BCE his teachings became the official religion of the mighty Persian empire. Apart from an intermission caused by Alexander's invasion, when control of Iran passed temporarily into the hands of his Seleucid successors, Zoroastrianism remained the state religion until the Muslim invasion in the seventh century CE. As the hold of Islam tightened, so the traditional religion of the Iranian plateau became steadily marginalised, and oppression and persecution of its followers became ever more acute. Hence in the tenth century CE a small band of the faithful set out to find refuge elsewhere: the eventual result was the foundation of a new Zoroastrian community on the north-west coast of India.

The only account we now have of this process of migration and settlement is the *Qissa-i-Sanjan*, a semi-mythical tale not committed to writing until 1600.[2] Although not strictly a historical source, the tale provides a clear picture of the way in which the descendants of these Parsi immigrants viewed themselves and their sojourn in India. The text relates that their initial departure and their stays in successive resting places took place under the direction of a wise astrologer-priest. While at sea in their frail boat a life-threatening storm arose, and they therefore prayed for deliverance, vowing that if they reached land safely they would consecrate a great fire temple as an act of thanksgiving. The wind moderated and they did indeed arrive safely. Once ashore in India they approached the local Hindu prince for permission to settle and build a temple. Their request was granted, subject only to the conditions that they learned to speak the local language (Gujarati), observed the marriage laws of the country, wore

---

[1] For a masterly overview of Zoroastrianism see Mary Boyce, *Zoroastrians: their religious belief and practices* (London: Routledge, 1979).
[2] On the *Qissa-i-Sanjan* see Mary Boyce, *Textual Sources for the Study of Zoroastrianism* (Manchester University Press, 1984), pp. 120–3, and Paul Axelrod, "Myth and Identity in the Indian Zoroastrian Community", *Journal of Mithraic Studies*, vol. 3 (1980), pp. 150–65.

local dress and refrained from carrying weapons. The settlers accepted these conditions and sought to reassure the prince that their presence would not be disruptive by producing a series of statements, *shlokas*, about their religion and way of life. These highlighted, amongst other things, the close congruence between their own traditions — particularly their purity laws and their reverence for the cow — and many aspects of Hindu practice.

The Tale of Sanjan neatly underlines Parsi attitudes towards their sojourn in India: their arrival and settlement was, they believe, "written in the stars", involving as it did a divinely guided journey and a miraculous rescue, which freed them from their previous persecution. The journey brought them to a land where they were free to settle, and where minimal demands — scarcely reaching beyond those necessary to ensure a peaceful society — were made upon them. It also emphasises the common symbols and values which Zoroastrianism and Hinduism share. For most Parsis their Indian experience contrasts sharply with that in Muslim Iran, for a millennium of persecution left scars in the communal memory not unlike those of the Holocaust amongst contemporary Jewry. Thus despite their strong attachment to India, most Parsis are very insistent that they should not be mistaken in an unqualified way for "Indians" or "Pakistanis".

Zoroastrians in British India

Until the arrival of the European travellers and traders in the seventeenth century, the Parsis were a peaceful and unobtrusive caste-like component of the population of Gujarat. They made a living either as farmers, or more usually as merchants; many specialised in the textile trade. However when the British began to develop Bombay as a major port and commercial centre, Parsis began settling there to take advantage of the many new opportunities. They were by no means the only group to do so, for migrants soon flocked into Bombay from all over western India. As a community they were, however, very successful, and soon began to make a mark in the growth of Bombay. It was Parsis who built and owned the Bombay dockyard; they were heavily involved in the China trade; and when Western-style education became available to Indians in the 1820s, they provided many of the pioneer students, as well as pouring in funds to establish schools and colleges. This early investment in education allowed them to dominate almost all the careers facilitated by Western education. In engineering, textiles, banking, commerce, journalism, law and medicine alike, Parsis were among the earliest and most influential Indian professionals. From the 1880s onwards they also made their mark in politics, notably in the Indian National Congress.

Many of the most renowned figures in early twentieth-century India were Parsis. They included Sir Pherozeshah Mehta, the so-called "uncrowned king of Bombay"; Sir Dinshaw Watcha, Secretary of the Indian National Congress for nearly three decades; Dadabhoy Naoroji, four times President of Congress, and the first Indian to become a Westminster Member of Parliament; Jamsetji Nusserwanj Tata, the founder of India's steel industry; and Sir Dinshaw Maneckji Petit, the textile magnate and philanthropist. As middlemen in trade and commerce and as leaders in many branches of Indian society, the Parsi community flourished hugely during the British Raj. Parsis thus typically view British rule in India in a positive light. This was further reinforced by the accounts of early travellers discussed below, and influenced the expectations of most of those who emigrated to London. Prosperity thus provided Parsis with a springboard for a new diaspora, for although Bombay was and still is their power-base, they have by no means limited themselves to that city. They have also spread out to other commercial cities in India such as Karachi, and onwards to a global diaspora. Hence Parsis were — and often still are — leading professionals and merchants in the many overseas Indian communities which have sprung up in China, East Africa, the United States and elsewhere.[3]

Early Visitors and Settlers in Britain

The first known Parsi visitor to Britain was Naoroji Rustomjee, who came to London in 1724 to protest — successfully — against the way in which his family had been treated by officials of the East India Company in Bombay. However, it was opportunities for education and training which gave the strongest initial spur towards travel to Britain. The first Parsi schoolboy arrived in 1823, and in the 1830s and '40s a series of visitors arrived, aiming to inform themselves about British industrial methods, particularly in textiles and shipbuilding. The earliest such visitor of whom a positive record can be traced was A.J. Wadia, who arrived in 1840, to be followed by his cousins, the brothers Jehangir Naoroji and Hirjeebhoy Meherwanji Wadia, in 1841. The first Parsi to study at a British university was Dhunjibhoy Naoroji, who began a degree in theology at Edinburgh in 1843, having converted to Christianity. Many more Parsis arrived during the 1860s

---

[3] On the Parsis in India in general see Eckehard Kulke, *The Parsees in India: a minority as agents of social change* (Munich: Weltforum Verlag, 1974). On Anglo-Parsi relations see John Hinnells, "Parsis and the British", *Journal of the K.R. Cama Oriental Institute*, Bombay, vol. 46 (1978), pp. 5–64. A study of the China trade and the East African Zoroastrian communities will appear in my forthcoming *The global Zoroastrian diaspora* (Oxford University Press).

to gain a university education, usually in medicine or law. Most studied in Edinburgh or London.

Parsis were also commercially active in Britain from an early date. The first Indian firm in Britain was set up by a trio consisting of Dadabhoy Naoroji and the brothers K.R. Cama and M.H. Cama, who opened offices in London and Liverpool in 1855. In 1857 R.B. Desai came to study the soap industry before returning to set up his own firm in Bombay, while R.M. Darukhanawala visited Oldham to study engineering in 1860. In 1865 J.N. Tata, later one of India's most successful industrial entrepreneurs, came to Britain to study the Lancashire mills. Parsis in the mid-nineteenth century thus saw Britain as a land of educational and industrial opportunity.[4]

Tourists and Travelogues

One of the most striking differences between the Parsis and their successors — the less wealthy and often poor migrants who followed them to Britain after the Second World War — is that as members of a comparatively wealthy and strongly urbanised community many of the earliest visitors came to Britain as tourists. The earliest appear to have been B.D. Cooper and his family, who visited Britain in 1858. Four years later Cursetji Maneckji Shroff brought his two daughters to Britain in order to equip them to move in "high society"; he arranged, amongst other things, for them to be formally presented to Queen Victoria. In 1865 three more families arrived (those of Dadabhoy Naoroji, D.R. Colah and J.B. Wadia) to be followed by J.B. Vacha's a year later. In 1868 the great educational reformer K.R. Cama sent his daughter on an educational trip around Britain.

From early in the nineteenth century a number of leading Parsi families began to take a relatively relaxed attitude towards social mixing, and their willingness to allow their wives and daughters to have some contact with British society and its institutions is in marked contrast to the ideas and assumptions of many later South Asian migrants to Britain. Even more striking is the way these pioneer travellers used their literary skills to circulate written accounts of their

[4] See John Hinnells, "Parsis in Britain", *Journal of the K.R. Cama Oriental Institute*, Bombay, vol. 46 (1978), pp. 65–84. The details for the dates and details of the events and awards here summarised will be expanded upon in *The Parsis in British India: their history and religion* (forthcoming, jointly written with K.M. JanamaspAsa). It is a pleasure as well as a duty to record my profound thanks, as ever, to Dastur Dr K.M. JamaspAsa of the Anjuman Atash Bahram in Bombay for his help and guidance for nearly twenty years with the Gujarati sources. Thanks are also due to Cyrus P. Mehta, Burjor and Zarin Avari for their ready and kindly help with the same. I would further like to express gratitude to Manchester University for funding all my research visits to India to consult sources, as well as the services of a research assistant.

impressions and experiences in Britain for the benefit of their fellows back in Bombay.[5] The main theme which emerges from these accounts is the speed and bustle of life, the crowds, the advanced technology, and the love of royalty and pageantry. Their flavour is conveyed by one of the earliest such narratives, written by J.N. and M.H. Wadia:

We were greatly surprised to see the amazing number of ships going out and pouring in to the Thames, and steamers every now and then running backwards and forwards; we cannot convey to our countrymen any idea of this immense number of vessels, and the beauty of the sight. You will see colliers, timber ships, merchantmen, steamers, and many other crafts, from all parts of the world, hastening, as it were, to seek refuge in a river, which is but a stream compared to the Ganges and the Indus . . . We thought it a great wonder that such a small and insignificant a speck as England appears on the map of the world, can thus attract so many nations of the world towards her.

After discussing the persevering habits, labour, skill and perfectionism of the English, the Wadias concluded that these have been achieved "by knowledge and science put in practice, because knowledge is power; and it is by the power of knowledge *alone*, and not by force of arms, that she has so many means of attracting the world to her."

They wondered at the speed of the railways and the miracle of trains travelling in tunnels under cities; they were struck by such oddities as English gentlemen gardening with their own hands, and of the strangeness of a ballerina who stood "for a long time like a goose upon one leg" — although they also loved the sumptuousness of the theatre. In general the early tourists gave glowing accounts of English society, but for one prescient warning: "We would inform our countrymen that the majority of the lower orders in England are very rude in their manners and behaviour towards strangers, whom they do not like to see in their own country."

Industry in its many forms also fascinated them, especially the use of steam to power machinery in its manifold forms. A visit to the Gallery of Practical Science near Charing Cross in London drove them to exclaim:

Oh! happy England, possessing within yourself this source of employment, of manufacture and wealth, old happy England you are, and long will be, the wonder and envy of the world, you possess materials that enable you to

[5] The earliest of these was the diary of Ardeshir K. Wadia in 1840, followed in 1842 by the more flowing text of his cousins J.N. and M.H. Wadia. Later came *The Travels in Great Britain* of D.F. Karaka, published in 1861, while J.H. Kothari produced an account of his travels in Europe, the United States, Canada, China and Japan, published 1889.

work machinery, that allows you to bring cotton from India, thousands of miles, to manufacture it into fine muslin, and send it back to India and to sell it there *much cheaper* than it can be made there.

Parliament both impressed and amused them, and they give a somewhat sceptical account of the construction of the English peerage. Attempting to explain why people were elevated to the House of Lords they asserted:

After sometime admirals of the navy and commanders of the army were made noblemen and sent to the House of Peers, sometimes persons have been made noblemen for lending their lives to the King, sometimes if a person has been very troublesome in the House of Commons and been constantly asking for information not pleasant for the Government to give, he has been made a nobleman; if a minister wanted votes upon a particular measure which he was anxious to carry, a peerage has been conferred upon a person to abstain from voting against the question; and if a man held a little place in the ministry was found to be of no use, and would not resign his situation, he was made a nobleman and sent to the House of Peers.

Nor were they much impressed by the House of Commons:

We had expected to have seen the representatives of all the wealth, all the talent, all the resources of the country, better dressed and a different looking set of men. We saw them with their hats upon their heads for the last two or three hours sleeping in all directions, and only opening their eyes now and then, when a cheer louder than common struck upon their ears.[6]

However, Parsi literary efforts were by no means limited to travelogues of this kind, for in addition to works written primarily for consumption within their own community, they also wrote books about their own people and religion which they hoped would inform and impress the British. Amongst the earliest of these were two by Dosabhoy Framjee, *The Parsees: their History Manners and Customs* and *The British Raj, Contrasted with its Predecessors*, both published in London in 1858. The former was later expanded and republished in two volumes as *The History of the Parsees*, dedicated to the Prince of Wales. It was produced with the conscious intention of projecting a favourable picture of the Parsis to an educated Western readership. Later a number of books on specifically religious themes appeared, including S.A. Kapadia's *The Teachings of Zoroaster* (1905).

Anglicising Tendencies

Besides their very positive attitude to British rule, a further important

---

[6] Jehangir Naorojee and Hirjeebhoy Merwanjee Wadia, *Journal of a Residence of Two Years and a Half in Great Britain* (Bombay: Private Publication, 1841), pp. 24, 103, 110, 134, 171, 182 respectively.

reason why Parsis were so eager to travel to Britain and to project a positive image of themselves to British audiences was their view of themselves as the most British-like of all the "races" of India. Hence they eagerly adopted European behaviour over a wide spectrum, including the use of knives and forks at the dinner table, wearing European clothes and playing English sports: it was Parsis who brought the first Indian cricket team on tour to England in 1866. By 1901 at least two histories of Parsi cricket had been published.

One of the main reasons why Parsis thought and behaved in this way was because they believed that there were many parallels between their own religious values and those of India's new rulers, most notably a common commitment to ethical monotheism. They also believed that the British had a particular respect for Parsis, since a number of European travellers had identified their community as one much given to charitable generosity, professing high ethical standards and, perhaps most crucial of all, fair-skinned.[7] The Parsis themselves were extremely fond of quoting such judgements.[8]

The Parsis also believed that they had themselves made a considerable contribution to British rule in India, and indeed to Britain itself. Thus there are records of Zoroastrian charity extended towards British people in Britain, for example to the poor and unemployed mill-workers of Lancashire in 1862, to famine victims in Ireland in 1822, to various hospitals and educational establishments, and to the Lord Mayor of London "poor box" from as early as 1848. The contributions of manpower (mainly to the medical corps) and funds to the Allies during the two world wars were enormous. In addition to charitable work among the poor of their own community,[9] Indian Zoroastrians were noted for the way they funded hospitals and schools, dug wells, built roads, and gave magnanimously to disaster victims and orphans of all communities.

Parsis in British Politics

A further facet of their history of which all Parsis are proud is their community's contribution to British politics, notably in the persons

---

[7] Nora Kathleen Firby, *European Travellers and Their Perceptions of Zoroastrians in the 17th and 18th Centuries* (*Archäologische Mitteilungen aus Iran*, Ergänzungsband 14, Berlin, 1988).

[8] In 1897 J.J. Motivala and B.N. Sahiar published such a collection of views entitled *Enlightened non-Zoroastrians on Mazdayasnism* (a term for Zoroastrianism).

[9] *The Fifth Commandment: Biography of Sharpurji Saklatwala* (Salford: The Miranda Press, 1991). On Parsi charity in general, and in Britain in particular, see John Hinnells, "The Flowering of Zoroastrian Benevolence: Parsi charities in the 19th and 20th Centuries" in *Papers in Honour of Professor Mary Boyce* (*Acta Iranica*, vol. 24, Leiden: E.J. Brill), pp. 261–326.

of Britain's first three Indian Members of Parliament: Dadabhoy Naoroji, who represented Central Finsbury for the Liberals from 1892 to 1895; Sir Muncherji Bhownagree, the Conservative Member for Bethnal Green between 1895 and 1905; and Shapurji Saklatvala, who represented Battersea between 1922 and 1929, first for Labour and then as a Communist. As one might expect the three differed greatly in their political work and in personality.

Naoroji was a pioneer in numerous ways. As mentioned earlier, he helped found the first Indian firm to be established in Britain, and was the first Indian professor in a British university — of Gujarati at University College, London; but he also kept firm roots in India, where he was elected President of the Indian National Congress three times. As a Westminster M.P. he campaigned on some local issues such as Home Rule for Ireland, but he was particularly vocal on Indian issues, arguing that although Britain had indeed invested money and manpower in India, it had drained even more resources away from the country through the imposition of unreasonable taxes, which were often used to finance activities which had nothing to do with Indian concerns, such as military adventures in Abyssinia and Afghanistan. He also protested about the obstacles placed in the way of Indian candidates wishing to present themselves for the Indian Civil Service entrance examinations, and acted as an adviser to Mahatma Gandhi in the early stages of his campaign for the rights of Indians in South Africa.

Bhownagree, by contrast, was a vigorous critic of the Indian National Congress, not least because of his belief that British rule had made an unquestionably positive contribution to India's economy and welfare; what has been much less documented, however, is his leading role as an advocate of the interests of Indian settlers in South Africa.

Of the three, Saklatvala was by far the most outspoken. Though unfailingly courteous in tone, he was a vigorous critic of the Raj, arguing that it harshly and illegitimately suppressed the interests of Indian people for the benefit of an alien power.

Parsis therefore typically believe that they made significant contributions to the government at the heart of the Empire. They also point out that that contribution was formally recognised by the British: three of the four baronetcies conferred on Indians before Independence went to Parsis, and sixty-three received knighthoods.[10]

---

[10] See David Mellor, "The Parliamentary Life of Dadabhai Naoroji, the Great Parsi Patriot between 1885–1895", *Journal of the K.R. Cama Oriental Institute*, 1984; Candida Monk, "The Role of the Parsis in the Emergence of the Indian National Congress", *Journal of the K.R. Cama Oriental Institute*, 1984; C. Hancock, "Shapurjee Saklatvala", *Journal of the K.R. Cama Oriental Institute*, 1990; M. Squires, *Saklatwala: A political biography* (London: Lawrence and Wishart, 1990).

The Growth of the Parsi Community in Britain[11]

As the Parsi presence in Britain grew, so its members, whether students, visitors, businessmen, professionals or politicians, gradually felt the need to organise themselves both religiously and socially. The first such formal move came about when Muncherji H. Cama, a leading businessman, was joined by Dadabhoy Naoroji in writing a circular letter to all the fifty Parsis then known to be resident in London, suggesting that the time had come formally to establish a Parsi Association. The first meeting was held on 13 November 1861, when a constitution was approved and it was agreed to set up six "Religious Funds of Zoroastrians of Europe", to be used: to purchase land for the burial of the dead; to help stranded indigent Zoroastrians; to purchase and produce books on Zoroastrianism; to fund research on Zoroastrianism; to establish a House of Prayer; and to establish a general fund for miscellaneous expenses.

In taking this initiative, the Parsis of London were anything but parochial in their thinking: rather they sought to organise themselves in an international setting, conscious of their location at the heart of the British Empire. Thus although the Association was initially composed solely of Parsis, they actively campaigned on behalf of their fellow Zoroastrians in Persia. Thus on the six occasions when the Shah visited Britain, deputations of Parsis waited on him to plead the cause of their oppressed Persian co-religionists. Given the weight of British influence in Persia at the time, and the regular presence of one or other of the MPs (either Naoroji or Bhownagree) in these deputations, it came to be understood that, at the very least, Iranian Zoroastrians had some powerful international friends.

In forming their Association these Parsis also had some specifically religious concerns, particularly over their burial requirements. While deaths were relatively rare, they nevertheless posed a major problem. As Zoroastrians they could not be buried in a Christian cemetery; to conform to their purity laws they needed access to a special plot where their dead could be appropriately buried, hence their first priority was to obtain land for this purpose. The second fund, to provide assistance to destitute Zoroastrians throughout Europe, is characteristic of their community's long tradition of benevolence, reinforced by a concern that none of its members should ever have to call on non-Zoroastrians for aid. Equally characteristic is the priority given to education. From

[11] I am deeply indebted to the Managing Committee of the Zoroastrian Trust Funds of Europe Inc. for their kind permission and ready help in my study of their files, and to Cyrus Mehta, Dr (Mrs) S. Kutar, Ervad Keki E. Kanga and Mrs Ruby Contractor for help with the Gujarati papers, also to Shapuhr Captain, Mr Modi and Russi Dalal for their help in tracing the papers used in preparing this section.

their inception, the Trust Funds have been used to aid Zoroastrians studying in Britain, and to support scholarship in general.

The Establishment of a Zoroastrian House

The first property bought explicitly for the community's collective use was Broacha House in Edinburgh, which Sir Shapurji Broacha endowed in 1909 for use as a hostel by Zoroastrian students. However all the trustees, with the exception of Sir Muncherji Bhownagree, were based in India, and this caused major administrative problems: for a long period the House's Scottish landlady refused to accept Parsis and admitted only white students! The house was eventually sold in the 1940s, and the funds passed to the London association. Moves towards finding a property which would provide a collective base for the community in London were first made as early as 1914, and a house in Cromwell Road was eventually bought in 1920. The property was larger than the community needed, so part of it was rented out as a maisonette; however, none of the rooms proved suitable for use as a prayer hall, and the lease was sold in 1924. Another house (11 Russell Road, Kensington) was bought five years later, and remained the centre of Zoroastrian activity in London for the next forty years.

When a new wave of immigrants arrived in the early 1960s, however, the resources of this house were overwhelmed. The increase in numbers raised the community's religious consciousness as well as its financial resources, and in 1969 a new property was acquired in Compayne Gardens, where Zoroastrian House has been located ever since. Right from the outset the new House included a separate prayer room and sanctuary, closely modelled on those in Bombay. An extension was added in 1983 to cater for increased numbers attending major functions.

The opening of a formally designated Zoroastrian House with a prayer room, and which served just as much as a community centre as a focus for religious activities, was part of a wider set of developments which began early in the twentieth century. Until 1909 the Zoroastrian Trust Funds actually operated as little more than a burial club, and as a means for friends to meet informally; they usually met in Naoroji's house until he returned permanently to India in 1906. Thereafter Bhownagree took over, and was re-elected President every year until his retirement in the 1930s. Under his leadership the "Religious Funds" were formally reconstituted as "the Incorporated Parsee Association of Europe", and its activities were dramatically transformed. Over the years Bhownagree regularly welcomed members of the British nobility, parliamentary figures, Indian princes, and diplomats such as the Persian chargé d'affairs, to the Association's dinners and banquets, his aim evidently being to project as positive an image of the Parsis as possible to the higher echelons of English society. The functions he organised gave London Parsis a strongly enhanced sense of community, rather than an informal group of friends and associates catering only for the direst needs of Zoroastrian travellers, as they had been in the early days.

At this point something must be said about the character of the community's leadership. Not only were Naoroji and Bhownagree political opponents, but many of Naoroji's supporters regularly and fiercely condemned Bhownagree for what they saw as his cravenly pro-British attitudes, and his unquestioning acceptance of British rule in India. In private, however, Naoroji and Bhownagree collaborated with no apparent difficulties: and each at some time chaired a meeting held in honour of the other. No doubt this was because the Parsi presence in London was then so tiny (records of attendance at social functions suggest that their number hardly exceeded 150 during the 1920s) and they felt that, whatever their public differences, there was an overwhelming need to set them aside in private.

But if Bhownagree achieved quiet cooperation with Naoroji, his relations with Shapurji Saklatvala were more difficult. Besides being a Communist, Saklatvala had married outside the community and had been baptised — though he stressed that he had done so simply to sample the experience, not because he had become a Christian. But he was not totally cut off from the community, for after lengthy negotiations his children were initiated according to Zoroastrian rites at a grand social occasion in Caxton Hall on 22 July 1927.

The Resurgence of Religious Tradition

While Bhownagree, as President of the Parsi Association adopted an elitist and largely secular strategy, the professionally qualified Parsi migrants who arrived from the 1940s onwards had very different priorities. Their influence soon brought about some major changes in the character of the community, especially a revival in religious traditions.

One of the most influential of these new migrants was Dr Sohrab Kutar, later to become Britain's first *dastur* (high priest); indeed he was the first and as yet only person resident outside either Iran or the Indian subcontinent on whom such a rank has been formally conferred, and whose status was recognised by Bombay's religious leaders. Having obtained his medical qualifications in Bombay, Sohrab Kutar arrived in Britain in 1939 just before the Second World War, and immediately volunteered for the Royal Army Medical Corps

— and was decorated by Field-Marshal Montgomery for his services in North Africa. After the war he practised in London, but medicine was by no means his only interest. For the local Parsi community his commitment to the revival of Zoroastrian religious practice was far more significant.

Before leaving Bombay, Dr Kutar had been deeply involved in religious activities, and during his medical training spent most of his vacations serving as a *mobed* (priest) in the Poona temple. He was thus virtually unique amongst priests in the diaspora in having previously officiated in an Indian fire temple. In London during the 1950s and '60s he organised an increasing number of ritual activities, most notably the *mukhtad* — a five-day ceremony to honour the souls of the departed. He provided these services readily, regularly and without charge, steadfastly refusing all (traditional) remuneration. Other priests later joined him. The devotional life of the community grew ever more active, and he was eventually rewarded by having the shawl of authority of a high priest, *dastur*, bestowed on him on 17 January 1965. As *dastur*, Dr Kutar had an immense influence on the community, not so much through powerful oratory or forceful leadership but rather as a quiet, rather shy but evidently sincere and holy man. But so great was his influence that there were few disputes over religious matters within the community during his period as *dastur*, which ended with his untimely death on 20 April 1984.

The Growth of the Community's Presence in Britain

Broadly the history of the Zoroastrian (as opposed to the specifically Parsi) community in Britain can be divided into four main periods. Until 1861, when the Trusts were formed, there was no community as such, but only a constant flow of travellers and visitors to Britain; but despite the lack of institutionalisation, the experience of individual visitors during this period laid the foundations of later community attitudes. In the second phase, from 1861 until the mid-1960s, there was the gradual evolution of a formal body, as well as in the size of the community, though numbers were in the hundreds rather than thousands. Typically, new arrivals came in search of education, either formal higher educational qualifications or, more informally, to learn about technological innovation, especially in the textile and shipping industries. It was during this period that many of the institutional structures for the organisation and preservation of the community began to evolve. Besides the formation of the Trusts themselves, these included the acquisition of buildings and the development of religious provisions, including a prayer room, priesthood and liturgical practice. While there was a slow but steady increase in numbers

throughout this formative period, including a significant but unquan-
tifiable boost through an influx of doctors after the Second World
War, numbers rose much more rapidly during the third period, from
the mid-1960s until the early '80s. This was largely the result of
increased migration from India and Pakistan in the early '60s, and
from East Africa thereafter.

During this third period the community became increasingly differentiated internally, as various informal groupings emerged. So, for
instance, there was some degree of tension between the majority of
Indian Parsis who came from cosmopolitan Bombay, and those from
rural Gujarat. Likewise there were differences between those from
India and those from Pakistan: some families had even fought against
each other in their respective national armies in the Indian-Pakistani
wars. Another factor was that while Indian Parsis came almost wholly
through the "pull factor" of Western education, many of those from
Pakistan were subject to the "push factor" of fear of oppression in a
militantly Islamic society. In yet another contrast the East African
Parsis were typically more traditional (or perhaps more nineteenth-
century Indian) in attitude than those who had remained in Bombay.
Finally the community's numbers gained an additional boost from
the arrival of a number of Iranian Zoroastrians after the fall of the
Shah in 1979, as a result of which the British Zoroastrian community
became a far more diverse grouping than ever before.

In the fourth and final period, lasting through the 1980s to the '90s,
inward migration has declined greatly (although it has not quite
ceased), as most Zoroastrian emigrants have preferred to settle in the
United States, Canada and, more recently, in Australia, all of which
are perceived as offering greater opportunities than Britain. Even so,
the size of the British-based community continues to grow because
of its younger age structure, at least in comparison with that in India;
births substantially outnumber deaths. However, given the small size
of most families, this trend may only be short-term.

Self-Perceptions of London Zoroastrians in the 1980s[12]

Although the typical Parsi perception of India and Hinduism is of a
tolerant and accepting society, Parsis have no wish to be confused
with Hindus, or to have their distinctive identity submerged in this

[12] One of the problems in discussing the community's presence in Britain is the very
name by which it is to be identified. A book I was writing jointly with Rashna Writer,
based on material from a large-scale survey and interview schedule, was to have been
entitled "South Asians in Britain: The Zoroastrian Experience", but without exception
all those with whom I discussed the project objected to the title on the grounds that
they were not South Asians.

way. In general, respondents found it much easier to say what they were *not* (not Hindu, Muslim or "Paki") than to identify themselves positively. British ignorance further compounded their problem: how can one identify oneself as a Zoroastrian when hardly anyone in Britain has ever heard of Zoroastrianism? In the face of such difficulties, many respondents asserted that they were "the true Persians", expressing a strong sense of pride at belonging to an ancient and historically influential tradition.

Some of these issues, as well as the strengths of the Parsis' concerns about the dangers which they face as a result of being a tiny minority, are clearly illustrated in an appeal for funds for the new Zoroastrian House which was circulated around the community and in India in September 1959:

In the midst of highly organised and liberally subsidised Proselytising Religions, we Zoroastrians are fighting a losing battle . . . As our people are naturally inclined towards religion, they inevitably drift into one or other of the highly organised religions which keep open doors and receive you with open arms. They have so much more to offer with their powerful resources in the way of highly paid, learned lecturers and priests, wonderfully furnished and well appointed Churches and places of worship . . . In the absence of religious instruction in our own institutions, our children naturally learn and adopt other religions in schools and in social contacts. The first generation of Zoroastrians who came to live in Europe generally have the necessary training and knowledge to follow their own religion. The second generation is rarely properly instructed, and the process of merging with others becomes evident. The third generation is almost completely lost to our religion. This process has been going on for the last Hundred Years and we have lost some of our best sons and daughters to other communities . . .

Our Great Religion has contributed very largely to the subsequent religions including Judaism and Christianity; and the Greek Civilization owes a great debt to our Religion . . . We are, therefore, naturally anxious to preserve our heritage to posterity . . . All Great Religions have a common purpose, but owing to our different backgrounds, we all feel more at home in our own religion and further we are likely to make quicker progress, ethically and spiritually, by following our own religion in which we are born. It is part of our make-up, therefore we must preserve and not destroy that which is of spiritual value to us.

In order to understand the concerns of the Parsis, it is important to appreciate what the term "religion" does and does not connote for them. Zoroastrianism does not, at least in this context, necessarily have a strong spiritual dimension. For some, being an atheist is not incompatible with being a Zoroastrian, while others spoke of it as being "in the blood" or "in the genes", a view further reinforced by the belief that members of the community are heirs to a specifically Zoroastrian culture of ideas, conventions and values deriving from pre-Islamic and non-Arab Iran. Not only is there widespread support for the view that is to follow the religion and culture into which one was born, as the document quoted above suggests, but also that this can only be passed on by birth rather than through study, however deep and long. Thus when a change in the adoption laws was being considered by the Government of India, three Parsi *dasturs* presented a petition to Prime Minister Indira Gandhi seeking exemption for Zoroastrians; they argued that if a Zoroastrian family were to adopt a non-Zoroastrian baby, the child could not be considered a Zoroastrian or become one in adulthood, however brought up.[13] The term "Zoroastrian" thus has strong racial or ethnic connotations and not simply religious ones.

Religion and the Diaspora Community.

Many Zoroastrians in Britain have commented that they practise their religion more in Britain than they did before leaving India. Although such an assertion can only be tested by observing individual activity before and after migration, the assertion is credible, because those who find themselves in the midst of a vast sea of change often find religion a reassuring identifier to which to cling. More active religious involvement has not only given Parsis a link with familiar practices "back home", but has made it easier for them to draw together with other Zoroastrians.

It also appears that those who arrived in Britain during the third phase of settlement from the 1960s onwards tended to be more "traditional" in their religious orientation than most of their predecessors, although they seem also to have been socially mobile and strongly westernised. What is also important is that by the late 1960s the settlement reached a "critical mass", when it was able to generate a far more "traditional" community infrastructure than had been possible earlier when numbers were so much smaller.

Thus, all who arrived before the 1960s faced particular difficulties, with the very existence of their community and faith virtually unrecognised. In consequence they took an active part in the 1960s in Inter-Faith Dialogue, readily accepting invitations to talk to interested groups and welcoming visitors to Zoroastrian House; this seemed the most effective way to present a more positive image of their community and their religion to the public. The result was that the highly westernised, fluent few became spokesmen for the community as a whole, and gained considerable status within it. Later arrivals often

[13] John Hinnells, "Parsi Attitudes to Religious Pluralism" in H. Coward (ed.), *Modern Indian Responses to Religious Pluralism* (Albany: State University of New York Press, 1987).

vigorously criticised those who had stepped into these roles in the earlier period for being too ready to adapt to Western and Christian expectations — thus prompting the newcomers to adopt much more "orthodox" positions. Since religion offers an effective means of marking and preserving one's tradition and identity, it is plausible to suggest that many Parsis have become more religious since their arrival than they were before.

Changes in Religious Practice

Have the religious practices of the Zoroastrians changed since they settled in Britain? Most do indeed believe that change has taken place. Some changes in practice were of course inevitable, not least because of the absence of a consecrated fire temple and of a full-time priest. A few settlers act as priests in their spare time, at considerable personal cost and with great devotion, but few previously served as priests in an Indian temple, and fewer still ever did so regularly. Before their arrival most such part-time priests had no idea that they would ever be called upon to fulfil this role.

This apart, the whole concept of worship in a traditionally Protestant Britain differs greatly from that in India: there it is thought vital to recite the prayers in the original language because of the "aura" they create and the spiritual power they contain, and for many Parsis the whole purpose of worship is the realisation of the divine presence in the spirit and objects of the ritual itself. This is in marked contrast to the Protestant emphasis on congregational worship, intercessory prayer and the idea of prayer itself as "talking with God", so that it is deemed essential to understand the meaning of the prayers which are otherwise thought of as becoming "mumbo jumbo". Thus young people brought up in the West, and especially those who have attended a primary school, often have very different perceptions of the nature and purpose of worship from those of their parents. In these circumstances a protestantized Zoroastrianism could eventually emerge.

In India worship is usually an individual act of pilgrimage, involving a visit to the temple to pray before the permanently burning fire, and thus to stand in the presence of God and receive the divine blessing. But in the absence of a permanently burning fire, British Zoroastrians cannot make such a pilgrimage. Instead the *jashan* has been developed as the common community ritual, and is part of both the ancient and the living Zoroastrian tradition. As in the Christian Mass, the intention of the rite can easily be modified, for a slight change in some of the prayers can transform it into an act of celebration (as for the installation of a *mobed*), a thanksgiving (as for victory in war), a blessing (as for a new home) or a petition (as for rain in a drought). Because the *jashan* is not tied strictly to a temple and can be celebrated in a hired hall or a private home, it is more often used as a vehicle for congregational activity in Britain than in India. The *jashan* is best understood neither as a new ritual nor as a new concept, but rather as a development of the received tradition adapted to meet the needs of new circumstances. As such it may prove to be an exemplar of the character of change in other aspects of Zoroastrian practice, but only time can tell what these other adaptations will be.

A Religious Generation Gap?

While it appears too simple to talk of a generation gap between migrant parents and their British-born children, younger people certainly pray less often and in a less traditional manner than their elders. Likewise fewer affirm belief in an afterlife, while many more describe themselves as non-practising. Even so, more than half of young Parsis affirm that they engage in at least some religious practice, for example by saying the prayers; and some are *more* traditional than their elders, as in the vigorous support which at least some of them give to the exclusion of non-Zoroastrians from the prayer room. As one explained, "Every day of my life I am in a multi-cultural situation at school. I want one place where I can go and be myself." Likewise more of the youth than the elders thought the purity laws should be maintained, that prayers for the dead were necessary, and that the link between race and religion should be preserved.

There are also some marked differences in attitude towards their roots: rather more younger people than settlers who arrived in the 1960s feel happy visiting the "old country". It would seem that whereas many of those who arrived in the '60s have come to terms with their new environment, their offspring have begun to look to their religion and to the "old country" for inspiration in their quest for a sense of identity and rootedness. Cautious though we must be about this conclusion,[14] it is clear that it is unsafe to make unqualified statements about the prospect of the second and third generation inevitably abandoning their religious and cultural heritage.

It appears that women play a crucial role in the transmission of the tradition. They are more frequent attenders at Zoroastrian House (although those men who do go tend to do so more regularly); they tend to pray more often and more traditionally; and more women than men want to sustain the link between race and religion. But within this broad pattern, there are further differences between those women

---

[14] It was far easier to interview young people who had kept in contact with the community, so the sample is probably somewhat skewed.

who are housewives and those who go out to work, for the positions taken by the latter are rather closer to those of the men. Where grandparents live with a family, they would seem to reinforce tradition, and in this context grandmothers often play an especially vigorous role.

Parsis and the British

Long before their arrival, Parsis had already formed impressions of the British — from direct experience of their rule, travellers' accounts and the steady accumulation of popular legend. But how have they found the British in Britain? Although many believe their relations with the host population to be excellent, most nevertheless have formed a number of negative impressions about the character of British society, and comment unfavourably on the perceived "lack of morals" amongst the native English, especially their tendency to engage in pre-marital and extra-marital sex. Virtually no elders want their children to grow up "like the British".

Just under half of persons questioned admit to having been subjected to racial discrimination, but this proportion is almost certainly an underestimate, for there is also reluctance to talk about it. One man who denied having encountered racial prejudice later described how he had suffered from "Paki bashing". Some young people do not tell their parents about such experiences in order not to distress them, while others claim to be "above that sort of thing" because they are so westernised.

The popular expectation is that the most likely victims of discrimination are the least integrated, the less well educated, and those with limited fluency in English. However, those who report experiencing prejudice are as academically well qualified as those who do not, their career patterns are no worse, and their attitude to their nationality is not significantly different. Prejudice, rather than being triggered by the "failings" of its victims, lies entirely in the attitudes of the discriminators. Of those reporting personal experience of prejudice, almost all had faced it at school — mostly from fellow-pupils, although some also criticise their teachers and the structure of the syllabus. Employment is the second main area where discrimination is reported, though rather fewer believe they have encountered it on the streets, in shops or from the police. Interviewees were also asked about the effect which prejudice might have on themselves and their community; few would seek to avoid it by assimilation, rather the result is to precipitate a stronger sense of community.

This apart, there is also a widespread and forcefully expressed belief in the difficulty of getting close to the British, who are often described as "cold", "distant" and "patronising". However there is also a significant difference in attitude between those who arrived in the 1960s and both their children and the more recently arrived elders. The longer established, middle-aged settlers tend to offer the least vigorous criticisms, while both young people and the more recently arrived elders are much more consistently negative. Similarly, professional "high-flyers" tend to be the least critical of the British, and housewives to be most strongly critical.

Since the Zoroastrians were the first of Britain's many South Asian communities to be formally reconstituted in their new environment, their experience is particularly illuminating, for although many aspects of it replicate in microcosm that of their successors, they also show some significant differences. First, the great majority of Parsi immigrants were well qualified educationally before their arrival and so expected to have professional careers. Secondly, the very small size of their community, both in Britain and India, has posed specific problems: given the low indigenous birth-rate and high emigration rate of Indian Parsis, there is a real possibility that if those in the new diaspora fail to preserve their identity and culture, the world's oldest prophetic religion could become extinct within a few generations.

Against a background of such concerns, debate on the merits of various survival strategies has become quite intense. Although most London Parsis believe that survival is possible, few do so unreservedly, because the educational achievement which has made their community materially so successful is also seen as a threat to their religious and cultural survival. Most parents are alarmed at the prospect of their children growing up behaving in the same way as their English peers, fearing that excessive freedom and independence may take them outside the community. They also foresee a degeneration of morals in the context of Britain's secular society; indeed these issues arouse far greater concern than racism. Another highly sensitive issue is the perceived reluctance of the wider society even to recognise their existence as a distinct group.

There are all sorts of paradoxes here. Parsis arrived in Britain with high hopes based both on their experience in British India and on the reports of early travellers; and in material terms most have fulfilled those hopes. Theirs is now a very prosperous community. As a result, despite some onward movement to the United States and Canada, most now see their future as being firmly grounded in Britain, and hardly anyone now envisages returning permanently either to India or to Iran. The widespread concern over the community's ability to maintain a distinctive identity has led to the formulation of a wide variety of survival strategies. At the most local level, many local groups now enable Zoroastrians in Britain to stay in touch with one another; and at the other end of the organisational scale efforts are being made to establish a worldwide Zoroastrian Association. Hitherto all attempts to do so have foundered on deep-rooted conflicts of interest between the community's Bombay-based and diaspora-based components, but the fact that such efforts are being made indicates the increasingly crucial role of the diaspora in the survival of Zoroastrianism itself.

Since educational success tends to be associated with religious doubt, it is significant that several London-based groups are making great efforts to develop programmes of religious education to counter the subtle forms of religious indoctrination to which their children are exposed at school. Yet these efforts are matched by a fear, common to young people and their elders alike, that they themselves know too little about Zoroastrianism to pass it on successfully to the next generation. No one disagrees that change is needed to enable them to meet the challenge of their new environment. But how, when, where and by whom this is to be done remains a matter of intense debate.

CAUGHT IN AN ETHNIC QUANDARY

INDO-CARIBBEAN HINDUS IN LONDON

Steven Vertovec

"To be an Indian or East Indian from the West Indies is to be
a perpetual surprise to people outside the region."
— V.S. Naipaul[1]

The great majority of Britain's best-known group of South Asian
"twice migrants" — the large body of people of Gujarati and Punjabi
origin who came to Britain from East Africa during the late 1960s
and early '70s — swiftly took advantage of the social networks and
cultural institutions already established by their counterparts who had
migrated directly from India to Britain. Besides ensuring that the
newcomers tended to cluster in those towns and cities where settlers
with regional and religious origins similar to themselves were already
established, these patterns also ensured that their links with the subcontinent would continue to influence the subsequent course of their
adaptation and identification.

However, a second group of "twice migrants" arrived in Britain
at much the same time by way of the Caribbean. These Indo-Caribbeans, whose very existence is still often overlooked, faced — and
still face — a much more perplexing situation. They had lived much
longer overseas, their regional origins in the subcontinent were different and they had had some distinctive experiences as overseas
settlers. As a result, they felt they had no connection with, and indeed
were often discouraged from participating in, the networks and institutions dominated by direct migrants from South Asia. Their almost
complete severance from the subcontinent, which had been initiated
in the middle of the nineteenth-century, meant that their "Indian-ness"
often seemed open to question. This chapter explores these and other
aspects of the unique ethnic quandary in which Indo-Caribbeans,
particularly the Hindus among them, have found themselves since
settling in Britain.[2]

[1] V.S. Naipaul, *The Overcrowded Barracoon and Other Articles* (London: André
Deutsch, 1972), p. 33.
[2] After field research in Trinidad in 1984–5, ethnographic research on British Indo-
Caribbeans was done in London on a "commuter" basis throughout 1988–9. Regarding
work in the latter context, I wish to express my sincere thanks especially to Ganesh

The roots of this problem can be found in a confusion of categories — just as evident amongst the native whites as amongst their British Asian peers — about the association between social boundaries, cultural practices and racial traits. Whites, taking no cognizance of their distinctive accents, styles and mannerisms, tend to lump Indo-Caribbeans into the generalised category labelled "Asian". Even when aware of Indo-Caribbeans' differing backgrounds, most white people still make this generalisation: Indo-Caribbeans are "Asian" because this is how they *look*. Yet there are other circumstances in which Indo-Caribbeans fall into a quite different social category: for official purposes they may well be "West Indians" because the West Indies was where they were born.

Meanwhile those South Asian settlers who have come to Britain either directly or by way of East Africa also tend to perceive Indo-Caribbeans at best as an enigmatic group, and at worst as a somewhat menacing one. Though physically similar to themselves, they often talk, dress and act in unexpected ways. Hence for many Indians from India, confrontation with a hitherto unknown but unremarkable fact — that some people of Indian descent have lived for generations in the Caribbean — generates confusion about how they should react to their long-lost cousins. This is highlighted in V.S. Naipaul's description of an encounter in an airport lounge which parallels the experience of most Indo-Caribbeans in Britain:

> There was another Indian in the lounge . . .
> "You are coming from — ?"
> I had met enough Indians from India to know that this was less a serious inquiry than a greeting, in a distant land, from one Indian to another.
> "Trinidad," I said. "In the West Indies. And you?"
> He ignored my question. "But you look Indian."
> "I am."
> "Red Indian?" He suppressed a nervous little giggle.
> "East Indian. From the West Indies."
> He looked offended and wandered off to the bookstall. From this distance he eyed me assessingly.[3]

While Indo-Caribbeans are regularly identified as "Asians" by most whites — and therefore regularly subjected to racial exclusionism — they are often simultaneously excluded (or at best regarded as a low-status, adjunct group) on social and cultural grounds by most other "Asians". Yet if most Indo-Caribbeans therefore have strong

---

Lall, Mazrul Bacchus, Jim Jinkhoo and Tamesh Lilmohan, as well as to numerous others in the British Indo-Caribbean community for their willing participation, continuous encouragement and splendid hospitality.

[3] Naipaul, *ibid.*, p. 30.

reservations about unambiguously identifying themselves as "Asian" in a British context, most have even less wish to be identified as West Indians, despite their recent arrival from Trinidad and Guyana. They regard the term "West Indian" as having strong *Afro*-Caribbean connotations, and, quite apart from negative British stereotypes about this group, there is, in the Caribbean itself, a long heritage of Indian antipathy towards people of African descent.[4]

How, then, do Indo-Caribbeans in Britain see themselves? We must now take a closer look at their background, their process of immigration, and their subsequent patterns of settlement and adjustment.

Indians in the Caribbean

The first Indians to arrive in the Caribbean were brought to British Guiana in 1838, as part of the global transplantation of Indian indentured labourers to European tropical colonies after the abolition of formal slavery.[5] Indian indentured labourers were introduced to Trinidad in 1845, Jamaica and the French West Indies in 1854, Dutch Guiana (Suriname) in 1873, and other, smaller Caribbean colonies such as Grenada and St Vincent intermittently. For decades, colonial planters were keen to obtain additional Indian indentured labourers. Despite the costs of recruitment and transport, Indians were regarded as a cheaper and more controllable source of labour than free wage-earners, which the ex-slaves of African descent had by then become. When the indenture system was finally halted in 1917, well over half a million Indians had been brought to the Caribbean. Of these, the

---

[4] A generally rather tense attitude toward Africans has existed among Indians in the Caribbean virtually since the Indians arrived in the region during the nineteenth century — cf. Bridget Brereton, *Race Relations in Colonial Trinidad, 1870–1900* (Cambridge University Press, 1979). Some scholars have suggested that, at least initially in the Caribbean, Indian distancing or outright prejudice against Africans was drawn from caste-based notions of pollution: since in North India the lowest castes were often associated with dark skin, it is suggested that the Africans encountered first in the Caribbean must have therefore been regarded by the immigrant Indians as a highly polluted people — Brian Moore, "The retention of caste notions among the Indian immigrants in British Guiana during the nineteenth century", *Comparative Studies in Society and History*, vol. 19 (1977), pp. 96–107. Others, however, emphasize the Indians' various, more recent experiences of structural inequality, largely at the hands of Africans, as a more pervasive influence on the former's distancing or prejudice towards the latter — cf. Malcolm Cross, "Colonialism and ethnicity: A theory and comparative study", *Ethnic and Racial Studies*, vol. 1 (1978), pp. 37–59.

[5] See, among others, Hugh Tinker, *A New System of Slavery: The Export of Indian Labour Overseas, 1830–1920* (Oxford University Press, 1974); Colin G. Clarke, Ceri Peach and Steven Vertovec (eds), *South Asians Overseas: Migration and Ethnicity* (Cambridge University Press, 1990).

great majority settled either in British Guiana (which received 238,909 Indians throughout the period), Trinidad (143,939) or Dutch Guiana (34,000).

Most Indian immigration to the Caribbean, as to Mauritius, Fiji and South Africa, was governed by a system of indenture contracts. Though the details of these contracts varied over the years and from colony to colony, their common features included: recruitment by indigenous agents who ranged over vast areas of northeast and southeast India; inducement to enter into a contract lasting at least five years to work on a plantation, usually cultivating sugar; transport to the port of embarkation (Calcutta or Madras) and thence abroad; receipt of basic pay (often on a task basis), rudimentary housing, rations and medical attention during the course of the contract; and a partly or fully paid return passage to India after the end of the contract (and often, for fully paid passage, a further five years' labour in the colony). Although the system appeared to provide an outlet for poverty-stricken people in economically devastated and famine-struck areas, indentured labour proved a harsh alternative, being often associated with poverty, disease, malnutrition and social oppression.

Yet despite the dire conditions, around 80 per cent of Indian immigrants in the three largest colonies opted to stay on once their period of indenture was complete. Not only was it expensive to return (especially in the later period when free return passages were no longer on offer), but opportunities to acquire land and achieve some degree of social mobility often seemed greater in the Caribbean than back in India. Former indentured labourers were quick to acquire land: well before the end of the century numerous settlements had sprung up throughout the cane- and rice-growing areas of Trinidad, as well as in British and Dutch Guiana. Subsequently Indians came to make up — as they still do — the backbone of the agricultural sector in each of these countries. But although still predominantly rurally based, they have moved into urban areas while Indo-Caribbean villages are now less isolated than in the early post-indenture days.

Indian cultural patterns in the Caribbean have evolved largely in response to local conditions,[6] in which scale, geography and poverty have often militated against the successful maintenance of pre-migration practices. In Jamaica and the smaller islands — where Indians are both widely dispersed and few in number — recognisably Indian

---

[6] Chandra Jayawardena, "Migration and social change: A survey of Indian communities overseas", *Geographical Review*, vol. 58 (1968), pp. 426–49; Allen S. Ehrlich, "History, ecology and demography in the British Caribbean: An analysis of East Indian ethnicity", *Southwestern Journal of Anthropology*, vol. 27 (1971), pp. 166–88; Steven Vertovec, *Hindu Trinidad: Religion, Ethnicity and Socio-Economic Change* (London: Macmillan, 1992).

phenomena have seldom been sustained. Meanwhile in Trinidad, Guyana and Suriname, where there have long been large Indian enclaves, recognisably Indian social and cultural features are much more widespread. Even so, these "Indian" patterns — which vary somewhat between the three territories[7] — are the outcome of processes of inadvertent permutation as well as of conscious manipulation which have taken place over the course of three to five generations, and are therefore distinctive in character.

In the first decades of immigration, there began a process of homogenisation which drew selectively on some basic Indian (and particularly Hindu) social and cultural institutions. Indentured labourers were recruited from a vast area of India, mostly ranging across what are now Bihar and Uttar Pradesh, in which socio-cultural and religious phenomena varied from region to region, district to district, and even village to village — hence common traits were few. This led to the spontaneous development of a creolised "plantation Hindustani",[8] based largely on a mixture of Bhojpuri and Avadhi dialects with English, by means of which a diverse set of individuals were able to create some sense of community. Through necessity the earliest arrivals devised a "lowest common denominator" of language and culture for organising generalized forms of address, formal and informal interaction, marriage, domestic practice, cuisine, music and art, ritual and religious belief.[9]

A significant feature of this process in Trinidad, Guyana and Suriname alike was the emergence of a sense of egalitarianism, thus attenuating the re-establishment of any clear sense of caste hierarchy.[10] As for caste, indentured labourers were drawn from all quarters of rural society; contrary to many myths, low-caste people were not overrepresented. But because they were of such diverse origins, having been recruited individually rather than as members of caste or kin groups, the loyalties of caste (*jati*), sub-caste (*biradari*) and

---

[7] Steven Vertovec, "'Official' and 'popular' Hinduism in the Caribbean: Historical and contemporary trends in Suriname, Trinidad and Guyana" in *Contributions to Indian Sociology* (in press).

[8] E.g. in Trinidad: Mridula Adenwala Durbin, "Formal changes in Trinidad Hindi as a result of language adaptation", *American Anthropologist*, vol. 75 (1973), pp. 1290–1304. In Guyana: Surendra Kumar Gambhir, "Diglossia in dying languages: A case study of Guyanese Bhojpuri and Standard Hindi", *Anthropological Linguistics*, vol. 25 (1983), pp. 28–38.

[9] See Steven Vertovec, "Hinduism in diaspora: The transformation of tradition in Trinidad", in G.D. Sontheimer and H. Kulke (eds), *Hinduism Reconsidered* (Delhi: Manohar, 1989), pp. 152–79; also Vertovec, "'Official' and 'Popular' Hinduism".

[10] See especially Barton M. Schwartz (ed.), *Caste in Overseas Indian Communities* (San Francisco: Chandler, 1967); also Vertovec, *Hindu Trinidad*, and Moore, "Retention of caste notions".

descent group (*gotra*), which have been such a vital focus of social organisation amongst free migrants to Britain, were soon forgotten on the sugar estates. Once they had gone, they could not be recreated. Thus when villages later grew up, it proved almost impossible to re-establish the ritual hierarchies and socio-economic inter-dependence so characteristic of village India. Given forced inter-caste proximity and commensality while crossing the "black waters" on board ship and later in the estate barracks, all the conventional boundaries of purity and pollution were confounded; the dictates of plantation labour also brought all traditional caste-based occupational and economic relationships wholly to an end. Gross inequalities in the sex ratio of immigrants (on average one female to three or more males) ensured that rules of endogamy were largely discarded, with only the extreme categories of Brahmin and Chamar (leather-worker) continuing to be recognised as having any attributional meaning. Today the Brahmins alone have sustained a hereditary occupation — the priesthood; and in doing so they have not only kept up their religious monopoly, but have retained a disproportionate influence in political and communal affairs.[11]

In keeping with other aspects of the local socio-cultural tradition, Caribbean Hinduism is strongly egalitarian.[12] Broadly North Indian in form,[13] its Vaishnavite orientation emphasises the *bhakti* tradition of personal devotion. Its sources are conventional, and focus mainly on Puranic literature (especially the *Shrimad Bhagavata Purana*) and Tulsidas' *Ramayana*, but where practice is concerned much has changed. *Pujas* (ritual offerings to deities), *satsangs* (devotional gatherings in which passages from the Ramayana are sung), *yagnas* (seven- to fourteen-day sets of readings and rites) etc. have gradually evolved into congregational events in which sermons are preached in English. *Hanuman Puja* has become one of the commonest domestic rituals, while the raising of coloured flags (*jhandi*), a tradition traceable to Uttar Pradesh, usually provides the ritual climax. Thus while the rites, texts and calendar of Caribbean Hinduism are clearly derived

[11] Peter van der Veer and Steven Vertovec, "Brahmanism abroad: On the development of Caribbean Hinduism as an ethnic religion", *Ethnology*, vol. 30 (1991), pp. 149–66.
[12] Chandra Jayawardena, "Religious belief and social change: Aspects of the development of Hinduism in British Guiana", *Comparative Studies in Society and History*, vol. 8 (1966), pp. 211–40.
[13] Before the 1860s, Guyana — and Trinidad rather less — received indentured immigrants from Tamil and Telugu areas of South India. Though in many ways suppressed by colonial authorities and North Indian immigrants, some South Indian forms of worship have persisted. Foremost is Kali Mai Puja, which in recent years has become popular in both countries, especially because of its emphasis on ecstatic, *shakti*-oriented healing. Nevertheless, it remains peripheral to the majority of Caribbean Hindus.

from India's "Great Tradition", local styles and procedures have acquired a distinctive pattern of their own, for the means and modes of Hindu practice in the Caribbean have been forged in conditions of racial and religious pluralism. The resultant forms are both "public"[14] and organised in such a way as to appear legitimate to local non-Hindus.[15]

The Indo-Caribbean Hindus' cultural identity has thus been forged in an ethnically plural society which has fostered the growth of communal sentiments.[16] While Trinidadian and Guyanese Hindi is now little used by younger people, most of whom have also been heavily influenced by British and American popular cultural styles, and although Indo-Caribbean Hindus have been strongly influenced by the cultural and linguistic styles of their Afro-Caribbean neighbours, they nevertheless retain a strong sense of ethnic distinctiveness.[17] This consciousness of Hindu ethnicity has become steadily more politicised since the early 1950s, when rival Indian and African-backed political parties were formed in both Guyana and Trinidad.[18]

In Guyana, the Indian- (mainly Hindu-) dominated People's Progressive Party enjoyed two brief periods of power (1953, 1957–64) over the People's National Congress — dominated by people of African descent and often too by Indian Muslims — before being toppled by pressure from the British and US governments. After race riots in 1963 and 1964 in which 150 people were killed, the PNC again assumed power and in 1966 led Guyana to independence; up till 1992, when the PNC was finally defeated in fair elections, it used intimidation and vote-rigging to consolidate its power. In Trinidad the Indian-dominated People's Democratic Party was all but indis-

---

[14] Chandra Jayawardena, "Culture and ethnicity in Guyana and Fiji", *Man* (N.S.), vol. 15 (1980), pp. 430–50.

[15] See Vertovec, *Hindu Trinidad*, chapter 2.

[16] Hindus number about 300,000 in both Trinidad and Guyana, thus comprising 34% of Guyana's total population of some 884,000 (or 61% of all Indians, who account for 55% of the total) and 25% of Trinidad's population of over 1.2 million (or 61% of all Indians there, who amount to over 41% of the nation's total).

[17] Drummond has usefully described the situation in Guyana (in many ways also applicable to Trinidad) as a "cultural continuum" or "intersystem" — patterned after a model of Creole linguistics — in which most members of the society are cognisant of much or all of the values and behaviour of numerous ethnic groups beside their own, and able to understand yet not necessarily to practise or master them — Lee Drummond, "The cultural continuum: A theory of intersystems", *Man* (N.S.), vol. 15 (1980), pp. 352–74. During the conference which preceded the publication of this book, Roger Ballard referred to Drummond's article and the Caribbean society it describes by way of suggesting this may represent a context in which people — despite mutual ethnic tensions — are actually "being multicultural".

[18] Steven Vertovec, "Religion and ethnic ideology: The Hindu youth movement in Trinidad", *Ethnic and Racial Studies*, vol. 13 (1990), pp. 225–49.

tinguishable from the Sanatan Dharma Maha Sabha, or national Hindu organization; but it never tasted governmental power, for the Black- and Muslim-backed People's National Movement (PNM) retained total control from the mid-1950s, through independence in 1962, until 1986. Indian perceptions of social and economic changes and oppor- tunities in both Guyana and Trinidad have therefore been heavily influenced by these racial and political confrontations.

Their fears were not groundless. Heavily concentrated in rural areas where poverty and underemployment were rife, Indians had the lowest incomes of any ethnic group throughout the 1950s and '60s, as well as the highest number of unskilled workers and the fewest professionals. Lacking patronage, they were under-represented in the civil service and subjected to blatant discrimination in many other sectors of the job market[19] — although from the 1950s they increas- ingly concentrated on education as a means of achieving social mobil- ity.[20] This particular combination of a strong sense of ethnic identity, a powerful commitment to upward mobility, and a perceived ex- perience of socio-economic and political exclusion and oppression helps to explain the patterns of migration and community develop- ment that have emerged among Indo-Caribbeans in Britain.

Migration and Settlement in Britain

Indo-Caribbean migrants arrived in Britain as part of the much larger inflow of Caribbean people in the late 1950s and early '60s, largely in response to the employment opportunities then available.[21] But although there are many parallels between Indo- and Afro-Caribbean migratory patterns, they differ in several important ways. Despite the disadvantages just outlined, Indo-Caribbean migrants tended to have achieved higher levels of education and of occupational skill before

[19] Jack Harewood, "Racial discrimination in employment in Trinidad and Tobago", *Social and Economic Studies*, vol. 20 (1971), pp. 267–93; Malcolm Cross, *The East Indians of Guyana and Trinidad* (London: Minority Rights Group, 1973); Percy Hintzen, "Bases of elite support for a regime: Race, ideology and clientelism as bases for leaders in Guyana and Trinidad", *Comparative Political Studies*, vol. 16 (1985), pp. 363–91.
[20] Malcolm Cross and Allen M. Schwartzbaum, "Social mobility and secondary school selection in Trinidad", *Social and Economic Studies*, vol. 18 (1969), pp. 189–207; Sara Graham and Derek Gordon, *The Stratification System and Occupational Mobility in Guyana* (Mona, Jamaica: Institute of Social and Economic Research, 1977); Joseph Nevadomsky, "Economic organization, social mobility, and changing social status among East Indians in rural Trinidad", *Ethnology*, vol. 22 (1983), pp. 63–79; Percy Hintzen, *The Costs of Regime Survival: Racial Mobilization, Elite Domination and Control of the State in Guyana and Trinidad* (Cambridge University Press, 1989).
[21] Ceri Peach, *West Indian Migration to Britain: A Social Geography* (Oxford Univer- sity Press, 1968).

their migration. Highly motivated Indians often chose to come to Britain to work and study at levels which they perceived as not being available in Guyana and Trinidad because of either a lack of facilities or deliberate discrimination. Many migrants claim that their original intention was to return to the Caribbean once they had gained additional educational and professional credentials, and had saved some capital.

Due to the lack of an appropriate question in the Census which would allow Caribbean people of Indian origin to be separated from those with African roots, we can only guess at the size of Britain's Indo-Caribbean population. Using the available Census data, it is possible to arrive at a figure between 22,800 to 30,400 for Indians from Trinidad and Guyana,[22] but this is almost certainly an underestimate, for it takes no account of illegal immigration or of the unknown number of Indo-Caribbean migrants from Jamaica, Grenada, and St Vincent. Using the same methods, it is reasonable to estimate that around three- quarters of British-Indo Caribbeans live in the London region. But despite their small numbers, they have not gathered together in a single ethnic colony but are widely spread across the whole region, although with modest concentrations in Balham and Tooting and smaller ones in Brixton and Catford. While almost all appear to have moved many times since arriving in Britain, nearly all had simply moved from one part of London to another.

Since the bulk of British Indo-Caribbean migrants came to work and study, most did not have established families back in Trinidad and Guyana whom they planned to support with remittances. As individuals who "came to go back", set on gaining credentials, ex-

---

[22] Martin J. Boodhoo and Ahamad Baksh (in *The Impact of Brain Drain on Development: A Case Study of Guyana*, Geogetown: University of Guyana, 1981), indicate that between 1969 and 1976, Indo-Guyanese emigrants comprised between 31% and 47% of the total of Guyanese emigrants; there is little reason to assume the ratio would be drastically different in Trinidad, for the 1960s and early '70s at least, although later the Indians were probably less motivated to migrate since they fared so well from both the oil boom and from sugar price hikes; see Vertovec, "Oil boom and recession in Trinidad Indian villages', in C. Clarke, C. Peach and S. Vertovec (eds), *South Asians Overseas.*

Working from the 1981 Census, if we count as Indo-Caribbean a conservative proportion of between 30–40% of all Trinidad-born (16,334) and Guyana-born (21,686) persons, we arrive at figures of between 4,900 and 6,500 Indo-Trinidadian immigrants, and between 6,500 and 8,700 Indo-Guyanese immigrants in 1981. If we then roughly double these figures to include British-born offspring (following the figures in the Labour Force Survey (1986), which show that the total West Indian population is twice that of West Indians by place of birth), we obtain figures of 9,800–13,000 and 13,000–17,400 respectively. The total Indo-Trinidadian/Indo-Guyanese population would then lie somewhere between 22,800 to 30,400. I thank Ceri Peach for helpful discussions on possible numbers of Indo-Caribbeans in Britain.

perience and capital, most arrived unmarried, and married only after living in Britain for some time. Since their spouses came straight over to join them, their children — unlike those of many other early Asian settlers in Britain — are almost exclusively British-born and -raised.

The Early Pioneers

Very few of the earliest Indo-Caribbean pioneers came directly to Britain from rural backgrounds. Most had lived for some years in the urban environment of Port of Spain or Georgetown, where they gained a higher level and quality of education than most of their rural compatriots, and were able to accumulate the funds needed to finance the journey. Early settlers invariably found it far more difficult to obtain accommodation than a job, for in the mid-1950s "No Coloureds" signs were still often displayed in the windows of lodging-houses. A number of such houses in the Notting Hill Gate, Earls Court and Hammersmith districts of London were rather more liberal, however — often because they were owned by members of other immigrant groups — and many of the early pioneers initially settled there. Nevertheless racial discrimination was still a major problem at all but the most menial levels of the employment market: "You couldn't get a civil servant's job, or any job in fact, that was commensurate with your education." Hence trained teachers, accountants and administrators often washed dishes, worked on assembly lines, or even swept the streets.

Nevertheless the pioneers were soon acting as contacts for subsequent migrants, and thus at the centre of rapidly growing migrant networks. Potential emigrants in Guyana or Trinidad needed no more than a name and an address and the knowledge that it belonged to someone from their neighbourhood, the friend of a friend, a sister-in-law's cousin, or whomever to feel that it was as good as an invitation. Having received a letter announcing that so-and-so would arrive on a certain date, pioneer settlers would dutifully meet new immigrants off the boat train, put them up for a few nights and give them tips on making their way in a new and hostile society.[23]

Many of the earliest Indo-Caribbean migrants felt socially isolated; one such recalls that he "lived in a shell", circulating between work, school and studying while knowing only a few kindred souls. Some began to frequent the West India Student Centre in Earls Court, where they had meals and "limed" (hung around joking and chatting) in a more familiar West Indian way. Even so they often met ignorance

---

[23] An identical process among Afro-Trinidadian immigrants is entertainingly portrayed in Sam Selvon's, *The Lonely Londoners* (London: Wingate, 1956).

and exclusion from small islanders, especially the many Barbadians who, because their island never received indentured Indians, had not encountered Indo-Caribbeans before.

Before long, however, small groups of men, mostly Indo-Caribbean Hindus but sometimes also including Hindus who had migrated directly from India, began to meet in "bedsits" to conduct *puja* (ritual offerings to a deity); in the absence of a priest, they simply used whatever *mantras* (Sanskrit prayers) and other ritual procedures they happened to know. *Murtis* (representations of deities) were no more than pictures brought over from Guyana and Trinidad, and all other ritual accoutrements were equally makeshift since "in those days there was no Southall[24] where you could buy things". News of their meetings spread rapidly — not least among the non-Indo-Caribbean Hindus who by then were settling in London. By 1956 Lambeth Town Hall in South London was regularly being hired, and ceremonies were held under the supervision of a priest from Guyana and attended by Hindu immigrants from many parts of the world, including India, the Caribbean, East Africa and Mauritius. In 1957 this group established the Hindu Dharma Sabha, which raised funds and continued to rent public halls for the celebration of major festivals such as Shivratri, Navratri and Diwali.

The Sabha represented a significant stage in the evolution of Hindu institutions in Britain. It was, in all probability, the first such body, and the forms of worship it employed were ecumenical since they had to cater for Hindu immigrants from such a diverse range of backgrounds. Indo-Caribbean rites are of generalised North Indian origin and thus rather "basic" in character, being directed toward "Sanskritic" rather than regional or sectarian deities, and employing English, rather than any of India's regional languages as the *lingua franca* — thus they provided a convenient framework for mutual aggregation. This fusion did not last long, however. The rapid growth of the Hindu presence in London in the late 1950s caused organisational fission into regionally-based groups,[25] so that Punjabis and Gujaratis (and caste groups within their ranks) set up organisations to facilitate the celebration of their own rituals in their own tongue and in their own manner.[26]

---

[24] Southall: district in the West London outer suburbs, containing the metropolitan area's largest concentration of South Asian inhabitants.

[25] Trends of "fission" and "fusion" of migrant South Asian communities are discussed in Surinder M. Bhardwaj and N. Madhusudana Rao, "Asian Indians in the United States: A geographic appraisal", in C. Clarke, C. Peach and S. Vertovec (eds), *South Asians Overseas*.

[26] Cf. David Bowen, "The evolution of Gujarati Hindu organizations in Bradford", in R. Burghart (ed.), *Hinduism in Great Britain* (London: Tavistock, 1987), pp. 15–31.

As the others peeled off, so Indo-Caribbeans organised themselves rather more exclusively. Thus in the early 1960s the Hindu Dharma Sabha renamed itself the Caribbean Hindu Society, while continuing to organise the same events. As one founder member explained:

"We thought that if we could make it specifically Caribbean, it could go out and attract people who came from the Caribbean, because they were in greatest need for this kind of cultural contact. If a person from Guyana just saw the name 'Hindu Dharma Sabha', he would think it was something more for people from India, and that he wouldn't feel quite welcome."

Indo-Caribbean Hindus thereby gained an institutionalised basis for meeting socially as a distinct ethnic community, as well as for congregating religiously for the practice of distinct ritual activities.[27] But their place in British society was shifting at the same time.

Just as the majority of Indo-Caribbean immigrants had made frequent moves around the London area since their first arrival, so they also frequently changed occupation. This is particularly striking amongst those who arrived in the late 1950s and early '60s: they often took unskilled or semi-skilled jobs while studying for credentials (in law, nursing, accounting, engineering, etc.) to which they hoped British employers would be more responsive than to those they had gained in the West Indies. Later arrivals, often with degrees from the University of Guyana or the University of the West Indies and studying for advanced degrees from one of London's universities, were in a rather better position, and usually did not have to make their initial step into the job market at such a low level as their forerunners. Indo-Caribbeans, having now achieved a high degree of upward social mobility, can be characterised as a largely middle-class group with a range of professional, administrative and white-collar occupations: e.g. teacher, lawyer, civil servant, accountant, clerk, nurse, hospital technician, health visitor, economist, maths lecturer and master tailor. Yet although neither geographically nor occupationally clustered, British Indo-Caribbeans still form a distinct community socially, culturally and in their religion.

Some Current Characteristics

Though typically Indian, Indo-Caribbean social and cultural styles seem, at least outwardly, much more "Western" than those of first-generation immigrants from India. This is particularly evident among women, who tend to sport salon hairdos and department store dresses; only at major religious events are saris and Indian jewellery normally

[27] See Steven Vertovec, "Community and Congregation in London Hindu Temples: divergent trends", *New Community*, vol. 18 (1992), pp. 251–64.

worn. But it is in their language that the Indo-Caribbean background is most evident.

Like their Afro-Caribbean peers, Indo-Caribbeans are fluent speakers of local Creole speech-forms which, though based on English, are marked by distinct features of grammar and pronunciation.[28] To those unfamiliar with them, Creole styles of utterance and pronunciation are often difficult to understand, while the fact that they are based on English often makes the task of communication equally frustrating for the speaker and the unaccustomed listener, especially when both feel that it *should* be straightforward. Context matters, of course, and having lived in Britain for decades, most Indo-Caribbeans now use standard English when talking with non-West Indians. When they socialize together, however, Creole grammar, dialect, turns of phrase and forms of humour come to the fore.

Due to linguistic changes in the earliest years of their presence in the Caribbean, Indo-Caribbeans' use of Hindi is limited, and their pronunciation of Indian personal names is distinctive. It is these unique, creolised forms of English and Hindi which other British Asians find so confusing. Indo-Caribbean Hindus are also identifiable by their preferred form of greetings — "*Ram-Ram*" for the Guyanese, and "*Sita-Ram*" for the Trinidadians — both of which also attest to a heritage grounded in the traditions of North Indian Vaishnavite *bhakti*. Other Indo-Caribbean features which may be considered distinct in varying degrees from those of their Gujarati and Punjabi peers include: devotion to a smaller pantheon (largely limited to Ram, Hanuman, Durga and Lakshmi), heavy emphasis on popular lore backed up by a few key Vaishnavite texts (especially the *Ramayana* and *Bhagavata Purana*), use of a simplified sacred calendar, and above all the use of more congregational forms of worship in which prayers are often participatory and sermons are given in English. Yet despite its condensed repertoire of ritual activities, Indo-Caribbean Hinduism still has its own characteristics, such as celebration of the *Hanuman puja*, which is still uniquely concluded by the raising of coloured *jhandi*. Hence amongst Guyanese Hindus in Britain and the Caribbean alike, "having a *jhandi*" is regarded as synonymous with

---

[28] Structural complexities of Guyanese Creole are described in John R. Rickford, *Dimensions of a Creole Continuum: History, Texts, and Linguistic Analysis of Guyanese Creole* (Stanford University Press, 1987). Rickford (pp. 147–9) also provides lengthy examples and translations of Indo-Guyanese Creole, such as "*mii granfaada bin gat plees a filisiti bilid*" ("my grandfather had a place at Felicity village") and "*wails abii tuu o kom nou wi dis boot, mi tel am, mi se, naanaa, a somting an yu na waan tel mii. tel mii a waa!*" ("while the two of us were coming along now in this boat, I told him, I said, Nana, something is wrong, and you don't tell me. Tell me what it is!").

"performing *puja*". Such practices are well rooted in the Hindu tradition, so however unorthodox the details may be, direct migrants from India rarely have much difficulty in making sense of the symbols and practices in Indo-Caribbean temples. Indo-Caribbeans, by contrast, are often confused by the much greater intricacy of religious belief and practice amongst their Gujarati and Punjabi Hindu peers.

Similarly, while the Indo-Caribbeans' culinary practices are discernibly of Indian origin — involving as they do the preparation of various types of *roti* (flatbread), *dal* (lentils) and rice, and curried vegetables — long years of residence in the Caribbean has led them to evolve a cuisine of their own. So if the curries themselves are milder than many Indian ones, home-made hot pepper sauce — in the growing, preparation and sampling of which men take particular delight — accompanies most dishes as a condiment. Curries prepared in this regionally unique way are always served at the Caribbean Hindu Society, and have the effect of uniting the community socially. Many Indo-Caribbeans, and especially their British-born children, claim that they do not particularly like the "Indian food" served in local Asian-run restaurants; and, true to their West Indian heritage, most Indo-Caribbean men have a strong penchant for rum.

The music they prefer is mostly Indian: Hindi film music and playback singers singing *bhajans* are regularly heard on home stereos and car cassette-players. Language is a problem, however, and although they often watch Hindi films, they usually take care to select videos with English subtitles. And although Indo-Caribbeans tend publicly to disdain calypsos — the hallmark music of Trinidad — on the grounds that they are associated with Afro-Caribbeans, many can both hum the tunes and recite some of the most popular lyrics.

It is also striking that a whole range of unarticulated values, mannerisms and dispositions are expressed in the most subtle aspects of Indo-Caribbean culture, and these are clearly of Indian origin.[29] Thus they are fastidious over matters of bathing and the brushing of teeth, and in their aversion to spittle — and therefore to talking near food in preparation, and to sharing a bottle or glass. There are also certain characteristic hand and arm gestures, such as a gentle rocking of the head when signalling agreement or attention when listening to another person.

While Indo-Caribbean kinship networks in Britain are attenuated, thanks largely to their particular history of migration and settlement, their social networks tend to be extensive. Indo-Caribbean settlers tend to be acquainted with many others of their community; and when Indo-Trinidadians or Indo-Guyanese meet for the first time, it is usual

[29] See Vertovec, *Hindu Trinidad.*

for them within minutes to have not only placed each other's original part of the country and village, but also to have discovered some common acquaintance or even a common relative in those parts. And although return visits to the Caribbean tend to be rare, most people have kept in close touch with local and national developments back home, mainly by cultivating a wide social network in Britain.

Formal and informal associations facilitate the maintenance of those networks. In addition to the (largely Guyanese) Caribbean Hindu Society, a (predominantly Trinidadian) temple has been set up by a Brahmin *pandit* at his home in Catford (South-east London), while a further temple run by a Guyanese *swami* in Shepherd's Bush (West London) is frequented by Indo-Trinidadians and Indo-Guyanese alike. Indo-Caribbean Muslims account for most of the membership of a body called the United Islamic Association. Meanwhile in the secular sphere the Indo-Caribbean Cultural Association publishes a newsletter, organises social events and works to promote knowledge of Indo-Caribbean heritage and culture, especially among members of the community. Many Indo-Caribbeans in Britain are also actively involved in Caribbean politics as overseas members of most of the region's major political parties. Recreational groups also flourish, such as the Guyana Sports and Cultural Association which fields largely Indo-Caribbean cricket teams, and a league of card-players who take part in annual tournaments of "All Foes", an engaging team game played especially by Trinidadians.

These activities serve to integrate Britain's far-flung Indo-Caribbeans. Yet it is ultimately their white and British Asian fellow-citizens' perceptions of them which provides them with the most powerful goad towards maintaining their ethnic distinctiveness.

Inter-ethnic Experiences and Attitudes

The most revealing statements about those experiences are naturally those made by Indo-Caribbeans themselves. Hence this section contains a selection of brief but typical statements made by over forty people of both sexes, from both Guyana and Trinidad.[30]

On British whites, and experiences of their reaction to them as Indians from the Caribbean:

> "Initially they think that only blacks live in the West Indies. Most of them have never heard of Guyana. They're usually quite interested in knowing more, and most of them want to go there for a holiday."

---

[30] I contacted most of these informants through, and interviewed them at, meetings of the Caribbean Hindu Society, the Durga Mandir, and the Indo-Caribbean Cultural Association.

"Very surprised — some were interested."

"They just could not care, so we were all classified as Pakis or Sikhs."

"Nice to your face, but not in their minds."

"Ignorance — they ask "what part of Africa is Guyana?""

"Surprised that Indians from India and from the Caribbean share the same traditions."

"Surprised by my English."

"They make no distinctions — everybody's Paki."

On Indians from India, especially their experience of the reactions of Indians from India towards them as Indians from the Caribbean:

"I don't think they knew Indian Caribbeans shared their culture."

"Some very good, some snobbish."

"They don't see me as one of them."

"As an Indian from the Caribbean, they look on you as an oddity, mostly as an ignorant cousin to mould."

"Amazement at our fluency in English, rum-drinking, cricket . . . ."

"In their eyes we're classed as second-hand Indians."

"Indians don't know what to think of us but are sometimes surprised we have retained the culture."

"Their attitude toward me is one of surprise and nearly always confusion."

"That I'm not 'pure' Indian because I can't understand their language, the difference in food preparation, etc."

"I believe people from India know we're Indian by origin, but we're not regarded as true Indian."

"I haven't experienced negative attitudes — but I haven't met many of them."

Finally on their own attitudes towards Indians from India whom they have encountered in Britain, I was told such things as:

"Some are very nice, most are very arrogant and self-centred."

"Perhaps like an Indian would [be] to another Indian from a distant part of India where traditional activities are different."

"My attitude towards Indians from India who are living here is negative. I don't quite understand how they can be so prejudiced towards Indians from the West Indies. I think they consider me as being mixed with negroes. I don't know if they have any idea that the West Indies have Indians at all."

"We are of the same stock, having the same features, culture, etc."

"I admire the Indians from the subcontinent."

"We get on very well."

"On the whole we get along fine. There is always a language barrier."

"Not much contact — otherwise good."

"They are my brothers and sisters."

"No special affinity."

"I personally feel that I'm one of them when it comes to racial discrimination and would hope that they feel the same towards me."

There is clearly no consensus of inter-ethnic experiences or attitudes. On the whole, however, a sense of separateness is apparent. Immigrants from India who have had contact with Indo-Caribbeans tend to convey no overtly negative stereotypes of them, and to be impressed by their success in maintaining their cultural traits and sincere religious devotion. One Bengali man hoped his British-born descendants would be able to maintain traditions as well as the Indo-Caribbeans have done despite generations of separation from the subcontinent, while an elderly Gujarati woman was deeply moved at the celebrations at an Indo-Guyanese wedding, which reminded her of her childhood back in village India. Another Gujarati woman, a librarian in Balham and Tooting (South London) who has had much contact with Indo-Caribbeans, describes them in Gujarati as "*trishanku*", a colloquialism for "dangling" or "floating in the air". Other Gujaratis, she said, did not look upon them as Hindus, while the Indo-Caribbeans themselves "realised they were not part of us". Yet she also reasons that this has caused the Indo-Caribbeans "to take more energetic steps" to preserve their ethnicity, because "they ended up learning Hindi [referring to classes on offer at the Caribbean Hindu Society]; our children haven't bothered."

What is perhaps more important than the attitudes of other Indians toward them is the Indo-Caribbeans' perceptions (or projections) of themselves. It is common to find a kind of inferiority complex towards subcontinental Indians, due mainly to the inability to converse in an Indian language. Thus Indo-Caribbeans may mis-attribute to sub-continental Indians an arrogance or negative attitude which is not there. Others are more convinced of the reality of Indian assumptions of social superiority, gladly citing all sorts of unambiguous examples. In yet other instances, Indo-Caribbeans express their own superiority to Indian immigrants,[31] referring, for example, to the "peasant" background or behaviour of the latter compared to their own westernised, middle-class habits, and to Indians' "backward" caste sentiments in contract to the almost complete absence of caste in the Indo-Caribbean social tradition. They also claim that Indians cringe in the presence of whites while they feel confident enough to treat them as equals, and suggest too that present-day Indians have degraded many Hindu devotional practices which they themselves claim to have kept pristine during their Caribbean sojourn. Either way, perceptions of "exclusion" — according to either their own Indo-Caribbean criteria or those of others — remain strong.

---

[31] Cf. Naipaul, *The Overcrowded Barracoon*, p. 38.

Conclusion: Indo-Caribbean Identifications

How, then, do the Indo-Caribbeans identify themselves? As all the other groups discussed in this book similarly reveal, ethnicity is related to a person's situation, and gives rise to level upon level of identification. Thus, while British Indo-Caribbeans are identified as "Asian" by most members of the dominant white majority, they are by no means fully accepted as belonging in that category by other South Asians. Indo-Caribbeans in Britain are not means unique in being faced by such a quandary: a wide range of other post-indenture, twice-migrant groups including Indo-Fijians in Vancouver,[32] Indo-Caribbeans in Toronto,[33] Indo-Caribbeans in the Netherlands,[34] and Indo-Mauritians in London[35] are in a similar situation. Hence it is no surprise that many Indo-Fijians and Indo-Mauritians in Britain have also gravitated towards Indo-Caribbean social and religious organisations and activities, rather than linking up with groups that have migrated directly from the subcontinent.

The longer-term future of the British Indo-Caribbean community is far from certain. Organisations like the Caribbean Hindu Society and the Indo-Caribbean Cultural Association do their utmost to foster and preserve a unique sense of identity — thereby expressing cultural resistance to the exclusionist tendencies of both British whites and British Asians. Yet internal fission amongst the Indo-Caribbeans themselves — whether between Muslims and Hindus (a pre-migration phenomenon) or between Trinidadians and Guyanese[36] — is already well established. How these even smaller groups will maintain Indo-Caribbean activities remains to be seen.

The ultimate orientation of British-born Indo-Caribbeans is at present unpredictable: current trends indicate lack of identification with either the Caribbean or with India. Many seem, instead, to be

---

[32] Norman Buchignani, "The social and self-identities of Fijian Indians in Vancouver", *Urban Anthropology*, vol. 9 (1980), pp. 75–97.

[33] Subdas Ramcharan, "The social, economic and cultural adaptation of East Indians from the British Caribbean and Guyana to Canada", in G. Kurian and R.P. Srivastava (eds), *Overseas Indians: A Study in Adaptation* (Delhi: Vikas, 1983), pp. 51–67.

[34] Peter van der Veer, "East Indians from the West Indies in the Netherlands: Identity as disposition and instrument", paper given at the Conference on the Dynamics of Ethnicity in Eastern and Western Europe (University of Utrecht, Netherlands, June 1987).

[35] Sam Lingayah, *Mauritian Immigrants in Britain: A Study of their Hopes and Frustrations* (London: Mauritius Welfare Association, 1987).

[36] Given the social, historical, demographic and economic differences between the countries, such intra-Caribbean fissioning is common and is characteristic of Afro-Caribbeans as well. See Ceri Peach, "The force of West Indian island identity in Britain", in C. Clarke, D. Ley and C. Peach (eds), *Geography and Ethnic Pluralism* (London: Allen & Unwin, 1984), pp. 214–30.

adopting a generalised British Asian youth culture (symbolised by *bhangra* music), which cuts across the cultural divide which faced their West Indian-born parents. Moreover in sharp contrast to their parents, many young Indo-Caribbeans are almost equally at home in British Afro-Caribbean cultural contexts. Young Indo–Caribbeans therefore represent an important new group who are successfully "being multi-cultural" in Britain.

What seems clear is that while British Indo-Caribbeans feel themselves to be very "Western" and "British" in class and habit, they are also very conscious that other South Asian settlers may regard them as a kind of pariah group. Hence they are somewhat alarmed by the prospect of being subsumed into a single overarching "British" or "Asian" cultural identity or categorisation. Instead, Indo-Caribbeans see themselves as forming a important but neglected part of the South Asian diaspora, and as one that should remain unique and unforgotten. These sentiments are exemplified in comments by one of the leaders of the Caribbean Hindu Society, who underscores the communal importance of the organization:

"We's swallowed up by the Asian community because we is so small. But that is why a place like this is so important. A number of times people have raised the question "Why don't you change the name back to something that's wider?" It will serve in some years to show that there was a Caribbean element, a presence here, that contributed to the larger Asian presence . . . It's not being parochial — it's a historical fact."

BIBLIOGRAPHICAL KEY

Adams, C.J. 233
Adams, C. 143, 146
Ahmad, M. 80
Ahmad, A. 69
Akhtar, S. 81, 86
Alavi, H. 45
Ansari, S. 65
Anwar, M. 35, 153
Ashok, S. 123
Aurora, G. 13, 95, 110
Axelrod, P. 251

Ballard, R. 7, 16, 68, 104, 113, 153, 204, 220
Banks, M. 231, 234, 240, 249
Bannerji, S. 140
Barot, R. 169, 214
Barrier, G. 89
Barton, S. 59, 82
Barz, R. 172
Bauman, G. 139
Beteille, A. 216
Bhachu, P. 18, 23, 97, 204
Bharadwaj, S. 282
Bharati, A. 214, 217
Bowen, D. 214, 220, 282
Bowker, J. 224
Boyce, M. 252
Brereton, B. 274
Brooks, D. 106
Buchignani, N. 289
Burghart, R. 214, 282

Caleb, M. 122
Cashmore, E. 2
Cheema, A. 84
Cohen, R. 175
Cole, O. 134
Cross, M. 274, 279

Dahya, B. 14, 35, 59, 143
Darling, M. 38
Deedat, A. 77
Desai, R. 13, 183, 216
Drummond, L. 278
Dumont, L. 25
Dundas, P. 233

Durbin, M. 276
Dwyer, R. 170

Eade, J. 143, 162
Eaton, R. 61
Ehrlich, A. 275
Engineer, A.A. 169

Faruqui, Z. 64, 65
Firby, N. 258
Fryer, P. 6

Gambhir, S. 276

Haq, M. 64, 65
Hardiman, D. 178
Harewood, P. 279
Helweg, A. 22, 96, 124
Helweg, U. 22
Hershman, P. 134
Hinnells, J. 251, 255, 266
Hintzen, P. 279
Hiro, D. 119
Holmes, C. 3

James, A. 96
Jayawardena, C. 275, 277, 278
Jeffery, P. 20, 35, 42
John, D. 107
Joly, D. 79
Jones, M. 53
Jones, K. 63, 119
Juergensmeyer, M. 121

Kabbani, R. 53
Kalsi, S. 123
Kessinger, T. 94
Khan, M. 64
Khurram, M. 76
Knott, K. 60, 225
Kulke, E. 254

Lapidus, I. 60, 67, 70
Lawrence, B. 61
Lingayah, S. 289
Logan, P. 225

MeLeod, W.H. 88, 92, 121
Mahar, P. 216
Makdisi, G. 60, 62
Mangat, J. 236
Mehmood, T. 81
Mellor, D. 259
Metcalfe, 62, 63, 64, 66
Michaelson, M. 184, 185, 215, 228, 232, 238
Modood, T. 60, 74
Monk, C. 259
Moore, B. 274
Morris, H. 169, 180, 214, 217, 237, 246
Mottadeh, R. 82
Munir, M. 66

Nagar, A. 121
Naipaul, V. 272, 273, 288
Nesbitt, E. 122, 123
Nevadomsky, 279
Nicholson, R. 61, 62

O'Connell, J. 89
Oberoi, H. 124

Parmar, P. 228
Peach, C. 279, 280, 289
Phillips, D. 242
Pocock, D. 171
Powell, A. 77

Quigley, D. 25
Qureshi, R. 80

Rahman, F. 73
Ram, P. 120
Ramcharan, S. 289
Raza, M. 66, 81
Redington, J. 172
Rex, J. 53

Rickford, J. 284
Rose, E. 7
Rose, H. 93

Saugave, V. 237
Saifullah Khan, V. 59, 83, 142, 191
Salter, J. 5
Schimmel, A. 62
Schwartz, B. 276
Selvon, S. 281
Shackle, C. 168
Shah, A. 213, 232, 236
Shaw, A. 36, 37, 40, 47, 52, 54, 66, 83
Singh, K. 19, 89
Sivan, E. 67
Sobhan, R. 143
Squires, M. 259
Syed, A. 68

Talbot, I. 61
Tambs-Lyche, H. 184, 198, 214, 228
Tinker, H. 24, 179, 181, 274

Usborne, F. 80

Van der Veer, P. 289
Vertovec, S. 275, 276, 278, 280, 283, 285
Visram, R. 5

Warrier, S. 191, 223
Watson, J. 30, 59
Wedon, F. 53
Werbner, P. 18, 191,
Westwood, S. 223,
Williams, R. 72, 175
Wilson, A. 191

Zarwan, J. 235, 236, 237
Zimmer, H. 121, 136

INDEX

adaptation, strategies of, 141
Ad Dharmis, 121
Africanisation, 181
Afro-Caribbeans, 274, 285
Aga Khan, 168
agriculture, 38
Ahmadiyyas, 51, 69, 76, 86, 121
Akhtar, Shabbir, 81, 86
Al Falah, 85
Arains, 38
army, (British) Indian, 37, 94, 124
Arya Samaj, 64, 115, 118
Asian Youth Movement, 85
assimilation, 5, 54
Australia, 147
Ayodhya, 186

Bakshi Ram, Pandit, 120, 121
Bangla (music), 162
Bangladesh, 142–64 *passim*
Banias, 170
Barelvis, 50–2, 66
Bedford, 127, 129
bhangra, 34, 84, 139, 140, 289
Bhatras, 93, 94, 111, 112
Bhindranwale, Sant Jarnail Singh, 92, 113, 114
Bhutto, Benazir, 86
bilingualism, 30
biradaris, 4, 27, 36, 37, 40, 43, 45ff., 54, 59, 276
Birmingham, 26, 34, 127, 129, 148, 217, 221
Bombay, 5, 10, 26, 135, 169, 253, 254, 256, 262, 264
Bradford, 3, 21, 53–87 *passim*, 148, 183, 185, 209, 217, 220
Brahmins, 25, 173, 277
Bristol, 98
British born, 29–30
Buddhism, 167
burial, 260
Bury, 72, 87

Calcutta, 5, 146–7, 176, 275
canal colonies, 38
Cardiff, 98

caste
  associations, 129, 184, 208–10, 221, 243, 245, 282
  divisions, 38, 118–20, 123, 137, 169–71, 180, 183–5, 193, 209, 248, 253, 276–7, 282
  Islam and, 43, 168
  status competition, 44, 110, 121
  vitality of, 4, 24–7, 91, 118, 169–71, 193
  see also zat
census, 7, 19, 280
Chamars, 277
Christians, 20, 21, 122
citizenship, 180–1
code-switching, 30–3, 284
colonialism, 62, 145
Commission for Racial Equality, 78
Communist Party, 106–8
community leadership, 52
Coventry, 3, 117–41 *passim*, 217
Creole, 284
culture conflict, 30

Delhi, 167
Deedat, Ahmad, 77
Deobandis, 50–1, 63–4, 72–4, 86
Dewsbury, 72–3, 87
Dhaka, 10, 148

East Africa
  business in, 179–80, 195–6, 217, 233, 235, 236
  emigration from, 25–7, 197, 236, 239
  railway, 124, 179
  settlement in, 97, 179, 180–2, 195, 217, 236
Eastern Europe, 6
Edinburgh, 254, 261
education, 30, 152
  female, 49, 78, 152
  secular, 55, 266
  religious, 49, 55, 72–5, 82–5, 189, 244, 271
  higher, 103, 152, 223, 244, 254, 261, 263, 270, 279, 283

employment
  female, 198–200
  manual, 14, 40, 94, 148, 197, 281
  self-employment, 100, 151, 183,
    223
  see also entrepreneurship
endogamy, 45, 140, 193, 213, 230
entrepreneurship, 9, 14, 36, 151–3,
  183, 211, 223
ethnic colonisation, 2, 13, 19, 28–9
ethnicity, 8, 266, 271, 278
exclusionism
  caste, 111, 118, 127, 137–8, 141
  double, 127, 137, 228, 286
  racial, 2, 33, 52, 85, 106, 114, 160,
    253, 258, 269, 273, 279, 289

Faisalabad, 38–9
family reunion, 15, 41, 43, 48, 96
Fiji, 221

Georgetown, 281
Glasgow, 39, 98
Gujarat, Gujaratis, 10, 19–20, 21, 26,
  72, 79, 88–141 *passim*
gurdwaras, 109, 130
Guru Nanak, 91
Guyana, 24, 276

hajj, 47, 168
halal, 78
Hindi film, 135–6, 285
Hinduism, 112–33 *passim*, 165–6, 168–
  90 *passim*, 191–230 *passim*, 224–7
  Caribbean, 276–8, 282–3, 286
  domestic worship, 134, 174
  and politics, 185–6, 278
  sectarianism, 186–90
Honeyford, Ray, 79
household organisation, 200–6
housing, 16, 17, 29, 37, 41, 44, 104,
  219
Hull, 68

identity, 4, 85, 158, 163, 229, 251,
  289
imam, 49, 50
immigration control, 6, 40, 95, 148,
  181, 182, 197
Impact International, 74
indentured labour, 274
Indian Workers' Association, 106–9,
  128

Indo-Caribbeans, 24, 272–90 *passim*
Ireland, 6
Islam, *see* Muslims
Islamic Foundation, 74, 75
Islamic Youth Movement, 75
Ismailis, *see* Muslims
izzat, 13–14, 18, 90, 105

jahiliyya, 67
Jains, Jainism, 167, 233–5, 231–50
  passim
jajmani system, 193
Jamaat-i-Islami, 67, 86
Jats, 38, 93, 128, 218
Jullundur, 20, 124

Kampala, 179
Kanbis, 170, 184
Karachi, 10
Khalistan, 113
Khatm-i-Quran, 49
kinship, 11, 12, 15, 16, 26, 36, 40, 45,
  48, 59, 147, 148, 201, 206ff., 278

Lahore, 62
lascars, 146
Leeds, 3, 88–116 *passim*, 183, 213–30
  passim
Leicester, 4, 74, 75, 183, 187, 217,
  231–50 *passim*
lena-dena, 46–8
linguistic competence, 5, 49, 80, 113,
  188, 284
Lohanas, 170, 184, 192, 214
London
  Central, 4, 126, 251–72
  East, 3, 21, 28, 142–64, 187
  North, 3, 183, 188, 191–212
  South, 4, 279–90
  West, 108
Luton, 217

Madras, 275
magazines, 85, 221, 247
Manchester, 71, 148, 235, 239, 242
marriage, 45–8, 54, 134, 140, 144,
  156–8, 171, 173, 193–4, 205,
  232
  breakdown, 229
  'love', 140, 157
merchants, 26, 168, 253
Middle East, 48, 144
Midlands, 8, 98

migration
   causes of, 4–8, 9, 10, 37, 147, 264,
      279
   chain, 11, 39, 95, 147, 148, 218
   consequences, 149, 155
   costs, 12
Milton Keynes, 185
Mirpur, Mirpuris, 20, 37, 68, 83, 153
Mochis, 185, 213–30 *passim*
modesty, 13, 52
Mombasa, 179, 236, 238
mosques, 50, 68–75
Mughals, 62, 144, 167, 174
Muslims, 19, 20, 49–57 *passim*, 168–9,
      142–64 *passim*
   Bohras, 168, 169
   caste, 27
   conversion, 168–9, 217
   identity among, 53, 54, 57
   "Islamic fundamentalism", 35, 162–
      3
   Ismailis, 168, 180
   Khojas, 168, 169
   Memons, 169
   politics, 49
   sectarian affiliation, 50, 59
   social mobility, 21
   Sufi, 60, 61, 62, 144, 145
   Sunni, 49, 60
   youth, 78–85
   see also Satanic Verses, The
myth of return, 35, 36, 48, 52, 56, 153
Maharishi Valmik, 117–41 *passim*

Nairobi, 124, 126, 179
Newcastle, 40, 98
North America, 104, 147, 169, 261

Oldham, 149, 255
Oman, 179
Oswals, 192, 232–43
Oxford, 3, 11, 21, 35–57, 127

Pakistanis, 21, 35–87 *passim*
Parliament, Members of, 254, 259
Parsi Zoroastrians, 171, 251–71
      passim
Patidars, 171, 184, 192, 214, 223
peasant farmers, 10, 38, 91, 146, 154,
      184, 237
pedlars, 93
Pennines, 8
pioneers, 93, 98, 253, 259

Pir Maroof Hussain Shah, 69–71, 78
pirs, 50–1
pollution, 14, 118, 128, 177, 216
population, 6–8, 69, 95, 117, 127, 165,
      179, 184, 215, 231, 241, 280
Port of Spain, 281
Prajapatis, 185, 191–212
Preston, 133. 217
Punjabis, 19, 79, 88–141 *passim*, 218
purdah, 46, 53, 160
purity, 78, 176, 285
Pushtimarg, 166, 172–5

qawwali, 80
Qur'an, the, 49, 65, 66, 70, 73, 84

racial discrimination, 52, 269
racism, 13, 32, 137, 139–40, 163, 286–
      90
Ramayana, 131, 132, 136
Ramgarhias, 97, 111, 121
Ravidasis, 119, 123
recession, 78, 100
religious revivalism, 48, 69, 86, 161,
      162, 188, 262
remittances, 144, 149, 150
restaurants, 149, 150–3

Saifullah Khan, Verity, 83
Satanic Verses, The, 4, 33, 50, 59, 76,
      77, 79, 83, 86, 162
Shari'a, 60
Shraddh, 123
Sikhs, 19, 21, 27, 88–111 *passim*, 112–
      41 *passim*
silsila, 60
Singapore, 124, 126, 136
Somnath, 121, 167
Southall, 108, 127, 129, 132, 282
Southampton, 98
Sufi, *see* Muslims
Sultan, 85–6
Sunni, *see* Muslims
Swaminarayan, 175–90 *passim*
Sylhet, 19, 20, 142, 144, 145–64

Tablighi Jamaat, 64–6
Thatcher, Margaret, 28
Trends, 75, 87
Trinidad, 24, 275
twice migrants, 26, 207, 272
Uganda, 38
      see also East Africa

Ujala, 83
'ulema, 63, 72–87 *passim*
Untouchables (Scheduled Castes), 20,
    25, 118, 119, 121, 138, 178
Urdu, 49, 52, 63, 79

Valmikis, 21, 27
Vishwa Hindu Parishad (VHP), 185–6

Wahhabis, 50–1
Wellingborough, 217, 240
Wolverhampton, 127, 129

women, 43–6, 47, 54–5

Young Muslims U.K., 74, 77, 84,
    86
youth, 29–30, 33–4, 53, 85–7, 159–
    61, 268

zamindar, 44, 145
Zanzibar, 179
zat, 25, 27, 44, 118, 124, 126–7
    see also caste
Zia ul Haq, Gen., 61, 86